dear Martin

In friendship a ever

Tony

February 1998

Religions in Conflict

Religions in Conflict

IDEOLOGY, CULTURAL CONTACT
AND CONVERSION
IN LATE-COLONIAL INDIA

Antony Copley

DELHI
OXFORD UNIVERSITY PRESS
CALCUTTA CHENNAI MUMBAI
1997

Oxford University Press, Great Clarendon Street, Oxford OX2 6DP
Oxford New York
Athens Auckland Bangkok Calcutta
Cape Town Chennai Dar es Salaam Delhi
Florence Hong Kong Istanbul Karachi
Kuala Lumpur Madrid Melbourne Mexico City
Mumbai Nairobi Paris Singapore
Taipei Tokyo Toronto
and associates in
Berlin Ibadan

ISBN 0 19 563676 7

Typeset by Guru Typograph Technology, New Delhi 110045
Printed at Pauls Press, New Delhi 110020
and published by Manzar Khan, Oxford University Press
YMCA Library Building, Jai Singh Road, New Delhi 110001

For Brian Kember

Epigraph

Joffre's grave expression lightened. 'What kind of thing is sinful in Aclar, sir?

'Each man there would give a different answer', Palinor said.

'And your answer, sir?'

'There are many things I would not do', said Palinor. 'But no misdeed could be graver, it seems to me, than trying to increase one's own luminance by quenching the light shining from another man. There's a problem calling it sin, however, when it is committed most often by holy men, by revered teachers, priests, mullahs . . .'

Knowledge of Angels
Jill Paton Walsh

Preface

I always knew I was going to write a book about missionaries. As an undergraduate, through taking a course in Prelims entitled Historical Geography, I became fascinated by the story of Catholic Mission to the Americas. One of my unfulfiled travel plans is to visit Mexico and Peru, the locale for the clash of Mission with ancient cultures.

But there was an even earlier pipe-dream. As a schoolboy I had struggled with considerable mystification through A. C. Bouquet's *Comparative Religion*. This left a sense of unfinished business and a wish to look once again at the relationship between faiths.

The immediate origins of this book are somewhat different. At the University of Kent I taught a course on the comparative history of moral change, *Moral Codes and Their Critics*, and from this emerged a book, *Sexual Moralities in France 1780–1890*. I had foreseen an analogous text for India, taking up the theme of an emergent Indian feminist movement. But the course had always required an understanding of both the sanctions for morality as well as the role of its critics, and, in one way or another, I began to veer towards a study of the clash of religions. Having written a book on sexuality, why not, I decided, write one on religion.

Clearly the study of inter-faith relationships is a personal matter and an author should at some point put his cards on the table. I come to the subject as a church-going Anglican, attracted to the antiquity of the Church of England and to the grace of its services, a middle of the road Anglican rather than High Church, let alone Evangelical. In terms of inter-faith relationships, I'd see myself as a pluralist. There seems to be no other conceivable stand-point one could adopt in the late twentieth century. For a liberal intellectual, Mission poses problems. One cannot deny the right to proselytize, but one is appalled by the abusiveness of some Mission. On the whole, I share Gandhi's distaste for conversion and his belief that one should pursue one's religious quest through one's own faith.

The themes of Mission as ideology, of cultural contact and of conversion all naturally lend themselves to high theory. Indeed, I drew up a long reading list of anthropological writings, from Ruth Benedict to Clifford Geertz. But, in the end, the sheer fascination of the primary source material took over. In consequence, this is a text with a strongly positivist flavour.

I should begin by thanking those institutions which made research for this project possible: the University of Kent for three terms of sabbatical leave; the Colyer-Fergusson Trust for a grant subsidizing my stay at the College of the Ascension; a travel grant from the University Research Committee, subsidizing my visit to India in 1991.

I would like to thank the library staff of all these institutions in which research was undertaken: the Heslop room, the University of Birmingham; Rhodes House, Oxford (and I thank the USPG for permission to quote their records); the Angus Library, Regent's Park College, Oxford (Mrs Susan Mills was very helpful); the Selly Oak Library, Birmingham; the Canterbury Cathedral Library; the Mission Archive of the United Theological College, Bangalore (Dr J. Patmury and his staff could not have been more helpful); the Adyar Library and Research Centre, Madras; the archive of Madras Christian College; the library of the Ramakrishna Mission Institute of Culture, Calcutta; the library and archive of Bishop's College, Calcutta; the library and archive of St Paul's College, Calcutta; the National Library, Calcutta; the Carey Library of Serampore College; not forgetting the library of the University of Kent.

I would like to thank all those who gave me advice both outside and inside India. Outside: Michael Anderson; Christopher and Susan Bayly; Bert Breiner; Penny Carson; Nancy Cassels; Robert Frykenberg; Eleanor Jackson (she went to great trouble to introduce me to the world of Indian Christianity); Rev Roger Hooker; Sir John Lawrence; Julius Lipner; Peter Marshall; Bishop Lesslie Newbiggin; Rev Dan O'Connor; Geoffrey Oddie; Rev Bill Owen, former missionary to Kenya; Andrew Porter; Tapan Raychaudhuri; Eric Sharpe; R. S. Sugirtharajah; Christian Troll; Peter van der Veer; Andrew Wingate.

In India: in Bangalore: Dr Abraham Ayzookuzhiel (CSIRS); Father Augustine (Dharmaran College); Father Ephraim David; Professor Fred Downs (UTC); Roger Gaekwad; Professor Peter (St Joseph's College); Professor David Scott (UTC); in Madras: Dayanand Francis (General Secretary of the Christian Literature Society); Ambrose Jayasekaram (Madras Christian College); Professor Ramaswamy (former Professor of English, Presidency College); Father Sundaram (Loyola College); in Hyderabad: Swami Ranganathananda (Abbot of the Ramakrishna Math); Professor Syed Sirajuddin (Editor, *Islamic Culture*, and I thank Diane de

Souza for arranging this interview in the Henry Martyn Institute); in Calcutta: Professor Chakraborty and his colleagues (I thank Sujon Chanda for arranging this interview at the Rabindra Bharati University); S. Chatterjee (Serampore College); Binoy Chowdury; Somen Das; Barun De; Professor Mahmood, Presidency College (and I thank Professor M. Khan for arranging this interview); Swami Lokeswarananda; the late Professor Nisrithiranjan Ray; Alok Roy, Scottish Church College; Amales Tripathi; Rev Dr Yisu Das Tiwari and his father (Serampore College); in New Delhi: K. N. Panikkar.

I would like to thank all the societies and institutions which gave me the opportunity to present a seminar paper to test out my ideas in advance: International Congress of Asia and North African Studies (ICANAS), Toronto, August 1990; South Asia Seminar, the University of Cambridge, February 1991; Conference on the Sociology of Sacred Texts, the University of Newcastle, September 1992; 12th European Conference of South Asian Studies, Berlin, September 1992; South Asia Seminar, University of Oxford, November 1992; Work in Progress Seminar, University of Sussex, November 1993; 13th European Conference of South Asian Studies, Toulouse, August 1994; A Conference on Inter-faith Conversion, Selly Oak Colleges, Birmingham, May 1995.

I thank Jill Paton Walsh for permission to use a passage from her remarkable novel *Knowledge of Angels* as an epigraph.

There are many I should thank for help and friendship. I thank Dan and Juliet O'Connor and Geoffrey Cleaver for making my stay amongst the missionaries at the College of the Ascension so pleasant and enlightening. I made many friends but just mention Jesu Prasad, Perlita Ponge, Tony Hardiment, and Heather and Richard Scott (just back from being medical missionaries in Tanzania). Michael and Pru Stokes gave me much helpful advice and made many introductions for my trip to India in 1991. Surur Hoda also made some very helpful introductions. In Bangalore I enjoyed the hospitality of Roger Gaekwad and his wife (indeed, their excellent fare restored me to health) and of David and Corinna Scott. It was a great pleasure to meet Jesu Prasad again and he and his lawyer friends showed me much of the city. Mrs Aruna Sunderlal likewise entertained and was kind enough to book me in as her guest in the Bangalore Club. In Madras, I thank Radha Burnier, Mrs Norma Sastry and others for allowing me to stay at the Theosophical Society at Adyar and for so tranquil a visit; George and Meera Verghese, for their frequent and excellent hospitality, and I would like to thank the Indo-British Society for their generous provision of a taxi which made my x / *Preface*

journeys in Madras so much easier; Sarvepalli Gopal, for inviting me to the Madras Gymkana Club; Mrs Sarah Chunda for her hospitality; I enjoyed the company of Mark and Laura Bevir at Adyar. In Hyderabad, I met up again with Venkat Rao, who had studied at Kent, and who took me out for an excellent meal in Secundarabad. In Bhubaneswar, Professor Ganeshwar Mishra and his colleagues at Utkal University took me out to dinner. In Calcutta, I thank Swami Lokeswarananda for the invitation to stay at the Ramakrishna Mission Institute of Culture, and Naimi Mukherjee and Mr Hazra for making my stay so rewarding; in Sujon Chanda I found an engaging and endlessly helpful friend; I owe much to Jatin Ghosh, whose generous loan of his chauffeured car whilst he worked in the High Court made my visits to archives very much easier and who also offered very lively hospitality; Margaret Macgregor very kindly offered me lunch the days I worked at Bishop's College and kept me cheerful; Jatindra Biswas, whose meal in his railway quarters was the best I enjoyed during my stay in India; Debesh and Kamal Das, who paid me the honour of inviting me to give the Amritasya Putree Endowment Lectures at the Ramakrishna Mission and became my good friends .In Delhi I met up with former colleagues from the Jawaharlal Nehru University; Yogesh Sharma took me out to a fantastic meal in old Delhi and helped me expand my wardrobe; Aditya and Mridula Mukherjee entertained me on their farm in Haryana and together we all saw in the New Year at the JNU.

I would like to thank James Mayell and Robert and Lorraine Tollemache for letting me stay in their cottages in Robin Hood's Bay and Steep Marsh respectively where, in fact, a good third of the book was written.

Nearer home, I would once again like to thank Elizabeth Deighton for her unstinting and generous hospitality. I also thank William and Clare Fortescue and Dan and Lavinia Cohn-Sherbok for putting up with me more than most.

One of the saddest losses of current restructuring at the University is the College Secretarial office and the services of Mollie Roots. I owe her much.

This book is dedicated to Brian Kember. Over many years, he and his wife, Ivy, have looked after my needs and made themselves indispensable. I hope he likes the bibliography, always his favourite part of a book.

Canterbury ANTONY COPLEY
August 1995

Contents

MAPS

(between pp 136-7.)

Southern and Eastern Bengal Missions
(Baptist Missionary Atlas)

North West Provinces (Church Missionary Atlas)

The Punjab, Sind and the Afghan Frontier
(Church Missionary Atlas)

Part of the Telugu Country
(Church Missionary Atlas)

Mysore, Coorg and Madras States

ILLUSTRATIONS

(between pp 136-7)

Prologue

Over the last century the role of religion in Indian society has come to be seen as problematic. The rich mingling of faiths has bred warring parties. How seriously has the vandalism to the Babri Masjid mosque wounded Nehruvian secularism? Though it would be misleading to lay the blame for this deterioration and the rise of communalism on nineteenth-century Mission, there can be no doubt that Indian religions did learn from its ideology and organization, and Indian faiths have, in consequence, taken on a new militancy. There is contemporary cause to look back to the mid-nineteenth-century conflict among religions.

Three themes thread this text: the role of ideology, the nature of cultural contact and conversion.

Christians in post-colonial societies revere their European missionary predecessors.[1] Indeed, some Indian Christian I met believed that European missionaries were not only better leaders of the Indian church, they were more perceptive at reading the minds and souls of Indian Christians. They may look on an interpretation of Mission as a form of ideology with dismay.

But it is difficult to see how else to read this fierce assault on the strongholds of Indian religions. The ideology of Mission should be separated from a secular Imperialist ideology, though they threatened disastrously to converge by the 1840s and 1850s. One can come to a definition of ideology from a number of directions. One derives from Marxism and sees ideology as an expression of underlying economic and social interests, regarding the class, national, or even ethnic. Another emphasizes a 'cluster of ideas', driven by a wish to proselytize and convert. If we have to place Mission in the context of mid-nineteenth-century Victorian society, and see its links to Empire, the second better fits the ideology of Mission. At its heart lay a formidable, but intellectually narrow, millenarian, exclusivist theology.

To test out the character of this ideology, three missionary organizations have been researched. This is not a project on their administration and their British background, intriguing though this story would be. Its concern lies with the attitudes of missionaries in the field. This is the story of 'new' Mission, in many ways to be a radical departure from the 'old' at Tranquebar. First in the field was the Baptist Mission, 'the particular Baptist Society for propagating the Gospel among the heathen', founded on 2 October 1792, in a back parlour of a house in Kettering, Northamptonshire. The day William Carey arrived in India (10 November 1793) is possibly the more pertinent date.[2] Next comes the Church Missionary Society, formally set up on 12 April 1799.[3] Of greater antiquity was the Society for the Propagation of the Gospel.[4] It grew out of the Society for Propagating Christian Knowledge. The SPCK dates from 8 March 1699; the charter of the SPG, 16 June 1701. In contrast to the CMS, always a lay body, the SPG, from its beginnings, was closely linked to the Church of England. In the eighteenth century the SPCK had given its support to 'old' Mission, centred on Tranquebar. The key dates in the early nineteenth century were the founding of Bishop's College, December 1820, and the transfer of the SPCK Mission stations in the south in June 1825 to the SPG. But, predictably, this three-way relationship between a non-conformist, anti-establishment body, a Low-Church evangelical and a High Church organization was not always friendly. However, a variety of Protestant attitudes is represented here. The Scottish Mission vital for missionary attitudes towards education, is the fourth Mission under review. I will occasionally refer to other missionaries from other Missions, such as the London Missionary Society and the American Mission.

It is not always easy to grasp the scale of missionary endeavour. George Smith stated that between 1851 and 1890, the number of converts increased from 91,092 to 5,59,661, an increase of 4,68,569. Figures for communicants, from 14,661 to 1,82,722, may be more indicative. Less than half a million may not seem many, but, as Smith pointed out, by 1890 there were more Christians than Sikhs.[5] This resulted from the work of 868 ordained clergy, 118 non-ordained men and 711 unmarried women, a total of 1697 missionaries. By 1890, Smith calculated there was one missionary per 1,67,000 of the Indian population. A telling statistic for the future was an increase in this period in the number of Indian priests from 21 to 797.[6] In Smith's analysis, Mission was only getting into its stride at the point the Raj took over from the Company: 'the history of Christian India began in the year 1858; all before this was a preparation'.[7] If numbers did indeed increase, in reality, the full force of Mission had peaked. The real thrust for conversion on a mass scale came between the 1830s and the 1850s.

In the global village, cultural contact is an all-pervasive concern. In the nineteenth century, it was at its beginning. Here was a quite extraordinary clash between a small but disproportionately powerful group of foreign missionaries and ancient religions. If these had come under attack before, it was never by so relentless and inescapable an opponent. Can we read the cultural response of the missionaries themselves? They came remarkably ignorant of these religions. Were they moved to understand these religions? Was there to be anything analogous to the curiosity of an earlier, if secular, Orientalist generation of visiting Europeans? Did they remain merely confrontational in their response to Indian culture or did they begin to respond to its antiquity and strength? And, in a more limited theological sense, did their narrow exclusivism give way to a more liberal approach? Was there the glimmering of an inclusivist theology? In so embattled an encounter—and I have to say there was little or no evidence of a reverse acculturation, of Christians converting to one or other of India's religions—one would be surprised by a radical shift, but the situation remains all the more a test of just how far cultural contact under pressure can lead to change.

Those caught up in the cross-fire of this encounter were the Indian Christian converts. In this account, without in any way wishing to underplay the significance of so called mass conversions, more attention is paid to the conversion of the elite. This lends itself more readily to an account of conversion as a cultural migration, a journey from one faith to another, and possibly, but not necessarily, from one culture to another. Although they were a small and highly specialized group, considerable interpretative weight can be placed on their experience. They were in the vanguard of that clash between India and western culture which was to afflict the much larger westernized elite under Empire. To an extent they fit the paradigm of the proto-nationalist. Their experience anticipates that of the generation which formed the Indian National Congress in 1885. There is, of course, an intrinsic fascination as to why people change their ideas, certainly something as deeply rooted as religious belief.

But this is also to be a contribution to the history of Indian religions themselves. Not all have been included. There is nothing on Parseeism, Jainism Buddhism or Tribal religions. It is limited to Hinduism, Islam and Sikhism. Just how did they survive this onslaught? Did the traditional institutions and their personnel weather the storm, or should the credit go to the nineteenth-century reform movements? One of the contentions of this text is that the former should take the credit, and that, indeed, the reform movements, if anything, represented a kind of mimesis of missionary ideology and organization, a serious compromise with their opponents and a disturbing legacy for the religious life of India. Missionaries attributed their failure to the hold of caste, and another of the contentions of the text is that this was a latter-day perception and that they had set out in the firm belief that Christianity would overpower India's ethical and metaphysical systems. Rather than admit to the weakness of Christianity, they made caste the scapegoat.

Part I sets the context. In Chapter I there is an exploration of the social and intellectual background of missionaries and their theology. If an analysis of missionary strategy can pall, it, nevertheless, provides an intriguing commentary on the inflexibility of ideology. Individual missionaries began to have doubts about this attempt to bring about large-scale conversions through itinerating. Mission as a whole, however, continued stubbornly to set its sights on this means rather than put its faith in the alternative of the education of India's elite. In Chapter III there is a sketch of the intellectual context of both cultural contact and conversion. Missionary ideology has to be contextualized in the debate on orientalism, anglicism and secularism. It is interesting to off-set the intellectual approach to Indian culture of William Jones and William Carey as a foil to that of the later generations of evangelical Protestants. Mission and conversion should be placed in the wider context of a cultural encounter between India and the West.

In the four chapters of Part II, there are a series of missionary case-studies which look at both their attitudes to strategy and the nature of their response to Indian religions. This is a study of religions in conflict, but also an exploration of cultural contact. It is to embark on Eric Newby's journey in reverse,[8] setting out from the estuary of the Ganges and Calcutta, journeying up river to lower Hindustan, to Monghyr in Bihar, to Chunar, Benares, and then into upper Hindustan, to Agra, Delhi, Amritsar, Multan and so to Peshawar and the North West Frontier. In the south, Madras, Tinevelly and Masulipatam have been selected. In all cases, the choice has gone to the itinerating missionaries, though several of these started out as teachers. Here Mission was to be at its most confrontational, and this gave promise of greater insight into the character of the clash of religions and of cultural contact in the mid-century.

In Part III, the focus is on the Indian Christians. Here it is necessary to pose several questions. Were there predisposing factors in the religious backgrounds of Indian Christians which might explain their conversion? Were they peculiarly alienated in the south by its strong temple culture? Did the strongly Vaishnavite culture of Bengal predispose intellectuals towards Christianity? Was guilt over the alleged practice of idolatry or over sexuality the greater dynamic? In the south, those selected include the Vellala Pillai brothers, Rajahgopaul, a convert of the Scottish Mission, Manchala Venkataraman and Anantam, converts from Robert Noble's school in Masulipatam; in Bengal, apart from some Baptist converts, most attention is paid to Krishna Mohan Banerjea and Lal Behari Day. There is only a brief account of Indian Christians in the north, looking, in particular, at Nehemiah Goreh, and some Muslim and Sikh converts. The school rather than the bazaar here comes into its own.

NOTES AND REFERENCES

1. I felt this very strongly on attending a service of the United Society for the Propagation of the Gospel at St John the Baptist Church, Halesowen, Birmingham, 24 May 1995. This was to mark the completion of a mission to the UK by Christians from across the USPG Mission, world-wide.

2. We are fortunate to now have a very scholarly new history of the Baptist Mission: Brian Stanley, *The History of the Baptist Mission Society 1792–1922*, Edinburgh: 1922.

3. I have relied on the standard history of the CMS by Eugene Stock: *The History of the Church Missionary Society. Its Environment, its Men and its Work*, London: 1899. This study does not attempt to do justice to its home administrators. Most exceptional was John Venn, its secretary, 1841–72, and the recipient of all correspondence from India.

4. The official history of the SPG remains that of H. P. Thompson: *Into All Lands: The History of the Society for the Propagation of the Gospel in Foreign Parts 1701–1950*, London: 1951. Again, I fail to do justice to its home administrators. Clearly I should mention Ernest Hawkins, Assistant-Secretary, 1838–43, Secretary 1843–64, recipient of all SPG correspondence from India.

5. George Smith, *The Conversion of India*, London: 1893, p. 204.

6. Ibid., pp. 206–7.

7. Ibid., p. 143.

8. Eric Newby, *Slowly Down the Ganges*, London: 1966, one of the most engaging travel books on India.

PART I
Mission Ideology in Context

CHAPTER 1

Ideology and Strategy

The years between 1830 and 1880 marked a distinctive phase in the history of Protestant Mission in India. It is necessary to assess the character of its ideology and the strategy by which it sought to proselytize, for these determined the context in which the missionaries responded to Indians and their culture. At no other time, with the exception of six-teenth-century Goa, was the confrontation between Christianity and Indian religions so fierce. No other foreign agency came into such close, if confrontational, contact with Indian society as did British Protestant missionaries in this period. Did the missionaries learn from this experi-ence? Did they modify their attitudes towards Indian religions? In this chapter I will simply try to describe and explain the peculiar features of missionary ideology at this stage, and look at debates on how to imple-ment this ideology at a number of regional conferences of missionaries in these decades. In subsequent chapters I will trace the response of indi-vidual missionaries, for it was almost certainly their cumulative experi-ence which explains any real changes in attitude and policy.

IDEOLOGY

It is not, of course, an easy task to achieve any kind of critical distance from missionary endeavour. No liberal intellectual can feel at ease with the distasteful arrogance and intolerance inherent in any attempt to bend the minds of others to a new set of beliefs. Norman Lewis has provided a simply horrifying tale of the activities of modern American Protestant missionaries in South America, those of the Summer Institute of Lan-guages and the New Tribes Mission, with their active collaboration with right-wing South American governments, particularly those of Paraguay and Venezuela, in the enforced development of the rain-forest, at the ex-pense of its Indian population.[1] Describing a visit to one missionary camp, Cecilio Baez, amongst the Ache Indians in the Chaco region of

Paraguay, he writes of 'something in the atmosphere here . . . the most sinister experience of my life. It was impossible not to be reminded of Jonestown, Guyana.'[2] Recruiting Indians into modern industrial schemes has become but another form of slavery. The American missionaries defend themselves by saying they are merely accelerating an inevitable process. Saving the souls of Indians from eternal hell-fire is worth the price. Disturbingly, Lewis sees here a clear line of descent from such missionary enterprise as that of the London Missionary Society to the South Pacific in the later eighteenth century, with that same threat to a traditional way of life, a common emphasis on guilt, and salvation from sin.

It is hardly surprising that some historians of nineteenth-century Mission in India cannot suppress a sense of anger. One such is Susan Bayly, in her brilliant and controversial study of south India.[3] Her theme is of the wanton carelessness of nineteenth-century missionary activity, both Protestant and Catholic, with its disruption of the social equilibrium between the Christians and Hindus in south Indian society. At its worst, such disruption bred a communal divide on a par with that between Hindus and Muslims in the north.

One villain of the story is Colonel John Munro, British Resident in Travancore from 1810 to 1819: 'a fervent evangelical Christian with all the familiar qualities of the early nineteenth-century reformer-official—boundless energy, rock hard prejudices against "heathenism", "native superstition", and "popery" and a fierce drive to reform and "uplift" Indian society.'[4] She traces the consequences of this encounter between 'super-charged evangelical Protestantism'[5] and this integrated society: an alienation between caste Hindus and Syrian Christians, much accelerated by the mass conversion of low-caste Hindus at the end of the century, so that by the 1880s Syrians were excluded from Hindu festivals, with a breakdown in the authority of the metrans, hereditary archdeacons and a fragmentation of the Syrian community. Her most serious indictment is to point to 'the innumerable riots'[6] between Hindus and Syrians in the 1880s and 1890s.

Although it is difficult to see how missionaries were solely to blame, she points to a fundamental change in the character of south Indian society. 'At no time,' she claims, 'in the immediate pre-colonial period was there a clear and unambiguous process at work by which the boundaries between different South Indian groups or communities were being irrevocably hardened.' Under the East India Company, 'its system of rule had severed the ritual relationships and schemes of "honour" and incorporation which had integrated the earlier kingdoms: the result was the emergence of more rapid and exclusive "communal" boundaries'.[7] Maybe as interesting an insight is the way the missionaries became the mere plaything of one or the other Indian social group: fatal catalyst they may have been, but not, in a sense, the determining agency. Still, to charge them with acting as a catalyst for communalism is a serious accusation to bring against the missionaries.

What was the relationship between this Christian ideology and the more powerful, if less obviously focused, secular ideology of Empire? Were they divergent or concurrent? Andrew Porter's answer is a 'qualified yes', to whether or not there was any systematic connection between religion and Empire: 'to grasp the pattern of that ambiguity,' he acknowledges, 'will test the inspiration and ingenuity of any historian.' Missionaries were under many strong compulsions, especially millenarian, to distrust government and go their own way. On the other hand, they also looked to government to provide them with a means of self-defence. If Porter is ready to challenge a view of religion 'as the flimsiest of ideological stucco on the imperial edifice', he still points to a constant resurfacing of 'the original missionary sense of self-sufficiency, their disdain or suspicion of imperial politics and government'.[8]

The story of the resistance of the East India Company to pressure from the Clapham Sect and the Evangelicals, William Wilberforce and Charles Grant the Elder, and to missionary presence in Company Territory, is a familiar one. But, as Penelope Carson has shown, missionary access did not become very much easier between the granting of licences in the 1813 Charter and the lifting of their requirement in 1833. Military men and governors, often themselves military, feared for the loyalty of Indian sepoys and threats to public order, should missionary activities be encouraged. An angry public response in Travancore in the 1820s to the pro-missionary policies of Colonels Macaulay and Munro justified their fears.[9] The conflict may have been eased with the failure of English missionaries to come forward in large numbers at this stage: missionary societies had to rely on recruits from Germany. From the 1830s onwards, however, the all pervasive influence of Evangelicalism brought Church and State together. As a result there was to be greater sympathy between Missionary and Company officials. However, this was also the time when missionaries were driven by a greater romantic impulse to independence, and so tensions of a kind remained. The connections between the missionary and evangelical officials, especially in the North Western Provinces and the Punjab, will be explored.

It is of course an intrinsically interesting question whether mission-aries were more involved and receptive to Indian society and culture than were civilians. Would one attribute to missionaries the same limited response as Bernard Cohn does for the civilian in Benares—he is writing of the 1830s—'the officials were recruited at an earlier age and went to India with an idealized adolescent view of their own society and culture. This adolescent view tended to become fossilized in India. It was to this idealized culture that British officials compared their segments of Indian culture with which they came in contact.'[10] The cut and thrust of mis-sionary interaction with India, especially in the decades from the 1830s to the 1870s, undermined any such rigidity, or so this study hopes to show.

There is also the danger of reductionism, the tendency to conflate, rather than separate, different strands in any one enterprise. It will make more sense if we attempt to define the missionary endeavour as a discrete set of values. At no stage did Empire ever challenge Indian religions and social institutions, and above all, caste, in the way Mission did. There was a fierceness and a wide scope to the challenge posed by Mission which compels its discussion as a distinctive ideology.

To make sense of this ideology, we must first grasp its theology. The Christian Church is in essence a missionary one: 'go ye therefore and teach all nations.' If the specific objective in this text is to characterize the nature of Protestant Mission in the mid-nineteenth century, we have still to place it in a larger context. Michael Nazir-Ali warns against too provincial an approach, too narrow a focus on a western European mis-sionary story.[11] We have also to recognize the role of the Church of the East, the Coptic Church, the Ethiopian Church. 'A proper appreciation of the most recent missionary history of the Western family of churches will only be possible', he argues, 'when it is seen as merely an episode (albeit a very important episode) in the missionary history of merely one family (albeit a very important family) of Christian churches.'[12] Indeed, the Reformed Churches of the Reformation were little interested in mission: 'it is not too much of a caricature to say that at the time of the Reformation it was widely believed that if God wanted the heathen to be saved, *He* would provide the means for their salvation;'[13] 'It is quite asto-nishing for us in the twentieth century to see quite how much energy was expanded in arguing *against* Mission.'[14]

The counter-reformation more than compensated for such Protestant neglect, and maybe this is the place to comment on the specifically Protestant focus of this text. The Roman Catholic Mission, which indeed did experience a recovery in the mid-nineteenth century after a period of decline in the eighteenth, was substantially concerned with the care of its existing Christian communities, and was caught up in conversion movements only by the 1890s. In consequence, it is a far poorer indicator in mid-century of how foreign Christians responded to Indian religions and society. Far too much of the energy of Catholic Mission was spent on that continuing internecine struggle between the Padroado, the Portuguese claim to authority, and the Roman Congregation, De Propaganda Fide, the Vatican's. This was a period of decadence in Catholic Mission.

If so much of Protestant Mission tends to be seen as low-church, it will be as well to introduce here another of Nazir-Ali's correctives and to highlight a specifically high-church, Anglican contribution, a 'Catholic' one, rooted in the seventeenth-century non-juror rebellion, but given new life by the Oxford movement of the 1830s. It was both an assertion of the autonomy of the Church from the State, of episcopal authority, and also of the universality of the Church. Here was a missionary impetus that 'led to a commitment to those who were disadvantaged in society and who had been neglected by the Church'.[15]

The real thrust for Protestant Mission came with the evangelical revival of the eighteenth century, one that was to touch all denominations. Our concern here must be to characterize an evangelicalism from the 1830s onwards, rather than to explore its origins. Here was the source of that exclusivist theology that was to type the nineteenth-century Protestant missionary movement. D.W. Bebbington both argues for a break in missiology in the early eighteenth century—the evangelical impulse was new—and for new attitudes in the 1830s.[16] Common throughout would be that 'quadrilateral of priorities':[17] conversionism— there had to be a conversion experience, be it sudden or spread over time; biblicism, though 'no wooden literalness',[18] and not a fundamentalist approach—be Bible Christians not system Christians, said Charles Simeon—to encourage devotion rather than impart a doctrine; activism, that led to Mission; crucicentrism, that led to a major shift of emphasis from the incarnation to the doctrine of atonement.

In Bebbington's intriguing and persuasive analysis, the eighteenth-century evangelical revival, far from being a reaction against the Enlightenment, a form of enthusiasm that jibed at an age of rationalism, shared many of its assumptions. It was rooted in the sensationalist psychology of Locke. Its epistemology was likewise empirical and rational. Still, it had to lay claim to an extra sense, a moral sense, to explain man's access to God's grace, and this seems something of a cheat. Once experienced, conversion could not be lost: this was the crucial 'doctrine of assurance'; as much as anything this gave a less troubled content to Christian conviction. It permitted a 'calmer, sunnier, devotional life'.[19] All this brought Christianity within a framework of rationalism and this does much to explain how rational-minded Hindus of the stature of Ram Mohan Roy were able to enter into a dialogue with Baptist missionaries in the early nineteenth century. If there was millenialianism, it saw the second coming of Christ post the millenium, and a Carey could argue that the millenium would only come, anyway, after the conversion of the 'heathen'. Here was a doctrine of providence quite compatible with an eighteenth-century belief in progress.

Had the mood of evangelicalism remained thus, the nineteenth-century story would surely have been very different. But Bebbington posits a change. About 1830, its 'careful pragmatism' gave way to a new mood: 'they were more confident, more outspoken, more assertive.'[20] 'There was a new appreciation of the dramatic, the extraordinary and the otherworldly element in religion.'[21] Romanticism had touched evangelicalism, with that deeply romantic figure, Edward Irving, as the force behind this transformation. As part of the romantic inflow into evangelicalism, millenialism changed its character: it became pre-millenialism. Evangelicals now believed in the immanent advent of Christ. This 'heightened supernaturalism'[22] encouraged a greater belief in the inspired nature of the Bible, though not, in Bebbington's analysis, to deteriorate into fundamentalism: 'If fundamentalism as a theological phenomenon is defined as belief in the inerrancy of scripture, fundamentalism had not prevailed among evangelicals by this date (1861).'[23] Conviction of the absoluteness of Christ led to a belief in the universal power of the Atonement: here was an anti-Calvinist belief in the salvation of all, *the* critical input into the missionary movement.

In his critique of the London Missionary Society, Irving had attacked a missionary's dependence on his institution. Missionaries should put their faith in God alone. Here was a highly romantic view of the missionary, battling it out on his own.

But this leaves a sense of paradox. If Romanticism was in the air, with its love of the strange and the exotic, should this not have inspired a shift away from an exclusivist theology, and a growing fascination with Indian religions for their own sake? Bishop Heber's positive response to Indian religions, for example, has identified him as a romantic. We will have to see in our study of individual missionaries whether this was the case. But clearly some more negative elements in evangelical theology have yet to be emphasized.

One such constituent was the belief in hell. If we restrict comment to the Protestant Churches—and it was the rejection of the Catholic concept of purgatory, unacceptable for its association with indulgences, that left Protestants with the only alternatives of heaven and hell—the fiercest input into the perceived reality of hell came from the Calvinist doctrine of predestination: only the elite, or saved, went to Heaven, the rest into eternal hell-fire. Social conservatism inevitably reinforced such a theology: hell, as punishment, became a cardinal means of social control. It was a modified Calvinism, more so Arminianism, that broke free from this appalling elitism into a belief in the salvation of all, and this was to have profound implications for Mission. If the heathen were still indeed condemned to hell for their idolatry and disbelief, they could yet be saved through spiritual enlightenment.[24]

Brian Hatcher has very engagingly shown how this nineteenth-century debate on eternal punishment related to the missionaries in India, especially those of the CMS.[25] They proved curiously resistant to that more liberal theology emerging amongst Unitarians and, above all, the broad churchman, F. D. Maurice, with his beliefs, derived from Coleridge, that there was in every individual some faculty for apprehending the divine, and that Revelation was a continuing process through time. Maybe missionaries felt that there would be no justification for their missionary presence in India were they not there to save souls from hell.

There is no doubting the sincerity of this belief. James Long, a CMS missionary, for example, in a letter of 12 October 1838, explaining his missionary vocation, agonized: 'the thought of 800 millions passing into eternity every 30 years without a ray of hope often overwhelms me, then I ask myself the question, am I doing my part to avert these dire consequences?'[26] Brian Hatcher suggests that 'the years 1864 to 1867 appear to represent the high water mark of CMS polemics against broad Church liberalism'.[27] Even so, this view of Hell took some time to fade. Only in 1882 did T. E. Slater, an LMS missionary, in his *Philosophy of Mission*, 1882, state: 'the ghastly argument drawn from the appalling picture of the future misery of the heathen which once aroused missionary assemblies has been abandoned.'[28] Interestingly, a utilitarian emphasis on punishment as reform had given way in the 1860s, in the writings, in particular, of James Fitzjames Stephens, to a renewed emphasis on punishment as retribution.

Social attitudes markedly influenced this theology. And given that Hinduism is as much about social relationships as metaphysical beliefs, an examination of the social prejudices of missionaries goes a long way to explaining their exclusivist theology. In the late eighteenth and early nineteenth centuries many missionaries came from a comparatively humble social background, more artisan than middle class. This was particularly the case with the LMS, and Kooiman has made much of this in his study of Travancore.[29] Geoffrey Oddie shows how this was to remain relatively true of the LMS throughout the century. Yet, from his analysis of 71 out of 146 candidate papers for the period 1845 to 1888, at least a third, it emerges, were from a professional background. S. Piggin demonstrates how missionaries were, in fact, very much an upwardly mobilizing group: 'most missionaries come from occupational groups which were campaigning for greater recognition in the industrializing society to which they owed if not their origins then their increased importance.'[30] To quote again: 'the social classes from which nearly all were drawn were among the most dynamic, aspiring, discontented and restless in a society which was in itself in the process of change.'[31] Education was one means for upward mobilization and an increased Oxbridge recruitment in the 1830s and 1840s points to a more assured middle class intake. Admittedly, only 27 per cent of Oddie's sample had university degrees, but the LMS missionaries were in this respect well below those of the CMS and the Presbyterian, and Oddie, anyway, insists that lack of a university training proved to be no bar to later intellectual achievement. Piggin suggests the dangers of this arrivisme: their class consciousness was potentially harmful: 'it could create a psychological desire for underlings, a role which the convert might be expected to fill to the detriment of his integrity and independence.'[32] Social climbing may clearly have been one possible motive for becoming a missionary and this would do much to explain missionary ambivalence towards the social establishment of Company and officialdom.

But feelings of insecurity went deeper. F. M. L. Thompson, in a brilliant synthesis of current thinking on Victorian social mores, points, as one indicator of moral insecurity, to an obsession with the decay of the family: 'middle class fears of the fragility of their own family ideals, unless these were protected with constant vigilance by elaborate ramparts of morality, modesty, reticence, sexual segregation, parental discipline and male dominance.'[33] Does this explain that almost pathological missionary critique of the extended Indian family so different from their own?

No society was undergoing such drastic social change as nineteenth-century Britain and missionaries surely projected onto Indian society just those same anxieties about shoring up social structures. Did not that same non-conformist Victorian distrust of fairs and their goings on, 'denounced for their disorderliness and gross immorality with even more lurid vehemence than the cruel sports',[34] underlie missionary hostility to the popular world of Hinduism, its fairs, its pilgrimages? Have we not here a desperately frightened attempt to maintain standards in the face of a place so alarmingly alien?

If missionaries were to concern themselves with social questions, did they do so in a spirit of humanitarianism or merely out of moral outrage? Bebbington argues that the Evangelicals simply attacked sin: they 'did not display a blanket humanitarianism in politics. Rather they mounted periodic campaigns against particular evils.'[35] Anything that stood in the way of the propagation of the gospel was denounced as a sin. Theirs was a 'negative policy of reform', their 'campaign was often explicitly anti'.[36] This explains an opposition to slavery and paganism as much as to sexual wrongdoing and drunkenness. It may also explain their attitude to caste.

No other factor seemed so impenetrable a barrier to the spread of Christianity in India. In fact, missionaries were ambivalent about caste and one argument of this text is that a more outright condemnation of caste was only forthcoming by mid-century when it became clear that Hinduism was not, after all, going to collapse. Missionaries made caste the scapegoat for their failures.

Given the social tensions of their own background it is not surprising that missionaries proved so uncertain in their response to so complex a social structure as caste, an affront to their own social ambition and egalitarianism, yet affirmative of an equal quest for a more ordered society. Maybe their obsession with the conversion of Brahmins reflected a certain snobbism. Duncan Forrester has well portrayed this ambiguity, one shared by Indian Christians and by European and Indian lay commentators.[37] It is possible to quote out and out condemnation of caste by the likes of Alexander Duff and Keshub Chunder Sen. Yet there was a far more extensive discourse on the possibility of differentiating between caste as mere social practice, and hence acceptable amongst converts, and as religious belief, and hence unacceptable. Max Mueller was ready to interpret caste as not so very different from class. We will have to see how caste eventually became a decisive issue amongst missionaries by the mid-century. If Indians, particularly Indian Christian converts, responded positively to Christianity for its apparent humanitarian social attitudes, and they were clearly entitled to their own reading of a Christian critique of caste, maybe they were wrong to do so: caste was attacked, not for its invidious social exploitation, but as an obstacle to conversion, as a sin. Even so, paradoxically, missionaries, ostensibly so hostile to caste, were almost obsessive in classifying Indian society along caste lines.

If Exclusivism takes its meaning from a sectarian belief in the superiority of Christianity over other religions, and a refusal to accept that Christians had anything to learn from other faiths, how likely was it that missionaries in the mid-century would have any apprehension of the true nature of Indian religions? Missionaries who went to India received just the same grounding in Classics and Theology, no more no less, as other ministers of religion. Theirs was a call to convert: seemingly, it was not necessary that they should be instructed in these alien faiths. 'One vainly searches the writings of evangelical ministers', comments Piggin, 'for any favourable reflection on non-Christian religion and it is not surprising that the prevailing attitude towards Hinduism for most of the nineteenth century was one of hostility.' 'The decided negative response to other religions appears to have been determined by biblical condemnation of idolatry and the reports of missionaries, shocked even more than they had anticipated by their exposure to epiphenomenal Hinduism.'[38] John Pemble puts this even more strongly: 'few people really doubted that beyond the bounds of Southern Europe the role of the British was to civilize others, not to civilize themselves. There was little that India could teach them and Asia generally was an area of darkness.'[39] Missionaries set out in ignorance. 'It is simply useless', observes Eric Sharpe, 'to criticize the early Evangelical missionaries for not seeing what they could not have seen and for not reading what few Hindus and only a handful of Western scholars even knew existed—the scriptures of the higher Hinduism.'[40] It is the slow unfolding of just this discovery, however, that makes a reading of the journals of the mid-nineteenth-century missionaries so intriguing.

It may help to allay a legitimate sense of Indian anger at such obscurantism if it is shown that India was not its special victim. British travellers to the Mediterranean, Italy in particular, were to display just the same kind of prejudice towards Roman Catholicism. They looked on all the aspects of popular Catholicism—belief in the power of relics, indulgences, images, etc., and the practice of idolatry—as forms of corruption or deviation from 'the authentic Christianity of the early Church'. They were 'a supine surrender' to paganism. Theirs was a horror of mendicancy: 'it removed the salutary stigma of shame from begging and it encouraged charity for the able bodied.' Material evidence of political decline heightened their sense of moral disgust: ruins seemed a visible proof of punishment for some former crime or iniquity. Yet, in Pemble's analysis, this horror in part sprang from a jealous recognition 'of the tremendous proselytizing power of the Roman Catholic Church'. 'Difference', he interprets, 'was the traveller's joy and the writer's inspiration and difference existed only so long as ordinary humanity, the common denominator was held at bay.'[41] The Victorians both experienced and invented the south. Victorian travellers to India arguably did much the same. India merely confirmed their presuppositions or needs. Given that many missionaries found it difficult to distinguish between 'popery' and Hinduism, this comparison takes on some edge. But missionaries were not to keep their distance: on the contrary, they threw themselves into this alien landscape. It is this which makes them so intriguing a case-study of cultural encounter.

So here was a fiercely embattled, bigoted ideology. Bebbington writes of 'the stern moral absolutism' of evangelical crusades: 'their demands were immutable, sacrosanct, certainly not open to negotiation.'[42] This inner-directed, exclusivist, theology was to be infused by secular Victorian values, the very uncertainties of which added an even more compulsive element to the quest for a more ordered, spiritualized society. The end was salvation, the means conversion. It was, of course, as much a personal pursuit of fulfilment as one for the luckless Indians. How was this ambition to be fulfilled?

STRATEGY

Given the enormity of their task, let alone its arrogance, missionaries in mid-century, as before and after, were locked into an often bitter dispute about the best means of conversion. Means are clearly as important as ends in realizing any ideology. So Gandhi was to argue, and, indeed, one of the more intriguing aspects of the way missionaries set about proselytization is their anticipation of Gandhi's own means of propaganda on behalf of his constructive programme. From the late eighteenth century, Protestant missionaries entertained various alternative strategies, overlapping, but with the possibility of emphasis or preference.

At the outset, Company chaplains, circumscribed in their missionary role, fell back on improving the moral tone of Europeans: here, at the least, an example might be set for Indians. Baptist missionaries put their faith in the translation of texts into Indian vernacular and classical languages. William Carey was a formidable linguist, and such translation was always to be a key element in the missionary enterprise. By the mid-nineteenth century, with the development of the press, this approach was to gain a new lease of life, with a demand for a new Christian vernacular literature, a reaching out, through school text-books and newspapers, to a mass audience. In the mid-century, however, the great debate lay between itinerating, the dramatic and direct confrontation with Indian religions, by word of mouth, in the bazaar, the mela, the village, and the slow, more indirect, but less erratic, reliance on education, above all of India's new anglicized elite in secondary education.

It is extraordinary how powerful a hold itinerating was to retain over the minds of missionaries. It was not until the 1880s that the majority came to recognize the greater need to win over the minds of the new élite, and so finally share that sense of priorities which Alexander Duff had promulgated in the 1830s.

The vanity and naiveté of the itinerating endeavour, that the Christian message should and could be spread to all and sundry, everywhere, is incomprehensible without recognizing both a millenarian belief that the British were in India for just this missionary purpose—it was for this that Providence had spared England defeat at the hands of Napoleon—and an almost apocalyptic faith that Indian religions were in terminal decline. One had but to blow the trumpet and the walls of Jericho would come tumbling down.

As an outcome of this missionary activity there was the tentative beginnings of an Indian Protestant community; only grudgingly did European missionaries come to accept a need to spend more time cultivating this emergent church, above all by training an Indian priesthood. By mid-century any distraction from the call of itinerating was resented.

One way into this debate is to look at a series of missionary conferences, held between the 1850s and 1880s, telling the story chronologically, the better to trace that slow shift towards education, but, above all, just to see the way missionaries sought to realize their ideological purpose. But two issues will be surveyed: the debate over strategy between itinerating and education; and the role of an Indian clergy.

The first of these conferences, the first indeed to be held after sixty years of Mission in Bengal, took place in the town hall of Calcutta, from 4–7 of September 1855.[43] Revd J. Mullens opened proceedings with a paper, *On the Progress made by Christian Missions in Bengal.* Hinduism, he persuaded himself, was 'going downhill': 'we have obtained a real hold on the country'; the Company secured any advances they had made. He

did express worry, however, at the dependency of the young church of
Bengal: 'we have not yet one church supporting its own pastor.'[44]

Fellow L. M. S. missionary, Revd A. F. Lacroix, followed with a
paper, *On the Peculiar Difficulties Encountered by Missionaries in Bengal*.
Here was an all too sadly familiar critique by the English of the Bengali
character: their 'distressing unimpressibility', 'levity', their turning 'the
most solemn truth into ridicule', 'obsequiousness, plausibility and apparent sincerity' (a reference to some ulterior material motive in approaching missionaries), 'their extreme timidity and their deficiency in nearly
all these qualities which constitute manliness'. There followed an interesting commentary on how with Hinduism, so interwoven with social
existence, missionaries, to make any headway, had to 'denationalize the
Hindus in many points'. Cultures with 'written books' were a far greater
challenge than those with an oral tradition. Hindu doctrine, above all its
pantheism, rendered 'preposterous' any apologetics for the atonement.
Lacroix enumerated all the obstacles in their path: caste, with its undermining of 'brotherly love' and its disqualifying converts, through their
becoming outcaste, as examples for caste Hindus; the tyrannical hold of
Brahmin priesthood; the social exclusion of women, normally a natural
constituency for the missionary; and the hostility of zamindars who
regarded their Christian tenants as troublemakers, and whose intimida-
tion bred that very 'mean slavish cringing disposition' which undermined the self-reliance of the new Christian communities. The Brahmos,
who saw the Christians as rivals to their own reform movement, were a
special challenge. Missionaries, being foreigners, were despised as im-
pure; native preachers, as outcastes, were little better. Poor mastery of the
vernaculars often led to misunderstandings. All these obstacles, it was
felt, should put missionaries on their guard against any expectation of
immediate success.[45]

In discussion, the Revd Lal Behari Day, one of the converts to be discussed, rallied to the defence of his fellow Bengalis; they were, he argued,
no more covetous than the English and, if timid, so were the other
Indians. They were, besides, 'undoubtedly the most religious people
on the face of the earth'. Fellow Free Church of Scotland missionary,
T. Smith, accused Day of betraying 'an unnecessary amount of zeal on
behalf of his countrymen', but then put in a good word on behalf of
education, especially female education and medical Mission, seeing here
the answer to caste.

On the following day, a Baptist missionary for Calcutta, J. Wenger,
took up the cudgels on behalf *Of Preaching the Gospel in the Native*

Tongues. Now battle was joined with the pro-educationalists. Whilst conceding that school children taught through the medium of English were 'more attentive, more intelligent and more free from prejudice and consequently better prepared for understanding the gospel than those we meet in the streets and market-places and at religious festivals', nevertheless, the gospel command was to 'preach the gospel to every creature and not only to educated young men'. 'If a distinction is allowable, a preaching missionary', he asserted, 'is the highest style of missionary'. One had still to put one's faith in European over Indian missionaries; 'frequently the enemies of the gospel insult native preachers with a malignity which they would never think of manifesting towards Europeans'. But Europeans needed their support, 'for out of door preaching in a hot climate and in the midst of a steaming crowd, requires an amount of physical exertion and endurance which the strongest man cannot sustain much longer than an hour at a time'. Besides, the joint activities of Europeans and Indians proved that Christianity 'constitutes a bond of brotherhood unknown to Hinduism'.[46]

There followed a very vivid account by Revd J. Stubbins of itinerating in Orissa. Here it was on horseback. The tent would be pitched amongst the villages, for some six weeks to two months, undertaking journeys from four to ten miles away: 'we sometimes travel as much as a thousand miles during a cold season'. To attract attention one sang a page or two from one of the poetical tracts; followed either by a passage from the same poem, 'a native sloka', a 'striking portion of scripture', or 'the remark of a bystander'. Nothing should be abstruse; it should always be personalized and in the vernacular: 'let him reserve his Sanskrit plumes for his tent or elsewhere!' If an audience goes dead, tell a joke, a story, 'bore him till he answers you'. Singing a verse or two will quieten an audience. 'Never manifest hurry or confusion, and never let it be seen that you are driven away, though such in reality be the case.' Introduce quotations from the shastras. And 'never go out without your bazar-book': 'this book should be the missionary's companion, whether in the bazar, market festival or study and everything should go in it.'[47]

The discussion ended with resolution placing the highest possible premium on itinerating: those who mastered the vernacular should devote all their time to preaching, and 'those who are directed to other plans should also give it as much time and effort as they can.' Itinerating should be extensive, regular and systematic. High claims for its efficacy were made: 'especially has it contributed to the marked change in religious views, both as to the character of Hinduism and the worth of Christianity, which distinguishes the present generation of the Hindu from those who have preceded it.'[48]

All this stung the pro-educationalists into a minority statement. Revd D. Ewart (Scottish Mission) took up the defence of English missionary education. It was, he conceded, education for the élite, for 'the middle ranks' of Indian society: 'middle ranks not as regards caste but middle ranks as regards wealth and worldly influence.' And if Brahmins did make up a quarter of those in English schools, who could quarrel with so influential a caste being imbued 'with the sound principles of modern philosophy'. But of scarcely less importance were 'the vast tribes of Ghoshes, Mitras, Basus, Dattas, Dases, Des and the like'. Only a few attended government schools and this was why a free education was so vital for attracting the rest. Such schools were to be in Calcutta or its immediate suburbs. The aim was to evangelize the pupils, and this could only be achieved with missionaries as teachers. The missionary gained attention 'by imparting useful and eagerly desired knowledge, call it secular if you wish, and follows it up by preaching the gospel to the impressible minds that surround him'. Missionaries were perfectly prepared that the arguments they brought forward for religion should be judged by just the same criteria as for secular learning. Such a missionary education led to 'the utter annihilation' of the major obstacles in the way of evangelism; it 'has a certain and powerful destructive tendency as regards all confidence in the Hindu shastras and all regard to the distinction of caste'. If outward conformity remained, 'the spell (was) effectively broken'. Even the consciences of unbelievers were 'Christianized'. He ended by demonstrating the success rate of conversion, highlighting Brahmin conversions.[49]

Later, E. B. Underhill, Secretary of the Baptist Missionary Society, on a visit to India, summed up these differences. He accepted 'that a general dissatisfaction seems to exist in all missionary bodies as to the results hitherto won by education for the gospel'. The verdict was in favour of itinerating: 'wisely or unwisely, they think they cannot safely depart from the direct command of the Lord to preach; to reach in the most direct, the simplest, the most effective way, every perishing sinner, to set before him with all the pathos of the human voice, and the eloquence of the human eye, and the warm passionate utterances of a heart on fire with the theme, the love of Christ and God.'[50]

It is something of a relief to come across in an appendix—he could not attend the conference—recognition by one of the most experienced CMS missionaries, William Smith of Benares, of how the itinerant preacher did grate on the ears of his audience: 'I tell them that I know very well they look upon us as officious intruders—that our very appearance among them as religious teachers is an insult to their understanding, to the wisdom of their forefathers and to the religion which they profess.' Still, he defended the activity: 'we desire as far as we know to do you good; though you, alas, look upon us as the greatest enemies you have.'[51]

Post-rebellion, the missionaries in south India met at Ootacamund from 19 April–5 May 1858. Given the much larger Christian community in the south one might have expected a somewhat different set of priorities. But the conference was to adopt a remarkably similar approach to the one in Bengal.[52]

The lead paper on itinerating came from Ragland, well known for his preaching tours in north Tinnevelly. Revd G. U. Pope, SPG, had already observed how his Mission had given more time to itinerating then ever before. Ragland gave eleven months a year to itinerating, even though the climate permitted but half an hour to an hour, morning and evening. They would try to visit each village at least twice a year, and some three or four times. There was no set plan. 'It is our endeavour in all our intercourse with the heathen to do what we can; to excite in their minds a feeling of responsibility, to correct their ideas of what God requires, and to convince them that they are sinners, and that nothing they are doing or can do is of avail to remove their guilt.' But as the audience was so unpredictable, 'the persons we meet are so varied in character, in circumstances and capability of understanding and the measure of attention we meet with is so utterly uncertain, that we can seldom reckon upon being able to preach as we intended'. All was ad hoc and contingent. 'We are utterly at a loss to say whether we ought to concentrate our efforts more or less. In general we are disposed to think that the Missionary's duty is rather to watch prayerfully and to follow humbly the indications of Divine providence than to lay down any previous plan except the circumstances of the district where his labours are peculiar.' The primacy of this activity was not in doubt; 'it seems essential to us that the Missionary should be entirely released from work of every other description.' Ragland was not so convinced of the necessity to master the vernaculars and understand local religions: 'the importance of these may be overrated. Before entering upon the work let no pains be spared; but after beginning to be actually engaged in it, let the work itself, not the acquisition of improved talents for it, be the *great* and I would say the *sole* object of attention.' Besides, we rarely encounter Indians 'who possess more than a smattering of this knowledge themselves'.[53] The conference gave itinerating its full approval.

The conference looked at education from several angles, but clearly education came off second best. Indians, argued Sargent, must be trained young: 'the Hindu mind seems to attain its prime of vigour under 30 years, beyond which there is generally speaking no progress.' The Revd W. Tracy of the American Madura Mission, saw little future for Duff's schools except in large cities: 'that they have been successful as converting agencies is not so clear.' The Revd D. Coles, LMS (Bellary), however, provided a somewhat surprisingly favourable apologetic for government schools. At the least, they trained the mind, and their secularism, though subverting superstition, could hardly be blamed for undermining 'a public morality which did not exist'. They 'loosen caste'. If the exclusion of the Bible was to be deplored, nevertheless, 'it is not to be overlooked that the area of what is commonly called English literature is more or less pervaded with the ideas and sentiments of Christianity'.[54]

There was a curious paper on attitudes towards Indian Christians and enquirers into Christianity. 'It is and has been too much the practice of professing European Christians in this land to call them by the contemptuous names of "niggers" and "rascals" and other terms of approach.' This did not deter the speaker from drawing attention to 'the dark part of their character, especially their lying, deceitfulness, ingratitude, dishonesty, idleness and uncleanness. Their gross apathy and neglect of the wants of the sick and distressed are also painfully manifest.' Here was a southern equivalent to the character assassination of the Bengalis.[55]

The Conference ended on a high note. The collapse of the rebellion was seen as creating new opportunities for missionaries. The government must revise its religious neutrality: there should be no more protection of idolatry and caste. 'The system hitherto *has been deference to idolatry and indifference to Christianity.* We plead for a reversal of this system.' The whole missionary enterprise must be reconceived. 'The means hitherto employed have been so utterly inadequate to the accomplishment of the end aimed at.' Yet, 'old Indian nationalities' have been defeated, and caste 'is being horribly battered and shaken'. Do we not see 'the Apocalyptic angel flying in the Heaven?' 'This great country is speedily destined to become one of the richest of the Redeemer's many crowns.'[56]

The next Conference opened up the story of missionary activity in the North West Provinces and the Punjab. It was held at Lahore, from

December 1862 to January 1863.[57] Islam and Sikhism featured alongside Hinduism. There were signs of a less confrontationalist approach. 'Bazar controversy', it was asserted, 'should be pertinaciously avoided . . . it nearly always degenerates and produces bitter fruits.' Itinerating still held the day, but with a revisionist edge.

The Revd Robert Bruce wondered if current modes of itinerating really worked: on longer journeys, little or no real contact was made; on more highly concentrated journeys, they simply lacked the labour power to achieve frequent contact with the villagers. Still, the latter was preferable and he himself regretted that he had not, like Ragland, given 'himself more perseveringly to a humbler sphere of systematic labour, instead of traversing such large tracts of country as I did'. Were one missionary to free himself entirely from all other commitments and be placed permanently in the field, Indians would no longer see itinerant preachers as bent on pleasure trips in the cold season. New churches should be backed up by an Indian pastorate.[58]

Education did not feature prominently but neither was it sleighted. The Revd Forman, American Presbyterian Mission, Lahore, thought Mission schools should freely admit their ambition for conversion. English schools in the cities exercised, in Robert Clark's judgement, a greater influence than acknowledged: the pupils carried the gospel message back to their homes. In fact, the major debate in the conference, and an interesting sign of the way missionaries had failed, to date, to address the question of how to handle the new churches they were creating, was on the native pastorate.

It was the Revd Herron who upset the applecart by exposing how poor in fact the relationship was between the missionaries and the Indian Christians. In the eyes of the Indian Christian élite they were seen as arrogant; of the majority, harsh and indifferent to their material needs. Many Indian Christians, indeed, looked on them as 'their enemies'. Too little time was given to their interests. Were missionaries to love them, they would master their languages, seek out their company, and 'overcome all the difficulties that arise from difference of race, civilization, education, manners and customs'. At the receiving end of this arrogance, the Revd Goloknath presented an even more damaging picture. There was a lack of fellow feeling; missionaries were too well-off; converts looked on them as but 'paid agents of a Religious Company'; once converted, missionaries no longer wished to know their converts. He quoted another received view: 'missionaries were much more friendly to the heathen whom they wish to catch in their net, than to their converts, whom they have already bagged.' Converts from poor backgrounds did expect material gain, but they were invariably disappointed. Missionaries were aloof and made it worse by having favourites.[59]

To give the conference its due, it recognized that here was an attack it had to confront. Many recognized how isolated and vulnerable Indian Christians indeed were. At the end of the Conference, the Revd Ferguson tried to scotch the rumours that there had been an attempt to stop this discussion. He then took the offensive. The fault lay with the educated convert: 'their intellectual training had been much more successful than their moral and religious training.' How could they not know that European missionaries, their spiritual fathers, loved them? He conceded, though, that the state of the Indian Christian churches did not reflect well on the way they had been trained.[60] This proved to be a sobering conference. Sir Herbert Edwardes concluded with the thought that God had not brought them to India for any material progress, but to 'conquer it for God'.

The Allahabad Conference in December 1872, whilst having much to say on Indian religions, seemingly sidestepped the debate on strategy.[61] The Revd Bhattacharja, Free Church Mission, Mahanad, Bengal, struck a relativist note: 'I think every Missionary should be left to choose that method of preaching the gospel which he, in his mature judgement, thinks best and for which he has a natural aptitude.' Missionaries now met a less violent opposition in the cities; in the villages they were listened to with respect. But they fooled themselves if they believed that Hinduism was on the wane: 'by far the vast majority of the nation is still Hindu in faith and practice . . ., I do not believe it will crumble to pieces so soon as many sanguine friends expect.' Brahmoism 'exerts just now a most pernicious influence in counteracting the efforts of missionary labours'. Admittedly, the Raj was supportive; the missionary 'may itinerate throughout the length and breadth of the land, and preach the gospel to as many people as he likes'. But the rate of conversion was frankly disappointing, however large the number of those 'who have not the moral courage to make a public confession of their faith in Christ'.

Robert Clark addressed the embarrassing issue of Indian churches. 'Our Native brethren', he accepted, 'will no longer brook being treated as children and rightly so'; their independence 'is the aim of our lives and the fruit of our toil'. However, echoing Macaulay's political views in the 1830s, he added: 'this is in the future. For the present, the Native Church of India can no more dream of such independence than a child at school can think he can live independently of his father's care'. 'Facts show that the foreign Missionary is still the originator, the organizer and supporter of almost every work. We cannot alter facts or go before nature.'[62] Clark was, as ever, the imperialist.

The Revd Sherring sought comfort elsewhere. It was remarkable that the number of foreign missionaries had not altered; it was 478 in 1861 and 486 in 1871. Yet educational statistics showed a dramatic rise: in 1861, there were 75,475 in Mission schools and by 1871, 1,22,372. His theme was to put less weight on conversion, and more on the moral influence of Mission. 'Generally speaking, there is a better appreciation of justice, morality and religion.' Even if there was not a single Hindu yet converted to the Christian faith, these moral and social changes 'would stamp the great humanizing work in which we are engaged as one of the most noble and beneficent that the world ever saw'.[63] This was a significant shift in perspective.

A. Mathew, however, sees the conference as a threshold one with regard to education. It was here that William Miller, Madras Christian College, made his seminal speech, with especial regard to Christian higher education, but covering secondary education as well, shifting the focus from direct evangelism to preparation, more a question of shaping mental attitudes than conversion. For Mathew, 1872 was a watershed in strategy.[64]

With the retrospective feel of both the final two conferences under review, we can have a sense of how missionary ideology evolved over the mid-century. At the Bangalore Conference of 1879,[65] the Revd T. Sargent started proceedings with a sense of the Mission exercise in a groove: 'I take for granted there are no discoveries to be made in the mode of missionary operations. We know exactly how the matter stands. There is no new story, no new lines on which we can move in reference to conversion.'[66] This certainly seemed the case with itinerating. The Revd Alexander, discussing the Telugu Mission, thought Ragland had got it right in Tinnevelly, with his separate itinerating agency. The more narrowly concentrated mode was best, though he retained a hankering for the longer journey; selling tracts over a long stretch of country reaped some dividends. Wives were an asset on shorter journeys: respectable women from the high castes would pay a visit, and 'have a look at the wonderful things of European art which an English lady always has with her'. Wives could also visit the homes of village officials, karnans and munsiffs, and of village landowners. Indian assistants were indispensable and Alexander pointed to a new conversion structure: catechists, preaching in or near a village; Readers, taking on 'more aggressive work' further afield; and Christian fakirs, 'generally men powerful in native song', who rely on the people for support, 'natural and true evangelists not hindered by notions which embarrass our more educated natives'.[67]

The debate on education was both of a higher order and indicative of its usurpation of itinerating as the preferred strategy. At an early stage William Miller, by now the doyen of Scottish educationists, argued for this 'slow thoughtful work that does not demand an immediate result': 'the Christian Church is too apt to think that the moment the Word is proclaimed, God is bound to bring about a result. There is too much thinking that the walls of Jericho should fall down the moment the horns are sounded.'[68] Fulsome acknowledgement followed of the work of such teachers as the blind Cruickshanks and Robert Noble, by Europeans and Indians alike. (They will be looked at in the chapter on Indian Christians in the south.) Conversion was not paramount. For Revd Hudson, Wesleyan, Bangalore, many students left Mission schools out of all patience with orthodox Hinduism: 'we shall never know the amount of secret discipleship.'[69]

Rajahgopaul, however, another Indian Christian to be looked at, entered a caveat. Many, he observed, passed through the whole curriculum of government and Mission schools 'whose moral nature is entirely unaffected and who have not been touched in their superstitions. They are as thorough going and orthodox Hindu as their forefathers; they as devoutly believe in all the puranic absurdities; observe good and bad days; they are terrified at bad omens and will retrace their steps if they meet at starting a Brahmin widow or an oilmonger or a cat, even the sneeze of an infant'. 'I believe there are at this moment more men studying Sanskrit works either in the original or more often in English than at any period before.' Some students, he conceded, 'break from idolatry and caste' but 'the majority do not and live false hypocritical lives'. 'It leads to terrible searing of conscience, deadening of all high thoughts and aspirations and as a final resort they sink into deism or neo-Vedantism.' It did not help that there were such impassable social barriers between Indians and Europeans. 'We seem to be on the verge of a great crisis in the history of India. Old things are passing away and the native is in a state of transition. Soon opinions and habits will be fixed. Such a change comes but once in a nation's history, offering alike glorious opportunities of moulding the character of the people and impressing upon them while still in a plastic state the stamp of Christianity.' The Revd Graeter, Bangalore, however, had little patience with those who did not come out and declare themselves as Christians. The difference with those who do so is 'between the moon and the sun'.[70]

There was yet another debate on the character of the Indian Church, with a focus this time on cultural norms. In this battle for the mind and soul of Hindus, how could one be sure that old values were not lurking behind Christian ways? There was the risk of formalism—might not that Hindu trust in mere external observances be carried over into Christian worship? Would one not have to insist on certain physical acts to be sure that old values did not still prevail, as, for example, cutting off the kudumi? As the Revd Burgess put it, 'as the clean shaven head is an undoubted sign of Mohammedanism and the kudumi an unmistakable sign of a Hindu, so the grown hair almost invariably points at least to the nominal profession of the Christian faith'. Should one insist on intermarriage between castes? Burgess cast doubts on the strength of any conversion: 'we have as a rule to deal with those who have no sense of sin, no realization whatever of pending evil, and consequently no yearning desire to flee from the wrath to come. It is not difficult to understand how such a people, naturally apathetic, and almost devoid of the power of perceiving spiritual truth, should content themselves with the bare fact of being connected with a Christian community and attending religious services.'[71] If this applied more to low-caste converts, it still suggests that missionaries had but little faith that their ideology had in any real sense prevailed.

A similar pessimism was expressed in the editorial conclusion to the Conference. If mere material motives did not explain low-caste conversions, their accession 'cannot be attributed to an enlightened spiritual awakening, or to a purely religious movement of any kind'. Might not the conversion anyway simply pave the way for sanskritization? Becoming Christian was but one foot up the caste ladder. Even so, the prospect was still entertained of the dissolution of Hinduism and the disintegration of Hindu society. Significantly, education was now given priority. 'All missionaries have become ever more deeply convinced of the necessity and importance of Christian schools as a missionary agency.' There was some progress on the question of means: 'different methods of missionary work are no longer set in opposition to each other and the adoption of one regarded as the disapproval of another.' But itinerating left much to be desired: 'in few instances, apparently, has provision been made for steady continuous development. Much power is thrown away by being dispersed over too large an area.' The future lay with 'evangelistic work amongst educated natives in the larger towns', and female education.[72]

If the Calcutta Conference of 1882 was to confirm the findings of the Bangalore Conference, it also expressed doubts on the ways to proceed.[73]

Itinerating likewise came under suspicion. For the Revd Mathura Nath Bose, Gopalgunge, preaching in the bazar got nowhere unless it was followed by home visits. Even so experienced a Baptist missionary as Revd T. Smith of Delhi queried the whole exercise. Confrontationalism was fiercely criticized: hearers leave 'with wounded feelings that never have another opportunity of being healed'. If preachers knew their Indian religions, less harm would follow, but often they did not: 'bazar preaching is an invaluable agency if carried on in a Christian spirit by men of needful attainments and qualifications, otherwise it is doubtful whether the good or evil proceeding from·it is greater.' He was a great believer in singing Indian bhajans and playing Indian music as a way of attracting a sympathetic audience. 'Above all the missionary should preach by his life'; he should be the opposite of the supercilious, racist, Europeans in India. Another very experienced missionary, Revd T. P. Hughes of Peshawar, argued: 'unless a man has some very special quali-fications for the task, he probably does more harm than good in attempt-ing to preach in the streets.'[74]

Just at the moment Mission was being won over to the primacy of education, the educationists themselves began to experience doubt. Paraphrasing the ideas of Alexander Duff, J. Wilson, Established Church of Scotland, Calcutta, did not believe Hinduism had been 'killed through its brain', only 'scotched' at best. 'The hereditary affection of many generations will not let it die.' If the educated class reject the Vedas and Tantras, they still clung to 'the sweet and precious kernel that remains', Hinduism as 'a beautiful religion'. One might hope that they will ex-perience 'a real sense of sin and guilt': but, for the moment, 'these refuges of lies, the accidental results of education, must have their day'.[75] R. C. Bose saw the new élite as but half way between 'heathenism and Chris-tianity . . . the most noticeable fruits of education more or less thor-oughly Christian'. He likewise bemoaned their lack of a sense of sin: 'they ought to be shaken out of the delusive notions behind which their secularity lies entrenched; and their consciousness of sin, deadened by false theories and continued self-indulgence, should be revived.'[76]

K. C. Banerjea, most eminent of the Bengali Christians, levelled an even more damaging critique: they were over-privileging the élite, giving them a false sense of their own importance. By challenging their logic and philosophy in kind, 'these educated men felt that they must never ack-nowledge that their logic is faulty or their philosophy false'. One should put one's faith instead in the Bible.[77] It is hardly surprising that at an-other meeting, W. Miller rushed to education's defence: 'there was no need for defending what all Christian men accustomed to consecutive thought were now completely agreed on.[78]

The problematic of the dependency of the Indian Church was once again addressed. W. T. Satthianadhan of the CMS, Madras, felt the answer, financially anyway, lay with small contributions from 'the poor many' rather than the 'rich few'. The CMS was embarking on a phased withdrawal of support, one twentieth of their grant per year. But he requested that it continue to carry the whole burden of educational costs. If the Indian priest was not properly trained, the whole venture would flounder. And he begged the missionary societies to adopt a consistent line; it would be fatal if some encouraged self-reliance, while others did not. The Revd Dutt, Khulna, felt the moment for withdrawal of support had not yet come. The Revd Mukerjee took up an old complaint: how could the Church not be stunted when missionaries neglected the needs of new converts?[79]

Signs of a major new departure in Mission was a paper on medical missions.[80] Over time the missionaries had acquired a guarded, suspicious attitude towards those they sought to convert. 'In few respects do young and old missionaries differ more', observed the Missionary Manual, 'than in the feelings which they listen to professional enquirers after the truth. The former in general regarded them somewhat like the Philippian gaoler, supposing them to seek out only the salvation of souls. The latter through bitter experience almost instinctively say to themselves, what temporal object have these men in view?' Nine out of ten would be so motivated. Large-scale, low-caste conversion had seemingly demoralized rather than encouraged missionaries. Still, the Manual observed, 'the instruction of sincere enquirers will form one of the most delightful parts of the Missionary labour'.[81]

There was a reluctant, but gradual, awareness of the frailty of the missionary endeavour. 'It is evident', conceded the Manual, 'that the evangelization of a country containing two hundred millions of inhabitants can never be affected by a handful of foreigners.' They were forced back on an alternative agency of Indian priests. Yet, all along, this had been given insufficient attention. 'Few errors', again conceded the Manual, 'have done more to retard the progress of Christianity in India than the overlooking of this most important department.'[82] Had European missionaries felt threatened by the prospect of such an emergent Indian priesthood? Was there here an analogy to the civilian distrust of the Indianization of the civil service? A continuing vanity that they could do it on their own? Or was it the problematic of fashioning a priesthood that would not merely be their mirror-image, but Indian?

This analysis has opened up key questions on the nature of Exclusivist theology, and around the central debate over means, between itinerating or education. It has exposed a serious gap in missionary awareness: its failure to take sufficient interest in the Indian Christian community itself, and in the need to train an Indian priesthood. All these themes will be dealt with in individual case-studies in Part II.

NOTES AND REFERENCES

1. Norman Lewis, *The Missionaries*, London: 1988.
2. Ibid., p. 174.
3. Susan Bayly, *Saints, Goddesses and Kings. Muslims and Christians in South Indian Society, 1700–1900*, Cambridge: 1989.
4. Ibid., p. 285.
5. Ibid., p. 285.
6. Ibid., p. 294.
7. Ibid., p. 459.
8. See his wide-ranging inaugural lecture, 'Religion and Empire: British Expansion in the Long 19th Century, 1780–1914', 20 November 1991, King's College, London.
9. P. Carson, 'An Imperial Dilemma: The Propagation of Christianity in Early Colonial India', *The Journal of Imperial and Commonwealth History*, vol. 18, no. 2, May 1990, pp. 169–90.
10. Bernard Cohn, see his essay, 'The British in Benares: A Nineteenth-Century Colonial Society', in *An Anthropologist among the Historians and Other Essays*, p. 458, Delhi: 1987.
11. Michael Nazir-Ali, *From Everywhere to Everywhere: A World View of Christian Witness*, London: 1991.
12. Ibid., p. 30.
13. Ibid., p. 43.
14. Ibid., p. 44.
15. Ibid., p. 53.
16. D. W. Bebbington, *Evangelicalism in Modern Britain: A History from the 1730's to the 1980's*, London: 1989.
17. Ibid., p. 3.
18. Ibid., p. 13.
19. Ibid., p. 47.
20. Ibid., p. 75.
21. Ibid., p. 81.
22. Ibid., p. 81.
23. Ibid., p. 91.
24. One way through this discourse on Hell is Geoffrey Rowell's *Hell and the Victorians*, Oxford: 1974.
25. Brian Hatcher, 'Eternal Punishment and Christian Missions: The Response of

the Church Missionary Society to Broad Church Theology', *Anglican Theological Review*, vol. LXXII, no. 1, Winter 1990, pp. 39–61.

26. Quoted in G. A. Oddie, 'India and Missionary Motives *c.* 1850–1900', *Journal of Ecclesiastical History*, vol. XXV, no. 1, January 1974.
27. Hatcher, p. 49.
28. Oddie, p. 69.
29. Dick Kooiman, Conversion and Social Equality in India: *The London Missionary Society in South Travancore in the 19th Century*, New Delhi: 1989.
30. S. Piggin, *Making Evangelical Missionaries, 1789–1858*, Sutton Courtenay: 1984, p. 36.
31. Ibid., p. 47.
32. Ibid., p. 31.
33. F. M. L. Thompson, *The Rise of Respectable Society*, London: 1988 (Fontana edn), p. 89.
34. Ibid., p. 135.
35. Bebbington, p. 133.
36. Ibid., p. 135.
37. D. B. Forrester, *Caste and Christianity. Attitudes and Policies on Caste of Anglo-Saxon Protestant Missionaries in India*, London: 1980. (I read this in manuscript.)
38. Piggin, p. 117.
39. John Pemble, *The Mediterranean Passion: Victorians and Edwardians in the South*, Oxford: 1987. My references are to the pb. edn, 1987, p. 60.
40. Eric J. Sharpe, *Faith Meets Faith: Some Christian Attitudes to Hinduism in the 19th and 20th Centuries*, London: 1977, p. 9.
41. Pemble, pp. 210–40.
42. Bebbington, pp. 210–40.
43. Proceedings of a General Conference, Calcutta, 1855.
44. Ibid., pp. 4–17.
45. Ibid., pp. 24–39.
46. Ibid., pp. 43–53.
47. Ibid., pp. 53–9.
48. Ibid., pp. 64–6.
49. Ibid., pp. 67–79.
50. Ibid., pp. 119–23.
51. Ibid., p. 171.
52. Proceedings of the South Indian Missionary Conference, Ootacamund, 19 April–5 May 1858, Madras: 1858.
53. Ibid., pp. 140–53.
54. Ibid., pp. 161–212.
55. Edward Porter, 'Essay on Native Christians. How many of their character and social position be raised?' ibid., pp. 242–8.
56. Editorial Committee's Statement and Appeal, Appendix, ibid., i–xv.
57. Report of the Punjab Missionary Conference, December 1862–January 1863, Lodiana: 1863.
58. Ibid., pp. 75–83.
59. Ibid., pp. 160–85.

60. Ibid., pp. 325–7.
61. Report of the General Missionary Conference, Allahabad, 1872–73, London: 1873.
62. Ibid., pp. 314–17.
63. Ibid., pp. 476–83.
64. A. Mathew, *Christian Mission Education and Nationalism: From Dominance to Compromise, 1870–1930*, Delhi: 1988, see Chapter 3.
65. The Missionary Conference, South India and Ceylon, Bangalore, 1879, London: 1880.
66. Ibid., p. 2.
67. Ibid., pp. 6–11.
68. Ibid., pp. 29–30.
69. Ibid., p. 79.
70. Ibid., pp. 105–15.
71. Ibid., 294–317.
72. William Stevenson, General Review, ibid., pp. 441–61.
73. Report of the Second Decennial Missionary Conference held at Calcutta, 1882–83, Calcutta: 1883.
74. Ibid., pp. 10–27.
75. Ibid., pp. 119–23.
76. Ibid., pp. 164–8.
77. Ibid., pp. 172–3.
78. Ibid., p. 331.
79. Ibid., pp. 251–77.
80. Revd W. Chester (Dindigal Medical Missions), ibid., 388–98
81. Indian Missionary Manual, 1st published 1864, pp. 266–9.
82. Ibid., pp. 291–307.

CHAPTER 2

Cultural Context

This is the story of a cultural encounter. To describe the nature of the interaction, be it of European missionaries with Indian religions and culture, or of Indians with Christianity, one has to undertake complex explorations of a contextualizing kind. How does a missionary's response compare with other kinds of European response to India? Do we need a distinct paradigm for the missionary? And how should one talk about the nature of conversion? This is primarily a study of a Christian elite and this encourages an intellectual rather than a sociological account: it is easier to say how ideas operated in the case of an individual as opposed to mass conversion. But no analysis can be undertaken along these lines that does not attempt to characterize Indian religions themselves. Their history has always proved elusive. Maybe a Hindu reluctance to engage in a linear view of history, with a preference, instead, for a cyclical and magical view of time, has lessened the likelihood of any convincing historical account of Hinduism. Between any exploration of missionary attitudes and those of converts one must insert some preliminary appraisal of where these religions were by mid-century. Hinduism, however, will be privileged at the expense of Islam and Sikhism.

ORIENTALISM, ANGLICISM, SECULARISM:
CONTEXTUALIZING MISSIONARY ATTITUDES

In order to describe European attitudes to India one has to engage in the current debate on Orientalism. In much the same way as have the concepts of modernism and post-modernism dominated the intellectual history of western culture, so this, likewise, threatens the intellectual history of modern India. At one stage historians were offered for the nineteenth century a two-track approach: an orientalist and an anglicist. This is in danger of disappearing in the all-embracing claims made for an orientalist discourse. Can missionary attitudes, given the variety of their response to India, be in any way attached to these possible clusters of ideas? How did the so called orientalists set about exploring Indian culture, and was there any kind of legacy that the missionaries were to adopt?

At first glance, Orientalism was simply a scholarly enquiry into India's classical culture. Many officials of the East India Company, the most famous being William Jones, took a passionate interest in this culture. The Asiatic Society was set up in 1784 to promote research in this subject.[1] Some historians have seen here the pioneering rediscovery of India's cultural past and a vital contribution to cultural revivalism and Indian nationalism in the late nineteenth century[2]. Any reading of this orientalist enterprise and of Jones' career which does not recognize their contribution to Indology would indeed be perverse.

Yet it would be equally naive not to query whether an outsider can ever wholly or impartially grasp another culture. Clearly, scholarship for its own sake did not alone impel the orientalist endeavour. There was a recognition that a better understanding of Indian culture would facilitate more effective government and trade. This has been taken very much further. Edward Said interprets Orientalism as an imperialist attempt to impose an invidious account of Asian culture, its failure to match up to western values; here was an urge to dominate which pre-empted the possibility of any genuine imaginative attempt to understand the 'other', the Indian 'other', to be reconstructed, instead, according to the value system of the West.[3] Said's text has prompted a spate of writing, so much so that anti-Orientalism threatens to swamp the study of modern Indian culture.[4] Fortunately, a post-Orientalism is beginning to surface. Commonsense claims are now to be heard on why we can, and should, accept the 'other', a recrudescence of cultural relativism, an approach which once again legitimizes a discussion of India in terms of its own distinct social and religious forms.[5] Javed Majeed writes of Said's 'rather monolithic and ahistorical conception of orientalism'.[6] And certainly Said's account, if less concerned with India than the Middle East, threatens to obscure our understanding of just how a scholar-administrator like Jones did try to understand Indian culture. In many ways his was the most admirable way to attempt an understanding of India and here its relevance is to ask whether missionaries were in any way to be his imitator. But here also is some exoneration for an orientalist tendency to impose essentialist categories such as caste and community on India.

It is just the way that Jones tries to understand India that sets him up as such an interesting foil to the missionaries. On his arrival in Calcutta, he immediately set to work with Arabic and Persian scholars in the mornings, and Hindus in the afternoons. He very soon fell under the spell of Indian classical literature; he found the Mahabharata as exhilarating as the Iliad. He was also fascinated by a Persian translation of one of the Puranas. But though he himself sought out Indian scholars, he was unable to persuade the Asiatic Society to grant them membership, and there was always to be some distance between Jones and the Bengali intelligentsia. However, his ignorance of Sanskrit remained, and in 1785 he took himself off to the centre of Brahminical learning at Krishnagar in Nadia, some sixty miles north of Calcutta. If one might read into this a political motive—Jones was concerned that European judges, through their ignorance of Sanskrit, were too dependent on the opinions of their pundits—Cannon claims that 'his enthusiasm of Sanskrit and especially the literary treasures had become a virtual drive'.[8] He enrolled in an ancient university, though one on the decline. Jones arrived during the vacations, and could only secure one Ramalocana, a vaidya or a doctor, and not a Brahmin, as his Sanskrit instructor. As Cannon acknowledges: 'a European' learning Sanskrit at that time was an extraordinary achievement.'[9] Perhaps of more relevance is how exceptional it was for an Indian to pass on this knowledge to an outsider. Jones was seduced: 'I would rather be a valitudinarian all my life than leave unexplored the Sanskrit mine which I have just opened.'[10] He was to write extraordinary poems in honour of the Indian gods.

By then Jones had made his way into the closed community in Krishnagar and was on familiar terms with the Brahmins. This greatly facilitated his legal enquiries and the translation of the laws of Manu. He drew on the services of pundits from Bengal and Bihar, including the Bengali pundit, Radhakanta, and the scholar, Jagannatha Tarkapanshanan, and those of the maulvis. Since he spoke Sanskrit so fluently he was looked on as a fellow pundit.

But he could still not persuade the Asiatic Society to admit Indians, despite the fact that most of its members employed pundits. It was not until 1829 that they gained admission. Cannon accepts that even Jones was not wholly free from the racism of his contemporaries.

Had he, indeed, anticipated cultural pluralism? Cannon sounds too rhapsodic: 'he sought East-West co-operation as mutual advancement in a spirit of universal tolerance . . . Here was a vital contribution to an India Renaissance.' He continues: 'His transmittal of cultural and linguistic Sanskrit knowledge to the West is comparable in its way to Marco Polo's opening of the magical world of Cathay to a startled Europe.'[11]

Clearly, this has to be qualified. There was always a self-interested or imperial dimension to Jones's work. If Jones was alarmed by this—'I tremble at the power which I possess'—and Cannon claims that 'from the outset he recognized himself as a helper rather than an exploiter'[12], he could write to Burke in April 1784: 'the laws of the natives must be preserved inviolate: but the learning of vigilance by the *English* judge must be a check upon native interpreters,'[13] Jones's motive for befriending the pundits was to acquire expertise to outwit them in the courts.

Was Jones, at the least, a liberal imperialist? Jones had expressed liberal sympathies for the cause of American independence, had admired Wilkes, and had even contemplated going to America. In a sketch for an Anglo-Indian Aeneid, he had a druid argue for an India governed by Indian laws, though still governed by Albion. And through the Cornwallis settlement, in which Jones was substantially involved, this was to be in part recognized. But was this doing anything more than legitimizing British rule, as Javed Majeed has suggested, in an Indian idiom?[14]

Yet the critique goes in two directions. On the one hand the attempt to impose common law in India, particularly for private property, was to marginalize both the pundits and the maulvis; on the other hand, this was seen to be an excessively Brahminical code, and one that contributed to the fatal process of essentializing Indian social and religious identities, caste, Hindu and Muslim, ossifying a society that would otherwise have been subject to the ordinary processes of change. This is the core of the anti-orientalist case. Did Jones unwittingly contribute to an imperialist ideology shaped by the orientalist discourse? If Jones was an almost impossible role model for the missionaries, from this perspective they do not emerge quite so poorly from the comparison.

Even more germane from the missionary angle was Jones's own Christianity. One could see Jones as essentially a humanist. In the name of humanism he was to attack infanticide and sacrifices to Kali. Here he was in a cross-cultural predicament. He saw such inhumanity as untypical of Hinduism, and he never publicly expressed disapproval of the caste system and of untouchability. Here was a Christian who trod very carefully on the awkward areas of Hinduism. Javed Majeed, indeed, sees his writings on the Indian gods as contributing to the essentialism of Hinduism, almost fashioning 'a new defined Hindu world.'[15]

Seemingly he rejected proselytizing: religious belief was 'each person's absolute property'.[16] Yet he was himself a devout man, much given to reading the Bible and to prayer. Admittedly, in his rejection of eternal punishment, he took up an anti-evangelical position: 'I would give up Scripture rather than embrace it. *Eternity* of pain if *Eternity* means for *endless duration* must be disproportional for any offence.'[17] Yet he was still keen that the most persuasive elements of Christianity, viz. Isaiah, evidence of the predictions, the life of Jesus, should be translated into Persian and Sanskrit, though he did not communicate this idea to missionaries then working in schools in Bengal. In all, his was a subdued faith, quite different from that of the Protestant missionaries to come.

Apart from the charge of his contributing to essentialism, here was an exemplary model of cultural encounter, scholarly, open-minded and perceptive. To what extent did the missionary approximate?

Claims are made for an 'orientalist' approach by the Serampore trio, William Carey, William Ward and Joshua Marshman, above all, Carey. We can further contextualize the attitudes of the mid-nineteenth-century missionaries towards Indian culture and religions by looking in some detail at Carey's response. However, just as doubts are raised about Jones's orientalism in terms of his ulterior legal purposes, so an initial question has to be raised about Carey's. How impartial a pursuit of knowledge can it be when the declared objective is the mass conversion of Indians?

At the outset, it is worth inspecting the difference in views between David Kopf, who has no doubts of Carey's orientalist credentials, and Brian Stanley, the latest 'official' historian of the Baptist Mission, who chooses to marginalize Carey's orientalist career at Fort William College, and concludes that even if 'the Serampore pioneers were more prepared than many later missionaries to see good qualities in Hindu culture, their essential conviction remained that Hinduism was a religion of darkness waiting for the light of the Christian gospel to dawn'. Even William Ward's *A View of the History, Literature and Religion of the Hindoos* is deemed a work essentially exposing the cruelties of Hinduism.[18]

No one can visit Serampore College today, with its impressive buildings on the banks of the Ganges, without a keen sense of just how far the Northamptonshire cobbler had come in Bengal. His was a curiously wordly success. This is not the place to narrate his Mission career, just to isolate his response to the exponents of Hinduism and to the faith itself. Did he shake off his initial reaction to Hindus in the 1790s as avaricious and servile and to Hinduism as satanic? Clearly he came up against social practices which repelled[19], and, for a man of the people, the high status of the Brahmins was an intolerable elitism. Here was missionary apologetics 'of an uncompromising and even confrontational character'. If growing familiarity with Sanskritic culture led to an awareness of the gulf between this classical culture and contemporary practice, and a recognition of the need to play down the merely confrontational in favour of a more positive affirmation of Christianity itself, 'nevertheless the change was one of strategy only, not theology'.[20] In Stanley's account, Carey involved himself in the orientalist Fort William College simply out of a recognition that the way forward for Mission in India lay in training a native priesthood and this necessitated translations of the Bible in as many vernacular languages, as well as Sanskrit, as possible.

But should we too readily discard a far more affirmative portrait of Carey as 'an excellent case-study of an eighteenth-century religious counterpart of the secular orientalists in Company service'?[21] In Kopf's analysis, in despair at the miserable rate of conversion, Carey interpreted his appointment to Fort William College in November 1800 as, at the least, a breakthrough in official recognition of Mission and the way forward. It would be a two way exchange: only Serampore could provide the Company with knowledge of the vernaculars; just as critically, through the skills of.William Ward as printer, Serampore would now be in a position to publish. By 1815, the Serampore Mission Press were publishing in Bengali, Urdu, Oriya, Tamil, Telugu, Kanarese and Marathi. But would it be correct to see Carey as 'a scholar entranced with his subject matter' and his view of Mission as 'flexibly accomodating'?[22]

His was an astonishing story of academic success. In November 1805 he joined the Asiatic Society. In July 1806, he succeeded Colebroke as Professor of Sanskrit. The Bengali language was his special love, one which he defended against the rival advocates of Hindi and Urdu, though Carey's vision of Mission reached beyond Bengal and was always expansionist. But Carey's was a quite specific quest, vernacularist and populist, a wish to strengthen primary education and hence fashion the means to spread useful knowledge to the Indian masses.

Orientalists divided themselves into the classicists and the vernacularists. Carey enjoyed friendly relations with the pundits. He got on well with the chief pundit in his Bengali department, Mrtyungay Vidyalankar, later to be an opponent of sati, and with Ramram Basu, a Kayasth, Carey's munshi since 1793, likewise appointed to the Bengali department, and, subsequently, to flirt with Christianity, though never to convert. Basu's was to be an unsparing exposure of the social and theological errors of Bengali Hinduism. Did Carey have a special insight into the mental predicament of a Ramram Basu? Carey himself remained driven by his initial challenge to Brahminism and its high Sanskritic culture.

By the time of his death on 9 June 1834, Carey must have been a disappointed man. Orientalism gave way to Anglicism, and they were largely eclipsed during the Bentinck era. Carey saw in Serampore the means of a replacement for Fort William: paradoxically, the Baptist college was to become more a centre of higher education than a means of promoting primary education.

To what extent should we see his Orientalism as suspect just because it was harnessed to his hopes for Mission? Christopher Bayly has recently suggested that 'the orientalist impulse was deeply implicated with Christian principles, a feature which has been underplayed in studies of Orientalism in both its historical and pejorative sense'.[23] Can we not see in Carey a kind of Christian orientalism and an exemplary model of cultural encounter for the next generation of missionaries in the 1840s and 1850s? Maybe it should be mentioned that Carey's stature as a translator has been questioned.

Intriguingly, missionaries do not feature prominently in Said's critique of the orientalists. In his recent *Culture and Imperialism* he has universalized his insights: 'the great imperial experience of the past two hundred years is global and universal: it has implicated every corner of the globe: the colonizer and the colonized together'.[24] Here is his underlying theme—the entanglement of the cultures of Empire and its subjects: 'cultural experience or indeed every cultural form is radically, quintessentially hybrid.'[25] Initially, missionaries do not feature in his demonizing list of imperialists who, in their own self-regarding culture, failed to recognize the role their subjects played in shaping a shared culture: 'scholars, administrators, travellers, traders, parliamentarians, visionaries, poets and every variety of outcast and misfit'.[26] Nor does Mission figure amongst the factors linking British trade and Empire—'cultural and social factors such as education, journalism, intermarriage and class'[27]—though here it is implied. Only in a list of those experts driven by a belief that the civilizing Mission of the West can save and redeem do they appear: 'missionaries, advisers, scholars'.[28]

Such charity quite probably flows from his own Palestinian Christian background. However, it has more to do, one suspects, with a wish to do justice to Palestinian Christians rather than to European missionaries, and to his belief in cultural hybridity. There is an interesting passage in which he comes to the rescue of those Arab Protestants who, after a century of conversion from Greek Orthodoxy, have been told to rejoin their former church: here was an example of a callous failure to recognize the mutuality of the imperial experience; to quote Gramsci, their sharing in 'a mutual siege'.

This creates an invaluable insight for this text, that one significance of Indian Christians lies in just their being contributors, in a distinctive and major way, to a shared imperial culture. And given Said's rejection of a view of a merely antithetical subject culture under colonialism, and his sharing Fanon's belief that the way forward lies not through a dogmatic nationalism but liberation—'a transformation of social consciousness beyond national consciousness'—[29] this leaves open the possibility that Christianity itself might have mitigated the excesses of colonialism.

Yet in this scenario, both missionary and convert are distanced from Said's version of orientalism. An agent of the Raj would put the question 'not whether something is good or evil, and therefore must be changed or kept apart, but whether it works or not, whether it helps or hinders in ruling the alien society'.[30] Missionaries, driven by a wish to convert, were subject to quite different imperatives.

The alternative approach of both Empire and Mission was Anglicism.[31] In terms of cultural encounter this was of less interest: with its arrogant assertion of cultural superiority, it bypassed the possibility of a debate between European and Indian culture. From the point of view of Mission and conversion, however it is critical. An Anglicist-inspired education proved to be one of the most likely routes, especially for the high castes, to conversion. Charles Grant, a trader, a Company official and eventually a director, whose highly polemical pamphlet, *Observations on the State of Society among the Asiatic Subjects of Great Britain,* had a decisive influence on the admission of missionaries to India through the revised charter of 1813, was its instigator.

So stereotypical has the linkage of anglicism with evangelicalism become that it is wise to enter a few caveats. We have already seen for Carey that the first choice for the transmission of Christianity was by an Indian clergy and through the vernaculars. The whole thrust of the itinerating tradition, to dominate Mission right through till the 1880s, lay in recognizing the need to master the vernacular languages. Something of Carey's vision continued to prevail. Anglicism was, in fact, to make heavy weather in Mission circles as a means of educating a new Christian elite. However pioneering some missionaries had been for an English education, above all Alexander Duff, quite probably it was to prevail, as Gauri Vishwanathan has argued, from a recognition by both Company and Raj, that an education with English literature to the fore, would instill the appropriate moral virtues of efficiency and loyalty into new generations of subordinate Indian civil servants. Yet here was a critical new ingredient in missionary ideology.

The character of the cultural encounter was to turn ugly. James Mill, rather than Charles Grant, should be held responsible for this. His *History of British India*, published in 1819, constituted one of the most condemnatory accounts of another culture ever written. It was to exercise considerable influence, if one hard to quantify, over both individual and official attitudes towards Indian cultures. Mill's standpoint is hard to place. Did he write from an orientalist or an anglicist perspective? Mill did not endorse the use of English in the administration. He was a vernacularist. But can one categorize as an orientalist a writer who knew no Indian languages? And he was himself a passionate anti-orientalist, his critique of William Jones his way of rejecting the attempt to graft common law onto Anglo-Indian law in favour of introducing Benthamite principles of legislation.

In Javed Majeed's attractive interpretation of Mill, his arrogant attack on India's religious and legal elite is seen as inspired by the radical programme of opening India up to the new universalist utilitarian ideology. Mill's was equally a critique of traditionalism in Britain. In this account, Mill would be neither the anglicist nor the orientalist, but rather the radical Benthamite.

It is a part of this project to see if mid-nineteenth-century missionaries, in many ways shaped by an anglicist approach, were, as a consequence of their cultural encounter with India, to gravitate to a more orientalist approach.

The length of their stay is important. Missionaries did not come to India as travellers.[32] Theirs was a commitment, at least for their working lives, to the subcontinent. Did not the itinerating missionaries necessarily find themselves in a position, however initially embattled their response to Indian culture and religions, analogous, in the sense that they were forced by circumstances to find out more about India, to that of the orientalists? Theirs was in many ways an even more prolonged physical encounter with India. If missionaries remained blind to the attractions of this culture, it would be a disturbing comment on the strength of the evangelical ideology which brought most of them to India. It would provide a very pessimistic commentary on the liberalization of attitudes under the pressures of cultural encounter. Missionaries who preferred an educational strategy to an itinerating strategy were more favourable to an Anglicist approach, though paradoxically, they were the more likely to take a critical interest in Indian culture. Here developed the background for the possible transformation of an exclusivist into an inclusivist theology.

Parallel to this debate on Orientalism and Anglicism, and in a sense incorporating both, was one on secularism.[33] This has always been an exceptionally difficult concept to define in the Indian context. Absent was the French understanding of secularism as laicism, a positivist and non-religious definition. One could speculate, though it would be hard to prove, that the Company, in the Cornwallis Settlement of 1793, adopted a secularist policy, but named it 'religious neutrality'. They did so out of sympathy with the orientalist approach, or, at the least, in a spirit of eighteenth-century latitudinarianism. (As it happened, of course, the Settlement, with its introduction of a Whig concept of private property and its quasi-liberal administrative reforms, can, alternatively, be read as the first step towards anglicism.)

Yet it was notoriously difficult to implement. If the state had itself been, in a religious sense, indifferent, it would have been much easier, but it was to come under increasing pressure to act as a Christian state. However, it was well aware that if it showed any preference for Christianity, and hence betrayed its protective stance towards Hinduism and Islam, its reputation would be immensely harmed.

Here lay the grounds for an often antagonistic relationship between Mission and the colonial state. Missionaries were peculiarly opposed to the way the Company took on the role of regulator of Indian religions. In their eyes, the state became tainted by such an association. It also made their endeavour to overthrow these religions all the more difficult. The colonial state, however, was not to be so easily deviated from its secularist path by these evangelical pressure groups.

A particular grievance was the Company's protection of temples—it has taken under its wing eight thousand in the Madras Presidency alone—the way it recruited labour for the temple car festivals and its collection of the pilgrim tax, most notoriously for the great Jagannath temple at Puri. The abolition of the tax in 1840 was seen as a triumph for the evangelicals. But Cassels has shown how it could alternatively be seen as a concession to the Hindus: earlier, Bentinck had thought of its abolition as possible compensation for the outlawing of sati in 1829. When it went in 1840, it did so 'as part of routine Government business deliberately disassociated from evangelical propaganda'.[34] Yet there can be no doubt that Hindus still felt this to be a betrayal and that the Company's new policy of leaving temple management in the hands of Hindus rather than is own officials was seen as a threat to the status and efficacy of religious institutions.[35]

The Company was to introduce further legislation favourable to the evangelical cause, most critically, the 'Emancipation' Act or Lex Loci of 1850, granting rights of inheritance to Christian converts, and the permissive Widow Remarriage Act of 1856. The rebellion of 1857 brought home to the Company the folly of such an undermining of its declared policy of neutrality.

But the 1840s and 1850s had seen a growing convergence in outlook of missionary and Company officials. Stephen Neill has with sadness recognized the extent to which, by mid-century, Mission had assumed many of the attitudes of colonialism, its paternalism, its arrogance, even its racism. In general, however, through a divergence of views on secularism, the relationship of Mission and state was an uneasy one.

INDIAN RELIGIONS: HINDUISM

One of the most baffling questions facing the historian of Mission is: what was the contemporary character of the Indian religions it encountered? Was this, in the light of current revisionist writing, above all for the eighteenth century, a Hinduism in decline or one in the process of self-revitalization? The conventional wisdom has been of a decadent and medieval Hinduism, a great falling away from the Vedic period. This was certainly the view of Charles Grant. Whilst conceding the existence of the golden age, he railed against a Bengali society, riven by caste conflict and blemished by its maltreatment of women. James Mill was ready to make no such concession: Hindu culture had always been Gothic and crude. Today's revisionist historians of the eighteenth century make a plea, that society was, in fact, in a state of flux, as much through its own internal dynamics as through any forcing-house experience from the colonial state: 'the 18th Century', affirms Christopher Bayly, 'was a period of creativity in Indian religious life and culture, not a sultry pause before the "radiancy" of Hinduism and Islam in the next century.'[36]

It is, of course, an impossible task to provide a summary portrait of Hinduism at any one point in time across the subcontinent. Self-evidently, it was subject to a variety of regional expressions, and a regional approach will be adopted when looking at the story of Christian converts in the south and Bengal. Ainslie Embree makes the revealing point that much of the colonial state's invocation of Hinduism was drawn from its experience of Bengal alone: its pan-Indian statements may simply be a response to Bengal writ large.[37]

But Embree is also convinced that it was the strength of the Brahminical tradition which kept the subcontinent together and put up the most effective resistance to challenges from without, be it from Islam or from westernisation and Christianity. Hinduism had always essentially been an amorphous faith and it is hard for this earlier period to bring it into focus. In general, or at least it feels safe to argue, Hinduism has proved as inflexible in, or, rather, as defensive of its social structure as it has proved malleable in its intellectual response.[38]

In mid-century, missionaries tended to subscribe to a view of Hinduism in decline. This was clearly the best way of legitimizing its hostile propaganda, whilst reinforcing the fantasies of all those at home who had invested in missionary organizations expectations of a rapid rate of conversion. If missionary archives are indeed to be a source for the history of Hinduism from the late eighteenth century onwards, can we get behind their polemical approach to get at the true nature of Hindu institutions and personnel, to discover just how educated its priesthood were, just how resilient its philosophical and metaphysical traditions were, to establish, in fact, the true character of the opponents of Mission. Any answer to this enquiry is bound to be impressionistic. But given the bias of Mission accounts, especially in its exclusivist phase, we have to set out some kind of correctives in advance, the better to grasp the very angularity of the nineteenth-century cultural encounter.

One attempt to explain decline, in the conventional pre-revisionist way, was by P. N. Bose.[39] He pointed to a Puranic age, lasting from the eighth century to the nineteenth century. As a consequence of the Muslim conquests, Brahmins had lost the patronage of Hindu kings and depended, instead, on that of the lower castes. This led to an inevitable decline in standards. It encouraged 'gross forms of idol-worship and still grosser forms of guru-worship'.[40] But a decline was already in evidence in the late Vedic period, with a shift from philosophy to poetry and literature. Sanskrit learning continued to flourish in centres such as Mathura, Benares (Varanasi) and Nadiya. But, through the constraints of the caste system, access to Sanskritic culture became confined to Brahmins and Kshatriyas, and if a few Brahmins were to perpetuate this learning, 'the great majority of them became immersed in ignorance. The line of demarcation between them and the lower classes gradually became less and less sharp. To quote Bose:

Brahmins had no longer the strength of intellect which is begotten of self confidence: they had no longer the originality which is the sure indication of intellectual progress. The Brahmins were the greatest sufferers of the Mahommedan invasion. They must have considered themselves disgraced. No wonder they retired into moody silence and devoted their energies to the composition of frivolous stories about gods and goddesses. The lower classes were now almost their only customers. The Sudras and Vaishas now fed and clothed them. They had all along pandered more or less to the superstition of the mass of the people, who were mostly non-Aryans.

Interestingly, Bose went on to suggest that the greatest barrier to Mission was the Anglo-Indian administrator. He feared the missionary as a challenge to his authority: 'with that instinct which comes from self-defence he saw the missionary was the most dangerous of interlopers. If he succeeded and India became Christian, the profitable monopoly was at once destroyed.' Christianity was, of course, to make but few inroads. But Bose's own account is filtered too much through those negative accounts of Hinduism in the nineteenth century and we must still struggle to try and get a different interpretation into focus, one which more persuasively explains this very capacity for survival.

Orientalists could describe Hinduism in a very matter of fact way. In a sympathetic account of the Hindu pantheon, and one which owed much to William Jones, Edward Moor, for example, had considerable praise for the Brahmins: 'on the whole the Brahmins are I think the most moral and best behaved race of men that I ever met with.'[41] Unlike the shocked and prudish response of a later generation, he was quite un-abashed at the symbolism of the lingam: 'the external decency of the symbols and the difficulty with which their recondite allusions are dis-covered both offer evidence favourable to the moral delicacy of the Hindu character.'[42] Likewise, his describing shaktism and the worship of the yoni, or female sex organ, posed no difficulty. How different was the response of mid-nineteenth-century missionaries to erotic temple sculp-ture! His was a refreshing and perceptive curiosity: 'my real opinion is that there is still a great deal for the European world to learn and a great deal for it to unlearn before a competent knowledge be obtained of the religion, mythology, manners, customs, prejudices, etc., of the many mil-lions of our fellow subjects of Hindustan.'[43]

The leading orientalist of the 1820s and 1830s, Horace Wilson, was to display an even more factual and non-judgemental approach[44]. There was, for example, only the faintest hint of criticism in his description of maths (monasteries). These were scattered all over the country, attached to temples, varying in size and in their number of chelas or disciples: 'the tenants of these maths, particularly of the Vaishnavas, are most com-monly of a quiet, inoffensive character, and the Mahants (the chief of a set of monasteries) especially are men of talent and respectability, although they possess occasionally a little of that self-importance which the conceit of superior senility is apt to inspire.'[45] If his was an exploration of sectarianism, it was with the same caveat as Bose, that this affected but a minority. Vaishnavism prevailed over Saivism. In the north, Siva had failed to touch the popular imagination: 'as far as enquiry has yet been instituted, no work whatever exists in any vernacular dialect in which the actions of Siva, in any of his forms, are celebrated.'[46] In the south, however, the Brahmins did worship Siva. And here is an important clue as to why Sankaracharya and Vedantism proved to have so limited an all-India influence in the nineteenth century. Tulasi Das was much more widely read at the time. We can begin to understand why missionaries often encountered such low key and garbled accounts of Vedantism, especially in the north.

Wilson can sound sceptical about the yogis. He accused them of overlooking the received view that in the Kali yuga their yogic power would not prevail. One sect, the paramahansas, went naked, did not speak, did not beg: 'it must be supposed that not infrequently there is much knavery in their helplessness, but there are many Hindus whose simple enthusiasm induces them honestly to practice such self-denial.'[47] With a kind of discrimination that missionaries were often to lack, he pointed out that often the Brahmins despised these ascetics. The findings of these Orientalists endorse the revisionist case.

To move from such a dispassionate portrait to that of a disillusioned missionary, Abbé Dubois, is to cross a cultural frontier. Yet Dubois did separate observation from judgement and was always honest about the limits of his information: 'everything that I have been able to ascertain', he wrote 'has been founded more or less on conjecture.'[48] Would that Grant and Mill had displayed such humility. Not that Dubois camouflaged his prejudice: he put pen to paper in the belief 'that a faithful picture of the wickedness and incongruities of polytheism and idolatry would by its very ugliness help greatly to set off the beauties and perfections of Christianity'.[49] Yet Dubois's findings are in many ways the fullest account we have of Hinduism in the first half of the nineteenth century. His was a regional study, based on personal knowledge of Mysore, south of the river Kistna.

He could be complementary about caste: 'in many respects the chef d'oeuvre, the happiest effort of Hindu legislation.'[50] But for caste, Hindus would have been dragged down to the level of the pariahs. It fulfilled the role that other authority figures, princes and parents, had failed to undertake. All this was strikingly different from the opinion of the evangelical protestant.

Dubois had much to say about the Brahmins and, indeed, they dominate his account. They are seen as being above sectarianism. He discriminates, in ways which many Protestant missionaries failed to do, between swamis (monks) and priests. Monks were the gurus. Each caste and each sect had its own gurus and were, he acknowledged, held in high respect. Mahants, such as those of Tirupati, could exercise influence throughout the peninsula. Ordinary temple priests, or purohitas, had far more limited roles and skills, reciting mantras, quoting the almanack. On the whole, however, he believed, Brahmins were ignorant of high Sanskritic culture: 'the very few Brahmins who were able to read the sacred books in the original only do so in secret and in a whisper.' They may know the four vedas by heart and pillage them for mantras: yet 'out of 20,000 Brahmins I do not believe that one could be found who even partially understood the real vedas.'[51] Just a few Brahmins in Brahmin villages, or agraharas, were Sanskrit scholars and taught in tols. Some rajahs founded schools, but, in general, Brahmins, he claimed, were averse to learning. If lip-service was paid to Vedantism, 'most of the Brahmins of the present-day who wish to pass themselves off as learned men blindly embrace its principles without understanding'.[52] This would help to explain the often highly unsatisfactory nature of encounters on Vedantism in the south between missionaries, themselves struggling to get a glimmering of understanding of its philosophical content, and Brahmins. There was to be even more of a chasm in the north.

In the end Dubois gives way to a characteristic missionary invective against the Brahmins, but does at least suggest some explanation for their moral limitations: deceit was but a natural defence mechanism against continual oppression. Here was an élite driven by the profit motive. To fill one's stomach one had to play many parts. Dubois conceded how successful they were in the pursuit of public office.

Dubois saw Hinduism as a mere formulaic faith. In its theology sin was pollution and could be absolved by penance or by ablution. Reading the puranas, going on pilgrimage, even looking at high mountains, would all suffice. Dubois was here at one with Protestant Mission's denial that Hinduism possessed any theory of sin, atonement, grace, salvation. Yet he made the surprising observation on how indifferent the Brahmins themselves were to the content of their own faith; 'though this assertion may appear paradoxical, I should say that of all the Hindus, they care the least and have the smallest amount of faith in them (the gods). There is no limits to the blasphemies, curse and abuse which they hurl at them under these circumstances.' But given the absurdity of the puranas, how, asked Dubois, could it be otherwise?[53] They did not despise Christianity; it was a part of Hinduism to see virtue in other faiths. But this gave way to hatred once custom, above all, caste, was threatened. One can easily see from Dubois why Mission in the nineteenth century should have been so non-plussed by Hinduism.

Professor Chakraborty and his colleagues at the Rabindra Bharati University in Calcutta shed light on just how learned a response missionaries would have encountered from Hindus in the mid-nineteenth century. As the texts were not written till the twelfth century, only thereafter would they have become available as literary texts. Their study would have been perpetuated, if by mere rote learning. Even in the worst of times, there would have been some learned men, products of the tols, attached to monasteries. But the great majority of the population would have had no knowledge of the Vedas. The great religious classics, the Mahabharata and the Ramayana, were written in less archaic Sanskrit and would have been more accessible. Some version of the Bhagavad Gita would have been known to the Bengalis. Bhakti had prevailed over jnana (knowledge).

Schools of philosophy were not central to the Vedic tradition, but it seems likely that it was their exponents, with their logic-chopping and pedantry, who had confronted the missionaries in the nineteenth century. It is difficult to escape the conclusion that this was a relatively low-level intellectual defence. And maybe just as well for the missionaries, given their own relative illiteracy in this tradition. Equally certainly, however, here in this encounter was the catalyst for the revitalization of the Vedantic tradition, Ram Mohan Roy its leading instigator.[54]

So far the trend of this account has been towards a view of Hinduism as decadent at this time. Can the revisionists demonstrate that Hinduism did have the wherewithal to counter a Christian critique, one founded on concepts such as suffering, sin, atonement, grace?

Missionaries were constantly to argue that the core Vedantic belief, the identification of the atman—loosely, man's individual soul—with Brahma, was a recipe for moral irresponsibility, a denial of any personal sense of sin. There was, of course, no reason why Hinduism should lay claim to concepts such as sin and guilt. In my conversation with Swami Ranganathananda, he became quite passionate in his rejection of a Christian concept of guilt: it sprang, he asserted, from pathological emotions. Nothing was worse, according to Vivekananda, than calling a man a sinner. Everyone had to find his own way to God[55].

But Hindus clearly do have a sense of sin, be it as a breach of the cosmic law or through action born of ignorance: 'the need, for penance' to quote one interpreter 'to wipe clean pollution and in a failure to be "real", an imperative of "being" rather than "doing", the real Vedantic quest'.[56]

Hinduism approximates to Christian concepts of grace and love through its bhaktic tradition, an emotional expression of faith, with a personal deism and offering a form of grace. It was particularly influential in the south and in Bengal.

Is this an approximation to the atonement? In Stephen Neill's analysis, the nearest Hinduism comes to Christ's redemptive power is Siva's drinking the poison that emerges from the churning of the oceans. Evil—not the same as original sin—was a product of anavam, 'the land of finite ignorance'. But other world faiths have always found it incomprehensible that an incarnate God could experience temptation and evil. In this formulation, Hinduism cannot accept the atonement: Brahma is beyond pollution through man's wrongdoing or sin. When man sins, he does so ultimately and finally against himself.[57]

In many ways bhakti was a reaction against the austerities of the yogis and just this cold abstraction of Vedantism. Because love, rather than awe, informed bhakti, it treated God more genially, God as joy rather than suffering.[58]

Can one reclaim the puranas? Here was one nineteenth-century indictment: 'the Puranic stories are at once rank and suited to the taste of the people who cannot digest better intellectual food, are told with a vehemence which is not creditable to the masses of India. The Vishnu purana exaggerates the powers of the god Vishnu and linga-purana of Shiva. Their obscenity is disgusting.'[59] But Ludo Rocher has made an intriguing revisionist bid. 'They preserve', he claims, 'in an encyclopaedic fashion every possible aspect of Hindu culture and civilization . . . More than the Epics, they are the scripture of popular Hinduism.' Possibly their sectarianism on behalf of either Vishnu or Siva has been exaggerated, they derive from some earlier Brahma purana, and are closely linked to the Vedas: 'I submit it is not possible to set a specific date for any puranas as a whole.' His is an emphasis on the complexity and variety of puranic religion.[60] Such a reinterpretation of the Puranas goes some way to meet their belittlement by nineteenth-century missionaries.

Clearly the decline in learning was a weakness in Hinduism. The neo-Vedantic movement of the late nineteenth century was to rectify this. Whether its puranic character was also a weakness is a matter of opinion. But nineteenth-century Mission would have been wise to take on board Swami Ranganathananda's view that Hinduism is never weak, only, at some times, stronger. Vivekananda and Gandhi were both to lend it that strength. This would have given the lie to their foolish millenarian belief that Indian religions were on the point of collapse and Indians ripe for large-scale conversion. Hindu social structures and religious institutions were to be proof against the most brutal challenge they had had yet to endure.

INDIAN RELIGIONS: ISLAM AND SIKHISM

If the non-Hindu religions of India are given shorter change in this study, this is in no way to question their significance. My research has tended to focus on south India and Bengal and away from the heartlands of Indian Islam and Sikhism in the north-west (though Bengal has, of course, a substantial Muslim population). But the limitation is in part out of a recognition that no one person can sensibly take on the whole of the Mission story, and others have already admirably examined the missionary encounter with Islam in the North Western Provinces.[61]

In India, Islam was, chameleon-like, to take on many of the features of Indian religions and so become significantly at variance from its Arabian progenitor. Yet Islam in its Indian context was doubly anomalous: on the one hand, it failed to acculturate Indian society to Islam, its usual triumph in subject lands; on the other, Hinduism failed to absorb Islam, its customary response to the challenge of rival faiths. But there was substantial syncretism.

To make sense of any Muslim susceptibility to Mission we have first to discover how responsive Islam proved to be to its Indian environment. There was to be no wholesale Muslim colonization. Instead, there was a gradual influx of small groups of Muslim settlers, permitting and rendering more probable a degree of assimilation. Here was the making of a Muslim elite, the so-called Ashraf community. But the majority of converts came from within, either from Buddhism, as in Bengal, or mainly from the low castes. With converts coming from inside the orbit of Indian religions, there was a corresponding tendency to syncretism. But there was always to be tension between those elements in Indian Islam which sought to defend orthodoxy and those which were attracted by a more eclectic faith. A strong element within Sunni orthodoxy always tried to preserve Islam in this alien setting. This had become so engrained by the nineteenth century that thereafter, to quote Anne-Marie Schimmel, 'barely a development or a deviation of thought was ever attempted'.

Yet, of course, there was to be an extraordinary symbiosis between Sufism, Islam's mystical tradition, and India's bhaktism, especially in its Vaishnavite form. From the twelfth century onwards, with the entry of such orders as the Chistiya and the Suhrawardiya, Sufism was very influential, above all in the Punjab and Sind. Its most conspicuous expression was Pirism, the worship of Sufi saints in their tombs. It was to be the inspiration for a mystical, vernacular literature which deeply pervaded India's illiterate rural population. In many ways this was an anti-intellectual, emotional, expression of faith, a reaction against an orthodox belief in a transcendent God, and one which shared a Hindu view of the world as illusion, or maya. It was never consciously heterodox, but the orthodox looked on it with suspicion, and it may always have been a predisposing factor for syncretism and heterodoxy, and the cultural milieu from whence subsequently Christian converts might have come.[62]

The revisionist historians also make a case for the vitality of Indian Islam in the eighteenth century, despite the collapse of the Mughal Empire.[63] Not only was there a continuing intellectual debate in Delhi, new centres of learning were emerging in the successor states, most famously, the Firingi Mahal ('the European quarter'; the school had previously been owned by Dutch merchants) in Shia Lucknow. Popular culture continued to flourish. But before examining the strengths and weaknesses of these institutions and personnel within Indian Islam which were to meet the challenge of evangelical Christianity, we have to attempt some account of the Muslim-Christian encounter over time.

A little ironically, Islam, in its purer, more orthodox form, was better equipped to meet a challenge from Christianity than the more syncretic version of Indian Islam. The Muslim-Christian encounter was always going to be significantly different from the Hindu-Christian encounter. The two religions were so entangled. Islam saw itself as the fulfillment of the religions of the book, Judaism and Christianity. It is a striking irony that the mid-nineteenth-century missionaries were so bitterly opposed to this fulfillment claim when a later generation were to fall back on just such a fulfillment theology for Islam and Hinduism in Christianity. Orthodox Islam had a considerable defensive armoury against Christianity. They could lay claim to Abraham as an ancestor of their faith, with a line of descent from his son, Ishmael, to Mohammed. Both Moses and Jesus were seen to be precursors of Mohammed; the Holy Ghost, or paraclete, was likewise a forecast of Mohammed. The Christian scriptures were in part incorporated into the Islamic. Central to the nineteenth-century encounter was the accusation that the Bible had been corrupted, the charge of tahrif. The social egalitarianism of Islam and its extreme monotheism were a far better means of meeting the Christian challenge then an Indian Islam which had taken on some of the trappings of caste and some aspects of Hindu polytheism as, for example, in the worship of saints. Maybe it was just because Islam did betray some grasp of the person of Christ, however imperfectly in the eyes of Mission, that missionaries experienced so strong an imperative to set the record straight, and to bring Muslims to the 'true faith'.[64]

This was an ancient encounter. In many ways the old stereotypes of 'the other' were carried over from medieval Christendom into the nineteenth century: 'the old attack on Islam as violent was paralleled by the image of cruelty and tyranny and corruption. The old attack on Islam as lascivious was paralleled by the image of romantic eroticism'.[65] An element of amused contempt had entered into European response, prompted by its attitudes to Turkey, but one that was to be carried over to Indian Islam. Here was an assumption of superiority based on no more than a more advanced western technology, but expressed in terms of the superiority of a Christian culture over an Islamic culture.

It is not easy to disentangle what was specifically a response to Indian Islam in this encounter. But Daniells shows how the nineteenth-century imperialist feared Islam, and certainly the Company had, in the eighteenth century, faced its most serious challenge from Muslim Mysore. One could draw as a plausible conclusion that its policy of religious neutrality did not derive from any high-mindedness, but simply from a gesture of appeasement to Indian Islam. Certainly a key element in the Vellore mutiny of 1806 had been a bid to restore the former ruling houses of Mysore.

At the turn of the century attitudes within Christian theology towards Islam were polarized between a liberal, partially orientalist approach, and an embattled, reactionary one. The latter was very much to be in the ascendant with mid-century Mission. Godfrey Higgins (1771–1833), with his *Apology for Muhammed*, published in 1829, was a contributor to the former; Charles Forster (1787–1871), with his *Mahometanism Unveiled*, published in the same year, was another. Bishop Heber wrote sympathetically of the Muslims: 'they have a far better creed (than the Hindu) and though they seldom like the English or are liked by them, I am inclined to think they are, on the whole, the better people.'[66] Forster saw Heber as 'the most accomplished observer, after William Jones, who ever visited India from this country.'[67] If Forster drew on Gibbon's revisionist writing on Islam, he was to reject his secularism and scepticism. He wrote from a perspective of faith in revealed religion. And his was as much a response to Islam in Africa as in India. But here was a distinctly unorthodox Christian approach. Islam, he argued, relied more on Mission than the sword. He shared its faith in providence. Islam was not so much a rival to Christianity as a sister faith. Islam was drawing nearer to the gospel; the two faiths might reunite. If fault was found with Mohammed's precepts, they should be compared to those of the Old Testament: 'objectionable features of Islam find sufficient precedents and parallels in its punitive precepts and carnal ordinances.' One should also remember that Christianity in Arabia at the time was 'totally corrupt'.[68] A similarly liberal account was forthcoming in John Davenport's *Apology for Mohammed in the Koran* (1869). Here were writings to be eagerly pillaged by progressive Islamic thinkers, such as Sayyed Khan, in mid-century. Subsequently, Forster was to wonder if he had gone too far: 'if I shunned to put more confidently before the public my own private belief that Muhammed may have been the subject of a Satanic inspiration, I may have erred.'[69]

Others readily adopted a far more intransigent line. This is not the place to repeat Avril Powell's excellent account of the CMS missionary, Karl Pfander's munazara or debate (and the CMS believed it had a self-appointed task to confront Islam) with the Muslim intelligentsia in the 1840s and 1850s. In his central text *The Mizanu'l Haqq: Balance of Truth* maybe more so in its revised version[70], Pfander sought to palliate Muslim feelings. Yet this was simply an assertion of the superior claims of Christianity.

Another leading protagonist was the scholar-administrator, Sir William Muir, Company civil servant, district magistrate and collector, secretary to the Lieutenant-Governor of the North West Provinces. He was to found Muir College, the future University of Allahabad. If anything, he took up the cudgels of Henry Martyn and Pfander in a narrower evangelical way.

Muir's exclusivism carried over into the next generation of missionaries: William St Clair Tisdall, for example (he became Principal of the CMS training school at Amritsar in 1885) branded Sufism as heterodox and non-Islamic, saw the Koran as of merely human inspiration, and Islam as a faith 'essentially opposed both to human progress and the Christian faith'.[71] Likewise he rejected the reformed Islam of the Indian modernists. Not surprisingly, Muslim writers preferred Higgins and Forster to Muir and Tisdall. Whereas Forster and his school had tried to discover the true character of Islam, Muir and his followers sought to deconstruct: 'they believed that if they could demonstrate the human origin of Islam, Muslims would be induced to abandon Islam in favour of Christianity.'[72]

How well equipped was Indian Islam to meet this challenge?[73] Initially, its response was one of indifference. There was nothing new about an attack from Christianity. This was an old conflict and had been dealt with elsewhere. Besides, Muslims could always shelter behind the Company's policy of neutrality. It was only when the Company during the 1840s or possibly earlier, showed signs of reneging on this pledge that they began to sense danger. As former rulers, Indian Muslims had, of course, most to lose from the rise of the colonial state. Even so, their cultural heritage was kept alive in centres such as Delhi and Lucknow. Muslim reaction also varied from one region to another. Muslim elites were a great deal more at risk in Bengal than in the North-West Provinces.[74] Here, maybe, is a good example of the way the Raj projected the experience of Bengal on to the whole of India. But even if one can point to the ashraf elite holding on to junior posts in the civil and judicial administration in the North-Western Provinces, the political climate had altered, and the élite had every cause to feel uneasy. For example, in the Company implementation of law, Anglo-Mahomedan law was not the same as the shariat and its hanafi tradition, and it was forseeble that the colonial state would in time do away with the services of the court-maulvis, even though this was to be delayed till 1864.

Indian Islam largely put its faith in its educated class, its ulamas, drawn from all sections of society, though largely from those of ashraf status. They could be Sunni or Shia. They were still the products of a traditional education, in the madrassa (religious seminary). They would go on to specialize as quazis (judges) or minor state officials. Many opted to teach in the madrassa or in the maktab (the boys primary school). Many were not highly educated. They were able to read but not understand Arabic and would have learnt the Koran by rote. Many lived obscure lives in villages. Ye it was just these humble men, supported by waqfs, tax-free endowments, who were to meet the challenge of the itinerating missionaries. However, a minority of the ashraf ulama community were very much more sophisticated, would have travelled, were a genuine elite, and one well able, as demonstrated in the Agra munazara, not just to hold their own with the CMS missionaries but to outwit them through their greater familiarity with continental European biblical scholarship. Here was the makings of a Muslim middle class.

Theologically, the interesting development in Indian Islam at this stage was a growing interdependence between the orthodox, with their respect for the shariat, and the sufi. The typical response of an Islam in danger is to look to its roots, to reassess the original vision, to query the accretions. Such was the character of the Wahabi movement, and their missionaries were another group which were to confront the Protestant missionaries. As with Hinduism, it seems to have been the traditional elements in Indian Islam which had to absorb the full impact of the evangelical challenge in mid-century: only subsequently did the liberal reformers, associated with Sayyed Khan and the Aligarh movement and with the new Deoband seminary, play their part. But there was one sovereign irony to this confrontation. The very selective way the Company and the Raj set about fashioning Anglo-Mohammaden law had the effect of drying up the pragmatism and natural flexibility of the tradition, creating a much more rigid and bureaucratic version of Islam in the process, breeding a 'scripturalism' which was to be the inspiration for a far more thoroughgoing reassertion of Muslim culture and identity in the late nineteenth century.

Mission's relationship with Sikhism betrays even more clearly than its relationship with Hinduism and Indian Islam the self-deluding nature of its millenarian belief that Indian religions were in terminal decline. Following the defeat of Ranjit Singh's kingdom and its annexation in 1849, missionaries foresaw the collapse of Sikhism and its likely reabsorption within Hinduism. Out of such demoralization they anticipated large-scale conversion. Though it was not an unreasonable assumption, it was to turn out otherwise.[75]

In the fluctuating political fortunes of eighteenth-century India, the Sikhs assumed a far more considerable presence: Ranjit Singh (1780–1839) imposed on the Sikh misls (military bands) his own imperial state. The Sikhs, then a community of one and a half million, comprised but 12 per cent of the kingdom's population. Sikhs, however, held the greatest share of jagirs. Persian remained the language of government. Both Persian and Sanskrit were still studied, and Hindus, mainly Brahmins, dominated jurisprudence. But the vernacular, Punjabi, was taking on the trappings of a literary language, and the specific Sikh script, Gurmukhi, was becoming more visible. Ranjit Singh set aside 7 per cent of state revenues for religious endowments, but 60 per cent of this was for the Sikh religion.

Would the collapse of the Sikh state in 1849 drag down Sikhism in its wake? Certainly Sikh jagirs were at risk. The Punjab was to be exposed to rival Mission movements, first Christian, then from Dayananda Saraswati's Arya Samaj. But the revolt of 1857 came to the rescue of the Sikhs, both through the role they were to play in its suppression, and in terms of subsequent rewards for their loyalty. The khalsa was substantially reconstituted. Many Sikh jagirdars were reinvested. The Raj sanctioned a higher proportion of grants to Sikh religious foundations. Already in the 1850s the Sikh faith had reasserted itself, partly through Baba Dayal's radical protest group, the Nirankaris, to be taken over by his sons on his death in 1853, and by the even fiercer Namdhari movement, led by Baba Ram Singh, seen as highly threatening by the Raj, and to be brutally put down. The future lay with the more moderate reform-minded Singh Sabha, to be dated from 1873, another form of Sikh reaction to the multiple challenge of Islam, Hinduism and Christianity. This initiated educational reform, most famously through the foundation of the Khalsa College of Amritsar in March 1892, and, as a reform movement, sought to control the gurdwaras or Sikh temples. This was the beginnings of the Akali movement.

Far from declining, the Sikhs emerged much the stronger from the crisis of the 1850s. Reverence for the Granth Sahib strengthened Sikh identity, and the Guru Granth equipped the Sikhs with the means to fend off the challenge from foreign missionaries.

CONVERSION

The clash between the ideology of Christian Mission and resistant Indian religions led to the conversion of just a few Indians in mid-century. Substantially different explanations are required for conversions from the poor or low caste, so-called mass conversions, and those from the elites.

In the past considerable numbers from the backward castes, mainly untouchables, had converted to Buddhism and Islam; for very similar reasons they were to convert to Christianity. Mass conversions were a feature of Mission in this period, one which took Mission by surprise, bred false expectations, and then, in the aftermath of disappointment, often left them suspicious of motive. Mass conversions were later to be a far more prominent aspect of Mission. Again, it is in no way to underplay their significance if in this text the emphasis is on the élite. Here some preliminary exploration is undertaken for élite conversion, less to explain the conversion itself and more to place it in its cultural context.

Through the exclusiveness of mid-nineteenth-century Mission, converts had to make a radical choice. It was almost impossible to reach out initially for some half-way house between the faith in which they had been brought up and Christianity. In this sense, conversion took on the aspect of a cultural migration. We will see later that converts did struggle to find some retrospective contact with Indian religions and maybe the break was never as radical as it had appeared. Nevertheless, conversion only initially makes sense in terms of this wider clash between European and Indian culture.

There is a relatively developed historiographical debate on Indian conversion, I have myself already argued for a more merely descriptive approach,[76] adapting the push-pull model, conventionally used by social anthropologists as a tool for explaining migration,[77] for conversion, rather than some more formulaic explanation. In other words, do push factors from their own culture—various forms of alienation—do more to explain conversion than the pull—the attractive aspects of European and Christian culture?

Of course, one common reply is to emphasize the merely economic or materialistic in the Indian context. Conversion opened up better job prospects, be it in the missionary organizations themselves, or, putatively, though this was to be some time coming, in the Company administration. Indeed, to the contrary, there is no evidence that becoming a Christian in any way enhanced employment prospects in the civil administration. There was so much entrenched hostility amongst European officials to the babu, the anglicized Indian, let alone the Christianized, that it was probably a handicap to be a convert. The babu always constituted a threat to the official, better equipped as he was in terms of language and familiarity with India to do his job.

Conversion acted at a quite different level to the economic. It operated at a psychological, and above all, cultural level. Given the enormous hostility which conversion engendered in the community one had left, it also required real courage. Hindus fell back on their most powerful sanction, caste ostracism. A convert became a non-being. Within Islam, conversion, or, as the faithful would see it, apostasy, was traditionally deemed a capital offence, though the convert was granted a period of time in which to abjure. If British rule removed so punitive a sanction, it was indicative of the severity of Muslim attitudes. It has always been acknowledged how many more Indians were attracted to Christianity than were actually converted: Hindus, certainly, found it easy enough to sympathize with another faith, but almost impossible to break caste. The best way into this issue is to locate conversion within the general cultural clash which affected all members of the elite before addressing the reasons why, out of this tension, only a few Indians were to convert. Just how did

British and Indian cultures encounter one another? Can we point to anything specific about this cultural encounter in the mid-nineteenth century? A few interpretations of this encounter are addressed.

Percival Spear saw the clash between East and West as essentially one of culture and civilization. It bred tensions of the mind: 'cultural problems, the great quo vadis' of the Indian mind.[78] An interaction was under way, but how deep was it and where would it go? If Spear wrote in terms of synthesis, he seemed to be saying that for most Indians a choice had to be made. Hindu values are largely alien from those of the West. Can they mix at all, or must Hinduism be rejected? Indian Islam, on the other hand, is much closer to the West, and a synthesis is plausible: 'for Muslims and Christians life is a probation for the next world and therefore supremely important; for the Hindu it is doing time in "illusion" and therefore without significance.'[79] His metaphor for the nineteenth-century Indian was of a chess player (did this inspire the title of Satyajit Ray's film?), 'absorbed and exhilarated in an exciting mental problem'.[80] In Spear's scenario, for the Hindu there appears to be a crippling choice between poverty and his own culture or worldly success and westernization. But might not a new civilization, he queried, emerge from the travail and distress of this conflict? If this has more the feel of a question for the twentieth century, rejection of his own tradition or search for a synthesis was at the heart of the predicament which faced the convert.

K. M. Panikkar had an altogether more abrasive and confident account of the encounter. It is also one highly germane to this project. He was quite clear that Mission was at its centre: 'it may indeed be said that the most serious, persistent and planned effort of European nations in the nineteenth centuries was their missionary activities in India and China, where a large-scale attempt was made to effect a mental and spiritual conquest.as supplementing the political authority already enjoyed by Europe.'[81] Reaction against the missionary challenge set India on the road to necessary change, a recognition, along with other Asian powers, that it needed western expertise to acquire strength: a wholly utilitarian response to the West. It could do so without betraying its traditional culture. His was a wholly affirmative account of the nineteenth-century Hindu reformation; 'one of the great movements of the age which by its massiveness and far-reaching significance takes its place with the most vital developments of modern history.'[82] Through Ram Mohan Roy's revival of Vedantism, Hinduism was to undergo a fundamental change: 'India started on her long adventure in building up a new civilization as a synthesis between the East and the West.'[83] It also worked at the popular level.

Here is an analysis of India's recent cultural history, without any of Spear's doubts. It points to a cultural renewal driven by self-interest and the pursuit of power. But it tends to marginalize those Indians who were attracted by the humanism of nineteenth-century European culture and, more particularly, by its Christianity. In his overview, converts would seem to be rather aberrant individuals, who failed to see how India could emerge the stronger from this encounter in a merely material sense.

Although the focus of Von Laue's interpretation is the twentieth century, he directs our attention elsewhere, and this is worth analyzing.[84] If his thesis is clear, his solution to the encounter is self-contradictory. There has been a world-wide revolution of westernization, he argues: even those who most vigorously opposed the West did so to seek alternative ways to achieve the same results (this endorses Panikkar). Whether one is looking at fascist or communist movements, they are driven by the same imperative of westernization, call it modernization or development. But the West fails to see the huge social and cultural cost which this has imposed on the non-western world. In his assessment, the strain is intolerable and the attempt doomed. Cultures are intrinsically different and it cannot work. It is for the West to make a supreme effort, though one that has but a 50 per cent chance of success, of grasping the intrinsic difference between cultures. Only then, and this is where he appears to be self-contradictory, can one begin to find ways in which a more gradual process of equalizing material standards of living world-wide be realized. He seems, in the end, to be saying that the non-western world cannot escape the demands of westernization.

In this account of cultural encounter, frustration, anger and anguish have intruded. India itself is seen to be in retreat from modernization, the better to spare itself this suffering. Indian Christians in the twentieth century have certainly moved very strongly towards the spirituality of their own cultural traditions. It would have been hard in the nineteenth century to forsee just how high a price collusion with the West would entail. They were always reaching out for what it had to offer in a religious sense.

In all three of the above accounts, a dialogue is seen to take place. In Wilhelm Halbfass's revisionist interpretation of the encounter, more narrowly focussed on philosophy and religion, India is seen to be a non-participant. Halbfass shares Von Laue's doubts on the West's capacity to comprehend another culture: we have both to recognize Indian as alien

or 'the other' and to accept that any unprejudiced or objective understanding is beyond our grasp. In the nineteenth century, through the
peculiar character of Protestant Mission, the European endeavour to
understand India took on a quite new complexion: 'its absolutism and
exclusivism as well as its missionary zeal created entirely new conditions
for European approaches to India.'[85] Here was an attempt to rediscover
the light that had once shone in India but had since dimmed; behind
Hindu philosophy lay an original Christian awareness, a 'Christian
Vedanta'. If Europeans were enthusiastic about the nineteenth-century Renaissance they hoped it would restore India to Christianity, an
inclusivist approach, though one that encouraged a western quest to
understand India. Halbfass's revisionism is to query whether Indian
intellectuals made any reciprocal effort to understand the West.

One might fairly respond that on those terms Indian intellectuals
might very reasonably have chosen not to enter into a dialogue. Traditionally Hindus have not sought, Halbfass claims, to understand other
cultures: 'the situation of the encounter and dialogue between India and
Europe is an uneven, asymmetrical one.'[86] Classical Hinduism had
developed 'a complex extremely differentiated framework of orientation,
a kind of immanent universe of thought, in which the contrast of the
"indigenous" and "the foreign", of identity and otherness, seems a priori
superceded, and which is so comprehensive in itself that it is not
conducive to any serious involvement with what is different and apart
from it—i.e. the "other" in the otherness.'[87] This was not, he argues, to
change and was to characterize neo-Hinduism and neo-Vedantism. To
deny Ram Mohan Roy's curiosity about the West seems extraordinary,
but in Haldfass's analysis, Roy was simply concerned to defend his own
culture by utilizing the West. By universalizing his own tradition, he
preempted the need for any exchange.

India's own inclusivism, seen, for example, in the writings of Keshub
Chunder Sen and Vivekananda, was, in fact, but a means of denying the
need for any dialogue: 'its very openness is a form of self-assertion; and
it proved to be one of the major obstacles to the efforts of Christian
missionaries.'[88] For Vivekananda, this very 'inclusivism' became the basis
of his mission on behalf of Indian spirituality to the West. Hindus
themselves had no need for conversion: 'the remaining religions are all
in truth encompassed by Hinduism . . . Hinduism already anticipates all
future developments within itself . . . In a sense the world has already
been conquered by Hinduism without knowing it.'[89] (This is Halbfass'
explication of Vivekananda.) And yet, Halbfass concludes, but for India

being forced into a response by the challenge of global westernization, there would have been no neo-Hinduism.

Halbfass's insights underpin recent interpretation of Hindu inclusivism as, in fact, a form of exclusivism, and the basis for current expressions of Hindu fundamentalism. But can we go along with this view of the missionary encounter with neo-Hinduism and, by implication, all of Hinduism, as an attempt at a dialogue with Hindus who would not listen?

Interestingly, in this negative account of the attitudes of Indian intellectuals to the West, converts come out well. They become an intriguing and significant minority of Hindus (and those from other faiths) who did embark on a positive encounter.

Having set the cultural context, this text now turns, in Part II, to a whole series of case studies, to see exactly how missionaries did respond to Indian religions, and, in Part III, to see where Indian Christian converts fit into this story of the conflict of religions.

NOTES AND REFERENCES

1. The most sensible account of this research is by O. P. Kejariwal in *The Asiatic Society of Bengal and the Discovery of India's Past 1784–1838*, OUP, New Delhi: 1988.

2. Most prominently David Kopf in *British Orientalism and the Bengal Renaissance: The Dynamics of Indian Modernisation 1770–1835*, Calcutta, 1969 and *The Brahmo Samaj and the Shaping of the Modern Indian Mind*, Princeton: 1979.

3. See Edward Said's two texts, *Orientalism*, London: 1978 (paperback edn, London, 1985) and, *Culture and Imperialism*, London, 1993 paperback edn, London, 1994). Said sees himself as an anti-essentialist, and has recently sought to defend himself agains the charge of uncritical occidentalism, let alone his seeking to legitimize an Islamic fundamentalism. . . . See his essay in *The Times Literary Supplement*, 3 February 1995.

4. If often critical of Said, one such text is Carol A. Breckenridge and Peter van der Veer (eds), *Orientalism and the Post-Colonial Predicament*, Philadelphia: 1993.

5. To quote Peter Robb: 'the ubiquity of internalized but divergent voices allows us after all to imagine the other.' See his introduction to *Dalit Movements and the Meanings of Labour in India*, Delhi: 1993, p. 35

6. Javed Majeed, *Ungoverned Imaginings, James Mill's The History of British India and Orientalism*, Oxford: 1992, p. 5.

7. For Jones's career in India, I have relied on a strongly apologetic text, Garland Cannon, *The Life and Mind of Oriental Jones: Sir William Jones, the Father of Modern Linguistics*, Cambridge: 1990.

8. Ibid., p. 299.

9. Ibid., p. 230.

10. Ibid., p. 232.
11. Ibid., pp. 360–1.
12. Ibid., p. 201.
13. Ibid., p. 211.
14. See his chapter on William Jones in *Ungoverned Imaginings*, though his finding fault with Jones may be a necessary move if he is to sustain his account of James Mill, himself an anti-orientalist, as a radical reformer.
15. Majeed, p. 37.
16. Cannon, p. 268.
17. Ibid., p. 281.
18. Brian Stanley, *The History of the Baptist Missionary Society 1792–1992*, Edinburgh: 1992, p. 47.
19. E. Daniel Potts writes well on this. See ch. 7, 'Certain Dreadful Practices', in *British Baptist Missionaries in India 1793–1837*, Cambridge: 1967.
20. Stanley, p. 46.
21. Kopf, *British Orientalism*, p. 51.
22. Ibid., pp. 79–80.
23. C. A. Bayly, 'British Orientalism and the Indian "Rational Tradition"' c. 1780–1820', *South Asia Research*, vol. 14, no. 1, Spring 1994, p. 8.
24. Said, *Culture and Imperialism*, p. 313.
25. Ibid., p. 68.
26. Ibid., p. 8.
27. Ibid., pp. 85–6.
28. Ibid., p. 158.
29. Ibid., p. 278.
30. Ibid., p. 186.
31. This is a subject that has attracted a substantial amount of literature. Here it will suffice to mention the best of the biographies of Charles Grant by Ainslee Embree, *Charles Grant and British Rule in India*, London: 1962, the most perceptive of its interpreters, Francis Hutchins and his *The Illusion of Permanence: British Imperialism in India* Princeton: 1967 and the controversial and original text by Gauri Viswanathan, *Masks of Conquest: Literary Study and British Rule in India*, London: 1989.
32. The 'traveller' is another paradigm against which one could measure and compare the missionary. Bishop Heber fits well into the paradigm of a traveller. But it is of course just the way missionaries did stay on that rules out categorizing them as travellers. See K. K. Dyson, *A Various Universe: A Study of the Journals and Memoirs of British Men and Women in the Indian Subcontinent 1765–1856*, Delhi: 1978.
33. In the light of the Ayodhya dispute, there have been new atempts to define secularism in India. However, the most helpful introductory account is by Donald Eugene Smith, *India as a Secular State*, Princeton: 1963. See also Nancy Gardner Cassels, *Religion and Pilgrim Tax under the Company Rule*, Riverdale: 1988. This is the clearest account of what the Company intended by religious neutrality.
34. Cassels, p. 150.

35. Geoffrey Oddie explores this theme, if just for south India, in his *Hindu and Christian in South-East India*, London: 1991.
36. C. A. Bayly, *Indian Society and the Making of the British Empire*, Cambridge: 1988, p. 39.
37. Ainslee, Embree, *Imagining India: Essays on Indian History*, Oxford: 1989. See ch. 7, 'Bengal as the Western Image of India'.
38. It would be silly to attempt a bibliography here, so I will just acknowledge a debt to two helpful and clear accounts. Sarvepalli Radakrishnan and Charles Moore (eds), *A Sourcebook in Indian Philosophy*, Princeton: 1957, and Eric Lott, *Vedantic Approaches to God*, London: 1980.
39. P. N. Bose, *Hindu Civilisaion and British Rule*, vols I–III, Calcutta: 1894. He was a superintendent of the geological survey of India.
40. Ibid., vol. I, p. vi.
41. Edward Moor, *The Hindu Pantheon*, London: 1810, p. 359.
42. Ibid., p. 385.
43. Ibid., p. 345.
44. H. H. Wilson, *Religious Sects of the Hindus*, rpt. edn, Varanasi/Delhi: 1972. Originally published in *Asiatic Researches*, 1828, 1832.
45. Ibid., p. 27.
46. Ibid., p. 107.
47. Ibid., p. 123.
48. Dubois and Beauchamp, *Hindu Manners, Customs and Ceremonies 3rd Edition* Oxford: 1924 (first edn 1897. But the book first appeared in French in 1848. There are now arguments that Dubois took the credit for a work largely compiled by another French missionary working in Mysore in the eighteenth century. This could explain that dichotomy in the text between a more objective description and a subjective interpretation)
49. Ibid., p. 9.
50. Ibid., p. 27.
51. Ibid., pp. 171–4.
52. Ibid., p. 407.
53. Ibid., pp. 296–7.
54. Personal conversation, Calcutta, 5 December, 1991.
55. One of my most enlightening conversations in India. Hyderabad, 27 November 1991.
56. There is an interesting exploration of this theme in Henry Lefever *The Vedic Idea of Sin*, Travancore: 1935.
57. Stehen Neill, *Bhakti: Hindu and Christian* Madras: 1974, p. 80.
58. A. J. Appasamy takes this up in his *Christianity as Bhakti Marga: A Study of the Johannine Doctrine of Love*, Madras: 1930.
59. This is quoted from K. M. Kunte, *The Vicissitudes of Aryan Civilisation in India*, Bombay: 1880, p. 516. This was a typical denunciatory account of Hinduism at the time; 'at present there is complete social and religious national prostration and lethargy in India, awaiting the action of the civilising influence of the Western Aryans, the Europeans.'
60. Ludo Rocher *The Puranas* Wiesbaden: 1986, pp. 16, 103.

61. I am thinking in particular of Avril Powell's definitive *Muslims and Missionaries in Pre-Mutiny India*, London: 1993.

62. Here I have been drawing on a useful survey of Indian Islam in ch. 41 and 42 in Haridas Bhattacharyya (ed.), *The Cultural Heritage of India vol IV: The Religions*, Calcutta: 1956 and Anne-Marie Schimmel *Islam in the Indian Subcontinent*, Leiden, Koln: 1980.

63. Bayly, op. cit., pp. 40–3.

64. The best attempt to contextualise Islam and Christianity in the history of mission is K. Cragg *The Call of the Minaret*, New York: 1956.

65. Norman Daniells, *Islam, Europe and Empire*, Edinburgh: 1966, p. 23. Daniells is just as indignant as Edward Said at the intolerance of the European response to Islam.

66. Quoted in Clinton Bennett, *19th Century Christian Views of Islam: Evidenced by Six British Approaches*, unpublished Ph.D. thesis, University of Birmingham, p. 27. This opens up aspects of Christian/Muslim encounter little touched on elsewhere.

67. Ibid., p. 43.

68. Ibid., pp. 75–6.

69. Ibid., p. 182.

70. C. G. Pfander, *The Mizanu'l Haqq: Balance of Truth. Thoroughly revised and Enlarged by W. St Clair Tisdall*, London: 1910. First composed in Persian, 1835.

71. Bennett, p. 259.

72. Ibid., p. 342.

73. Here I am relying on ch. 2 of Powell, Michael Anderson, 'Islamic Law and the Colonial Encounter in British India', in Chibli Mallet and Jane Connors (eds), *Islamic Family Law*, London: 1990, and conversations with Dr Nizami, Director of the Centre for Islamic Studies, Oxford, 5 September 1991, Professor Syed Sirajuddin, editor of *Islamic Culture*, at the Henry Martyn Institute of Islamic Studies, Hyderabad, 28 November 1991, and Professor Mahmood, Presidency College, Calcutta, 23 December 1991.

74. It was, of course, Sir William Hunter who drew attention to the plight of Muslims in Bengal. Inerestingly, Daniells shows how Hunter felt that the best recourse for the Muslims was to look on India as dar-al-harb, e.g. a land where the faith could not be practised, but still to recognize that Islam was protected by the Raj and that there was no need to rebel. Daniells, pp. 275–8.

75. For this all too brief account of Sikhism I have relied on, J. S. Grewal, *The Sikhs of the Punjab (The New Cambridge History of India, vol. II, 3)*, Cambridge: 1990, and W. H. Mcleod, *The Evolution of the Sikh Community*, Oxford: 1976.

76. Antony Copley, 'The Conversion Experience of India's Christian Elite in the mid-19th century', *Journal of Religious History*, vol. 18, no. 1, June 1994, pp. 52–74.

77. Two texts which adopt this model are Vaughan Robinson, *Transients, Settlers, and Refugees: Asians in Britain*, Oxford: 1986, and James I. Watson (ed.), *Between Two Cultures: Migrants and Minorities in Britain*, Oxford: 1977.

78. Percival Spear, *India, Pakistan and the West*, Oxford: 1967 (first edn 1958).

79. Ibid., p. 47.

80. Ibid., p. 112.
81. K. M. Panikkar, *Asia and Western Dominance*, London: 1959 (first edn 1953), p. 314.
82. Ibid., p. 240.
83. Ibid., p. 242.
84. Theodore von Laue, *The World Revolution of Westernisation: The Twentieth Century in Global Perspective*, Oxford, New York: 1987.
85. Wilhelm Halbfass, *India and Europe: An Essay in Understanding*, New York: 1988, p. 21.
86. Ibid., p. 173.
87. Ibid., p. 187.
88. Ibid., p. 227.
89. Ibid., p. 238.

PART II
Mission and Cultural Contact

CHAPTER 3

Missionary Case-Studies: Bengal

In 1852, there were but 102 European missionaries in the Presidency of Bengal, but 59 in the North-Western Provinces. In eight of the districts of Bengal there were none at all, in five others, only eight.[1] With so small a sample, one might reasonably have attempted an analysis of them all. However, only three societies have been looked at, the Baptist, much the strongest mission in Bengal, the SPG and the CMS. Given that the objective is to learn about the ideology of Mission and the character of its cultural encounter, preference has been given to the more confrontational, itinerating missionary over the educational. But as all missionaries, educational as well, took to the evangelical trail, they have sometimes been included. These all become case-studies in ideology. If these were missionaries who set out with a conviction in the rightness of itinerating, several were to experience doubts about this strategy, and were to begin to ask the questions, were they the best people to be undertaking this task? Might not Indian missionaries do it very much better? And might not their energies be better served as educationists?

These are also case-studies in cultural encounter. To a quite extraordinary degree, the mid-nineteenth-century missionaries were symbiotic with Indian religions: wherever Indians went to celebrate their own faith, be it the ghats, melas, pirs, pilgrimage sites or great centres of learning, the missionaries followed. It is no accident that the thread that linked so many Mission stations in Bengal and north India was India's most sacred river, the Ganges.

If the mid-century missionaries did not match a Reginald Heber as travel writer, nor indeed, his tact, their's was not an imagination primed by another Asian country: Heber had already travelled extensively in Russia before taking up his appointment as Bishop of Calcutta in 1823.[2] For the most part, after the long sea journey via Madeira and round the Cape, they were pitched straight into this alien land. As we have already seen, they brought with them all kinds of prejudices. Was their experience of India to break down this prejudice? Were they to exhibit curiosity, even tolerance, towards Indian religions? Were they, in other words, to share in any way in that scholarly and enlightened outlook of the orientalist?

They came at a time when these religions were seen to be 'medieval' and decadent, a view which has only recently come under fire from the revisionist historian. However polemical and biased their accounts of these Indian religions were, the missionary archives are one of the best sources for discovering the true character of these religions, and indeed, to discover, to the contrary, just how resilient and vital such traditional religion really is.

Compartmentalizing Mission in eastern and northern India can be tricky. The most natural boundary is between Bengal and Bihar, one that divides a Bengali-speaking area from a Hindi and Hindustani, and, to a degree, constitutes an ethnic divide. But in the new administrative boundary drawn up in 1836 between the Lower Provinces or the Presidency of Bengal, incorporating Bengal proper, Bihar and Orissa, and the Upper or the North-Western Provinces, this more natural boundary was obscured: Bihar remained within political Bengal. If this political boundary was to be the one to respect, the Baptist Mission station at Monghyr would have to be included under the heading of Bengal. However, the decision here is to place it under the heading, Lower Hindustan, though the statistics given for Bengal will include Bihar and, indeed, Orissa. Through the extensive coverage to date of Orissa, with the writings of James Peggs, and the whole debate over the pilgrim tax at Puri, it has not been included here.

Bengal's was overwhelmingly an agricultural and village-based economy. But 5 per cent of its population was urban. As it happened, a quite disproportionate number of missionaries, 37, lived in Calcutta. Villages were far from uniform: in the deltaic area, they would often be strung out along the river bank while in south Bihar, they would be clustered together. The average population of a village was 335. Hindus constituted 63 per cent of the rural population and Muslims, 33 per cent. In Calcutta itself, it was 65 per cent to 29.4 per cent. The Baptists believed the proportion of Hindu to Muslim to be four-fifths to a one-fifth, which may explain their relative neglect of Islam. Interestingly, in terms of language, Bengali speakers in Calcutta did not greatly outnumber Hindi speakers: 4,35,000 to 3,19,000. In the province of Bengal as a whole, there were 15 castes with over a million each, 66 with 1,00,000. Somewhat surprisingly, given their status as elite castes, in Calcutta, Brahmins,

83,000, and Kayasths, 67,000, were the most numerous. No missionary at the time seemed to have any awareness of the complexity of Bengal's caste structure. Two-fifths of India's Muslim population lived in Bengal.[3] Even more surprisingly, no missionary seemed to have grasped the extent to which this large Muslim population was at the time stirred by a reform movement.

In brief, this had been initiated in the eighteenth century by the Sufi philosopher, Shah Waliullah (1703–82), and given further impetus by Sayyid Ahmed Drelvi (1786–1831). Further stimulus in the nineteenth century came from the Faraizi movement, in East Bengal linked to Haji Shariat Allah (1781–1840) and even more dynamically to his son, Haji Muhammed Muhain (1819–62), in West Bengal, from Titu Mir, a follower of Sayyed Ahmed, and subsequently from Wilayat Ali and Enayat Ali of Patna. Here was a specifically Bengali Islamic revivalist movement, Wahabi in spirit, seeking to purify Indian Islam of its Hindu accretions.[4]

THE BAPTISTS

If Baptists take pride of place in Christian Mission to Bengal in the mid-century, this was a deeply troubled Mission. Serampore fell out with the home authorities, opening up a division between an older and younger generation of missionaries. The break came in 1827 and they were only to be reunited in 1837. Even then, Serampore College was to stay apart, and this obscured the way the earlier generation had pioneered a new approach to Mission: they had seen that the future lay in the translation of texts into Indian languages and a reliance on an indigenous ministry. The younger generation of the 1830s and 1840s went with the tide and accepted, instead, the strategy of itinerating, one heavily dependent on the European missionary. It took a visit to India by the secretary in charge of foreign affairs, E. B. Underhill, from 1854 to 1857, to cast doubt on some of this strategy, and to press, once again, for a greater reliance on 'native agents'. The earlier tilt towards education could only resurface once Serampore College itself had come back within the orbit of the Society, which it was to do in 1855, though, even so, the policy was to concentrate on primary education. It was to take all of Underhill's powers of persuasion in the 1890s to save the college as an institution of higher education at all. By going with the grain from the 1830s to the 1850s, the Baptists lost the initiative in new thinking on strategy.[5]

To elicit the character of Baptist encounter with Indian religions, we will look at Mission in the suburbs of Calcutta, Thomas Morgan at

Howrah, George Pearce at Entally; drop south into the deltaic area, looking at Pearce's Mission in the Sunderbans, centred on the villages of Luckyantipur and Khari; and fan eastwards to J. C. Page at Barisal.

Thomas Morgan: Howrah

If Howrah was 'as much part of Calcutta as Southwark London',[6] nevertheless, it was deemed to be Bengal's second largest town. There had been a Baptist Mission station here since 1820. Born on 21 November 1809, Calvinist methodist by background (his maternal grandfather was a minister), it was the Baptist faith of his employers in Swansea that led to Thomas Morgan's enrolment at the Baptist College in Bristol. In the 1830s, new recruits to Mission had turned to the West Indies, not to India. Only four went to India between 1832 and 1839. But Morgan was to accompany William Pearce (George's brother) to India in May 1839, and to be posted to Howrah. As one visitor to Calcutta put it: 'he is a missionary indeed in the strictest sense of that important office'.[7]

Morgan was an excellent Bengali speaker, familiar, as his obituarist[8] was to claim, 'with native thought and modes of illustration'. This ability to empathize with the Indian mind, and Mission believed Indians had a different manner of thought, was highly rated by missionaries. Was he tactful? 'While unsparing in his exposure of the evil in various religious systems he encountered, there was a most scrupulous avoidance in both act and speech of all that might unnecessarily offend national prejudices.' Howrah had a fluctuating migrant population: distribution of tracts in Howrah gave promise of their diffusion elsewhere.

During the cold season he would itinerate the banks of the Ganges. Here he came into contact with the religious life of the river. Brahmins gave him a mixed reception. One 'took a tract from my hand, tore it to pieces and then deliberately threw it in my face.' To Morgan's question of why, he replied that he 'only wished to know whether or not I was perfect and his standard of perfection was freedom from anger'. Another Brahmin sat him at some distance from the idols, but when Morgan announced that he was a padre, 'immediately placed me near the idol, procured me a chair and we entered into conversation'.

If Brahmins were hostile, the people listened. They laughed when 'last week a brahmin told me the sahiblog were great drunkards. I took the opportunity to tell him the Kulins are now employed in making rum, contrary to the shastras'.[9] (The kulins were a Brahmin sub-caste, notorious for their privelege of practising polygamy.) No missionary could hope to survive without the capacity for such badinage.

Clearly puzzled by Hindu faith in the salvific powers of the river, he was delighted when a Brahmin at death's door showed an interest in one of his tracts: 'the fact of a dying brahmin in the sight of the Ganges reading a Christian book seemed to fill all with astonishment.' Not quite so promisingly, an elderly woman expressed the belief that one could not be saved by bathing in the Ganges but 'by fixing the mind on God'.[10]

Morgan put great faith in tracts: 'I wish there was a small Bengali tract, containing some of the most obvious astronomical, philosophical and moral falsehoods contained in the shastras, including a reference to the shastras themselves.' Once, at a Jagannath festival, he approached the car, thinking 'it would be rather a novel thing if his lordship would permit Christian books to contaminate his throne'. He gave tracts to those on the car and soon 'the very shrine of the god was covered with tracts from one extremity to the other'.[11] Such faith in the talismanic power of tracts has an almost Hindu feel to it.

Almost uninterruptedly (he returned to England in 1856 and again, for a longer spell, in 1868) Morgan kept up his Mission till 1882. He died on 16 August 1885. There is here already evidence of that curious mirror image in missionary attitudes, the way it took Hinduism so literally.

George Pearce: Entally and the Sunderbans

George Pearce, one of the most prominent Baptist missionaries of the younger generation, combined the roles of teacher and evangelist. He was to enjoy a quite considerable success rate of conversion in the various schools he ran, first at Chitpur, then Howrah, and, finally, in the more salubrious suburb of Entally. Here, on 3 February 1840, the Calcutta Native Christian Institute was opened. Conveniently, it was near the Baptist Mission press, and also, intriguingly, the Kalighat temple. The story of the Baptist converts will be told later. Here we will look at Pearce's preaching, in both city and village.

George Pearce came out to Calcutta in November 1826, joining Eustace Carey at Chitpur in February 1827. Clearly, this was a shock, and a five week spell of dysentery did not help: 'this is, indeed', he wrote, 'the stronghold of the princes of darkness. If any place his dominion is visible, it is in this country. I had heard and read much of the depraved character of the inhabitants of Hindoosthan but truly I can say the half had not been told me, nor can I conceive it possible for any person to form anything like an adequate idea of Indian wickedness without actual intercourse with the people.' No group was excluded. 'Falsehood, dishonesty, lasciviousness, superstition and idolatry seem to be inseparable from their nature.' Exposure to these matters had, he believed, brought on his dysentery.

As a preacher he was soon to experience a communication gap. 'One of the greatest difficulties that a missionary feels', he reported, 'is the want of first principles in the minds of his hearers.' You cannot assume that they believe in the 'unity and holiness of the divine being, the responsibility of man, etc.' 'Perhaps one reason for the want of success here is taking too much for granted', yet what could one expect, he wondered, when one's hearers listened for no more than ten minutes. This brevity was an unpleasant truth which itinerating missionaries were reluctant to recognize.

Pearce was himself to be an early, though still rare, convert to an alternative strategy of education. Teaching at his school had still to be defended against the greater dictate of preaching: teaching he would only undertake 'in the heat of the day when I cannot with prudence be exposed to the weather'.

There was an amusing account of an encounter with a Brahmin, on whom he had placed some hope, until he brought with him Paine's *Age of Reason* 'which he tells me he received from the celebrated Ram Mohun Roy with his commendatory remark'. As an educationist, Pearce saw himself as undoing the damage done by the Hindu College, Calcutta's most prestigious English-medium college. By 1830 he had a tolerable knowledge of Bengali and had begun to learn Hindustani: if a majority spoke Bengali, 'there are thousands not acquainted'. In the 1830s, his base was the native chapel in Saum bazaar, Chitpur. He sensed a spirit of enquiry among his audience: 'it is true that the multitude hesitate to embrace the gospel, but that thousands know its superiority there is not the shadow of a doubt.' From his obituary, we learn that he 'was always an attractive speaker to the natives though his voice was somewhat feeble and unequal to large and crowded audiences'.[12]

Pearce was always to be one of the optimists of the Bengal Mission. On 12 Febru6ary 1831, he wrote: 'but do not I beseech you give up on India in despair . . . tho' sometimes cast down I have never despaired.' To the Home Committee he declared in July 1834: 'Hinduism was 3000 years old, supported by an extensive, interested, and influential priesthood.' There was caste, no doubt but Ireland had received the gospel only 1000 years ago and 'where was the state of that country?'[13] Ill-health forced him to take home leave in 1834 and again he was to be away from 1838 to 1842, but on 7 December 1837, he could assert, 'my expectations of the missionary efforts in Bengal were never higher'.[14]

On his return in 1842, he was posted to Entally. Yes, he conceded, compared with the West Indies the East Indies Mission was slow work: 'so it is, but what shall we say? Conversion work is God's.'[15]

His was also a Mission to the villages of 24 Parganas, to the Sunderbans, centred in the villages of Luckyantipur and Khari. These were Mission stations he had himself helped to initiate in 1830. This was an extraordinary terrain, forest and swamp, running some 170 miles along the Bay of Bengal, from the estuary of the Hooghly to that of the Meghna, extending inland for some 60 to 80 miles. At this stage, the only means of communication was via the maze of tidal creeks and cross-channels. Its population was largely low caste and Muslim. Only in the late eighteenth century did the Company issue contracts for the reclamation of the forest, though these met with opposition from the local zamindars.[16]

Pearce, and this was a feature of Baptist Mission, quickly sympathized with the economic plight of the village peasantry. He saw how gangs employed by the local zamindars fleeced the villagers of any profit they made from fishing or farming: zamindars 'generally exceedingly dislike missionaries as they are afraid of their instilling sentiments into the minds of the people unfavourable to their interests'. In a letter of 12 October 1829, he reported the murder by a zamindar of a native preacher, Kam Kissore, a product of Serampore.[17] Not that zamindars were necessarily alienated by Mission: indeed, so regular were convert peasants in their payment of rent, some zamindars offered them as much land as they could cultivate.[18]

Quite apart from the difficult terrain, Pearce encountered a popular religion which posed a real test of nerves. To a description of attending a Churrak (hook-swinging) puja in April 1827—'a little old man dressed in the most indecent manner, his body besmeared with red paint, his eyes and countenance had all the appearance of a confirmed drunkard'—he added, 'do'nt send men with tender feelings to India for these things will break their hearts, and yet if they have them not they will be of no use in this country'.[19]

The local Brahmins, for they too, like the zamindars, felt their livelihood to be under threat, were hostile: 'their rude behaviour, ridiculous questions, clamour' destroyed the good effect of missionary preaching. Brahmins, Pearce observed, may seem respectable and polite when they seek a favour from Europeans, 'but see them in situations where they are completely independent of you, where they have nothing to expect or fear and they exhibit a very different character'.[20] In Pearce's estimate, local Brahmins were ill-educated, largely ignorant of the shastras, and unable to defend Hinduism against the rival claims of the missionaries.

But Pearce also reported the sincerity of Brahmins. He had witnessed a sacrifice by a Brahmin on behalf of someone saved from cholera. 'I could not but observe', he wrote, 'how intent he was on his work: he took not the least notice of me during the whole time I stood, perhaps ten minutes, looking on. Between the Brahmin and the people assembled stood two men holding up a long piece of cloth to hide him and the ceremonies from the spectators. I nevertheless took the liberty to stay and observe what he was doing.' He went on: 'I left the place not a little grieved and I may say mortified at what I had seen, especially as the principal persons concerned in it had often conversed with me on religious subjects and confessed the vanity of idolatry and the truth of Christianity.'[21] Here was a reluctant admission that a local Brahmin went about his religious functions with a proper professionalism.

Pearce also betrayed some insight, however captious, into popular Hinduism. In every field, bar Muslim-owned, there was the figure of a local god, Dokyin Roy, propitiation for rice and fish. The village had saved enough money to build a temple to Krishna. But the villages admitted to its inefficacy: 'I do'nt know how it is, but the fact is certain that everybody that builds a temple, instead of getting rich as he expects comes to poverty.' Somewhat smugly, Pearce added: 'I have often been surprised at the pleasure which has been manifested when the inconsistencies and abominations of Hindooism have been exposed. The people appeared as though they have been wishing to throw away the load which oppressed them and they had now found reasons for so doing.'[22]

Pearce was not always regular in his visits to the villages: 'the journey is somewhat perilous for excepting in the dry season it would be probably fatal to one's life to travel by water as the way is thro' the dense and pernicious forests of the Sunderbunds.'[23] Three years of dearth had led to a major backsliding of village Christians. Several had joined in songs to a local deity, Seeb, at the annual Churrak festival. Pearce's response was tough: the backsliders were to be refused entry to the chapel at Lockyantipur, return to where they had worshipped Seeb and there 'in the presence of their brethren to express their sorrow for their crimes and abjure idolatry, ere their brethren would receive them again'. For Pearce, who attended this act of repentance, 'this was one of the most solemn and affecting occurrences that I have witnessed since I have been in the country.[24] It was from these villages, from this highly populated area, that most of the children attending the Native Christian School came.[25]

With seniority, Pearce's itinerating became more extensive. In the cool season of 1851–52, for example, he undertook an 800 to 900 mile journey across the deltaic area to Barisal and back. There was no let up in his optimism. 'The confidence of the people in Hinduism has gone,' he reported. One Hindu responded to his sermon in this manner: 'You have but one Bible, one way of salvation and one hope for the future. But with us nothing is certain, for our shastras are many and contradictory: we have many gods and many ways; we are divided by innumerable castes, hence all our confusion, uncertainty and despair. Of the world to come, we know nothing.' Even the Muslims, Pearce felt, formerly seen as a 'very hopeless class', were changing: many had converted at Jessore. The Baptists, he recommended, should concentrate on this their own preserve of the deltaic area. There was a large Christian gathering to welcome him at Barisal: 'the tout ensemble, was, so I felt at the time, one of the happiest that I have ever witnessed in this country.'[26]

Pearce was to stay on in Calcutta till 1861 when he retired to Ootacamund. Despite erratic health, he not only remarried in 1877, but lived on till the ripe old age of 86, dying on 6 June 1887.

John Chamberlain Page: Barisal

Barisal, headquarters of the Backergunge district, was a major rice growing area. It was connected by the delta's intricate network of river and canal to Dacca and Calcutta.

To the Mission station at Barisal in 1848 came a missionary even more committed to the Sunderbans. Indian born, at Monghyr (in Bihar) on 28 November 1822, he came from a military background; his father was a Captain in the Company's army, his mother, a Colonel's daughter. His father had befriended one of the most famous of the older generation of Baptist missionaries, John Chamberlain, and named his son after him. After an education in England, the son returned to Monghyr, came under the influence of the missionary, Andrew Leslie, travelled to Serampore, and, in April 1841, himself turned missionary. He married the widow of J. I. Thomson, the eldest son of the BMS missionary to Delhi, J. P. Thompson. He had died but six months after marriage, leaving a posthumous son. Page's first assignment was to be to the villages south of Calcutta and he was never to leave the Sunderbans.[27]

His was an uncomfortable beginning at Barisal. He replaced the Revd S. Bareiro, dismissed on grounds of adultery with an Indian Christian, Parbati. It had not helped that she was a non-attender. George Pearce, along with two other missionaries, had drawn up the report on the matter. Subsequently, Bareiro married Parbati. Sixteen years later, he sought his revenge. He joined the SPG and they set him up in a rival station in Barisal. Page saw a clear threat to steal his converts: 'solemnly and in the presence of the God of missions I protest against the SPG acting at all.' All the latent antagonism between the non-conformist and the Church of England flared up: 'I never knew a man called Lord Padre (and this is the appelation assumed one way or another) do any good among the natives in the vicinity of a mere padre, but a vast deal of harm.' How, queried Page, could poor Christian peasants understand doctrinal differences between baptists and Anglicans? They would merely respond to Bareiro's promises. But he proceeded to contradict himself by claiming that they had transferred their loyalties through his refusal to condone child marriage, marriages other than under the law, adultery and breaking the sabbath: 'had they regarded the Baptist Mission with anything approaching to Christian feeling, they had never played the part they had done.'[28] But the SPG were to regret this poaching. In 1874, they dismissed Bareiro and disbanded their Mission. In all, a troubling example of interdenominational conflict.

Page was to be caught up in extraordinary battles on behalf of his Christian peasantry. Most highly publicized was his defence of fourteen Christians from the village of Baropakhya. Kidnapped by agents of an indigo planter and a local zamindar, they had been shunted around for some five to six weeks. When the case came to court, the Christians won in the local magistrate's court, but lost on appeal. They were found guilty of deliberately fabricating the whole story so as to get their own back on the zamindar. Eventually, the courts upheld the initial verdict, but as the verdict of the magistrates could not be reversed, this was but a moral victory. With a despairing recognition of the immense indifference of the House of Commons to Indian affairs, a memorial was drawn up, with signatories from all the Mission societies, and submitted to the Lieutenant-Governor. Maybe Page should not have been so despondent. Two parliamentary deputations were to visit Barisal during Page's time. Here was continuing evidence of the struggle between a Christian peasantry and the zamindars.[29]

It must have been a great relief for Page and fellow missionaries, Martin and Anderson, to take up the more familiar task of preaching at Hindu and Muslim festivals. There is a vivid account, provided by Martin, of one Hindu festival near Barisal, stretched out a mile along the river, boats set back four or five deep. If the din was so great that Martin could not hear the native preachers speak, it provided him with 'a better notion of the true character of the work of an evangelist than anything I had ever seen or heard'. They were to attend a Muslim festival at Kali-suri, some 1,50,000 in attendance, an opportunity for the local popula-tion, as Martin recognized, 'to eat, buy and sell grain'. Here all three preached every day for five days, from seven till ten in the morning, from three till sunset. They came to the conclusion that Muslims were more civilized than Hindus, for they did not worship idols, and whereas three or four hundred prostitutes had attended the Hindu festival, but four or five the Muslim.

Mindless cavilling rather than any serious dialogue was the outcome of their evangelizing. If they distributed books, they did so with little confidence that they would be read; the Brahmins were literate, but that was about all. They read into such occasions the enfeebled nature of Hinduism: 'it is impossible to make even one visit to these gatherings and return without a strong conviction that the Hindoos have very little or no faith in the efficacy of their own systems. They do not in their hearts believe that they shall obtain salvation by the performance of any cere-monies . . .' Idols were acquired much as an English lady would purchase dolls: 'if they worship these things it is more the result of long-established customs, of the influence of caste, of their stereotyped notions which forbid change, than from a conviction that they shall derive any real or substantial good from the works of their own hands.' The Bengali, they averred, was indifferent to serious discussion: he took nothing seriously but 'rupees, his hookah and his food'. No serious debate took place on sin and guilt. 'It is somewhat different with the Mussulman: he will admit to a large degree of Scripture truth, but tell him that Mohammed was a false prophet and that Jesus is the only saviour and you at once rouse his indignation and his enmity.'[30]

One is struck above all by the errant blindness of the missionaries. Here were innocent folk simply out to have a good time at the fair: engaging in kill-joy conversations with importunate missionaries was the least of their wishes. Missionaries also entertained the most bizarre expectations of the metaphysical skills of ordinary country folk.

Page was to be disappointed in his converts. Steadfast they may have been, but 'they are as they were'. There was no development in the 'divine life'. 'We cannot rest satisfied with mere harmlessness.' There has to be 'a living, growing transformation of character'. 'Christianity is aggres-sive, not in the sense of Mohammedanism. It must *grow* or our Lord's parables do not teach aright. It must *attack*, or the kingdom of heaven is not taken by force.'[31] If his Christian villagers were grateful for his taking up the cudgels on their behalf in land disputes, the quid pro quo must have been a fairly torrid time in the chapel.

Page was to devote twenty years to the Barisal Mission, eventually retiring to Darjeeling. He died on 22 November 1895.

One of Bishop Middleton's objectives in founding the college—its foundation stone was laid on 20 December 1820—was to train an Indian missionary priesthood: by the 1840s, this had not been realized. But the college itself had a watching brief over the SPG's Mission in Calcutta and its environs. Apart from Gossner's Chota Nagpur Mission (in Orissa and not included in this project), the Society's Mission in Bengal was tentative and understated. During the mid-century, Bishop Daniel Wilson, Calcutta's longest serving bishop (1832–57), a leading evangelical spokesman, the principal of the college, Professor Withers, and Professor Street, all wrote on the society's involvement in Mission. But the Anglican establishment was in something of a muddle.

Bishop Wilson was confident that the Anglican model would work for India. 'All the institutions of our reformed Protestant Church', he rather patronizingly proclaimed, 'so settled three centuries since by our Cramner, Hooker and their noble compeers, are eminently adapted to languid, prostrate India . . . the whole visible form and aspect of our religion, all give just that aid to the Native convert which he needs.' But Wilson had the insight to see that Company chaplains and European missionaries were not the answer, and that Bishop Middleton had got it right: 'we want besides these, Christianity to be fixed in the soil—a body of permanent Mission clergy with adequate maintenance, independent of distant and fluctuating bodies of subscribers. We want an indigenous clergy—we want the native converts to be instructed by a native clergy'.[32] Later, Wilson was to attempt a partial implementation of such a vision with his special mission attached to the new St Paul's Cathedral, though both European and Indians were to participate. This touches on the story, told below, of K. M. Banerjea.

The prospects of SPG Mission lay mainly with stations south of the city, Jhangera, under Mr Jones, and Baripur, under C. E. Driberg. Wilson became very excited when something akin to the karta bhoja conversions, which had made such a big impression in 1838, looked as if they might be repeated in these stations in 1842. A representative of the karta bhojas had been in touch with one of Driberg's catechists. Rather touchingly Wilson wrote on 5 November 1842: 'I write as from the margin of the tomb and my humble desire and prayer is that I may be permitted before I go home and be no more seen, to behold our Episcopal Reformed Church established in India more firmly and widely as the bulwark of Christianity amongst our shifting Christian society.' But it was a false promise, and Wilson was to learn to be more sceptical of the durability of such mass conversions in the future.

If it takes us some distance from Mission, these were issues which deeply troubled missionaries at the time, and we have to give some space to doctrinal dispute. There was always a sectarian feel to Wilson. He was genuinely horrified that the Vatican was at work in Calcutta: 'the gross idolatry of Popery is being ingrafted on the kindred idolatry of heathenism. Our well informed Protestants, of the Indo-European class chiefly (presumably a reference to the Eurasians, those of Portuguese descent), are seduced by glitter and gorgeous apparel and incense and pilgrimage and relics.' But, of course, such was also the outlook of the Anglo-Catholics, and Wilson had to face such attitudes nearer home.

He was shocked by Professor Street's sermons, published in 1850. Looking back through his file, he discovered that Newman had been one of his referees in his application for a post in the college in 1839. One explanation for Wilson's passionate anti-tractarianism lay in its 'virtual overthrow of Justification of Faith only as taught by St Paul, as held by our churches and the supercession of the supreme authority of Holy Scripture for the traditions of man.' And, of course, such a view point does have a bearing on Mission: it does much to explain why an evangelical was at odds with faiths which set such store by custom and tradition. Wilson hoped that Withers's replacement as principal, Professor Kay, would keep Street in check. Wilson was clearly unbalanced by Street: 'the thorough persuasion he has that he is right and his martyrlike spirit, his patience and silence when disconcerting events occur, and unremitted pursuit of his plans, remind me of the Romanist's zeal—he is Ignatius Loyola in a small way.' Could Wilson seriously have cast Street as the spearhead of a movement amongst chaplains, missionaries and laity, 'not only of Calcutta but of the Provinces . . . which look up to him as the standard of truth and oracle of wisdom.'?[33] Street's premature death, following two nights of exposure on the river whilst on Mission work, led to kinder words: 'his fine talents, his sound scholarship, his general knowledge, his kindness and tenderness of heart, etc.'[34] Yet one has the sense that the Bishop may have launched his St Paul's Mission just to escape the influence of Street, and such fractiousness could not have helped the cause of SPG Mission.

Both Principal Withers and Professor Street were to have serious doubts about SPG Mission in Bengal, in particular, over its Indian personnel. This was Withers: 'I never have had but a mean opinion and have now a still meaner of the whole apparatus of sircars, readers and catechists and all the native assistants as a body.' One could not delegate. 'Unless these instruments are put aside altogether or replaced by better ones the Missions must be in a rickety state.'[35] Street was particularly despondent about the calibre of the current student body: 'how unpromising one's toil with the listless, unenergetic Eurasians we now have.' But he made their apologies: 'what can be more sordid, more destitute of all that could rouse by records of the past or the deeds of the present than is the life of India.'[36]

Street's was both the most perceptive analysis of the weaknesses of SPG Mission and the most constructive proposals for its change. Physically fit, intellectually able, but thirty at the time, his was a promising appointment in 1839 to the college. He was soon to express his disillusionment with Mission.' I have used the great health and strength and insensitivity to heat which it has pleased God to help me', he reported, 'in exploring at intervals the Society's Missions.' If he had seen but a few, 'the impression on my mind is a strange mixture of joy and pain': joy at the calibre of the European missionary, pain at their exposure and lack of support. Then came his true feelings: 'the natives are so deficient in energy that I am disheartened'.[37]

The Mission station at Barripur was unusually depressing. It was quite impractical. Half the year it was under water, enforcing journey by sallees (canoe), 'a tedious and most comfortless mode of conveyance; the other half, one had to ride, exposed to all the fierceness of the sun.'[38] Clearly Street was not drawn to the Sunderbans. He found it a dismal prospect: 'and so one goes on from one swamp-girt hamlet to another, the bearer of the temporal good in some measure certainly, one must hope too of eternal good.' Not that he could explain the choice of the Sunderbans. Conventionally, the SPG Mission had chosen the city over the village. But 'we cannot withdraw. We have for better or worse baptised so many hundreds of men, women and children and how can they be left without a shepherd?' Towns, in fact, he looked on as a lost cause.[39]

Street's instinct was to rein in expansion and to centralize. He was one of several prophets of a new style of celibate missionary. Even if he recognized that it might be visionary to suppose missionaries could remain single, he saw the College as the source of missionaries, sending them out in pairs on special assignments.

The SPG he felt was ignoring the real challenge. It confronted neither the Brahminical priesthood nor the wealthy. Near Barripur was Rajpur: 'a hotbed of Brahminical bigotry. I think there are ten temples to Shiva in it and there are three just behind it. Had we the men to spare I would commence work there . . . Undermanned as one is at present and with such wretched subordinates as the native Readers we must be content with anything one can find anywhere and be happy to hold what one has got.' Until Mission addressed the wealthy and the high caste, 'the propagation of the Gospel will not be the easygoing bloodless occupation it now is'.[40]

C. E. Driberg: Barripur and the Sunderbans

Over time, and his was to be a long stay at Barripur, Driberg came to see the misguided nature of missionary strategy.

Barripur is sixteen miles south of Calcutta. He came there as Deacon in October 1845. Wisely he was to bypass Rajpur en route, with 'its hideous car of juggernaut and numerous lofty Temples with the trident of Shiva displayed'. It was a relief to catch his first glimpse of the church, the pinnacle, then the tower, 'and then the East end comes in sight with the Sacred Symbol of our holy Truth'.

Under his care was a community of some 6000, a quarter of whom were pan-cultivators or barrins. It had ceased to be a civil station. In consequence, Barripur was not exposed to 'the scandalizing examples of dissolute and abandoned Christian men'. It was distant enough from the city 'for quiet and retirement and yet not so far as to deprive us of the benefit of constant counsel and advice'. There had been a dissenter in the area, but, with his language skills, he had found civil employment and 'I was left unmolested'. Dwarkanath Tagore had lent, rent-free, a small house near the Mission for divine service. An initial attempt to set up a Bengali school at Rajpur had been shouted down, but once the headman had been won over, it went ahead.

The converts who had reverted to caste practices proved to be Driberg's most recalcitrant opponents, 'turning away with contempt from any attempt to recover them from their dreadful state of apathy and decadence to the things pertaining of the ever lasting peace'. In one village, led by 'an apostate christian', he and his catechist, Mr Moore, had been *gheraoed* in the chapel for two hours. On the whole, though, the atmosphere was friendly, especially among the ryots, who looked on him as 'some sort of protection and security against the zamindars'. The high castes saw the advantage of learning English.[41]

Ten years on, we get a clearer picture of his Mission. Driberg denied that it was 'aggressive': so busy were parochial duties, they left 'but a fraction of their time for direct aggressive operations'. However, he had nudged his way into Rajpur, 'teeming I may say with a Brahmin population with their colleges for the education of pundits and vernacular schools for the common people, crowded with temples and ghats presenting to the missionary work enough for his whole life'. He described one encounter with a Brahmin. Initially, he let him choose the ground: 'he carried me away with him and lost both himself and me in a sea of metaphysical speculation and we separated after a drawn battle.' On their next encounter, Driberg chose the ground: 'I kept him to the point and made him talk by rule.' Maybe he was not convinced but 'the eagerness with which he enters into conversation shows that he takes an interest in it. His tone and manner too have changed very much for the better. Instead of endeavouring to stop my mouth as he did at first by loudly repeating Sanskrit slokas he listened attentively and with respect till I had concluded what I had to say and always professed great respect for me personally'. A knowledge of Sanskrit was essential: 'in fact it is often difficult to get a pundit to converse with you at all if he knows that you are ignorant of the language of the gods.' Driberg himself felt the want of this knowledge, 'especially when you go into a village such as Rajpore'.[42] Driberg had come to appreciate the educated character of his Brahmin opponents.

But Driberg was to lose faith in missionary strategy. How could there be progress without a native priesthood? 'We visit our people three times a week but what is really wanted in order to produce a lasting impression', he recognized, 'is the daily ministration of a village pastor.' To date European Mission stations were but 'an oasis in the desert'. Shall we be so absorbed in these little spots already reclaimed as to make us forget the vast moral wilderness that lies before and around us?' Only native missionaries, who would not stand on their dignity, 'will penetrate into the lowest and darkest corners of the native character and find out what it is that keeps them from adopting Christianity and their desire to eradicate it . . . The longer I labour as a missionary the more I feel the overwhelming nature of the work and the more sensible am I of the weakness and inadequacy of the instruments.'

Did Mission make any impact at all? Admittedly people listen, for to interrupt would be 'a breach of good manners', 'but you look in vain for the earnest and anxious enquiry as to the purport of the message you deliver—and how it affects their position—how the hearing of it adds to their responsibilities.' And if 'many are prepared to give an objective assent to Christianity, until the heart is touched and consciousness of the truth is produced, we cannot expect to see any satisfactory results from preaching—it is not that kind of assent which is given to mathematical demonstrations that will do any good, not head convictions but convictions of the heart that is wanted'. In many ways, this was the peculiar flaw of the whole evangelical endeavour, its appeal to the emotions, to some quite specific temperamental change, call it spiritual, rather than an appeal just to reason. Why should those from another culture share that wave length? Driberg ended on a gloomy note: 'One is sometime tempted (I know I am). I think that all is lost labour—because we see no immediate fruits—"what has all our preaching produced" is a question one often puts to oneself, forgetting', and here all missionaries had to fall back on some such answer if they were, indeed, not to give way to despair, 'that we have nothing to do with results—we just have to do our duty.'[43]

There is an interesting general statement on how to set about Mission, revisionist in tone, not by Driberg, but reflecting his more cautious approach. Greater emphasis should be laid on good manners. The missionary should not 'betray any self-complacency on the score of belonging to the race of conquerors'. He should not consider his house to be too good to be frequented and his furniture too neat to be used by his Hindu friends. Europeans should not set themselves aside as a caste: 'no obstacle could be so formidable to conversion as this.' Above all, we must practice what we preach: 'the missionary must show the Christian and unlearn the mere Englishman as much as he can.' These were all timely reminders of how colonialist, even racist, missionaries were in danger of becoming.

But by what means was Hinduism to be addressed? Clearly here was a missionary who was rattled. 'The system is so complex, so full of seeming as well as real contradictions, that one is at a loss to where to direct the battery of reason and scripture against it.' 'Experience has however', and here again one sees how a missionary could draw liberal lessons from the religious encounter, 'shown that hasty sweeping charges fail to produce the desired impressions.' Merely attacking Hindu polytheism could backfire on one, and 'provoke their opposition to the Trinity'. Without a proper familiarity with the Hindu system, a European 'incurs great danger . . .' Take careful stock of your opponent: 'I repeat that the

Hindus might not practically be considered as one people and every combatant must determine with what class he is talking before he frames his attack.' But the conclusion was optimistic: 'a historical and scientific education connected or unconnected with religions has been known to batter down almost magically the fabric of the Hindu mythology—and so far the work of destruction is concerned, no method has succeeded better.'[44]

Slater, O'Brien Smith and the SPG Hindustani Mission

In 1832, Corrie had initiated a Hindustani Mission in Calcutta. If very ill-qualified for the post—he had only started to learn Hindustani at the time of his appointment—Samuel Slater took on the assignment on 15 February 1847.

He was to discover a rather miserable congregation, only twelve, poor and ignorant, in a house in Wellesley Street. The inadequate way the Portuguese catechists performed services put off the better educated. Only a minority were sincere Muslims: the majority, reported Slater, had no faith at all, 'not infidels but people living evil lives who care for no religion not because they hate it, but simply because they never think of it'. Just like the population at home, he commented, a commonsensical observation, and one often overlooked by missionaries.

In an encounter with a Rahaman Ul Huqq, he detected a Muslim love of controversy for its own sake, in this case, over denominationalism.[45] But Slater soon gave up the Mission on his appointment to the second professorship at Bishop's College.

O'Brien Smith was his successor and this was to be a more serious encounter with Islam in Calcutta. He was surprised to find but two mosques in the city with a khatib or preacher attached. And they, to allow Muslims to trade on a Friday, only preached on a Sunday. Clearly, colonial rule imposed its own constraints. O'Brien Smith always felt that educated Muslims preferred to meet him in the streets rather than in 'calm and fair discussion'. Educated Muslims would seek a delay in any conversation, 'to enable them to study the Pentateuch and Gospel which they have not read for a long time'.

Calcutta had become home to dispossessed Muslim élites from the North West and O'Brien Smith took up a lively correspondence with one of the former Amirs of Sind, Meer Hosein Ali Khan, detained at Dum Dum. O'Brien Smith's response to the insistence that Mohammed's riselut (divine mission) was proven by the frequency of his miracles was to quip: 'it never seems to strike Mussulmans that if Mohammed's whole life were one uninterrupted series of miracles as they represent, these miracles must have been patent to all and would have been a sufficient answer to the Querishi and others who doubted.' Clearly, the respective claims of both faiths to a monopoly in miracles still mattered. O'Brien Smith was stopped in the streets by a Muslim from Kashmir who looked to him to give proof of the powers of Christianity by performing a miracle in the church in Park Street: 'it is very strange', he said 'if you are a preacher of a true religion, why can you not perform a miracle and thus convince me at once.'

Apropos his correspondence with the Amir, he pointed out the problematic, as he saw it, of any controversy with Muslims: 'their extremely imperfect acquaintance with historical facts and their inability to discriminate between fabulous legends and true history . . . their deep-rooted prejudices and predetermination to admit nothing against Islam and nothing in favour of Christianity.'

Clearly O'Brien had come up against an impasse.: 'One feels also that with Mussulmans there is no religious element, no spiritual feeling to work upon. No heart, no conscience to appeal to. It is merely a hard intellectual struggle.' Could the Amir produce 'a single text from the Qu'ran in which Mohammed lays claim to miraculous power or any passage from which it could be distinctly shown that he professed such power?'[46] Had he encountered the Muslim intelligentsia in Agra and Delhi, O'Brien Smith might have been less condescending to Indian Islam's defendants, but one can see how the peculiar and, in many ways, emotional character of Protestant Mission at this stage simply could not get round a hard-edged, legalistic, faith. Islam can indeed feel cold.

The Revd Jones at Tollygunge, a largely Muslim town, where the princes from Mysore were confined, also had observations to make on Indian Islam. During the year of the Rebellion, the town became off limits. Even with the presence of European troops, 'the sullen and sinister countenance one meets with especially amongst the followers of the false prophet are an index to their true feelings'. But Jones still felt there was a case to be made for an Urdu-speaking Mission, 'armed for the Muhammedan controversy'. But he had come to doubt the value of the once or twice weekly visits by European missionaries. He entertained, instead, the rather fanciful notion of supporting an Indian priesthood endowed by Christian zamindars.[47]

Samuel Hassell: The CMS Mission at Nadia

This is to take us some sixty miles north of Calcutta, to the birthplace of Caitanya and into the centre of Bengali Vaishnavism. If neighboring Krishnagar attracted more attention in Mission circles through the startling nature of the karta bhoja conversions, Nadia (Nawadwip) was the seat of one of the great centres of Hindu learning, and the mid-century missionaries always relished such a challenge. Hassell was to discover advantages in simply being stationed at such a traditional and still respected centre of scholarship: just to mention the name Nadia would attract favourable attention in its neighbouring villages.

Hassell came out to India in 1847. We take up his Mission story during his winter tour, 1856 to 1857.[48] Here was another adverse landscape. One could not stay all the year round. Once the rains came, with Nadia at the confluence of two rivers, the land became 'almost like a mixture of sand and water. The smallest hole made with a stick in the ground at once filled up with water'.

This winter tour was to prompt feelings of despair: 'how such a mass of ignorance and inequity can be enlightened by the present machinery it is impossible to say. We are but the drop in the ocean. A visit to a neighbourhood like this, once a year, is only just one degree better than doing nothing.' Surveying the visit to fifty-six villages on his return, he reflected: 'except for a few places, the work is scarcely begun even in our own neighbourhood—thousands have never heard and village after village has never been visited. Do what we may, our efforts are puny, compared with the magnitude of the work.' And what would it profit to convert, anyway? 'At present', he ruefully observed, 'there is no prospect for any man, of even comfortable subsistence and social fellowship, when he leaves Hinduism, so that none but the really in earnest take the decisive step. The feeble enquirer just feeling after truth in the dim twilight of doubt and uncertainty is, I believe, often checked in his enquiry by the reflection—"if I believe I must of necessity lose my all".' He entertained no greater hopes for Nadia itself; 'a sort of cold philosophical acquiescence in the truth of the gospel appears to be about the limit of the ground gained; but beyond this man has no power. We look for conversion of heart and that involves a miracle.' Hassell was but another missionary who came to believe that the only way forward lay with Indian missionaries, 'not so much highly educated as faithful, fervent and holy'.

Nevertheless, some of his exchanges in the villages were positive: 'not the mere captious queries of half-educated ignorance but of simple enquiring earnestness.' Audiences could be attentive: 'I never get such a crowd to address without feeling as though I need to have my capacity of enjoying happiness enlarged that I might grasp it more fully.' And given the proximity to Nadia, something of its sophistication, he hoped, might have rubbed off on the village Brahmins.

One exchange was over the role of the guru. Here Hassell could play to his low caste audience: 'nothing so much delighted the common Hindus as a vigorous attack on their gurus, afterwards they will listen attentively to the gospel tale of the true guru who is the way, the truth and the life.'[49] To make the point that caste was no natural distinction, he pointed out that some gurus were in terms of their appearance indistinguishable from ordinary folk: 'they rose most indignantly and said enough—so many years have we done according to our father's religion and shall we now foresake that and be unsettled by you.'[50] Observing a poor man prostrate at the feet of his guru, Hassell declared: 'such solemn adoration should never be paid by any one mortal to another'; the guru replied: 'he would do all for those who thus trusted in him.'[51]

Brahmins were, of course, anxious to protect their professional interests. One young pandit was to stir up the village against them, 'mocked and blasphemed at the name of Jesus': 'he felt, I imagine, that his craft was in danger from our preaching.'[52] Two Brahmins, father and son, the father 'short and unnaturally fat, with all the indications of a luxurious and lazy life', the son, 'educated at one of the best tols in Nuddea', and with 'all the politeness of his class and much more than the usual amount of candour', refused to sit near them, lest they be defiled. Hassell rather sourly noted that, contrary to the shastras, to save costs, they hung onto the idol after its ritual drowning in the annual festival.

Observations of a similar kind peppered his exchanges with Brahmins. One elderly pandit 'said we were guilty of irreligion in trying to make them foresake the habits of their forefathers'. Hassell's retort was to point out how he himself broke those traditions: the scarlet broadcloth wrapper he wore was made in Europe, likewise the white cloth he held in his hand; 'this type of argument regularly demolishes the notion of observing the forefather's religion. Young pandits now wear shoes of cow's skins—eat potatoes—wear clothes made with seams—dress in flannel and hundreds of other things which their forefather's never dreamt of.'[53] Clearly Hassell had not thought through the moral implications of Bengal's trading relationship with the Company.

There were theological exchanges. Idolatry still held sway in the villages. To the analogy that they were as necessary for reaching the gods as deroghas, magistrates and judges were for reaching the Governor-General, Hassell replied that God was everywhere and 'all their subordinate deities were only in the way'. The pandits laughed and said: 'be that as it may, we are Hindus and wo'nt be anything else.'[54]

One pandit, in a discussion on the atonement, asserted: 'meditation was sufficient to purify our souls and render us acceptable to God.' If this had so far failed in his case, the explanation lay in his failure to meditate properly.

Hassell saw Hinduism as 'entirely objective. Personal knowledge of the power of religion no Hindu seems to have.'[55] When one pandit went so far as to concede, 'no Hindu can be saved by observing the smritis', and Hassell pressed him to convert, his reply was: 'in all plainness and sincerity, here I have many disciples and much wealth and am surrounded by the family I love. All this is visible and certain to me—the future of life is uncertain—with you I shall be poor and dependent, lose my family and all and hence I have resolved to stay where I am but still I like to have intercourse with the missionaries.' There was not very much Hassell could do about such pragmatism.

On his journey Hassell had other encounters. He met some former servants of Carey, no longer so well paid: 'none of them, however, are friendly disposed towards the truth.'[56] There were two Calcutta babus, one who had spent fifteen years in Dr Duff's Institute, the other fourteen years at Serampore. They had opened a school. Neither had converted, but 'strange as it may appear at first sight Hindu teaching Hindu the gospel, it is cause for deep thanksgiving'.[57] There were Brahmos: 'like all such cavillers the Deists of Bengal borrow half of their knowledge from the Bible or Christian books and then disown it.'[58] Clearly, the mofussil on occasion did not lag so far behind Calcutta in the lively variety of its ideas.

He even encountered proto-nationalism. Three excellent English speakers were to accuse the Company of holding down Bengal: they 'sighed for a revolution'. In his rejoinder, Hassell was to anticipate many like-minded future British accusations against Indian nationalists, that Bengal's top educated 10,000 displayed no independence of mind and that they were merely imitative of the West: all that they knew of medicine, law, even religion, came from the West. If, for example, they had rejected idols, 'except in their father's and mother's presence', they had merely uncritically taken on board western atheism or unitarianism: 'we talked for hours until it was quite dark and the good men discovered that some Europeans were friendly to the natives, although they were not blind to their follies, nor could they flatter their vanity.'[59] Was that, indeed, the impression he would have left?

On his return to Nadia, Hassell, when he met with the new enrolment of students in the tols, was 'kindly received': 'there is manifestly an improvement in the tone of the young men and I believe it is humanly speaking to be attributed to the degree of Christian influence.' Not that Hassell had any expectations of conversions, but here he also was taking one step back from despair.

But post-1857 the situation did not improve; 'there appears to be, however, a sort of solid indifference in the minds of most of those who know the general features of the gospel . . . it seems as if the spirit of slumber had seized the whole people for they do not even oppose vigorously.'[60] Missionaries always feared indifference more than retaliation. Yet Hassell did not abandon hope that he was exercising a good influence over the young pandits of Nadia. And, like almost all missionaries working in the mofussil, he became strongly attached to his station: 'Nuddea is a peculiar place and requires able earnest devoted men: a more important field of work I do not know.'[61] He left India in February 1863 and he died on 5 June 1879.

CONCLUSION

Any account of Mission in Bengal which narrowly focussed on itinerating to the exclusion of education would, of course, be seriously skewed. All the missionaries just reviewed would, anyway, have been, to some degree, involved in education, be it in a Bengali or English school, normally an elementary one, though Pearce's Native Christian was obviously at the secondary level. Given the role of Carey at Serampore, and even more of J. C. Marshman, together with that of the stormy petrel of Mission, Alexander Duff, the educationists held their own. Even so, itinerating in Bengal was still held to be the primary task.

However, this has not sought to be a balanced account. It has quite deliberately set out to discover from the evidence of itinerating just how faiths and cultures did encounter one another. Here was evidence of an aggressive assault by Christianity on Bengali Hinduism and Islam, only gradually tempered by a perception that this was counter-productive, and a growing despondent awareness that it was getting Mission nowhere.

In the villages, Mission came up against a Hinduism, as much popular as high Sanskritic, though, as modern anthropologists have made us aware, these were interdependent. We should not be too surprised if missionaries failed to talk in terms of a Great and a Little, or folk, tradition. At Nadia, Hinduism had one major centre of Sanskrit culture, and Hassell's observations do not suggest it was quite so petrified as some accounts have suggested.[62]

In Bengal, Christianity met a distinctive form of Vaishnavism, a tradition of bhaktic Hinduism, going back as far as Caitanya, even earlier, and the Christian message of a personal saviour may have induced a special, more favourable, Bengali response. (This is discussed more fully when I tell the story of Bengali Christian converts.) But Bengali Hinduism did just enough to bend under the evangelical assault, without making any serious concession; an effective form of resistance. Sometimes there would be an angry response, wholly excusable, considering how heavy footed the evangelical protestants could be. More often, it was a polite, even an indifferent, response. There is little evidence that in the villages the missionaries met a more sophisticated opposition from the Brahmo reformers, always, anyway, an elite movement.

Just occasionally, confrontation with Islam, though in the mofussil and not in Calcutta, was of a higher intellectual content, and this may indicate the influence of the Faraizi reform movement. If so, it was not perceived by the missionaries.

The exponents of a traditional Hinduism and Indian Islam in Bengal seem effectively to have smothered an embattled Christianity. Would Mission be any more successful in the north?

NOTES AND REFERENCES

1. Figures taken from *The Missionary Herald* (hereafter M.H.), vol. CLXXII, Nov. 1852, pp. 166–7. The Presidency of Bengal then included Bihar and Orissa.
2. Reginald Heber, *Narrative of a Journey through the Upper Provinces of India*, vols I–III. I will in the text refer to the rpt. edn, Delhi: 1985. But see also M. A. Laird (ed.), *Bishop Heber in Northern India: Selections from Heber's Journal*, Cambridge: 1971.
3. I have taken these statistics from the entry on Bengal in *The Imperial Gazetteer of India*, vol. VII and on Calcutta, vol. IX, rpt. edn.
4. For a succinct account of the Islamic reform movement, see J. N. Sarkar, 'Islam in Bengal', in section III in N. K. Sinha (ed.), *The History of Bengal 1757–1905*, Calcutta: 1967.
5. Here I am largely summarizing ch. V of Brian Stanley's recent account, *The History of he Baptist Missionary Society 1792–1992*, Edinburgh: 1992.

6. *Imperial Gazetteer*, vol. VII, p. 224
7. Mr Evans, M.H., vol. LVI, January 1844, p. 218.
8. *Baptist Handbook*, London: 1886, p. 130.
9. M.H., vol. XXIX October 1841, pp. 153–4.
10. M.H., vol. XLII, Dec. 1842, pp. 389–90.
11. M.H., vol. XXI, Feb. 1841, p. 20.
12. *The Baptist Handbook*, London: 1888, p. 111.
13. An address to the annual Home Meeting, M.H., vol. CLXXVII, July 1834.
14. All the references for Pearce's early career in Calcutta are from correspondence in IN/29 (BMS, Regent's Park College, Oxford).
15. M.H., vol. XXXVI, May 1842, p. 259.
16. See entry on Sunderbans, *The Imperial Gazetteer*, vol. XXIII.
17. George Pearce, IN/29 (BMS, Regent's Park College).
18. Baptist Periodical Accounts, 9, London: 1839, p. 13.
19. Ibid.
20. 24 July 1829, ibid.
21. M.H., vol. CLVII, Jan. 1832, p. 2.
22. M.H., vol. CLVII, Jan. 1832, pp. 2–3.
23. Ibid.
24. M.H., vol. CLXXIII, June 1833, p. 50.
25. M.H., vol. XII, May 1840, p. 178.
26. M.H., vol. CLV, April 1852, pp. 57–9.
27. See his obituary, M.H., 1 January 1895, pp. 7–8.
28. See his letter to C. B. Lewis, 30 April 1864, IN/32 (BMS, Regent's Park College).
29. For obvious reasons—it was good publicity for the humanitarian endeavours of Mission—this took up a great deal of space in missionary journals. See 'Persecution of Native Christians in Barisaul', M.H., vol. CXCIX, Jan. 1856, pp. 1–7; 'The Case of Persecuted Christians at Barisaul', M.H., vol. CCVIII, Oct. 1856, pp. 150–4; contd, M.H., vol. CCIX, Nov. 1856, pp. 165–70; 'The Persecution in Barisaul' The Baptist Magazine, vol. XLIV, Jan. 1857, pp. 6–10; 'The Persecution in Barisaul: The Zamindari System', *The Baptist Magazine*, vol. XLIX, pp. 73–8.
30. *The Baptist Magazine*, vol. XLIX, Jan. 1857, pp. 51–5.
31. M.H. Sept. 1858, p. 587.
32. Bishop of Calcutta to Revd A. M. Campbell, 7 April 1842, Correspondence Local Received 12 (SPG, Rhodes House).
33. Bishop of Calcutta to Archbishop of Canterbury, 30 May 1850, pp. 263–70, CLR 13.
34. Bishop of Calcutta to Archbishop of Canterbury, 30 May 1851, CLR 13.
35. Revd Principal Withers, 16 March 1843, CLR 12.
36. Professor Street, 18 January 1843, CLR 12, p. 100.
37. Professor Street, 7 February 1842, CLR 12, pp. 12–13.
38. Professor Street, 26 November 1845, CLR 12, p. 288.
39. Professor Street, 6 June 1844, CLR 12, pp. 199–200.

40. Professor Street, 18 June 1843, CLR 12.
41. C. E. Driberg to Professor Street, May 1845, C. Ind 1 (46 AC) (SPG, Rhodes House, Oxford).
42. C. E. Driberg to Revd Professor Slater, n.d. 1854, Printed Ecclesiastical Gazette, 6 October 1854, C. Ind 1 14.
43. C. E. Driberg to Revd Vallings, 28 May 1861. C. Ind 1 (14).
44. Anon, 'The Character of the Pagan Mythologies and Superstitions', C. Ind 1 (1) 48.
45. Revd Samuel Slater to Professor Street, 9 June 1847, C Ind 1 (51 A–D).
46. W. O'Brien Smith to Professor Slater, Various letters, 25 November 1853, July 1854, C. Ind 1 (14).
47. Revd Jones to Revd Hawkins, 23 November 1857, to Rev Kay, 26 December 1857, C. Ind 1 (14).
48. Revd Samuel Hassell, His Journal for Nuddea, 1 October 1856 to 31 March 1857. Dated 1 April 1857. CMS CI 1/0133/12 (CMS: Birmingham).
49. 6 December 1856, ibid.
50. 3 December 1857, ibid.
51. 9 December 1856, ibid.
52. 19 December 1856, ibid.
53. 6 January 1857, ibid.
54. 3 December 1856, ibid.
55. 9 December 1856, ibid.
56. 3 December 1856, ibid.
57. 15 January 1857.
58. 20 January 1857, ibid.
59. 24 January 1857, ibid.
60. He was describing his preaching at Chapra, December 1858/January 1859. Report dated 30 September 1859, CI 1/0133/22.
61. Hassell, 30 September 1860, CI 1/0133/23.
62. For example, M. A. Laird writes of the tols as 'concerned with the perpetuation of traditional classical culture in a somewhat petrified form', *Missionaries and Education in Bengal 1793–1837*, Oxford: 1972, p. 50.

CHAPTER 4

Missionary Case-Studies:
Lower Hindustan

In crossing from Bengal to Bihar, missionaries were entering the heartlands of Indian religions, Benares (Varanasi) for Hinduism, Delhi, Lucknow and Lahore for Islam, Amritsar for Sikhism. In part they were following the ever expanding frontier of Company rule, through the Doab, to the Punjab, to the North West Frontier. Yet the imperative was only incidentally political. Missionaries did not follow the flag. Indeed, they were often hostile to political authority. They were driven, instead, by the millenarian delusion that, were they to penetrate the strongholds of Indian religions, these would soon collapse and mass conversions would follow. Probably never before or since has inter-faith contact been so confrontational and continuous in northern India.

Once again, this cannot be a comprehensive approach; it has to be selective. The same three mission societies have been chosen. As we journey further up the Gangetic plain, the CMS, the most highly organized of the three and the one, in some ways, most favoured by the Church of England at the time, begins to come into its own.

To contextualize the mid-century missionaries to Bihar, to Chunar and to Benares, I need to say something of the missionary journeys of Bishop Heber, a marvellous foil to the experience of the following generation, and to the pioneering role of the 'pious chaplains'.

Bishop Heber

No Christian account of Mission to north India matches Bishop Heber's for its humanity and tolerant curiosity.[1] His is seen to be a romantic's response to India, a delight in its variety and exoticism. (He would not, therefore, necessarily find favour with the anti-orientalists.) The degree to which the next generation was able to match this imaginative response becomes a yardstick for measuring the quality of their own cultural encounter.

Heber was struck by the agricultural and commercial prosperity of the lower Gangetic plain, from Patna to Benares, and the impoverishment of the Doab, the territory that lay between the rivers Ganges and Jumna.

This is not the place to elaborate on Heber's tolerant account of Indian faiths. It took him time to recognize that the dominance of Islam in the cities gave a false impression of its overall strength: 'there are so few pagodas of any importance visible that I thought I had bidden adieu to the followers of Brahma.'[2] Contrastingly, following his visit to Delhi, he was surprised how little Islam did in fact dominate: 'through all the country, indeed, notwithstanding its proximity to the capital of Islam in the East, Hindooism seems to predominate in a degree which I did not expect to find.'[3]

Not that the missionary in Heber lay so far below the surface. Had he been too charitable in his account of Indian religions, he wondered: 'we are all much impressed with religious ceremonies to which we are not accustomed, and while as passing and casual spectators of a worship carried on by persons in scene and dress, words and posture, all different from our own, but all picturesque and striking, we may easily overlook those less conspicuous instances of listlessness and inattention, which would not fail to attract our notice, where the matter and manner were both familiar.'[4] He was quick to see opportunities for evangelism, especially for those tribal populations he met in the Rajmahal hills near Mongyhr. For all his generous response to Benares, he could still write of its 'awful and besotted darkness', and that 'God may have much people in that city'.[5] And in drawing attention, quite rightly, to Heber's hostility to the arrogance of Empire and its racism—he wrote of that 'exclusive and intolerant spirit which makes the English, wherever they go, a caste by themselves, disliking and disliked by all their neighbours'[6] —we are in danger of overlooking that he came to India as a missionary bishop.

Yet nothing differentiates Heber so emphatically from the next generation than his rejection of the strategy of itinerating: 'the custom of street-preaching, of which the Baptist and other dissenting missionaries in Bengal are very fond, has never been resorted by those employed by the Church Missionary Society and shall never be as long as I have any influence or authority over them.' It might be 'safe among the timid Bengalees, it would be very likely to produce mischief here'.[7] Or was this just Heber, the high churchman, speaking?

The Pious Chaplains: Henry Martyn and Daniel Corrie

Pioneers of the mid-nineteenth-century missionaries to north India, maybe ironically so, considering how much missionaries were later to malign the Company chaplains as a group, were those early Company chaplains, christened 'the pious chaplains' for their missionary zeal, Henry Martyn and Daniel Corrie to the fore. Officially Mission lay outside their remit. They came to India to meet the needs of Europeans, particularly those of the military. But both Martyn and Corrie were strongly attracted to Mission and were determined to break beyond these constraints.

Born on 18 February 1781, Cornish by background, his father an ex-miner and a self-made man, Henry Martyn came under Charles Simeon's influence at Cambridge, and it was he, though his father's death played a part, who was to steer him away from an academic career, well within his sights, and towards Mission. He was ordained on 22 October 1803. Financial hardship, a consequence of the loss of his father, drove him to seek a Company chaplaincy—he wrote in his journal, 24 May 1805: 'I felt more than I had ever done the shame attending poverty'—[8] and he set sail for India on 17 July 1805.

With Martyn, we begin to encounter that nineteenth-century feeling of alienation from India. On arrival at Madras on 12 April 1806, for example, he 'felt a solemn sort of melancholy at the sight of such multitudes of idolaters'.[9] He was to experience his first sight of Hindu worship at a temple in Calcutta as a vision of hell.

Problems of strategy had to be addressed. He had been posted to the military station at Dinapore (Danapur) near Patna in Bihar. If his preference was to proselytize, he saw the need first to master the vernaculars and for translations. Martyn, in many ways, was in the Serampore mould. His long term reputation was as a translator and, at the time, he recognized that this task stood him in good stead: 'it seems a providential circumstance that the work at present assigned to me is that of translation; for had I gone through the villages preaching as my intentions led me to do, I fear by this time I should have been in deep decline.'[10] By 1808 his Hindustani translation of the New Testament appeared. He then applied himself to a Persian. Martyn's sense of Mission was always more consciously directed towards Islam.

Education was an alternative. He started a number of schools at Dinapore. Maybe they would make Indian children 'ashamed of the idolatry and other customs of their country'.[11] But neither translation, a 'merely intellectual' activity, nor teaching, could take the place of his wish to evangelize.

Whatever the nature of that initial sense of alienation, there was nothing arrogant, let alone racist, about Martyn. His first real encounter with Indians had been as munshis, or teachers of language, and there had been rows. En route to Dinapore, he thanked God he had not been born a Brahmin. But his morbid conscience drew him to Indians: 'I think that when my mouth is opened I shall preach to them day and night. I feel that they are my brethren in the flesh.'[12] The first encounters were demoralizing; they left him 'much discouraged at the suspicions and rebuffs I met with or rather pained'.[13] If he did attract an audience, it was only, he felt, through his being a 'sahib'. In Patna he sensed the hatred of Indians. One gesture of appeasement was to give up the use of the palanquin. There was despair; 'looking around the country and reflecting upon its state is enough to overwhelm the mind of a minister and a missionary.'[14]

Yet Martyn is looked on as a founder of Mission in north India, especially among its Muslim population. So lax did Indians strike him in their own faith that he thought a nominal conversion to Christianity would be easy to achieve. Only after his transfer to Cawnpore (Kanpur) did he take on the role of a street preacher. He preached to mendicants, often up to 800 at a time, who gathered outside his house. He was to baptize some forty adults and twenty children. There was one distinguished convert, Abdul Massih. But ill-health and his pursuit of Persian led him away from India and to Persia, and to an early death on 16 October 1812.

Daniel Corrie (1777–1837), Martyn's contemporary in India and close friend, was another early Company chaplain to make a pioneering contribution to Mission in north India, at Chunar, Benares and Agra. In time, the claims of the ecclesiastical establishment were to take Corrie away from Mission and he was to end his career as the first Bishop of Madras (1835–37).[15]

His likewise was an initial sense of alienation. 'These natives', he wrote, 'presented a most disgusting appearance to a stranger, especially to a European stranger.'[16] India was a benighted land in need of salvation: 'every day brings one acquainted with some new proof of that wretched slavery which they are under to the powers of darkness.'[17] But, quite quickly, Corrie registered a change of outlook. At Masulipatam, en route to Calcutta, he wondered why he no longer felt so great a hostility towards Hinduism.

Corrie's was an appealing personality. He saw himself as impulsive and sanguine. Yet India was to be a severe test. Its climate was enervating: 'I go on rather in the spirit of sullen obstinacy than under the influence of the constraining love of Jesus.'[18] It could induce despair: 'I am ready to be weary of what appears to be so hopeless a task as the turning of men, so incorrigible, from the error of their ways.'[19] But his was to be a life-long commitment to India: 'my views in coming to India I would hope have not altered; to live and die here; and to spend my strength and substance in this land is I think my purpose.'[20] By 1812 there was even cause for hope: 'notwithstanding the opposition of Government (and Corrie here referred to the great debate on the missionary clause in the battle over the renewal of the Company's charter), a work is working in this land.'[21] At one stage there was a temporary loss of personal faith: 'how seldom can I "take hold on God". I read and kneel in devotion, but too generally without apprehending or appropriating any benefit.'[22] And what were, he questioned, his real motives? 'It is often I doubt, fear for myself rather than love for the heathen that keeps me, in a measure, at the Missionary helm.'[23] But such morbid introspection was typical of missionaries in India at the time.

A less complicated person than Martyn, and more direct, Corrie's was to be the more practical contribution to Mission. On arrival at Calcutta, he sought out the Baptist missionaries at Serampore. But their denomi-nationalism put him off: 'I learnt that their prejudice against the Church of England will not suffer them to take one step beyond that narrow enclosure.'[24]

He was posted to Chunar, with its great fort. At first sight, his heart sank and he looked on it as his grave. Once a frontier fortress for the Company, then a garrison and hospital for the sick of the Company's army, Corrie's first responsibility was to the Europeans. But Corrie kept his social distance and rationed his time with them to three hours a week. Not only was there the largest Indian Christian congregation to date in north India to care for, there was the enticing challenge of a population of some 10,000 Hindus and Muslims. Downstream, there was the greatest draw of all, Benares, and Corrie began to explore the possibility of opening a Mission there, setting up a school in the suburb of Secrole. Here was its European population. He was to spend some time in Cawn-pore. Not until 1813 did he reach Agra, where again he was to be a pioneer in Mission. In 1818, he was appointed chaplain at Benares.

Like Martyn, Corrie had to think through missionary strategy from scratch. He also saw the prior need to master the vernacular languages. He learnt Hindustani and went on to tackle Persian. If conversion was the objective—'my life shall be devoted to the furtherance of this work'—[25] he soon became aware of its intractability: 'you can have no idea of the magnitude of the work of conversion.'[26] But there was as yet no fixation on itinerating and Corrie could be flexible in his approach.

Schools were one way forward. Particularly successful was Jai Narain's school for boys in Benares. Heber has a marvellous picture of the look on Corrie's face of 'calm but intense pleasure' when they visited the school later, in September 1824, and discovered how it had prospered.[27]

Corrie was also one of the first to recognize the essential role that Indians would have to play in Mission: 'ever since my arrival and short acquaintance with this country it has appeared that natives will be the great means of converting their brethren.[28]

If Corrie saw the risk of over-identification with Europeans, he was aware the harm that official indifference could do to Mission in a culture where the sircar counted for so much. With his own preferment through the ecclesiastical establishment, he began to doubt whether Mission could make much progress without greater official support. Later in his career he was to be at the centre of evangelical appeals to government to alter its rigid stance on religious neutrality.

If Corrie was to take itinerating a good deal further than Martyn, he did so with a sense of its superficiality. He had not been attracted to Methodist itinerating in England; 'bids fair to turn them all into preachers and no hearers.'[29] In India it struck him as an impossibility; 'you have heard of the population of India but you can have no idea', he wrote to his friend, Buckworth, 'of its immensity unless you saw it: so that a man may visit I cannot tell how many villages of three hundred, four hundred people and upwards, in a circle of six or eight miles; there seems little need of itinerating according to your idea of the word; but you may think to how little an extent all the whole of the missionaries now in India can do is likely to be felt.'[30] Such fears were not to beset the missionary generation of the 1830s and 1840s.

Corrie's initial response to Indian religions was highly disparaging. When a byragi (a Vaishnavite ascetic and mendicant) stood in his way to a temple, Corrie turned on him; 'he was a lazy man that could do no work, but only eat, and that God was angry with him, and that when he died he would go down to fire for ever.'[31] Corrie certainly shared the evangelical belief that non-Christians would go to hell. Another such holy man at Mirzapur struck him as 'strongly under Satanic influence'.[32] And it was the belief that Indian religions were on the wane that kept Corrie going. 'In general', he wrote, 'the spirit and fury of idolatry does not appear':[33] 'there is a general falling off amongst the Hindoos from

their former system.'[34] Temples were falling into decay. Religious practice appeared to be lax. But if Hindus make temple offerings 'at the time
most convenient to themselves' and Muslims did not attend Friday
worship at the mosques in large numbers, they turned out in large
numbers at one another's festivals: 'the whole country wears the appearance of a mountebank show.'[35] Only a proto-Victorian hostility and fear
of such expressions of popular culture could explain Corrie's readiness to
see this mixing of the two faiths as a further sign of decline.

But decline or no, Corrie felt he was up against impossible barriers of
communication. If he did have conversations with Brahmins, these were
but 'words spoken to the air: so deeply rooted is error in their minds and
so congenial are their lying idols to the corrupt nature of man.'[36] Just
because Indians were, in his view, so naturally submissive and so anxious
to please, he could never be sure if he had succeeded in communicating;
'they do not either acknowledge their ignorance or ask explanations';
'their duplicity makes it beyond measure difficult to know when they are
convinced or even silenced.'[37] 'This servile spirit does not give place entirely', he sensed, 'on conversion.' Only a 'common measure of understanding' and 'an intimate acquaintance with human nature' would do
the trick.[38]

Of course, at this stage, still confidently sheltering behind the shield
of neutrality, the Brahmins may have seen no cause to engage in any real
contact with these still very rare missionaries, and Corrie may have been
up against an especially opaque Indian mind. But in Corrie's response to
Indian religions we can detect the fading of a naive evangelical optimism,
and a dawning sense of the enormity of the task of Mission. Rather than
recognize the hopelessness of it all, the alternative was to take the
offensive.

Andrew Leslie, John Lawrence, John Parsons:
Baptist Missionaries at Monghyr

Some three hundred miles distant from Calcutta at Monghyr was
Hindustan's first Protestant Mission. The town itself was set on a pro-
montory on the south bank of the Ganges. Set in a fertile district, with
a dry climate, with the blue Rajmahal hills in the background, as civil
stations went, it was 'in some respects one of the most picturesque in
Bengal'.[39] In the 1840s there was a population of 30,000 Hindus and
Muslims. Many retired from the army to Monghyr and it became, as

Chunar, something of a town for invalids. Besides the civilians, there were some twenty European families. One missionary described it as 'an exceedingly smug, harmonious little station', but, compared to Calcutta, it 'is regarded as insufferably dull—one of the most intolerable spots in all India'.[40]

The Baptists had been here since 1818. Their mission spread in all directions, north and south into the neighbouring villages, drawn by the river as far west as Allahabad, and south west to the tribal populations of the Rajmahal hills. This can but be an impressionistic account of Baptist Mission in this area.

Andrew Leslie joined the station in 1823. More than anyone else he was to take the Mission to the hill people, be it in Bhagalpur, where they came down from the hills, or in the Rajmahal hills themselves. Heber had taken to him a good deal more than to his irascible predecessor, that great scourge of the Church of England, John Chamberlain. He saw him as a 'very mild, modest person, of a far better spirit and scarcely less diligent among the heathen than Chamberlain was'.[41] On grounds of ill-health Leslie left for Calcutta in 1841. John Lawrence had joined him in 1831 and lived out his missionary life there till 1874, dying in England shortly after his return the following year. Briefly, from 1841–42, until his death, G. B. Parsons was to work at Monghyr. His brother, John, replaced him, and worked there till his death in 1870. Andrew Leslie died in the same year.[42]

There was no dispute over strategy. This was a Mission committed to itinerating. Even so, it was one that could induce despair. One was clutching at straws. Leslie trusted that the hill people, several thousands each year, who attended the native chapel in Monghyr 'would take the message back to their villages some one to two days distance away'.[43] Two years later, he was close to surrender: 'my spirits are sometimes so overwhelmed at our little success that I am often ready to give up. Nothing can possibly be so disheartening as missionary work in this country.'[44]

Lawrence was quick to share these doubts. How could human agency hope to bring about conversion?: 'such abominable ignorance, superstition and pride the Spirit of God alone can remove.'[45] Again, one had to clutch at straws. There were always hearers in the bazaar: maybe one seed will bring forth fruit.[46] A more likely response was 'a stoical apathy': 'the prince of darkness sits enthroned in the hearts of all around us and exerts his destructive influence almost as much upon the Europeans as upon the heathen.'[47] Lawrence began to wonder if this was God's chosen moment for conversion: 'I am sometimes tempted to sit down in despondency, to regard myself as an unprofitable servant . . . Someone else should take on the role . . . At other times I am disposed to conclude that the Lord's time for converting the Hindus and Mussulmans is not come, but that it is my duty to labour in faith and patiently wait for it.'[48] Almost ten years on, he sounded no more cheerful: 'a lamentable deadness in regard to spiritual things prevails. Unbelievers come to the house of God and listen to the word, but go away unimpressed, or at least unchanged.'[49] But despite this indifference, Lawrence still felt that 'mission has loosened the fetters of superstition and brahminical tyranny. It has weakened the confidence of the people'.[50]

Given such demoralization, the openly confrontational style of the Monghyr Mission is all the more puzzling. They did not hesitate to proselytize the great melas. One was at Hajipur, north east of Patna. Leslie reported that the Brahmins were disinclined to take up the challenge, acknowledging the excellence of Christianity and the uselessness of Hinduism.[51] Here was the site for the Kartik puja—Kartik, the son of Shiva and Durga, a god of war. Lawrence came every year. In a matter of fact description of the ceremony of the worship of his image and its ritual immersion in the river, he reported: 'the beauty of Kartik is quite proverbial amongst the Hindoos, who when they wish to describe a handsome man or boy say he is Kartik personified.' Many barrins, pan producers, worshipped at the festival.[52] He got to know those who took their books, though had to recognize 'even in the most pleasing cases a perfect insensibility to the evil of sin and the necessity of the atonement of the son of God'.[53] He attended the Karagola mela near Colgong, to the east of Monghyr. The 100,000 strong crowd stretched three miles along the river; in two days he distributed some 250 gospels and 100 tracts.[54] One rather intriguing choice of where to preach was at Surajgarreh, the official collection point for opium.[55]

Most ambitious was their attending the great Kumbh mela at Allahabad (Prayag). This was a peculiarly sacred Hindu site, the confluence of three rivers, the Ganges, the Jumna, the Saraswati (in fact, underground and mythological). Here there was an annual pilgrimage. But every twelfth year there was the great Kumbh mela, and to this Lawrence came in 1835. Some 20,000 byragis were present. Lawrence reported his spending, rather brazenly, several hours each day preaching and 'was much encouraged by the friendly reception which I met and the attention with which they listened to my message'. By then he had mastered Hindustani, and 'nothing can exceed the delight which I experience when I see fifty or sixty of these poor deluded souls listening to the truths of the gospel of Christ'.[56] Here was Hindu forbearance at its best.

But encounters could turn violent. At Darbhanga, some 100 miles north of Monghyr, the inhabitants demanded that Leslie depart: 'the tracts and gospels which had been distributed among them were found torn to pieces in the streets.'[57] In the city of Soobah Behar, outraged at remarks which belittled the Prophet, Muslims threatened to attack Leslie and they beat a hasty retreat in the night, taking advantage of a full moon. When they visited villages for the first time, they were often mistaken for servants of the Company, hired to distribute tracts, with the aim of persuading 'all the different sects of the country to become one caste with Europeans'.[58] But Lawrence was to experience greater opposition from the villages he had already visited than from the new: 'in some instances those who had frequently heard the gospel showed much opposition and bitterness of spirit.'[59] Occasionally, a whole village would drive them out. More often, just the Brahmins would go on the attack.[60]

Theological exchanges could be odd. At the house of a zamindar, on Lawrence's insistence that Christ was the *only* saviour, Ram was held to be the incarnation of God and hence the equal of Christ. If this was reasonable enough, the claim that in the kali yuga the deity had been incarnated in the Company and hence the Company was Ram in another guise was a little more difficult to take. A pandit at Karagola told Lawrence that the Vedas contained the same truths as the Bible and that the self-sacrifices of Christ and the apostles were matched by those of the Hindu sages and ascetics.[61]

A more civilized debate took place with a maulvi, employed by a rich Muslim, in Sarsaram. Here was the mausoleum of the sixteenth-century Afghan emperor, Sher Shah: Lawrence found it one of the prettiest places he had visited. It was by way of a formal debate. Three types of discussion were deemed to be possible; one in which both parties were exhibitionists; one in which each tried to outsmart the other; one in which both sides sought the truth. Their's would be the last. The maulvi and Lawrence sat themselves down opposite one another. At the outset the maulvi prayed that God would show them the truth. Was Mohammed a true prophet? Was the Koran truly the word of God? The maulvi rejected the charge of tahrif (the corruption of text). Christ was indeed called the son of God. But he would not acknowledge his death and resurrection.[62] Clearly theological debate need not deteriorate into a slanging match.

The most promising field for the Monghyr Mission was the hill people, the Pakarias, of the Rajmahal hills. During his stay at Bhagalpur, Heber had been quick to spot how unprejudiced they were towards Christianity, and was all for dispatching a CMS Mission straightaway to one of their villages.[63] But the Baptist missionary Leslie should take the credit for starting Mission at Deoghar. In his first report, he stated: 'these people are quite in a savage state, but they do not worship idols, have no caste, bury their dead, and use bows and arrows as the instruments of their rude warfare.'[64] But an attentive audience led to no conversion. Subsequently, Leslie was to stay with their chief: a 'shrewd and intelligent man and I am sure he is no deceiver.' Leslie echoed Heber's verdict of the honesty of these people. 'A mild, frank, godly missionary residing among them would soon', he optimistically forecast, 'see the whole people turn unto God.'[65] Later, the Paharias were to be swamped by the Santals.

John Parsons was to make rather less of an impact on another tribal community to the north of Monghyr. They listened, they did not dispute inch by inch, Hindu-style, but they did not display 'any genuine contrition for sin or concern for salvation'. His audience were 'not much impressed by the new and important message'.[66]

However, tribal populations were to be receptive to Mission. Here was to be another example—compare the peasantry or low castes—of the way Indians would use missionaries for their own purposes. Missionaries were possible allies in the defence of their tribal lands. For example, the Kols in Chota Nagpur were ready to take full advantage of the Moravian Mission in the 1840s.

In the aftermath of the Rebellion, the Monghyr missionaries doubted the loyalty of both Muslims and Hindus. The great majority would rejoice in the downfall of the government. They put their faith in force: 'nothing but the strong arm of power will keep the mass of the people, especially the upper classes, loyal. Until they are Christianized they will be unworthy of confidence.'[67] Baptists had turned imperialist. Maybe it is not fair to the Baptists to end on a sour note, for, in many ways, they were at their best in this Mission, especially among the tribal populations. With a Baptist tradition of political radicalism, they were more attracted to these more democratic, tribal societies.

William Bowley: CMS Missionary to Chunar

It seemed to be Bowley's role to pick up where Corrie had broken off. Corrie had 'discovered' him in 1814 at Meerut, in charge of a small congregation of some twenty to thirty Indian Christians. Bowley was Eurasian by birth, his father an English soldier, his mother, an Indian. It has been one of the problematics of this text to decide whether such mixed ancestry subtly affects the whole attitude of a missionary to Mission, both in terms of the extent of the Englishness brought to the encounter, and in terms of the response to Indian religions. At Chunar he was to eschew the company of Europeans, though whether he did so through following the example of his mentor, Corrie, or unease as a Eurasian in their presence, is open to question.[68] In his early life he had been a drummer boy, by then a customary form of employment for Christians in the army, for they would not share a Hindu taboo against contact with leather. Corrie had taken him to Agra. But Bowley did not get on with Abd al-Masih. He became unhappy and thought of giving up being a missionary. But the Agra Mission foundered[69] and Bowley, instead, took over Corrie's role at Chunar.

And clearly things went better, for Corrie, on his return to Chunar in early 1818, found a congregation of some forty Europeans and some seventy to eighty Indian Christians: such numbers 'testify to the diligence and exemplary conduct of Mr Bowley and of the blessing attending his labours'.[70] At this stage, Bowley confined his attentions to the garrison and to the sick. He clearly had a way with Indian NCO's and their families. He could move them to tears, especially their wives. According to Heber, it was Bowley who had converted them from Hinduism, Islam and Roman Catholicism. In 1819, the Church of Holy Trinity was built, though not consecrated till later. Heber, on his visit to Chunar in September 1824, was also to be moved by a Bowley sermon: 'he speaks Hindoostanee with the fluency of a native and I was pleased to find that I could follow the argument of his sermon with far more ease than I expected.'[71] By then the numbers attending the native service had increased to two hundred, though these included Hindus and Muslims. Heber was to ordain Bowley as deacon on 30 November 1825. It has to be said that Corrie took greater pleasure in the ordination, at the same time, of Abd al-Masih.

The great Fort of Chunar had fallen into Company hands after the battle of Buxar in 1764. But as the frontier expanded, it ceased to be a bastion of defence and became, instead, as Corrie had found it, a hospital for European and Indian troops. If Corrie had dreaded the place, Heber rather took to it, reminding him, as it did, of a Welsh market town. He ferretted out the interesting information that in the uppermost part of the fort these was a Hindu palace, containing a large black marble slab: here, the Hindus believed, the Almighty sat for some nine hours a day, but in the other three he visited Benares, and only then, between the hours of six and nine in the morning, could the fort be taken.[72]

For Bowley, however, if Chunar was his base, the town and its environs were only of interest for the opportunity they presented to proselytize and Heber would, no doubt, have looked on him with a more cautious eye had he known that he had already, in his time as bishop, and in flat contradiction of his policy, begun to do so. As early as in 1822 Bowley conjectured a Mission up and down the Ganges, upstream to Mirzapur, downstream to Buxar, Ghazipur, and inland to Jaunpur. In time, he was to travel widely, to Allahabad, Lucknow, Cawnpore. Only Mission, he passionately held, would save Indians from hell: 'I am in a ferment and can almost weep for want of a hearing. Also it is hard living without it when thousands are perhaps for want of it dropping into torments annually.'[73] Avril Powell sees him as 'semi-educated'.[74] And, indeed, he could not have received much formal education. He resented time spent on his journal. His, he confessed, was not fit to read, 'since I hastily insert what has occurred without so much as looking over what I have written even to correct blunders, nor does a second person see it'.[75] Still, Bowley was to make a pretty good attempt at taking over in the late 1830s from the mysterious Joseph Wolff the munazara with the Muslims. And any self-consciousness over his journal was too trifling a matter to stand in the way of Mission.

Initially, Chunar proper was too great a risk and Bowley took, instead, to the ghats below the town and to the surrounding villages. Here he met pilgrims 'of a degraded, ignorant set', mendicants seeking 'a bare subsistence rather than obtain a livelihood by honest industry'.[76] Enquirers felt less exposed were they to collect his tracts in the villages or at melas. Even so, they were hesitant, and many tracts were returned. 'People little know', Bowley lamented, 'what obstacles we have to encounter to remove the prejudices against our books.'[77] They looked on the distributor of tracts as 'a great deceiver'. 'They want to take our caste.' 'Were we offering bribes?' were questions raised. Alternatively, the books 'will answer for paste-boards'. Bowley saw himself in a battle between the old man and the new: if the old were to prevail, he himself was not fit to be a missionary: if the new, 'he will have a tenfold inducement to redouble his labour'.[78]

In fact, Bowley was acquiring a bad reputation for distributing tracts too freely. This he was to reject,[79] and, indeed, from the beginning, he had insisted that enquirers should give evidence of an ability to read.[80] In the end, it all came down to a matter of cost. Indians, notoriously, took the tracts to read the extracts from their own scriptures and for their resale value. Clearly, one could not afford to be too cavalier in their distribution.

Not until 17 February 1826 did Bowley summon up the nerve to preach in the bazaar of Chunar: 'though I went trembling towards the place yet the scene was so encouraging that I was thankful for this beginning, a day which I had been longing for years.'[81] In fact, it did not work out too well. People were afraid to be seen by their neighbours listening, quite apart from the taboo that 'to hear is to become a Christian.'[82]

Meanwhile Benares beckoned. Here Bowley paired up with the Baptist missionary, William Smith (confusingly, he shared a name with the CMS missionary, to be discussed next). Together they embarked on a long career of distributing tracts. Admittedly, they ran up against the same problem of neighbourhood watch. One enquirer, for example, fell out with a nearby Hindu for his weeping over a Hindi translation of *Saint Matthew* and his neglecting the shastras and he would have taken his complaint to the magistrate had not another Christian intervened and reminded him of a Christian need for forbearance[83]. But, at the least, here a Christian seemed to have the upper hand.

Benares, indeed, was curiously accessible. 'The learned Brahmins of Benares' had no inhibitions about tracts: they 'did not hesitate to avail themselves of possessing them'.[84] One Brahmin went so far as to admit that Benares, far from being a holy city, was 'without exception the most wicked.'[85] In Benares, Bowley was always sure of an audience and of a lively feedback.

How to characterize the Hindu response? At Mirzapur, they saw the missionaries as coming to steal their dharma: 'one told us that not being content with wresting their country from them we now continue to deprive them of their dharm also.'[86] At Allahabad, they wondered if Christians were atheists.[87] In a village near Benares, they were greatly disappointed to discover that Ram and Christ were not one and the same.[88] Elsewhere, however, they cast the new rulers in an invidious role in the Ram Lila: Ravana was dressed as the Governor-General and his army in European military uniform; at Chunar they employed European troops to play the army's role; in Benares they merely whitened their faces.[89] Converts, they saw, as 'rice Christians', purchased by 'handsome presents'.[90] If they took Christianity rather more seriously when it was discovered that Christians, to the contrary, took on manual work, this merely induced the sentiment 'the time is drawing nigh when we shall all become Christians'.[91]

For Hindus in Lower Hindustan, missionaries were still a novelty, and they would not have seen Bowley as much of a threat. They could afford, on the whole, to be polite and leave him alone. Bowley put it somewhat differently: 'I find I have to deal with a people who are in a sound sleep in the lap of sin and indifference'.[92]

Muslims seem to have taken much more active steps of avoidance. Rather than stand up to Bowley and defend their faith, they would claim: 'thus it is written, thus they believed'.[93] Muslims would often declare that they were just too busy, 'absorbed in the cares of life . . ., to investigate these things'.[94] Some found the missionaries intolerably meddlesome. At a pir festival Bowley attended, the women turned on those who had listened to him: 'all their labours of coming for a distance of four days journey had been lost without their obtaining their boon.'[95] But Bowley was to make some interesting Muslim converts, one Nathaniel, a sepoy, and one Hyder Ali, former tutor to the nawab of Oudh (Awadh).

Given that they occurred on the hoof, theological exchanges tended to be scrappy. They were often but exploratory moves to find out the weaknesses of one's opponent. Bowley had to realize that many of the imperatives of his Protestant faith, that, for example, sin led to hell-fire, simply did not impress his Hindu audience. One Vedantist was ready to concede that inequality derived from transmigration and that sin was its explanation.[96] Bowley came to see that a Hindu reverence for all forms of life—that they all possessed the same soul—accounted for this belief in transmigration. Not many missionaries were to get their minds round, certainly with any sympathy, Hindu pantheism. It was, of course, one justification for idol worship: Hindus did not worship the idol, but God through the idol. But Bowley made no real concession to the Vedantic tradition. When a Sikh 'professed to render divine adoration to the soul', his response was to brand this 'the atheistical doctrine pervading the Vedant, the Geeta and the other shasters'.[97]

Which was the more rational faith? When one pandit fell back on the authority of the Vedant, another interjected: 'but the Vedas have nothing to do now, seeing that we are upon reasoning ground.' Bowley admitted that one Brahmin 'would reason me out of everything, only that he was checked at the outset'. But, as far as reason went, it was a mutual admiration society. Another Brahmin, an apologist of Krishna, acknowledged ' the Ferringhees as being noted for wisdom, they being men of reason'.[98] One sign of Hindu conciliatoriness was their conceding 'we possess a religion as well as they do, and that we admit the being of God upon rational grounds which(?) according to their various systems they cannot establish'.[99] Bowley was to capitalize on this concession: if only one of the three religions could be true, yet all claimed to come from God (he was no proto-inclusivist), 'in not exercising reason to settle the point we should prove soul murderers if we perished in a false religion'.[100] Bowley disparaged those Brahmins who 'only manifested a show of reasoning, while in reality they did everything in their power to turn the best things into ridicule'.[101] But defending Christianity on rational grounds was one thing, matching Brahmin skills in ratiocination was another, and most missionaries were here at a disadvantage.

In exchanges with Indian Islam, Bowley came up against the limitations of Christian rationalism. The Trinity was at issue. Here he had to concede: 'it is not in the power of reason to fathom the incomprehensible deity, it is more than we can grasp.'[102] Maulvis had a whole battery of replies to Christian Mission, if along familiar lines: e.g., the new testament had prophesied Mahommed, the Paraclete, etc. It is interesting that as early as in the 1820s some Muslims did see the need to match Christian apologetics. In his critique of Islam, Bowley fell back on equally stereotypical lines, tainting it as a carnal religion, with its endorsement of polygamy, taunting that if Muslims fasted by day, they feasted by night. It was a religion of the sword. On this occasion, Muslims chose evasion: the maulvies 'did not think proper to touch on the points above alluded to'.[103]

Bowley fancied his chances in a debate with Muslims, and as already mentioned, was drawn into the munazara initiated by Joseph Wolff at Lucknow. In Avril Powell's estimate, 'though boundlessly enthusiastic', he was 'clearly unequal to the task'.[104]

If no sophisticated theologian, Bowley was a tireless traveller. In Allahabad, he felt he had made a breakthrough: Brahmins seemed delighted to approach him and to treat him as a friend.[105] Less than generously, Bowley took pleasure later from the thin attendance at the mela in 1830.[106] Maybe Bowley has taken insufficient credit for pioneering Mission in Lucknow. He went there as early as in 1831, accompanied by the Muslim convert, Hyder Ali, determined to press into the hands of the dewan (chief minister), Mahdi Ali Khan, and the king, Nasir Al-din Haydar, copies of the Hindustani translation of the gospel. In the city Bowley did not drop the price of his tracts. He was carried away by the beauty of the city's architecture, by the Imambara, by Claude Martin's La Martinière, though he could not refrain from prophesying the destruction of the former, and from dwelling on Martin's private life.[107] On his visit to Cawnpore, he sought out the Hindu community at Bithur, gathered around the ex-peshwa, Baji Rao, of the Maratha confederacy.[108] Whilst still in post at Chunar, he died on 10 October 1843.

Bowley was a typical itinerating missionary of his time, something of a nuisance-maker, acting out his vocation. But the battle-lines between the religions were still being drawn up. How much more of a trial was it for the missionaries of the next decade in Benares itself?

William Smith and Charles Leupolt: CMS Missionaries to Benares

Never was evangelicalism's folie de grandeur so grotesquely on display than in the delusion that it could convert Benares, 'the ecclesiastical metropolis', to quote Heber, of India.[109] If Benares were to fall, and the historian of the CMS Mission, Eugene Stock, was clear that the conver-sion of the Brahmins of Benares would be 'more emphatically a miracle' than anywhere else, then all of Hinduism would follow.[110] Less ambitio-usly, they trusted that since Benares was the greatest of India's pilgrimage cities, should pilgrims hear the word, they would transmit the message back to all corners of India. In fact, and all too predictably, Benares was a constant source of disappointment to mid-nineteenth-century mis-sionaries.

More open-minded Christians felt the religious drama of the city. 'As the stream of worshippers flowed on and on, one seemed to get a glimpse', mused Charles Andrews, 'into the soul of the Indian nation and to understand better its inextinguishable passion for religion.'[111]

Neither Smith nor Leupolt emerge as particularly colourful person-alities. Smith is best known for his conversion of Nehemiah Goreh (though his role has been exaggerated), and Leupolt as an educationist at the Jai Narain school. But they were one of the best known missionary partnerships of their generation. In the judgement of LMS missionary, James Kennedy, 'in their respective departments, they had no superiors in India'.[112] How did they respond to Benares and its environs?

On his arrival in India in November 1831, Corrie took charge of William Smith and set him to learn Hindustani; Benares was his pros-pective destination. Initially sent to Gorakhpur, he arrived in the city in August 1832. He was to remain there until 1873. We get glimpses of family problems: the need to help his widowed mother, the death of one brother, the bankruptcy of another, worries over the education of his daughter in England. He was always to oppose the penny-pinching re-duction of missionary salaries during this period. There was strain: 'I feel a good deal the effects of the climate upon my nerves, in so much that two or three hours spent in arguing and setting forth the gospel to the people will produce a great deal of excitement as often to prevent my attaining a proper rest at night.'[113] He was overworked: 'I sometime feel almost as if I should go distracted. I often feel that the greatest cross I have to bear to be that I have not time enough for prayer.' Even so, he went on to write: 'notwithstanding all my discouragement, I am thankful to say I have none in the work itself.' He was another missionary who resented time spent on his journal. There could be gloom: 'I am working as hard as I can and sometimes am tempted to think I must give up in despair.' After twelve years, he had but two conversions to show for his hard work. 'The difficulties with which we have to contend are fearful and now that I know the natives and understand their habits, ways of thinking, etc, so well, they appear to grow in magnitude the nearer they are approached.' 'Oh the stretch of faith that is required to believe confidently that Benares will yet become a Christian city.'[114]

Yet, as was true of so many missionaries, he fell in love with his place of mission. At the end of his career, he made extraordinary claims on its behalf as a site for a new Training College for Indian priests. 'It is much more than the Oxford and Cambridge of the whole pennsula', he enthused. 'No higher title can a Brahmin aspire to among men than to be a Kashi (Benares) pandit.' Here was a city with 151 native Sanskrit schools and 1564 students. Through the new college, Hinduism would be replaced by Christianity, and Benares would 'become a head and fountain of truth and holiness as it has hitherto been of error and superstition and will flourish and prosper tenfold more'.[115] But the choice was to go to Lahore. After his thirty-eight years in the city, he agonized that there was no-one to take his place: 'the pioneer work here is done.'[116] When ill-health finally enforced retirement, on his return journey from Trieste, he wrote: 'here I am bodily though my heart is in Benares'.[117] My mind has been so filled with regrets and remorse ever since that I don't think I shall ever get over it and become myself again until I am back at my post.'[118] No one who has discovered the ravishing beauty of Benares can be surprised by such attachment; it is proof of the way India worked on the imaginations of these mid-nineteenth-century missionaries.

Charles Leupolt was a product of the seminary at Basle. Again, as with a Eurasian, one can but speculate how subtly different missionary attitudes became through this German background. He joined Smith on January 1833, and was also to remain till 1873. For the first seven years he was the superintendent of the Jai Narain school, as well as in charge of the Hindustani chapel in Secrole, the European suburb of the city. After eight years, Leupolt still felt 'how difficult it was to think as the natives and to speak as they speak'.[119] He and Smith shared responsibility for a new church opened in October 1847, in the western suburb of Sigra.

In time, Smith's example as an itinerating missionary was too powerful for Leupolt and he likewise turned preacher, for twenty-five years to Smith's forty-four. Less vulnerable than Smith, Leupolt's career demonstrates how at the time a missionary assigned an educational post found itinerating the more compelling.

In terms of missionary strategy, Smith was a committed itinerator. From Gorakhpur, en route to Benares, he reported: 'I am filled with the idea of spreading the gospel amongst these villages.' He deeply regretted that he was not more fluent in Hindustani.[120] At this early stage he saw the village as a more promising field than the city: 'the nearer we approach large towns and cities the manner and character of the people are more depraved; hence I conclude that humanly speaking the gospel is more likely to meet with success in villages remote from such places.'[121]

But he soon began to veer towards Benares. He felt 'an increasing interest and pleasure in my visits to the city because I feel we are gaining ground in the minds and consciences of the people'.[122] The city had to be the point of departure: 'they say in the country, whatever they do in Benares we shall follow.'[123] He set up some ten to twelve preaching platforms in the city. What did all this achieve?

In a typical year, Smith would visit some 450 villages near Benares: 'met with some encouragement but more discouragement. The fact is the work is yet scarcely begun.'[124] 'I feel deeply concerned', he brooded, 'that one year after another should pass away without our endeavours yielding any visible fruit'. Could not some 'competent man' come and assess the value of this activity?: 'I mean the direct work of preaching.' Intriguingly, Smith was beginning to place more faith in education: 'the schools so long as properly managed are humanly speaking sure to succeed.'[125] He saw the vanity of the itinerating enterprise: 'flying about from town to town and village to village is not wise, excepting on occasions. The people have drunk in the doctrines of their religion from their infancy in a much deeper manner, generally speaking, than Christians have theirs, and it is not to be expected that a passing harangue or two, one fourth of which is probably understood and one half of this misapplied, will be sufficient to eject the poison.'[126] Still, one had to go on.

Smith had little faith in Indian preachers. 'They are abhorred', he observed, 'not as Christians but as apostates, and often have I seen the natives turn from them with disgust while they have paid the greatest attention to a European teacher, merely because he is such.' Alexander Duff had got it wrong.[127] To a degree, Smith was just expressing doubts about the wisdom of employing Bengalis in north India; 'the Bengalis are despised here.'[128] He was happy to accept that Indians should be used in Mission to the tribal populations, 'the low, degraded aborigines of the unhealthy mountain ranges'.[129]

With hindsight, Leupolt was to show a more practical grasp of strategy. Not that he had any greater expectation of success. Lacking a sense of sin, Indians, he sensed, had no compulsion to listen to the missionary. 'I do not remember', he wrote, 'any instance of a convert having been baptized during the time the missionary was itinerating.' Even so, 'in Benares itself there is not a lane or a corner where the gospel has not been preached', and he had insisted that teachers in the Sigra school itinerated twice a week.[130] Clearly visits by Europeans missionaries were far too infrequent. One zamindar reported: 'it is now twenty-two years since I heard the same truths which you have told us from Bowley: when shall we hear them again? The intervals of your visits are so great that we forget what we have heard ere you come again.'[131] Leupolt saw that a catechist would have to be left in permanent residence.

Post-1857, the policy was adopted to play down the confrontational style. Too much of Leupolt's life had been dedicated to itinerating for him to deny its usefulness at the end of his career. But he came to recognize that the educated elite had become the key group: 'the mind of the educated Hindu in 1882 is certainly not what it was in 1842, much less what it was in 1832, when I arrived in India.'[132] He retired in April 1874 and died on 16 December 1884. His was an implicit recognition of the need for a change in strategy.

By the 1840s, missionary activity took on a greater political dimension. It was not unusual for Smith to meet bitter criticism of Company rule. A headman of a zamindar branded the English as 'wild men' and the Company as 'neither more nor less than banias, who farmed India to contract and altogether they and the English nation generally were a most dirty, filthy race'.[133] When an angry Brahmin in Benares harangued the missionaries—'depend upon it, if you were not our rulers, we should soon rid our country of you'—Smith's reply was to ask where the Indian gods were during the conquest: 'what, have our soldiers conquered Ram, Krishna, and the whole hosts of your god?'[134] All too often, exchange took on this soap box, Hyde Park corner character. Several times they were stoned in the villages. One strategem was for Smith to blackmail his audience with the reminder that, now, they had heard the word 'and would therefore have to answer for it and that I would bear witness against them in the Judgement'.[135]

Not that Smith had any great love for Company policy and did not believe that its commitment to secularism would do anything to raise the standard of government. It would help if Europeans were to exemplify 'a mild, peaceful, cheerful and holy temper.' One Christian nation fighting another in the Crimea, he was later to reflect, did the Company's reputation no good. The British were lucky that the Muslims had defiled the land before they came: 'a fact which tends in some measure to assuage the wrath of the brahmins against us.'[136]

When the rebellion of 1857 broke, Smith's first response was to blame English officers, with their indifference towards the sepoys, and the Company itself: 'presumption on the part of the government and a sort of reckless dependence on good luck.' North India would now have to be subject to a proper conquest: 'many many thousands of Mussulmans especially will have to be mown down by our cannon.' And were Mission itself to retreat, it would be seen as weakness, and who knows what demands Indians might then make? Maybe India should be required to pay for bishops and chaplains out of its own resources? But given the anti-Christian character of the rebellion, Smith, somewhat perversely, saw cause for pleasure, for was it not evidence that, after all, Mission had made an impact?[137] Besides, Indians would now have to recognize the superiority of the British: 'the collision has been rough and bitter but the issue will be good.'[138] Smith showed himself to be quite the imperialist.

Leupolt's was a more defensive reaction. Maybe Mission was to blame: 'the preaching of the gospel may have something to do with it. The Brahmins feel that they lose daily more of their hold on the people and Satan fears for his kingdom.'[139] He also came up with the interesting opinion that had missionaries been allowed to evangelize the sepoys, they would rapidly have disillusioned them of their fears of the greased cartridges. Conversion did not lie that way but by 'righteousness and peace and joy in the holy ghost'. Leupolt blamed 1857 on the Muslims. If Islam had been able to withstand pagan religions, 'it cannot stand before Christianity'.[140]

One would have hoped for a higher calibre of theological debate between Mission and Hinduism in Benares. But Smith was not impressed by the various versions of Vedantism he met: 'that he and I and everyone is God and that God is the author of sin.'[141] One way of countering Vedantism was to question one pandit 'whether it would not have been much better for all in every way if there had been no world and none of these things called creatures', and the pandit was to concede that one shastra 'plainly states that it does not know why God created the world'.[142] Not that Smith found dualists, 'just because they approach in some respect nearer the truth', any easier to handle.[143] In an exchange with the raja of Rewah, a dualist, whom Smith described as 'the most intelligent, candid and dignified ruler that we have met with', Smith would not grant that Ram, himself not free from sin, possessed the powers of atonement.

The Hindus became exasperated with the missionaries going on about sin. 'You are always talking about your sins. If you are such a great sinner', they expostulated, 'pray keep it to yourself and do'nt go proclaiming it through every street and land.' And when Smith pointed out a sloka which required Brahmins to acknowledge their sins in daily prayer, back came the riposte, 'yes, but we do'nt publish this to the whole world'.[144]

Smith did not take to the educated Hindu. Once a Hindu has 'imbibèd the doctrines of the shastras all fear and reverence of the deity are lost'.[145] For two days he had found more reward in the company of the byragis of Ayodhya, more sincere in their faith, and who had listened to him with patience and curiosity.[146]

And one begins to sense that Smith began to fall under the spell of at least some expressions of Hinduism. On arriving at Jabalpur on the Narmada, he recorded: 'the whole scene is magnificent and has a very solemnizing effect—I could not help but feel it to be a place peculiarly adapted for contemplation and prayer and for praise of the great Creator. I almost envied a byragi who I observed had taken up an abode on one of the cliffs.'[147]

Leupolt had run up against a similar abuse from Hindu opponents: 'such men would gladly stop our preaching by violent means if they dared.'[148] One arch-enemy in Benares, 'a very tall gossain (a spiritual adviser), made a point of disrupting any meeting where the audience seemed attentive. But ascetics practising self-torture by the 1860s were no longer visible in the streets of Benares. In his view, the Brahmins were more familiar with the six systems of philosophy than the Vedas. Educated Hindus rejected the Puranas and, indeed, questioned 'the whole of their gigantic system of idolatry'.[149] Europeans had become too obsessed with the mere exploits of Krishna and others in the great classics, and had failed to respond to 'the deep, moral lesson conveyed by those books'. This was progress in sympathy.

But he had little time for Brahmoism, but a 'halting place between Hinduism and Christianity', 'a Christianity without Christ', ignorant of the atonement, and an obstacle to Mission.[150] Many educated Indians were, he believed, pessimistic about the future of Hinduism, and feared that 'the gospel will and must finally prevail and that it is only the work of time'.[151] But Leupolt was drawing nearer to a more sympathetic approach towards Hinduism.

One could compare the views of Smith and Leupolt on Hinduism in Benares with the seemingly more friendly account of Hindus by the LMS missionary, James Kennedy. 'For many years', he wrote, 'it has been my settled conviction that Hindoos are vastly better than looking at their religion we would expect to find them, and that we on the other hand fall far below the excellence to which our religion summons us.' Still, his verdict was ultimately damning: Hindus 'have not arrived at the knowledge of even the first principles of theology worthy of God and fitted to direct, purify and guide them.'[152]

Curiously, caste featured little in the writings of both Smith and Leupolt on inter-faith relationships. If Leupolt came to see it as the greatest barrier to Mission, one has the sense that they had set out on Mission convinced that Christian apologetics would prevail over the metaphysics of Hinduism. It was only ex post facto, with the failure of this Mission, that caste became the villain.

Contact with Indian Islam was more negative. Smith saw this as good reason for choosing Hindu Benares as the site for the new training college rather than Muslim Agra. On his travels, he had reported seeing Muslims scanning the scriptures, trying to detect prophetic evidence of the coming of Mahommed. One Maulvi, caught in an argument on tahrif, felt 'it was altogether wrong to argue at all upon the subject of religion'.[153] But any attempt to prove the corruption of the Bible was proof of sorts that Muslims were now on the defensive. Initially, Leupolt was pretty contemptuous of Muslims: 'they are altogether most bitter and inveterate foes of Christ. They are too ignorant to comprehend a sound argument and too proud to listen to an explanation for it.'[154] But he recognized a change in approach. No longer did Muslims feel it enough to defend Islam on grounds of 'the elegance and beauty of the Koran': they referred to Mahommed's miracles and prophecies. Leupolt was a rare missionary who was to mention, if in passing, the Wahabi reform movement. Muslims sent their own preachers into the bazaars.[155]

Smith went further afield. He travelled to Awadh. He took to Lucknow: 'the whole presents a scene of activity, prosperity and happiness I have never seen equalled in this country.' Here there were lively encounters with Muslims. They sought out his literature. But there was an explanation for this openness. 'As in all places', he interpreted, 'where they have not tried their strength or found their weaknesses', they 'are very fond of disputing.' With some self-satisfaction, he continued: 'they found they had not quite so good, nor we quite so bad a cause as they had imagined.' So ascendant was Islam, Smith feared for the Lucknow Hindus, down to but one temple.[156] A later journey took him to Kashmir where the maharajah proved to be hostile to Mission, and to Amritsar, where he was much discouraged by the 'dogged hostility' of the Muslims.[157]

It must have been immensely dispiriting proselytizing so indifferent a Hindu stronghold as Benares. It says much for the strength of missionary ideology that these missionaries to lower Hindustan did not give up. It is in retrospect disappointing that there was not a more sophisticated theological encounter between Mission and Hinduism. Probably Smith was at his best in his exchange with Nehemiah Goreh. If, apart from Lucknow, they had not yet reached the heartlands of Indian Islam, Christian–Islamic exchange was along fairly predictable lines. But there was a stiffening of attitudes all round, and 1857 saw missionaries far more consciously the colonialists. Relationships between Mission and the Company were very much closer in Upper Hindustan.

Notes and References

1. Reginald Heber, *Narrative of a Journey through the Upper Provinces of India*, first edn, 1827. The references here are to the rpt. edn, New Delhi: 1985.
2. He was visiting Ghazipur at the time. Ibid., vol. I, p. 327.
3. Vol. II, ibid., p. 327.
4. Vol. I, ibid., p. 411.
5. Vol. I, ibid., p. 375,
6. Vol. II, ibid., 343–4.
7. Vol. I, ibid., pp. 395–6.
8. Quoted in Revd John Sargent, *A Memoir of the Rev Henry Martyn*, London: 1831.
9. Ibid., p. 169.
10. Ibid., p. 294.
11. Ibid., p. 239.
12. Ibid., p. 191–2.
13. Ibid., p. 201.
14. Ibid., p. 205.
15. For Corrie, I have consulted *Memoirs of the Right Revd Daniel Corrie* (edited by his brothers), London: 1847; Angus Macnaughten, *Daniel Corrie, His Family*

and His Friends, London: 1969; M. E. Gibbs, Daniel Corrie, *Indian Church History Review*, vol. IV, no. 1, June 1970.

16. Personal Journal, 27 August 1806, *Memoirs*, p. 35.
17. En route to India, Personal Journal, 24 July 1806, ibid., p. 33.
18. In a report from Chunar, 6 July 1807, ibid., p. 86.
19. Ibid., p. 124.
20. Personal Journal, 11 June 1809, ibid., p. 132.
21. Letter to J. Buckworth, 20 July 1812, ibid., p. 233.
22. Memorandum, Chunar, 6 July 1807, ibid., p. 132.
23. Letter to Sherer, 22 January 1827, ibid., p. 402.
24. Letter to J. Buckworth, 20 July 1812, ibid., p. 234.
25. Letter to J. Buckworth, 22 May 1807, ibid., p. 74.
26. Letter to J. Buckworth, 25 April 1808, ibid., p. 115.
27. Heber, vol. I, p. 371. Corrie accompanied Heber, in his capacity as Archdeacon of Calcutta, on tour. That they proved such good travelling companions speaks well for both men.
28. Letter to Revd T. Sargent, 1 November 1813, ibid., p. 259.
29. Letter to J. Buckworth, 14 February 1804, ibid., p. 11.
30. Letter to J. Buckworth, October 1811, ibid., p. 211.
31. Personal Journal, Plassey, 18 December 1806, ibid., p. 58.
32. Personal Journal, 24 August 1808, ibid., p. 117.
33. Letter to Revd D. Brown (another of the pious chaplains), Cawnpore, 1 January 1811, ibid., p. 186.
34. Letter to his brother, 6 April 1825, ibid., p. 378.
35. Letter to a friend, August 1814, ibid., pp. 276–7.
36. Letter to J. Buckworth, 22 May 1807, ibid., p. 75.
37. Letter to J. Buckworth, October 1811, ibid., p. 211.
38. Letter to a friend, August 1814, ibid., p. 279.
39. Entry on Monghyr Town, *The Imperial Gazetteer of India*, vol. XVII, p. 401.
40. G. Parson's Report. Letter to Revd John Dyer, 2 January 1840, *Missionary Herald*, May 1840, p. 184.
41. Heber, *Narrative*, vol. I, p. 299.
42. For an obituary notice on Andrew Leslie, M.H., 1870, pp. 669 –70; John Lawrence, M.H., 1 May 1875, p. 83; John Parsons, M.H., 1870, p. 323.
43. Annual Report, 19 June 1834, Baptist Periodical Accounts 9, London: 1839.
44. Leslie, 4 April 1836, M.H., vol. CCXIX, p. 18.
45. Lawrence, Digar, M.H., vol. CLXXXVI, June 1834.
46. Lawrence to Dyer, 11 January 1834, M.H., vol. CXCI, Nov. 1834.
47. Lawrence to a Member of the Committee, M.H., vol. CCXXIII, July 1837.
48. Lawrence, Digar, M.H., vol. CCXLIII, March 1839.
49. Lawrence, 12 October 1847, M.H., vol. CIV, January 1848, p. 3.
50. Lawrence, 14 April 1848, M.H., vol. CXIII, October 1848, p. 149.
51. Leslie, 2 February 1826, M.H., vol. XCIII, September 1826.
52. Lawrence to a Member of the Committee, 14–15 July 1836, M.H., vol. CCXXIII, July 1837, p. 49.
53. Lawrence to Dyer, 3 February, M.H., vol. CCXXXVII, September 1838, p. 70.

54. Lawrence, M.H., vol. CXII, September 1848, pp. 130–1.

55. Lawrence, 14 April 1848, M.H., vol. CXIII, October 1848, p. 149.

56. Lawrence, 9 February 1835, M.H., vol. CCII, October 1835.

57. Annual Report, 19 June 1834, Baptist Periodical Accounts 9, London: 1839, p. 14.

58. Lawrence, 12 October 1847, M.H., vol. CIX, January 1848, p. 4.

59. Ibid.

60. Lawrence, 14 April 1848, M.H., vol. CXIII, October 1848, p. 149.

61. Lawrence to a relative, 28 Sept. 1849, M.H., vol. CXXIX, February 1850, p. 21.

62. Lawrence to a friend, 10 February 1836, M.H., vol. CCXVIII, February 1837, pp. 11–12.

63. Heber, *Narrative*, vol. I, p. 412.

64. Annual Report, June 20 1833, Baptist Periodical Accounts 9, London: 1839, p. 14.

65. Leslie to Dyer, 25 February 1837, M.H., vol. CCXXVI, October 1837, p. 82.

66. John Parsons, M.H., vol. XCIX, August 1847, pp. 525–6.

67. Lawrence, M.H., September 1858, p. 585.

68. He felt very uneasy at seeing Europeans at a fair near Chunar. 'The most painful sight were the Europeans who crowded to the fair to make it a day of eating, drinking and merriment, and this became a gazing stock to natives from all parts.' April 1827, Revd William Bowley, CI 1/053/56B (CMS: Birmingham).

69. 'Abdul Massih and William Bowley had not surprisingly proved incompatible at Agra in Corrie's absence.' M. E. Gibbs, p. 25. See also Corrie, *Memoirs*, p. 280.

70. Corrie, ibid., p. 301.

71. Heber, *Narrative*, vol. I, p. 412.

72. Ibid., p. 400.

73. Bowley, 24 February 1820, CI 1/053/2.

74. Avril Powell, *Muslims and Missionaries in Pre-Mutiny India*, London: 1993, p. 128.

75. Bowley, 1829, CI 1/053/11.

76. Bowley, Journal, July 1820, CI 1/053/24.

77. Bowley, 1 June 1822, CI 1/053/29.

78. Bowley, at Azamghar, 27 October 1828, Journal, October–December 1828, CI 1/053/67.

79. 'I know that many years ago a prejudice has gone against me giving the books too freely and without discussion—but all who accompany can testify that it is not the truth.' Bowley to Corrie, 2 April 1830, CI 1/053/12.

80. 'We invariably made everyone whom we give books to read a portion. Consequently we refused hundreds who could not read fluently', Bowley, 11 July 1820, CI 1/053/24.

81. Bowley, 17 February 1826, CI 1/053/47.

82. Bowley, September 1829, CI 1/053/71.

83. Bowley, 8 October 1821, Journal, October–December 1821, CI 1/053/27.

84. Bowley, 4 June 1822, CI 1/053/29.

85. Bowley, July 1820, CI 1/053/24.

86. Bowley, Journal, 18 September 1820, CI 1/053/25.
87. Bowley, January 1825, CI 1/053/45.
88. Bowley, 29 October 1821, CI 1/053/27.
89. Bowley, 1828, CI 1/053/66.
90. Bowley, 8 February 1826, CI 1/053/47.
91. Bowley, June 1827, CI 1/053/57.
92. Bowley, 1828, CI 1/053/66.
93. Bowley, in a village near Benares, 29 October 1821, CI 1/053/27.
94. Bowley, June 1832, CI 1/053/91.
95. Bowley, near Jaunpur, 3 December 1823, CI 1/053/35.
96. Bowley, January 1827, CI 1/053/52.
97. Bowley, June 1832, CI 1/053/91.
98. Bowley, 5 November 1821, CI 1/053/27.
99. Bowley, January 1825, CI 1/053/45.
100. Bowley, 28 January 1831, CI 1/053/81.
101. Bowley, Bithur, Cawnpore, July 1831, CI 1/053/84.
102. Bowley, at Jaunpur, January/February 1822, CI 1/053/28.
103. Bowley, 15 December 1823, CI 1/053/35.
104. Powell, p. 130.
105. Bowley, January 1825, CI 1/053/45.
106. Bowley, CI 1/053/75B.
107. Not that he found the city well governed. 'Nothing appears so lawless as everything about us since we entered the city. Everyone seems for himself and the strongest seems to prevail. Hence the necessity of everyone carrying a sword, a pistol, a butcher's knife, a spear, our people seem much alarmed.' Bowley, Lucknow, February 1831, CI 1/053/80.
108. Bowley has some interesting information on the scale of Baji Rao's handouts to Hindus, his funding 'thousands of brahmins', and paying out large sums so that devotees could relinquish penintential vows. Bowley, March 1831, ibid.
109. Heber, *Narrative*, vol. I, p. 436.
110. Eugene Stock, *History of the Church Missionary Society, vol. II*, London: 1899, p. 167. However, Stock was making the point that such miracles did occur, either through Brahmins reading Christian scriptures, or their exposure to the teaching at Jai Narain School. Goreh was the prize example.
111. Charles Andrews, *North India*, Oxford; 1908, pp. 78–9.
112. James Kennedy, *Life and Work in Benares and Kumaon 1839–1877*, London: 1884, p. 305.
113. William Smith, 1836, CI 1/0265/71 (CMS: Birmingham).
114. Smith, 1 January 1844, CI 1/0265/8.
115. Smith, April 1868, CI 1/0265/95.
116. Smith, CI 1/0265/85.
117. Smith to May, 1872, CI 1/0265/43.
118. Smith to Venn, 9 May 1872, CI 1/0265/44.
119. Revd C. B. Leupolt, *Further Recollections of an Indian Missionary*, London: 1884, p. 271.
120. Smith to Corrie, 10 October 1831, CI 1/0265/46.

121. Smith to Corrie, on arrival in Benares, 7 August 1832, ibid.
122. Smith to Corrie, 26 March 1834, CI 1/0265/50.
123. Smith to Venn, CI 1/0265/17.
124. Smith, 26 February 1846, CI 1/0265/74.
125. Smith, October 1846, CI 1/0265/76.
126. Smith to Venn, CI 1/0265/17.
127. Smith, 16 September 1842, CI 1/0265/6.
128. Smith, CI 1/0265/11.
129. Smith to Venn, 10 February 1850, CI 1/0265/14.
130. Leupolt, *Further Reflections*, p. 266.
131. Ibid., p. 265.
132. Ibid., p. 36.
133. Smith, 14 February 1844, CI 1/0265/77.
134. Smith, 9 November 1832, CI 1/0265/64.
135. Smith, to a group of Brahmins at Mughal Serai, 26 February 1846, CI 1/0265/74.
136. Smith, Report, 1853–54, CI 1/0265/81.
137. Smith to Venn, 4 August 1857, CI 1/0265/22.
138. Smith, 4 June 1857, Report, 1856–57, CI 1/0265/83.
139. Leupolt to Venn, 2 May 1857, CI 1/077/54.
140. Leupolt, *Further Reflections*, pp. 350–1.
141. Smith to Corrie, 2 January 1832, CI 1/0265/47.
142. Smith, 23 August 1846, CI 1/0265/76.
143. Smith, 24 December 1844, CI 1/0265/77.
144. Smith, 18 August 1846, CI 1/0265/76.
145. Smith, 1836, CI 1/0265/69.
146. Smith to Corrie, 2 January 1832, CI 1/0265/47.
147. Smith, 1853–54, CI 1/0265/79.
148. Leupolt, *Further Reflections*, p. 97.
149. Interestingly, Heber likewise had sensed that the Brahmins of Benares were 'less intolerant and prejudiced than in most other places'. Had they grown weary, he wondered, at an endless round of ritual? Heber *Narrative*, vol. I, pp. 437–8.
150. Leupolt, *Further Reflections*, pp. 114 –17.
151. Ibid., p. 113.
152. Kennedy, pp. 71, 77.
153. Smith, 11 October 1846, CI 1/0265/76.
154. Leupolt, September 1834, CI 1/077/119
155. Leupolt, *Further Recollections*, pp. 20–30.
156. Smith, February 1844, CI 1/0265/52.
157. Smith, Letters to Revd Stuart, 27 May 1863 and n.d., CI 1/0265/55.

CHAPTER 5

Missionary Case-Studies:
Upper Hindustan

Mission was drawn to 'frontiers' and beyond. As the Company extended its direct rule in northern India, Church and State drew closer together. Hiving off the North-Western Provinces from the Presidency of Bengal and appointing a Lieutenant-Governor to Agra in 1835 was one way the Company handled its penetration of upper Hindustan. Mission followed—and here there is more substance to the charge that Mission followed the flag, though, in some senses, it was merely taking advantage of its shelter—and the CMS Mission to Agra was reactivated in 1837. After the second Sikh war and the annexation of the Punjab in 1849, Mission grasped its opportunity. Missionaries and civilians were now to become a great deal more intimate. In this more politicized context, Mission in upper Hindustan encountered the heartlands of Indian Islam and Sikhism, as well as some of the most sacred sites of Hinduism in Muttra, Brindaban and Hardwar.

One of the intriguing features of missionary journals from the 1840s was the perception of a decided improvement of moral tone among 'official' passengers on board ships that brought missionaries to India. But it cannot be surprising that so dominant a force as evangelicalism should in time influence the outlook of Company officials, particularly in the newly established North-Western Provinces and the Punjab.

John Thomason, son of one of the 'pious chaplains', is a classic example. His winter season tours have an uncanny resemblance to the missionary, all the more so, with Thomason taking all the religious services. Extracts from religious writings filled the commonplace book he compiled for his daughters. Here was a man whose 'pervading characteristic was Christian seriousness' and who 'would impress upon all alike the importance of their displaying a Christian standard in their life and conversation'.[1] He was particularly close to the CMS. Whether Indians were able to see the distinction he drew between his respect for the

Company's policy of religious neutrality in his public life and his commitment to Christianity in his private—he would not allow any religious instruction in government schools, for example—is open to doubt.

His disciples in the North West Provinces shared his evangelical faith and some, such as John Lawrence, Robert Montgomery and Donald Macleod, brought it with them to the famous Lawrence administration of the Punjab. Here, above all with Henry Lawrence and his close friends, John Nicholson and Herbert Edwardes, a particularly heady religiosity was to prevail. So cloying could this be, it is something of a relief to speculate that behind this highly-strung faith lay emotional, if probably, merely platonic, homosexual ties. However, in some cases, there is cause to suppose there was the practice of pedophilia with Indian boys.[2]

Muttra: Baptist Missionary, T. Phillips

Muttra (Mathura), a city of some 48,000, on the Jumna and the road to Delhi, some thirty miles north of Agra was, after Benares, the leading pilgrimage centre for Hindus. It was particularly frequented by Bengalis. Here Krishna, destroyer of the tyrant, Kani, became incarnate. Nearby was Brindaban (Vrindavan), some six miles away, another leading pilgrimage centre, where Krishna came of age. On the western side of Muttra district, to quote the Imperial Gazetteer, 'almost every grove, mound and tank is associated with some episode of his life'.[3] It was a leading centre of Vaishnavism, and hence its appeal for Bengal. Phillips's account of his visits to these sacred Hindu sites is a fascinating study in cultural encounter.

Initially posted to Agra, Phillips begged to be transferred to Muttra. In 1841 he had acquired a house near Muttra. By September, he was preaching regularly on both sides of the Jumna. By 1843, even in the hot season, he would make a four or five day visit, once or twice a month. A chapel had been built, its verandah a resting place for pilgrims. 'Missionary work', he reported, 'is quite easy and delightful here.' In contrast was Agra, 'where the people have heard the gospel for so long that they deride it'. He held the same expectations for Muttra and Brindaban as missionaries did for Benares. Its pilgrims would carry the word as far afield as Ceylon (Sri Lanka) and Lahore: 'a wide door of utterance is open to us and any influence exerted on Muttra would be felt for hundreds of miles.'[4]

But an initially friendly response was not to last. At first the Brahmins had appreciated the psalms in Sanskrit and 'had behaved very civilly'. Should the missionaries be interrupted, 'a well directed sloka' from the convert, Brij Lal, normally did the trick. Sometimes, though, 'the better informed . . . will quote without end, either to show the extent of their knowledge, to overwhelm the preacher with a torrent of words, or to ward off the force of his arguments'.[5]

By 1853, the atmosphere was startlingly different and clearly Phillips, a confrontationalist, was to blame. 'Every day', he reported, 'the opposition grows warmer. The people are becoming alarmed at our bold and regular attacks.' If there was a ready audience for tracts, the explanation lay in the government's requirement that all administrative and police employees should have a knowledge of Hindi. Phillips continued to distribute these free, though charged a small fee for the scriptures. On 4 February, outside the mosque, the pandits stirred up opposition. Phillips, revealingly, rejoiced at the first throwing of a brick. At the Swami ghat, by the 11th, 'opposition grows more fierce and more persevering'. One long-term opponent 'exulted that though for eight or ten years we have been preaching here, still Hinduism and Muhammedanism continued unchanged'. Why, they jibed, did he not perform any miracles? Krishna's had matched those of Christ and Krishna did not die. Phillips's come-back was to deny that Krishna and Ram ever appeared in the Vedas. 'In general', he claimed, 'the people display a very considerable ignorance of their own religious books, which gives us an advantage over them.' He had come armed with a copy of Wilson's translation of the Vishnu purana.

Some of his most vitriolic exchanges were with the ascetics, the Chaubis, in his view, fat, lazy and addicted to hemp. They were insular: 'India is the world to them. All books are false but their own.' Phillips took the offensive: 'We make it a principle never to be beaten in an argument.' They are to be 'convinced as well as silenced'. They could not believe we 'were not in the pay of the government', and attributed our 'new energy to stringent orders from government head-quarters'. Chaubis raised dust in their faces, a shopkeeper shook a floor-cloth at them, stones were thrown: 'this was the first time I had ever been so honoured.' Forever imprinted in Phillips's memory was 'the cunning, sinister, malicious and triumphant expression' on the face of a man who had tried to trip him up in some argument.[6] This was religious conflict at its worst and does much to explain the violence of 1857 to come.

After a long spell at home, Phillips returned to India, to resume 'his old labours as a herald of the cross to the heathen'. But clearly his health had not recovered. 'When extremely weak, he still insisted on preaching.' He died in Darjeeling on 16 May 1867.[7]

Monghyr Baptist missionary, John Parsons, in Agra for his safety during the Rebellion, was also drawn to Muttra and Brindaban, but for an interesting reason: 'it is not curiosity alone that would make one wish to see these places. it is often of use to be able to say to the natives that you have seen the places they deem the most sacred sites and seen they are no more free from sin than other places.'[8] Free of sin or not, as with Nadia and Benares, association with Hindu sacred places rubbed off to the advantage of missionaries.

Agra: Thomas French, CMS Missionary

Agra city, Akbar's imperial capital, with its great Moghul fort and mosque, and since its conquest in 1803, a frontier fortress of the Company—it bordered on Rajputana—became the seat of a Lieutenant-Governorship from 1835 to 1858. It was then transferred to Allahabad. In 1851 its population was 90,000. If not quite on par with a presidency capital, it was deemed, nevertheless, to be 'the finest city of upper India'.[9]

Here arrived, on 13 February 1851, Thomas Valpy French. In Charles Andrews's account, his was a career punctuated by ill-health and new beginnings. He had been appointed to Agra to open St John's College (the future University of Agra); in 1862, he initiated the Frontier Mission at Derajat; in 1869, he founded the St John's Divinity School at Lahore (the one William Smith had sought for Benares); in 1877, he became Bishop of Lahore. 'Seldom', asserted Andrews, 'in modern missionary history has there been shown such untiring and devoted zeal, combined with so clear a prophet's vision of the future, as is seen in the life of French.'[10]

His nineteenth-century biographer did not find him an easy man to read: 'this strange blending of natural reserve, keen sensitiveness, outspoken courage, and far-reaching sympathy, produced a character which was singularly attractive, but at the same time, exceptionally difficult to analyse.'[11] Here was the new-style CMS recruit, public school, Oxbridge. Born on 1 January 1825, he was educated at Rugby and University College, Oxford. Old Rugbeian and Andhra missionary, Henry Watson Fox, did much to persuade him to be a missionary. He was accepted by the CMS on 16 April 1850. It was an Oxbridge background that made it easy for him, on his arrival in Calcutta, to engage in conversation with the principal of Bishop's College, Professor Kay. His initial response to India was quasi-imperialist: to discover England 'mistress of so vast a territory. What', he exclaimed, 'a remarkable providence of God'.[12]

Quickly he became friends with the civilians at Agra. Several leading officials, including the Lieutenant-Governor, Thomason, together with his secretary, William Muir, were to subscribe to a scheme whereby a catechist could be employed to instruct their servants. Herbert Edwardes gave a talk to his school. Nearly a quarter of the schools's funds were at risk from the deaths (or feared deaths) in 1857 of Lieutenant-Governor Colvin, Henry Lawrence, and Mr Gubbins. Even in the Frontier Mission French made friends with the Europeans, mainly military personnel. Even so, he saw the risk of too close an association with Europeans: Indians would 'feel we did not desire their intercourse. I so dread the intrusion of an unmissionary spirit'.[13]

His was a strong commitment to learning Indian languages. 'I always spend', he reported, 'from three to four hours in the *direct* study of the languages daily, besides what I gain in teaching others and conversation in the bazaars. It is essential to a thorough knowledge of the languages that they should be learned in this practical way.'[14] Being holed up in the Agra Fort during the Rebellion gave him the opportunity to improve his Arabic and Sanskrit.

French was also to experience disillusionment. 'The lack of interest displayed by the majority is *appalling*', he admitted, 'and I have been filled at times with something not quite short of *consternation* at the gulf which has seemed to separate my hearers and myself.'[15] But 'consternation' is not despair, and if French was to drive himself to the edge, he always came back.

The CMS made it clear to French that he was appointed as an educationist, not an itinerator. In Calcutta he had visited the Scottish Assembly School and agurpura (Indian) schools. Such contact had convinced him that 'knowing the truth was a widely differing thing from embracing it'. What could his new school provide which was not already provided by the Government College in Agra? He had absolutely no wish to take over these government schools: they were indeed to be on offer to the missionaries in 1857. French had the makings of a great pioneering educationist, and he was later to realize these talents, but at this stage of his missionary career, the lure of itinerating proved too strong.

At first, he feared he might lose face with his students should he be seen preaching by chance in the bazaar, so the solution was to take them along with him. He came up with an answer that would, in his view, reconcile the competing claims of missionary strategy; teachers would spend five years in the school mastering the vernaculars, then be transferred to itinerating. He saw no point in preaching where Mission was clearly unpopular, and such was the case with Agra. They should go elsewhere, and here he betrayed his expansionist approach: 'were I asked, I should give my advice to transplant the Mission almost entirely to fields yet untried, or comparatively so, such as Ajmir, Muttra, Allighir (Aligarh) or even Peshawar.'[16] He envisioned teams, some four to five strong, well trained and ready to go immediately onto the offensive, for some two to five months. To provide for continuity, one of the notorious gaps of Mission, Indian catechists, 'the more intelligent of the new converts', should be left behind. 'This more arduous and hazardous missionary enterprise', and one that 'would arouse bitter enmity and persecution', had to be better than the status quo: 'our own nothingness seems to be forcibly impressed upon us by the failure of repeated effort.'[17]

He gave over his vacations to itinerating. With regard to a trip to the Rajput states, he wrote: 'the relief from the burden of school-work is intense, the climate is delightful. I trust to return thoroughly invigorated.' He also itinerated in the post-monsoon summer months. But Rajputana was to prove disappointing, in part for political reasons: he came up against the anti-English feelings of the people of a princely state. He felt he enjoyed greater success by going both east and south, towards the Ganges. On the eve of the Rebellion, he pressed for more missionaries for Agra: Calcutta, Tinevelly and Peshawar had had more than their fair share. In Agra they were but scratching the surface: they needed to be more 'boldly aggressive'.[18]

Post-1857, French almost drove himself to death on the Dejarat Frontier Mission. As his biographer vividly put it: 'he flung himself down on the barren plains of Marwat.'[19] He grew a beard to ingratiate himself with the Afghans. He tried to learn Pushtu. In December 1863 he was discovered 'stricken senseless in the jungle' (near Dera Ismail).[20] French confessed to his wife: 'my health gave way—became, in fact, wrecked and broken'.[21] Maybe it was all a futile gesture: it was such an ephemeral Mission. There was a romantic and masochistic side to French.

French's response to 1857 was to be oddly optimistic: 'the storm which breaks the serene uniformity and monotony of our work seems full of hope to me for the future.'[22] Anything, it would seem, was preferable to Indian indifference. Muslims would now have to pay more attention to Mission. He conjured up a vision of 'a missionary phalanx, destined to pull down some of Satan's strongholds in North Western India'.[23]

French enjoyed a scrap. This the Hindus would not offer. The sight of a Hindu temple in Calcutta was, for the uninitiated French, 'a heart-sickening sight'.[24] The very passivity of the Hindu would, he feared, rob the missionaries of their zeal. But might, he wondered, a greater concentration on God the Father rather than God the Son bring Mission more into line with Hindu reform movements? Still, it was the examples of Henry Martyn and Abd-al Massih that had drawn him to India and his preferred opponent was Islam. In his experience, Muslims were far more hostile, be they the maulvis, the urban elite or the village headmen. And the Baptist missionary to Agra, Richard Williams, would have agreed with him: the Muslims, he reported, 'are a very prejudiced people, much worse than the Hindus'.[25]

If Pfander was the recognized front-man in any confrontation with Indian Islam in the North West, French had been his number two in the *munazara* at Agra in 1854, and had, indeed, in Pfander's absence at Peshawar, initiated the encounter. Fortunately, William Kay, by chance on a visit, gave him support. In Avril Powell's account, French comes across as rather a mild man, a good deal less abrasive than Pfander and, in fact, a better biblical scholar.[26] But maybe abrasiveness is a relative quality. French certainly took more to the Afghan mullahs: 'far abler champions of Mohammedanism than I had looked for so far from the world's great thoroughfare.' He found them more friendly and more outgoing—always a preference of the British—than Muslims on the other side of the frontier. They would give him more of a run for his money. Maybe, he speculated, their Sufism had engendered 'a free-thinking spirit among them'. They seemed to hold Christ in higher esteem.[27]

J. I. Thompson, Baptist, and an SPG Mission to Delhi

Given the violence against Christians in 1857, it is worth exploring just how abusive Mission to Delhi had been. Since 1818 only one Baptist missionary had represented the Protestant Mission to Delhi. Serampore's Ward had spotted Thompson in one of the Company's offices in Calcutta. Apart from the years 1835 to 1839, when he returned to Serampore to see his Hindi translation of the New Testament, the Psalms and tracts, through the press, he was there till his death on 27 June 1850. Mission looked on him as its greatest Hindi expert. In the gap between his death and the appointment of Revd Mackay as his replacement in 1856, there was the beginning of an SPG Mission. It was their agents, the Revd Jennings, his wife and daughter, and the convert, Chimman Lal, who were to be murdered in the Rebellion.

Thompson's was a typical Serampore missionary career. Above all, he was a translator and distributor of tracts. In (old) Delhi, he would hire a room in the Chandni Chowk, its main thoroughfare, and invite people in for a talk. Some 600 dropped in in the course of two months in 1844. He would also drive around. He was a frequent visitor to melas, and went regularly to Hardwar, one of the most popular places of Hindu pilgrimage, further evidence of that symbiosis between Mission and Hinduism. Once Thompson took advantage of the presence of the Governor-General's encampment near Delhi, in February 1843, to proselytize. It was a wide-flung Mission and, in retrospect, the Baptists were to wonder if it would not have been wiser to have limited its scope. What, indeed, did people learn at melas? 'The confusion, riot and revelry of a fair are not favourable to the production of serious thoughts.'[28] But Thompson distributed tracts on a prodigious scale.[29]

Much of Thompson's religious encounter was in response to this literature. Many came in search of tracts containing texts of their own religions, but were to be disappointed. Thompson was perfectly happy to give tracts to the ascetics: supported as holy men, they would be under no temptation to retail them elsewhere.[30] Interestingly, those who scoffed at tracts in Hindi, were all too ready, out of reverence for the language, to receive those in Sanskrit.[31] One particularly receptive audience were Bengali employees of the audit and account's office, travelling up-country with the Governor-General.[32] One Hindu attributed sickness to his taking a tract home, and was relieved that there were no appropriate tracts for him to receive the next time he met Thompson.[33]

Curiously, evangelizing Hardwar, one of Hinduism's most sacred sites, where Krishna came to bathe, does not seem to have been thought offensive. Might receiving tracts, indeed, provide Hindus with an escape from their treadmill of reincarnation, 'exemption from the imaginary horrors of successive births and deaths': 'all expect to obtain light and relief from the words preached and the books offered them.'[34] Thompson distributed tracts in Persian, Kashmiri, Afghan and Hindi, though 'first ascertaining their ability to read'. His last missionary journey was to Hardwar. And there was later a pleasingly unprejudiced account of Hardwar in the *Missionary Herald*.[35]

Thompson's encounters with Indian Islam were no less tranquil. Even 'these bloodthirsty and haughty people', he reported, 'appreciate the Pax Brittanica': one applicant for his books hailed 'the spread of the gospel as an event that is to give a mighty impulse to Muhammedanism and revive its declining interests'.[36] Muslim merchants would take Persian and Urdu scriptures off him at Hindu melas. 'Asperities' had been 'softened down', and enquiries from Muslim employees in the courts and the police, even from zamindars, were more 'bland': whether they seek out these scriptures 'to be satisfied that Muhammed is the promised comforter or torture some passage of scripture in his favour, their anxiety for the word is undeniable'.[37] Pfander's tracts on the Mohammedan controversy were arousing interest.[38] Here is intriguing evidence, if it also points to revivalism, of a non-aggressive, Islamic response to Mission in upper India by the 1840s.

The SPG Mission set off in a quite different direction.[39] It was both more restricted in scope and put more emphasis on education. Company chaplain, Jennings, paved the way in 1851. Missionaries Stuart Jackson and Hubbard followed in 1854. The plan was to set up a missionary diocese in and around Delhi. This was to be the platform for 'a strong attack'.[40] But itinerating was delayed: 'churchmen are beginning to feel that they waste their labour and strength on the desultory and independent mode of doing missionary work which has been so much in vogue.'[41] Instead, Jackson and Hubbard set up an institute, the beginnings of the later, immensely influential, St Stephen's College. Jackson took on Persian and Arabic, Hubbard, Hindi and Sanskrit: both applied themselves to learning Hindustani. Maulvies and Pandits paid them a visit. None of this seemed too threatening. But, secretly, they gave lessons in religion to boys at the Government College. Lieutenant-Governor Colvin befriended them and even raised the possibility of transferring the Government College to the Mission: 'it would certainly be a very important thing to have the large (the only) college in our hands, the effect upon the population must surely be great.'[42] If, in the end, this was seen to be too costly a responsibility for the SPG and they were to apply, instead, by Easter 1856 for a grant-in-aid to set up their own college, here was evidence of governmental readiness to breach neutrality. Had rumour of this circulated, it would have been highly disturbing to a Delhi population, already very alarmed by the much debated conversions of Ram Chandra, teacher of mathematics at Government College, and assistant-surgeon Chimman Lal. Jackson luckily got out in time but others were not so fortunate. Subsequently Kay reported from Calcutta: 'it must have been a fearful trial to encounter the wild, unrelenting bigotry of the Mussulman crowd.'[43]

Neither the Baptist Mission nor the SPG were especially confrontational in Delhi. It is hard to read the murderous events of 1857 as hubris. But the Indian fear underlying the religious content to 1857 derived as much from a belief that the Company was reneging on its policy of neutrality as from any response to missionary offensiveness, and the SPG strategy may have unwittingly contributed to these deeper fears of governmental betrayal.

Punjab and the North West Frontier: Robert Clark, (CMS Missionary)

At this stage of the Mission story, civilians and missionaries were to be at their closest, and Mission itself took on a 'frontier', imperialist character. The Punjab civilians 'present', to quote the historian of the CMS, 'the most conspicuous instance in Indian history of a body of British rulers and officers going to work definitely as Christian men, scorning to hide their faith in the True God'. If Stock rhetorically sought to camouflage this breach of neutrality with the claim that 'the Sikh and the Hindu and the Muslim received from them all due respect', he almost rejoiced that 'the Lawrences and their leading followers were not ashamed to be known as devout Christians and not afraid to declare that they wished all men to be the same'.[44] No missionary was to take on board this Christian imperialism quite so affirmatively as Robert Clark[45].

Born to a clerical family but to start out in life as a businessman, in late 1844, whilst employed by a firm in Liverpool, he was to experience a vocation for the church, and later at Cambridge in 1850, for Mission. Initially slotted for Tinevelly, to work under Ragland, the CMS appointed him, instead, to the Punjab. Here, together with Thomas Fitzpatrick, he arrived in 1852. The American Presbyterian Board had preceded the CMS to Ludhiana in 1836. At a meeting of the local CMS committee in Amritsar, with Sir Henry Lawrence presiding, and Robert Montgomery also present, the CMS Punjab Mission was initiated.

A large fortified city, with a population of 1,22,000, the largest in the Punjab, Amritsar chose itself as the Mission station on two grounds. The large number of pilgrims who visited the city would help, or so the missionaries hoped, to spread the word. Merchants who plied the trade routes which transitted the city would likewise take the word with them into central Asia. It was also, of course, the holy city of the Sikhs. In 1853, a Mission site was found just outside the city walls.

But Clark was far too restless a personality to settle for just Amritsar. On 16 December 1853, this time with Colonel Herbert Edwardes presiding, and no doubt a point was made through this being on the same day as the local races, a new CMS station was started in Peshawar. It was an important garrison town. Edwardes made an astonishing speech. 'That man must have a very narrow mind who thinks', he opined, 'that this immense India has been given to our little England for no other purpose than that of our aggrandisement—for the sake of remitting money to our homes, and providing writerships and cadetships for poor relatives.' It was no coincidence that the Company was founded, he went on, and with an unusual reference to the early days of the Company, but two years after the English reformation: in India as in England, the task was 'to preserve the Christian religion in its purest apostolic form'; 'to the . Hindus we have to preach one God and to the Mohammedans to preach one Mediator.' This so self-evidently betrayed the spirit of neutrality that his speech had a hollow ring when he went on to ascribe this role of evangelism to 'the private Christian'.[46]

Peshawar fitted into Clark's imperialist vision for Mission. It would be one of a chain of Mission stations across the frontier. Both Clark and Pfander were to be transferred to Peshawar in 1855. In 1855, Clark went on a mission to western Tibet, reaching Leh on 24 July 1855. He was unimpressed by Tibetan Buddhism. Simple, pious, but not highly educated missionaries would do for the area. Absent in England during the rebellion, on his return in 1859, he went on a tour, up and down the frontier, escorted by Mahzebi troops, Christian converts from the Sikh scavenger caste. He likened the frontier Mission stations to a Punjab canal, 'made to irrigate and fertilize the waste and barren lands which lie on both sides of its course'.[47]

But Clark had been appointed as an educationist. Indeed, he was to open a school in Amritsar, teaching Hindi, Persian, Urdu and English, if, in fact, the Bible was to predominate. On 14 May 1855, he opened another in Peshawar, named after Edwardes, and soon to attract some ninety pupils. But, almost immediately, in both cities, Clark revealed himself to be the committed itinerator. The mere presence of missionaries in Amritsar was held to be 'a sermon in itself'.[48] Interestingly, his wife, Elizabeth Browne, made a major contribution to zenana Mission. And Clark, a little surprisingly, was to be an advocate of Indian agency.

Clark's encounters with Indian religions lacked all subtlety. The Indians themselves were all too anxious to discuss religion. Religious conflict had left the people of the Punjab peculiarly open-minded. But Clark went on the offensive. Christians should be open and unashamed about their faith. The way forward lay in tackling the Indian extended family. Missionaries should attack caste. The initial violent response, as, for example, when Kashmiri Muslims attacked an Indian catechist in

Amritsar, did not deter him. 'The hopeless, godless creed' of Buddhism could not meet the needs of Indians. Vedic Hinduism was dead, and not even the Arya Samaj could revive it. In the Punjab and the North West Frontier, Clark came up against, after Bengal, the second largest community of Muslims in India. Islam, he averred, was but a Christian heresy, off-spring of 'the ignorant, dead and apostate Christianity as it appeared to men in the time of Mahommed': 'if we would have Mahommedanism give way to Christianity, and it cease to be, as it has always been, a power for evil, the only true way is for us to present to the Mahommedans the light and life of Christianity as it is declared to us in the Word of God.'

Given such blindness to the true strengths of Hinduism and Islam, it is a little surprising that Clark did perceive that Sikhism had not been reabsorbed within Hinduism, following the defeat of Ranjit Singh's kingdom in the 1840s, as other missionaries had forecast. It was, in fact, as Clark could not help but recognize, experiencing renewal through the Singh sabhas and the new Khalsa College in Amritsar.[49]

Here, well beyond 1857, was a frightening example at work of a still absurdly simplistic, exclusivist theological approach. Whilst still in India, he died on 16 May 1900.

Agra and Amritsar: James Leighton (CMS)

James Leighton is a link figure in this northern tale. He was to move from Agra to Amritsar. He joined French at Agra on 15 December 1854. He came to admire French who had introduced him to itinerating: 'his noble example has been continually before me for three years and a half, an example which I desire to follow as long as my life is spared.'[50] Yet, for all that, subordination proved insupportable and Leighton is a good example of the Edward Irving/Anthony Groves model of the missionary who prefers to walk alone. This is how Leighton expressed it: 'I would recommend no such subordination to be made at all. It gives occasion to uncomfortable feelings; it hinders cordial union and cooperation; it increases the prohabilities of difference of opinion; it has an injurious effect upon the subordinate Mission's character; if prolonged it injures the Mission itself; and lastly it risques(sic) the continuance of the missionary in the employ of the Society.'[51]

His was a career plagued by ill-health. During the Rebellion, he and his family had been housed in the Fort at Agra, in 'a narrow, un-ventilated cell, like a poor native house', for four and a half months. He went down with 'a violent fever', and it clearly affected his mind. The stress of dependency and his mental imbalance were, in his mind, connected, for he attributed his recovery to his transfer in 1859 to Amritsar, 'to a sphere where responsibility rests directly upon myself'.[52] But he never really recovered. He had earlier returned to London in 1857 for his health. On his return to India he had gone down with cholera. In October 1859 he had to be placed under medical care in Simla: 'my nervous system is entirely deranged . . . I find my memory fails and my religious feelings are all unhealthy owing to the state of my mind . . . I am now useless.'[53] Here was one long-term casualty of the Rebellion, and there must have been others. Even so, in England he lived on till 10 August 1906.

Yet this very frailty makes Leighton an attractive figure. His was an almost morbid wish to get closer to Indians: 'to many this is difficult to do. It requires more laying aside of our European habits than most of us are able to bring ourselves to do. Yet without it we stand at too great a distance from the natives to bring our message closely to their minds.'[54]

He was another reluctant educationist turned itinerator. He accepted that the school at Agra was breaking down prejudice and preparing the way for Christianity. Even if the English education on offer at the school in Amritsar was slow to catch on in the city, surely, he felt, it would help to clear up misconceptions about the missionaries. Yet he always chafed at the constraints of being a teacher. 'A pious and educated layman' could easily take on his role: 'a missionary after all ought to be employed in preaching the gospel and in devising methods whereby it can be brought home to the hearts of the people.' His reasons reveal an admirable wish to become more familiar with Indian religions: 'I feel it is impossible to do justice to the school and become a thoroughly efficient preacher. It requires so minute and careful a study of the language; such a knowledge of Mahommedan and Hindu and Sikh religions; such a readiness in applying that knowledge, and such an ability to set the gospel before the people in an intelligent and vernacular light that I often despair of attaining it. It can only be done by ordinary men when they give themselves entirely to it.'[55]

He was to get his way in Amritsar. In the city, such was the opposition, especially from the Kashmiris, that he came to doubt his talent for bazaar preaching: 'I have been so pained with the blasphemies and the scorn of the rabble.' He preferred the Calcutta model of preaching chapels, covered sheds where private interviews could take place. Near the school, he erected a chabutra, a raised platform, on a site where 'Brahminic bulls used to congregate', shaded by a pipal tree, and in a pedestrian only thoroughfare. Here he found he could preach.[56] Even so, he was at his happiest on tour in the villages, preaching outside his tent. One under-estimates how great a demand as public performers fell on the mission-aries, though the choice was theirs.

And did Leighton reveal appropriate theological skills in these en-counters? When one Hindu levelled the all too familiar charge against the Christians as carnivores, Leighton pointed out that the shoes he wore, despite the shastric insistence that only leather from animals who had died a natural death should be used, almost certainly came from a slaughtered one. This was in a discussion on reincarnation. Leighton believed that Hindus all too often muddled up metaphysics and religion. Nor was he any the more keen to 'wrangle about their traditions' with the Muslims. To one Muslim, he observed, that unless he read the pro-phets and the gospel: 'he could not even be a good Musulman as these are commended in the Koran as inspired books.' The Muslim replied 'that one book, the Kuran was enough for him and that he should not be able to finish it in his lifetime.'[57] If he met Sikh policemen and discharged soldiers, this did not turn into a theological exchange.

Post-Rebellion, Leighton sensed a change for the better, and that he was listened to 'with more respect'. But the quality of the theological exchange does not suggest that Leighton had been wise to abandon school teaching in favour of proselytizing.

Amritsar and Multan: Thomas Fitzpatrick (CMS)

Here I must round off this exploration of India's North West. Thomas Fitzpatrick had accompanied Robert Clark to Amritsar in 1852. As a curate in Birmingham, in a clerical meeting, he had prayed for a foreign Mission, and in particular for the new CMS Mission to the Punjab, and he had been promptly snapped up by the Revd George Lee: 'Fitzpatrick, *you* are wanted for the Punjab.'[58] Clark was to be close to both Thomas and his wife: in them, 'he found the kindest of friends as well as loyal colleagues'.[59] In fact, Fitzpatrick was to be another 'loner'.

He grasped the risk of too overt a dependence on the civilians. One reason why Amritsar was preferable to Lahore as a missionary station was the less obtrusive nature of European society: 'a state of things which adds a little to the preference for Amritsar.'[60] If he and Clark were given pride of place at a meeting of government servants by Montgomery and McLeod: 'this was done as you can perceive simply in regard to our office and that as we go about through the country we may the better obtain all needful information, etc, from the several deputy commissioners.'[61] He was happy enough to work with the civilians in tackling such social malaise as female infanticide. But he was curiously reluctant to take up Montgomery's offer, post-1857, that Indian Christians should fill more posts in the administration: 'indeed self-respect and a sense of honour will make them jealous lest their protégés should fail of public approbation and still worse prove less faithful or useful than Hindu or Musulman . . . There should be no thrusting forward.'[62] Still, this seems to suggest he was less concerned at a charge of favouritism and more concerned whether Indian Christians would live up to expectations.

If in a minor key, Fitzpatrick, however, shared Clark's expansionism. He made a strong case, for example, for a Mission station at Sialkot: 'it must have a great influence upon a large division of the Punjab and ultimately on Kashmir.' And one at Batiala would link Sialkot and Kangra and 'complete as far as we can expect for a short time at least the whole of this immense population enclosed within a line drawn through Jullunder-Lahore-Vazeerabad-Sialkot and Kangra to Jullunder—this in a kind of a way'.[63] And the Punjab civilian ethos of independence and self-reliance clearly rubbed off on Fitzpatrick. He wanted the Punjab Mission to be wholly independent of the Corresponding Committee in Calcutta and either have one of its own or be free to liaise direct with the parent body.

Fitzpatrick took to Amritsar and the Punjab straightaway. It struck him as safe as 'any part of England' (as it surely was, under the Lawrence administration): ideal for itinerating. The more open city plan of Amritsar made it a more practical place for Mission work than Agra or Benares. The Punjab was healthy: 'I see no reason why missionaries should not live here with proper care and in good hands for years upon years.'[64] With that familiar pride that missionaries took in their own station, he added: 'it must at any time be superior to many if not most other parts of India in respect of climate and natural facilities for extended missionary tours.'[65] And when he was posted to Multan (it was Mcleod's idea it should have a missionary), leaving Amritsar was a wrench: 'to leave it will be leaving home, aye more than home.' But with characteristic evangelical fortitude, he added: 'the trial will be severe but so much the more profitable.'[66]

To the historian of Company rule, Multan is best known as the city where two English officers, Vans Agnew and Anderson, were murdered, casus belli for the second Sikh War. It was a city of some 87,000, to the south of the Punjab plain, subject to extremes of climate. It lay on the trade routes to Kandahar and central Asia. Nearby were famous Muslim shrines.

Fitzpatrick relished its challenge. He felt that his work in Amritsar 'had been getting of late somewhat too easy for me and that my staying would rather hinder the full development of the talents of my brethren'.[67] Shifting from Amritsar to Multan was 'something like removing from London to Birmingham, and being so and for other reasons also not altogether pleasing to ourselves.'[68] But Multan was, he believed, with a degree of masochism, 'universally considered the worst place in the Punjab'. Its population was variously described as 'intriguing', 'insubordinate', 'fearfully sensual and morally degraded'.[69] But he took to being on his own: 'those who came from Amritsar have all returned in succession, complaining of the unhealthiness of Multan. My being alone however often disarms opposition and I can generally preach without suffering much from the rudeness or prejudices of the people.'[70] But the enormous scale of the Mission, comprising, as it did, some two million people, began to get him down: 'I must not conceal it from you that Multan seems to me the hardest soil in India—French said it was worse than Agra—I am convinced it is much worse than Peshawar.'[71] By September 1860, ill-health enforced home leave.

Not until 1864 was he to return. On the way out he detected a drop in moral tone in the passengers, and he made himself unpopular by doctoring in his prayers those passages which expressed hope in present company. In the Punjab, however, he was struck by the way that 'unimpressiveness which we used to think unalterable in the natives has yielded manifestly—they have come much nearer to us in thought and habit'. He called on Sir Herbert and Lady Edwardes at Ambala. The Punjab, he concluded, 'is smiling with contentment and prosperity'. Once again he took to bazaar preaching in Amritsar, and was pleased to discover that his Indian vernaculars had become none too rusty after a lay-off of some three and a half years: 'for several reasons I am more than ever drawn towards these people and am led to hope that we are not far from the eve of a great movement amongst them in search of divine truth.'[72] But once again, on grounds of health, he had to leave India, and he died in 1866 in his Cumberland parish of Dalston.

In terms of missionary strategy, Fitzpatrick was yet another educationist turned itinerator. He accepted the role of schools: 'there is an immense multitude who we fear cannot be reached by books or preaching, they must be taught in schools and come under catechetical teaching in some other way.'[73] There would be no rivalry, according to the promise of the civil administration, between State and Mission schools. In Multan, however, Fitzpatrick decided at the outset against setting up any schools, the better 'to make our machinery as simple as possible'.[74] In Amritsar, the missionaries had scorned advice that they should delay preaching for at least four or five years. At first, Fitzpatrick left preaching in the bazaar to Clark. Besides overseeing the school, his role was to deal with enquirers. However, soon, and whatever the risk to health, he was out in the town in the hot season: 'we promise the committee that we will not settle down—we must go out and preach everywhere.'[75] He delighted in the experience: 'I would that every missionary in India could spend the whole of every day in the heart of the city or in the midst of the people. I feel almost impatient of any other plan.'[76]

Multan, however, was a different proposition. He had no trouble attracting an audience of 150 to 200 strong. Here Multan had the edge over Amritsar. But, in other respects, Multan was a far greater challenge: 'the difficulties are greater here than at any other place I have seen for the Punjab.'[77] Fitzpatrick was a pioneer. Outside Multan, it rapidly became obvious, with few exceptions, 'none had ever seen or heard of the "Sahib log" going about to preach their religion'. Surely, they felt, missionaries were here for some ulterior purpose? But Fitzpatrick was unimpressed by those he met: 'the ignorance and superstition of the people seems a shade deeper than those of Multan and those of Lahore and Amritsar.' Yet even here, so far off the beaten track, he still felt there was just enough grasp of Christianity to make it worth his while to stay on as a missionary.[78]

During 1857, preaching in Multan came to a standstill. (Only Pfander in Peshawar was to keep going.) Fitzpatrick himself turned down the offer of refuge in Simla. He did not believe many Europeans would lose their lives but 'the natives will perish in thousands'. In his interpretation, the origins of 1857 were both national and religious. The Muslims were to blame. 'I believe it will be the last effort', he forecast, 'of the Mahommedans of India—if our Government rise to the occasion and will only denounce their infidelity.'

But official policy was also at fault. In its educational policy, it had left schools largely in the hands of Muslims, and was 'avowedly infidel'. One instance of a government favouring of Islam, he cited, was its handing over a mosque in Lahore to the Muslims, said to have been polluted by Sikhs. Were Government to give up its hostile attitude to Mission, 'we would soon see a prodigious change in the course of a very short time';[79] 1857 might yet therefore prove to be a blessing, but what, he wondered in a letter to Montgomery, would Thomason have made of it all?[80] It is very revealing that a missionary in many ways so close to the civilians should still experience such a degree of anger at the official policy of neutrality, and it is a sign that the degree to which the Company compromised on this front can be exaggerated.

Fitzpatrick tended to conflate all those of other faiths as simply his opponents. There were three kinds; those 'who know a little of their religious system and argue reasonably'; 'the violent who would overcome by force'; 'those who ridicule and deride'. In Multan, Hindus and Muslims would put up a common front, declaring: 'we know two religions which are believers, but will never acknowledge a third.'[81] One hobbyhorse which Fitzpatrick rode, his distaste for polygamy and easy divorce, was, in his eyes, common to both Islam and Hinduism. He was appalled at the way Christian magistrates sanctioned such practices: 'it is an evil greater than the opium traffic.'[82] 'We do not serve the Lord Jesus Christ herein but Muhammed and the brahmins—never will the people rise from their degradation until polygamy be discountenanced if not altogether abolished and facilities for divorce greatly restrained.' He incited Montgomery: 'the women and children of India will call you blessed if you deliver them from this thraldom.'[83]

Fitzpatrick was just as actively engaged in a campaign against female infanticide. At the beginning of the Mission, a substantial durbah—'the largest ever seen in this country' —had sat in judgement on the issue. Marriage expenses would have to be reduced. It decreed that the practice was against the laws of God and that it was to be opposed to the utmost, 'even to the putting out of caste of any person known to be guilty of it'. (Clearly, the Company was ready to turn caste to the advantage of other measures of social reform.) And as Brahmins, or so Fitzpatrick believed, made money from the practice (and, it is true, priests were called in to offer ritual penance for the murder), its abolition would be a great blow against Brahminism[84]. In many ways, Fitzpatrick was exceptional as a missionary in giving so much attention to social questions.

The most serious theological exchanges occurred with those who were to convert. In Fitzpatrick's case, these were more commonly Muslim and Sikh than Hindu. Just occasionally, whenever his stay was longer, as, for example, for some seven days in November 1856, in Shujabad, just south of Multan, more elaborate theological debates took place. The tahsildar, descendant of a Pathan family of some two hundred years standing in the town, a reader of Arabic and Persian and an owner of a Persian Bible, took him up on a number of issues. Did not the Koran show that God was the author of both good and evil? Could one reconcile the Koran and God's

Maps
and
Illustrations

SOUTHERN AND EASTERN BENGAL MISSIONS

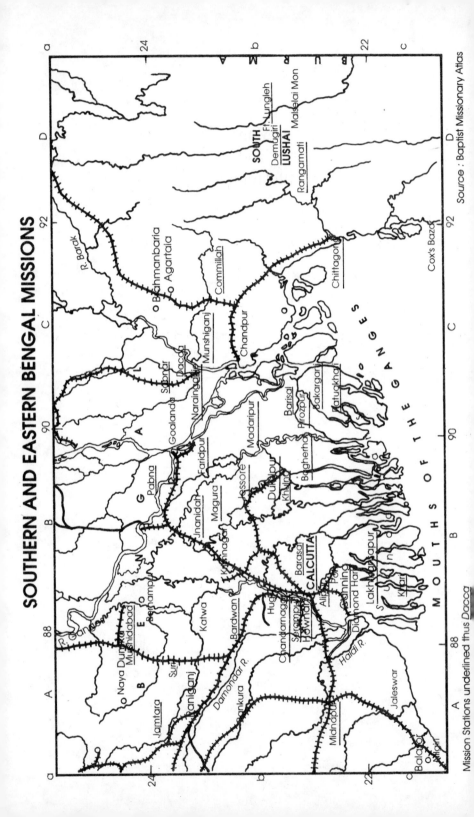

Mission Stations underlined thus Dacca

Source : Baptist Missionary Atlas

NORTH WEST PROVINCES

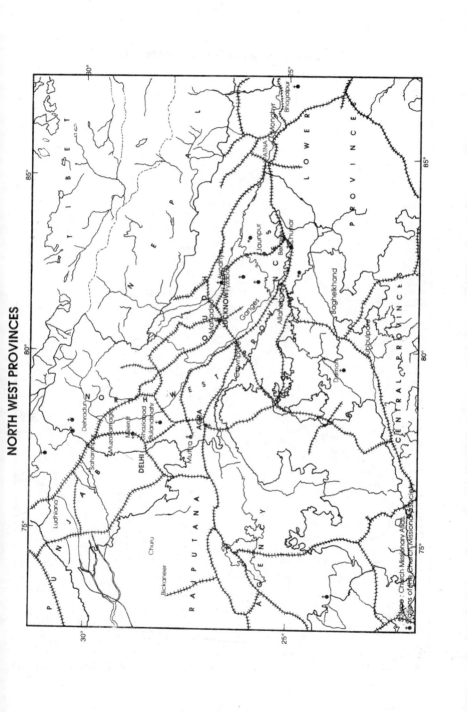

Source : Church Missionary Atlas.
Stations of the Church Mission Society.

THE PUNJAB, SIND AND THE AFGHAN FRONTIER

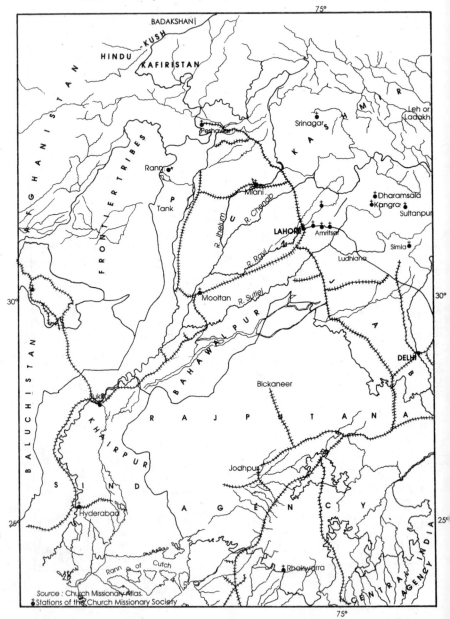

Source : Church Missionary Atlas.
● Stations of the Church Missionary Society

PART OF THE TELUGU COUNTRY

Source : Church Missionary Atlas.
♦ Stations of the Church Missionary Society

MYSORE, COORG AND MADRAS STATES

Source : Imperial Gazetteer Atlas of India.

1. Chapel at Luckyantipore

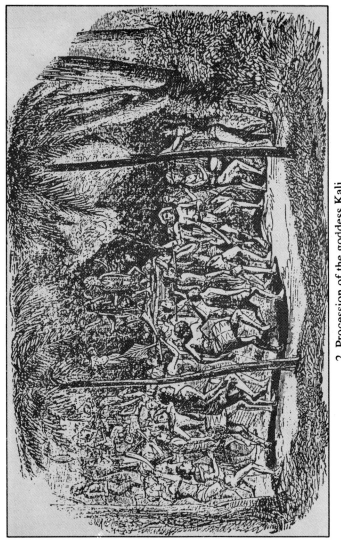

2. Procession of the goddess Kali

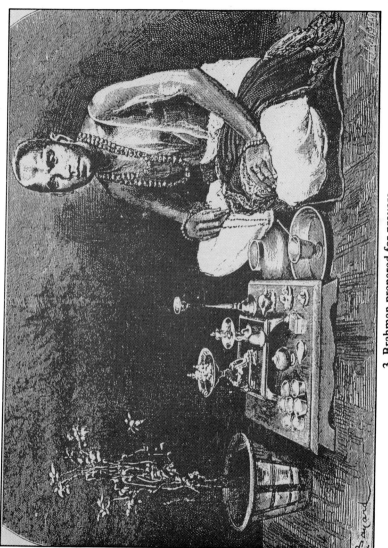

3. Brahman prepared for prayers

4. Brahmins and Hindoos of different castes

5. Rev. Dr. Krishna Mohan Banerjea

'providential arrangement of marriage'? There were fewer women than men but God had sanctioned more than one wife. He tried to prove Mohammed's powers of prophesy by quoting from the hadith (tradition). Fitzpatrick's rejoinder here was to assert that these had been written some 150 years or so after Mohammed's death. Miracles, the tahsildar asserted, were still being worked. Where, Fitzpatrick enquired, was the proof? They both agreed that there would be a second coming. For the Muslims, 'it will . . . be a great event'. But Fitzpatrick denied that Christ would receive the tahsildar, for he did not acknowledge him: 'you deny his Divinity and his meritorious death'. He continued: 'all the prophets declare that He is God and that in his human nature He bore the sins of all men on the cross—but Mohammed denied both and the Koran is the evidence.' It came as a matter of surprise to the tahsildar to learn that Fitzpatrick was not employed by the Company.[85] If necessarily inconclusive, and maybe this particular Muslim was willing to meet the missionary part of the way, this was another example of a civilized encounter.

One of the more pleasing aspects of this particular tour was the delight Fitzpatrick took in the appearance of Muslim tombs. 'One of the most exquisite buildings I have seen in this country' was his description of a tomb being erected for the late nawab of Bahawalpur. Failure to draw the worshippers into a conversation somewhat spoilt his enjoyment: 'I never saw a more bigoted people.[86]

One reason for selecting Amritsar over Lahore as Mission headquarters for the Punjab was the greater number of Sikhs in its population, some 10 to 20,000, as opposed to but one per cent. Here, in Fitzpatrick's view, was a community ripe for conversion, but they would have to hurry: 'I believe from what I see and daily learn in one way or another they are a broken sect—losing their religious distinction and lapsing faster than we would wish into the more powerful sect of Hindu and Musulman.' He continued: 'there is but a very small section in this city we are credibly informed who do not worship Hindu idols and we know that several have very recently embraced the faith of Islam.' His was that very British response to the Sikhs. 'They are a very ignorant but a frank, open, manly independent people—we always find it naturally agreeable to speak to them of Christ and of his salvation.'[87] And there were indeed converts (to be discussed later). The Akalis (a distinctive orthodox community, followers of Guru Gobind Singh) had, Fitzpatrick believed, all but disappeared; there used to be some 4000 in the city, but now 'it is rare to meet with one'. Their gurus were, he observed, elderly and, with their death, the system would collapse. He did not believe that attacking the gurus would rejuvenate the faith[88]. He saw a similar collapse of Sikhism in Multan: 'the few, very few Granthas that remain being very ignorant and utterly dispirited.'[89] Clark, who outlived Fitzpatrick, was to live long enough to learn how wrong this forecast of the collapse of Sikhism was.

Can we stand back from these individual case-studies and point to more generalized attitudes of Mission, both in ideology and in its response to Indian religions? As the Baptists confined their attention to Bengal and the north, they are the appropriate Mission to select for this purpose before turning attention to the south.

Ideology was sustained by a millenarian conviction that Indian religions were in terminal decline. Clearly it was not in Mission's self-interest, from the point of view of home consumption, to underestimate the opposition: 'next to the extinct mythologies of Greece and Rome never has Christianity had to do battle with a foe mightier than that it meets with in the plains of Hindustan.' Yet, in Bengal, Hindus no longer had any faith in Hinduism: 'a direct assault on the foundations of the Christian faith itself is deemed the only politic course. The Vedantists felt 'insecure'.[90] One indicator was the very large number of societies set up in defence of Hinduism. One example was the Hindu Charitable Institution, set up in 1846, paid for in part by Debendranath Tagore. 'Do you prop a firm building?' rhetorically enquired one long-standing missionary.[91] Another indicator was the decline in caste. Baptists took patriotic pride that whereas former conquerors 'gradually yielded to the power of Hindoo social institutions, for the first time, they are giving way. England's ideas of law, of right, and of morals, with England's Christianity, are mightier than they'.[92] In keynote speeches in February and April 1857, E. B. Underhill underlined these points of view: caste was shaken; only custom shored up Hinduism; 'idolatry has no hold on the heart of the people'.

But Underhill was also pleading for an end to that mere abuse of Indian religions: 'too great eagerness to shame the Hindoos and Mohammedans, by remarks on the follies of their respective beliefs, should not be displayed, while the missionary should, on the other hand, avoid a vague and too general statement and application of religious truth.'[93] It would be rebarbative to cite many examples of such abuse. There was a strange mix in Baptist journals in the accounts of Indian religions of the merely descriptive, the proto-anthropological, and the merely derisory. On the one hand, for example, perfectly informative accounts of Hindu mantras are provided; then we are told that the 'timid Hindu' at the midnight hour, 'retires to some cemetery, burning with revenge, repeats the above mantras with the intention of bringing destruction in all its forms upon a real or supposed enemy. How opposed to the spirit of Christianity'.[94]

There was just the glimmerings of a shift in ideology and attitudinal response to Indian religions, though an exclusivist ideology was clearly still in the ascendant. The gap between missionary intent and achievement was huge and it was all part of this delusion that Baptists looked on 1857 as proof of Christ's victory over Krishna.

How did the defence mechanisms of Mission stand up to the even more entrenched Hinduism of the south?

NOTES AND REFERENCES

1. From a biography by a contemporary. Richard Temple, *James Thomason,* Oxford: 1893, pp. 15, 129.
2. So Ronald Hyam speculates. *Empire and Sexuality: the British Experience,* Manchester: 1990, pp. 29–30.
3. *The Imperial Gazetteer of India,* vol. XVIII, p. 64. See also T. Phillips's account, *Missionary Herald,* vol. LIII, October 1843, pp. 167–8.
4. Phillips, March 1844, M.H., vol. LVIII, pp. 246–7.
5. Phillips, February 1842, M.H., vol. XXXIII, p. 216.
6. Phillips, August 1853, M.H., vol. CLXXI, pp. 124–7.
7. Brief obituary notice, M.H., 1867, pp. 557–8.
8. John Parsons to his sister, 10 September 1858, IN/8 (BMS: Oxford).
9. *Imperial Gazetteer of India,* vol. V, p. 84.
10. Charles Andrews, *North India,* Oxford: 1908, p. 124.
11. Herbert Birks, *Life of T. Valpy French,* vol. I, London: 1895, p. 11.
12. French Letter, 3 January 1851, ibid., p. 25.
13. Ibid., p. 39.
14. Ibid., p. 74.
15. French to Venn, February 1855, quoted ibid., p. 78.
16. French to Knight, 8 August 1853, quoted ibid., p. 53.
17. French to Venn, 2 May 1852, quoted ibid., pp. 64–6.
18. French to Chapman, 3 May 1857, quoted ibid., p. 87.
19. Birks, p. 143.
20. Ibid., p. 145.
21. French to his wife, 30 December 1863, quoted ibid., p. 145.
22. French to Mr Frost, 27 August 1857, quoted ibid., p. 106.
23. French to Mr Knight, 2 December 1857, quoted ibid., p. 108.
24. Quoted ibid., p. 25.
25. Richard Williams, Journal, 25 March 1838, IN/11 (BMS: Oxford). Still, he did find some Muslims ready to listen to the parable of the talents and he did attract some attentive Muslim audiences, anxious to learn about 'salvation'.

26. Avril Powell, *Muslims and Missionaries in Pre-Mutiny India*, pp. 238–42.
27. Birks, pp. 144–9.
28. M.H., October 1858, p. 645.
29. Between 22 November and 30 June 1844 he had distributed 562 volumes, 2387 gospels, 7612 tracts, in Persian, Urdu, Hindi and Sanskrit. M., LXX, March 1845, p. 36. At a fair and en route in 1850, 1472 scriptures and 4269 tracts were distributed. M.H., October 1850, p. 149.
30. M.H., August 1841, pp. 122–3.
31. M.H., vol. XXXVIII, May 1842, p. 265.
32. M.H., vol. LX, December 1843, p. 203.
33. M.H., August 1841, p. 122.
34. M.H., vol. LXXXVII, October, pp. 147–8.
35. M.H., October 1858, pp. 643–4.
36. M.H., vol. XXVII, August 1841, p. 120.
37. M.H., vol. XXXVIII, May 1842, p. 265.
38. M.H., vol. LXX, March 1845, p. 36.
39. For a summary account, see Thompson, *Into All Lands*, London: 1951, pp. 352–5.
40. Jackson, Delhi, 22 November 1855, CLR 14 (SPG: Oxford).
41. Jennings, Simla, 19 June 1854, ibid.
42. Jackson, 2 February 1856, ibid.
43. Kay, Principal of Bishop's College, Calcutta, 15 June 1857, ibid.
44. E. Stock, *History of the Church Missionary Society: Its Environment, its Men and its Work*, vol. II, London: 1899, pp. 201–2.
45. For Robert Clark, I have relied on Henry M. Clark, *Robert Clark of the Punjab: Pioneer and Missionary Statesman*, London: 1907. Robert Clark, *The Mission of the CMS and the CEZMS in the Punjab and Sindh*, London: 1904 (first published in 1885).
46. Quoted Robert Clark, *The Mission of the CMS*, pp. 178–9.
47. Ibid., p. 17.
48. Henry Clark, p. 63.
49. Robert Clark, p. 243.
50. Revd James Leighton, Annual Report, September 30 1858, CI 1/0176/12 (CMS: Birmingham).
51. Leighton, Amritsar, 10 March 1859, CI 1/0176/6.
52. Leighton, Annual Letter, 29 January 1859, CI 1/0176/16.
53. Leighton to Dr Maclean, 1 September 1859, Leighton to Mr Cuthbert, 1 October 1859, CI 1/0176/17.
54. Leighton, Annual Report, 30 September 1858, CI 1/0176/12.
55. Leighton, Annual Report, 30 September 1858, CI 1/0176/12.
56. Leighton, 18 April, 10 May 1859, CI 1/0176/11.
57. Leighton, 23 January 1859, CI 1/0176/9.
58. Robert Clark, p. 34.
59. Henry Clark, p. 56.
60. Revd Thomas Fitzpatrick, Journal, 21 June–5 July 1852, CI 1/0106/26 (CMS: Birmingham).

61. Fitzpatrick to Venn, 16 February 1852, CI 1/0106/3.
62. Fitzpatrick to Montgomery, 12 October 1857, CI 1/0106/18C.
63. Fitzpatrick to Venn, 16 February 1852, CI 1/0106/3.
64. Fitzpatrick to Venn, 4 November 1852, CI 1/0106/6a.
65. Fitzpatrick to Venn, 6 July 1853, CI 1/0106/8a.
66. Fitzpatrick, Annual Letter, 2 January 1856, CI 1/0106/30.
67. Fitzpatrick, 6 February 1856, CI 1/0106/14.
68. Fitzpatrick, 2 November 1856, CI 1/0106/15.
69. Fitzpatrick, Multan, Annual Letter, 5 January 1857, CI 1/0106/31.
70. Fitzpatrick to Venn, Multan, 22 October 1857, CI 1/0106/18A.
71. Fitzpatrick to Venn, 22 June 1859, CI 1/0106/20.
72. Fitzpatrick to Venn, 19 February 1864, Amritsar, CI 1/0106/22.
73. Fitzpatrick, Journal, 21 June–July 1852, CI 1/0106/26.
74. Fitzpatrick, Annual Letter, 5 January 1857, CI 1/0106/31.
75. Fitzpatrick to Venn, 10 May 1854, CI 1/0106/10.
76. Fitzpatrick, Annual Letter, 19 January 1855, CI 1/0106/30.
77. Fitzpatrick, 2 November 1856, CI 1/0106/15.
78. Fitzpatrick, Multan, 17 March 1857, CI 1/0106/17.
79. Fitzpatrick to Venn, 26 June 1857, CI 1/0106/16.
80. Fitzpatrick to Montgomery, 12 October 1857, CI 1/0106/18c.
81. Fitzpatrick, Annual Letter, 5 January 1857, CI 1/0106/31.
82. Fitzpatrick, 22 October 1857, CI 1/0106/18A.
83. Fitzpatrick to Montgomery, 12 October 1857, CI 1/0106/18C.
84. Fitzpatrick to Venn, 16 February 1852, CI 1/0106/3.
85. Fitzpatrick, 17 March 1857, CI 1/0106/17.
86. Fitzpatrick, 17 March 1857, CI 1/0106/17.
87. Fitzpatrick to Venn, 4 November 1852, CI 1/0106/6a.
88. Fitzpatrick, First Report of the Punjab Mission, 21 June–9 July 1852, CI 1/0106/26.
89. Fitzpatrick, Multan, 17 March 1857, CI 1/0106/17.
90. Progress of Missions in India, M.H., vol. CLXIII, December 1852, pp. 182–4.
91. Appeal on Behalf of the Baptist Mission in India by one of its oldest missionaries (J. Thomas) M.H., vol. CII, November 1847, pp. 162–5.
92. M.H., vol. CLVI, May 1852, p. 71.
93. Annual General Meeting, 30 April 1857, The Baptist Magazine, vol. XLIX, 1857, pp. 383–9, 445–50.
94. The Mantras in Popular Use in Bengal, M.H., vol. CLXXXIV, September 1854, pp. 134–5; October 1854, pp. 151–3.

CHAPTER 6

Missionary Case-Studies:
The South

Protestant Christianity took root earlier and was to penetrate deeper in the south than in Bengal and the north.[1] At the turn of the nineteenth century, the Indian Christian community, some 50,000 strong, was concentrated mainly in and around Tanjore (Thanjavur) and Trichinopoly (Tiruchchirappalli), within the old Lutheran Tranquebar Mission. But it was Christianity 'in a state of stagnation and decline'.[2] This was to change in the far south. The beginnings of the Protestant Mission to Tinevelly (Tirunelveli) can be dated from the visit in 1780 to Palamcottah (Palayancotta) of Christian Schwartz, best loved of the Tranquebar missionaries, at the time in the employ of the SPCK. It was a largely locally inspired movement, however, which took off in the 1800s. This fell into the doldrums and not until the arrival of Company chaplain, James Hough, did it acquire, from 1818 to 1821, a new shape. Under the leadership of yet another of the great Lutheran missionaries, Charles Rhenius, employed by the CMS, it underwent yet further expansion. Meanwhile the old Mission in Madras, centred in Vepery, had been revitalized by the 'pious chaplains', Michael Kerr and Marmaduke Thompson. In 1814, the CMS had instituted a Corresponding Committee in Madras: the SPCK followed suit with a Madras District Committee in 1815. The SPG took over from the SPCK in 1826 and potentially serious clashes of interest with the CMS were resolved by 1844. In the 1840s the CMS extended its influence north to Masulipatam, and two of the case-studies are drawn from the Telugu Mission.

Indian religion in the south was distinctive. Through the inspiration of Samkara (788–820?), Ramanuja (1017?–1137) and Madhva (1197–1276), in the great medieval reform movement, Vedantism, in its three forms of monism, qualified non-dualism and dualism, had come of age. Alongside was a remarkable period of temple building. Here was a realization of high Sanskritic culture at its finest. But it was also a continuing expression of Dravidian culture, Tamil, Telugu, Kanerese, and it is this mix that has led interpreters to highlight a distinctive southern Hinduism. The tendency today, however, is to reintegrate this Hinduism into an all-India perspective: Fred Clothey, for example, wonders if 'in short it may be time to deprovincialize the study of religion in south India and see it in the perspective of a contradistinction of that which occurs elsewhere'.[3] It is certainly one of the objectives of this project to open up a comparative account of Mission and Indian Christianity between the south and the east and north.

If not unique to the south, there was a peculiar tension there between high Sanskritic culture and the local or folk culture. Over time this has been variously described, as a high and a folk culture, the Great and the Little Tradition, but, once again, the tendency today is to underplay their separateness, and stress instead their interdependence and interaction. All this points to the quite astonishing pluralism.of Indian religions. Chris Fuller, for example, has shown how in the gods of the great Minaksi temple at Madurai, the Hindu pantheon and the local Tamil gods, the non-brahminical village deities or gramadevatas, have come together. Devi or Sakti, Siva's consort, has taken on many of the trappings of village goddesses. Siva himself has become more the husband and father, more 'tamed', and less the erotic and ascetic figure of northern Hinduism: 'Siva is more unity dissolving into localized forms, the goddess is more a severalty coalescing into a universalized form.'[4] Such hybridism of folk and Brahminical culture operates at all levels. Did the mid-nineteenth-century Protestant missionaries show any insight into such distinctive expressions of Hinduism in the south?

Part of the answer lies in their aesthetic response. Heber, as ever, responded to the drama of building and landscape. 'The ancient Hindoo temples', he wrote, 'though inferior in taste to the magnificent Mussulman buildings are in size, picturesque effect and richness of carving, for above anything which I had expected to meet with.' 'The country, the objects, and the people round me, are all of a kind to stimulate and repay curiosity more than most others in the world.'[5] The journey south was, of course, to cost him his life. Did the enthusiasm of later missionaries match his?

The old Mission had been attracted to the centres of Brahminical culture in the south, to Tanjore, to Madurai. Robert de Nobili, through the earliest attempt at a policy of inculturation, had gained a remarkable insight into this culture. The later Lutheran missionaries had, at the least, sought to read and understand the Hindu texts. Was the 'new Mission' to seek out any similar endeavour and understanding?

There was always something 'preposterous' and 'arrogant', and here

I am quoting Hugald Grafe, about the way missionaries paraded their exclusivist faith in the context of a culture where Indian religions had for centuries achieved a harmony of interests. Drawn to the vibrant popular culture of the village, missionaries simply saw their task as driving out 'devil-worship'. If missionaries took with them H. M. Scudder's Bazaar Book, with its collection of quotations from some of the great Tamil classics, such as the Tirrukaral, their's was 'a failure to look at such key Hindu concepts as dharma and karma, so no real understanding was possible'.[6]

But there was a paradox. For one, 'dialogue, discussion and debate had been part of open-air preaching'.[7] The level of this exchange will become apparent in the individual case-studies. And in time, especially through its later mass conversion movements, as well as through its schools and colleges, Mission proved to be a catalyst for social and cultural change. Through the Tamil expertise of some of its missionaries, especially those of Robert Caldwell and George Pope, Mission was to make a significant contribution to the Tamil Renaissance of the late nineteenth and twentieth centuries.[8]

John Tucker: Madras, CMS Missionary

Tucker, between 1833 and 1847, was the much respected secretary to the CMS Corresponding Committee in Madras. His correspondence is particularly interesting for observations on the confrontation between Hindu and Christian in Tinevelly in the 1840s.

In terms of strategy, Tucker was ahead of his time in prioritizing education. This probably reflected the quite extraordinary official interest taken in missionary education, above all in the 1840s, during the governorship of the Marquess of Tweesdale. Tucker fought hard, but was to lose, for the CMS Institute in Madras becoming the basis of a new seminary for the south. Raw provincials from the Christian hunting grounds of Tinevelly needed, he believed, some of the polish of Madras metropolitan culture, or rather, some acculturation to European ways: 'the practice of all of us is I believe here to ask our catechists, or any respectable native, to sit down in a chair, when we meet them after absence we shake hands with them, and with the Native students of the Institute we have still freer intercourse whilst we keep them to their native habits.' Were the seminary to go to Tinevelly or, indeed, students to Islington College, as the home Committee preferred, this would be in breach of promise and inflict a serious wound: 'nothing but a CMS

Institute at the Presidency can meet the wants and circumstances of the CMS in southern India.'[9] The seminary was, in fact, to open in Tinevelly on 9 December 1846, with Pettit in charge.

Tucker always pressed the case for founding new schools. There was the Native English School at Palamcottah, opened in 1844, with the blind Cruickshanks as the headmaster. Tucker made a strong case for the appointment of another schoolmaster from England for Noble's school at Masulipatam. He was well aware of the success of the Scottish missionary schools under John Anderson. If preachers e.g. itinerators should be multiplied tenfold, 'I cannot but deeply feel in common with others here', he averred, 'the increasing importance of extension and vigorous efforts to promote Christian education through English-medium schools, above all in the Brahmin, urban, elite'.[10]

Such apologetics was closely linked to his recognition of the need for an Indian priesthood. Yet this was combined with a quite exceptional animus against Indian catechists, though this may represent the views of the local committee as much as Tucker himself. Catechists took on many pastoral functions, but were seen to be 'utterly unfit for their office'. And just because they did take on this role, and so incompetently, they stood in the way of the real objectives of Mission, 'raising up a body of Native Ministers who shall be qualified fully and faithfully to preach the gospel to their countrymen'.[11] Guidelines were to be drawn up, limiting the number of catechists, 'and insisting on a monthly meeting with the missionary'. Tucker certainly entertained bleak thoughts were missionaries to leave their communities to their catechists and not to exercise their full interventionist powers: 'a cold and withering selfishness and indifference would it is to be feared prevail'.[12] But both the Committee and Tucker were being grossly unfair for, as Grafe has claimed, but for these catechists, mainly drawn from the Vellalas and the Maravars, Christianity would never have spread and, anyway, both the CMS and SPG advocacy of an Indian clergy proved rhetorical: European paternalism rather than Indianization was to be the norm.

By late 1845, Tucker got wind of the destruction of some twenty Christian villages in the district of Nalloor, near Tinevelly. His initial response was to play the problem down: 'I must caution you not to measure these movements and proceedings with English associations and feelings—here in themselves they would be of little consequence and cause no alarm—the people have too little principle to hold together in combinations and are too feeble to resist the ordinary exercises of authority.' However, he was forced to recognize that here was something new, and that the number of victims would have been higher 'had Pliny or some Roman more bitter than he been our Collector'.[13] In fact, here was a serious resistance movement, organized at the local Tinevelly level by the Vibuthi Sangham or Sacred Ash Association, and in contact with the Madras-based Four Vedas Society, based in Salai street—its inhabitants had already earlier successfully petitioned against the erection of a church in their street. Several Tinevelly participants had sought refuge with Christians in Madras, and this suggests that at least some of the protesters were lapsed Christians. There was a complicated judicial process and only the removal of one of the Appeal Court judges, Malcolm Lewin, who had little sympathy for Mission, and who had argued that Tinevelly through the Christian presence had become more prone to crime, did the case go the way of the missionaries, and the main figures involved get long prison sentences. In Tucker's estimate, so costly had Hindu attempts been to bribe the courts, there would be tranquillity for some time to come.

It was to flare up again in December 1858, Grafe makes a good case for seeing these further Hindu attacks on Christians as the south's equivalent of 1857. Interestingly, Tucker had reported Nalloor as 'the last occupied and least culturated of all our mission districts', and that 'the parts of the province which are in the most peaceful and orderly state are those where there are the greatest number of missionaries and native Christians, the south and the SE'.[14] This fits Eric Stokes's model of resistance in 1857 as most likely in areas of least penetration, a preemptive strike against a threatened and resented intrusion.[15]

Tucker, perversely, saw cause for satisfaction at this Hindu resistance; 'whatever rouses the Native Mind from its long cherished torpor is, so far, to be counted as a benefit'.[16] This was a reflection of that greatest missionary dread of all, Indian indifference. But Tucker had failed to see how this was evidence of effective Hindu opposition to the Mission enterprise[17]. Tucker retired from his post as secretary in January 1847.

Madras: James Joseph Haydn Louis (CMS)

There is just a hint of William Golding's sad parson, Revd Robert James Colley, from his novel, *Rites of Passage*,[18] in Louis's journal entries on his journey out. If he found the captain 'decidedly pious', the cadets frivolous, down below, in the forecastle, the crew 'are remarkably attentive'.[19] Seemingly objective accounts of Hinduism in Madras almost earn him the accolade of proto-anthropologist, were they not tied to conventional evangelical pieties. It is clear from his information that Hinduism had lost none of its momentum in the Presidency capital by mid-century.

In his journals, we find long, careful accounts of Hindus at prayer and at festivals. On arrival in 1838, he was immediately out and about, with his notebook. Here is an account of worshippers in a temple, heads bowed, fingers pointed upwards, 'after the manner of the recumbent figures on many ancient tombs of England'. There was 'the appearance of mental prayer'. There is a description of all the exchanges between worshipper and temple priest, the coconuts broken in two before the gods, the camphor burning in a brass dish, the application of ashes on the forehead, and all described without a trace of ridicule, only to add in mockery of priestly fees: 'the whole scene gave a strange idea of the mingled superstition and avarice exhibited in these disgusting places.'[20]

There was an account of a fire festival. Brazenly, they had entered the temple, to the consternation of the worshippers, and had been asked to retire some distance. This they had agreed to do, though they would not exchange the vehicle they had come in for two armchairs. The worshippers had wanted its removal from the court, but this would have required their walking 'some distance under a burning sun'. There was the sacrifice of a sheep. Then the gods were taken on a walk around the area, shaded from the sun by 'a faded pink parasol'. Walking on fire did not impress Louis. The ashes were almost spent and any embers on the feet would have been 'instantly extinguished in the water beyond': 'indeed there was manifest deception throughout the whole affair.' Still, some bystanders who picked up the ashes to rub on their faces found them too hot to handle. Louis was more impressed by the natural beauty of a palm-tree nearby and felt a positive relief whilst taking evening prayers for those Indian boys who had been rescued from such superstition.[21]

There is an account of a hook-swinging mela. He recognized a parallel with an English fair. In addition, there was a Hindu playing castanets, a man with a hawk, booths selling fruits and sweet-meats, etc. He provides a very exact account of the hook-swinging itself. 'I narrowly watched', he wrote, 'the countenance and deportment of the natives, but I could trace nothing of pity, admiration, even of surprise, a slight clapping of hands was heard, as the swinger rose, beyond all this was apathy'.[22] Did he understand that invariably someone of high caste was using the hook-swinger, generally of low caste, as a surrogate means of penance?

There was an encounter with an abbot of one of the leading Saivite mutts. He was about fifty, 'with a pleasing expression on his countenance'. There is a careful description of his howdah and those in attendance. Such visitations were to levy payments on Hindu worshippers. Louis observed: 'the more the idolatry of India unfolds itself as a system the more it seems adopted to bring the superstitious, timid, Hindoo into servile bondage.'[23]

All his evidence points to a Hindu faith still holding. 'In the city we look in vain', he reported, 'for symptoms of a decaying superstition in prostrate idols and crumbling pagodas; everywhere the house of the false god is carefully maintained.'[24] Repair work was in progress on several temples and tanks. Hindus, he sensed, saw the government as their backers: 'this I know sounds strange, that the natives continually when speaking of the machineries of their idolatries refer to government as favourable to them, especially if taxed with the folly of these.'[25]

Sited in a CMS chapel in Black Town, hook-swinging visible at a nearby temple, Louis seems to have had a few ideas on how to confront this Hindu challenge. He recognized how important it was to educate girls, in single sex schools, for it was women who did so much to shape the attitudes of the young. Caste, he saw, as a greater obstacle to Christianity than idolatry. But such an insight came late in his ministry,[26] and may reflect a feeling of defeatism before the institutional powers of Hinduism. But were he not to buoy himself with hope, the missionary could never have kept going. 'Yet it is manifest', he self-deludedly wrote, 'that a silent current is sapping the whole fabric of idolatry here.'[27] His journals provide clear evidence to the contrary of a continuing vitality in Hinduism.

Tinevelly: George Pettit, CMS

Pettit's missionary career got off to a worrying start. Recently married, he had had to leave his wife behind at Portsmouth on the journey out, and, over the next three months, agonized as to whether he would ever see her again. In fact, she journeyed out later with John Tucker. He himself arrived in Madras on 22 June 1833, only to be overwhelmed by the heat. But, with his wife restored to him, his morale improved: 'I believe there is not a spot in the world where all things considered we would rather be than where we are.' Even so, he was unimpressed by the Institute in Madras—Tucker would have to improve it—and he had to rein in his 'impatience' and 'bad temper'.[28]

On the first of June 1835 he set off, by palanquin, on the four hundred mile journey to Palamcottah, taking in, en route, the temples at Madurai and Srirangam. He was impressed. Pettit's career was to be one of troubles, but he was also to provide a careful, if arguably wrong-headed, account of popular religion in the far south.[29]

His first task was to sort out the quarrel with Charles Rhenius. It was tragic that so outstanding a career as Rhenius's should have been blighted at the end by his rupture with the Anglican church over his Lutheran insistence that, as priest, he had the right to ordain. But for his falling under the spell of Anthony Groves, he might have slipped quietly away. Instead, he stood his ground. The Tinevelly Mission was to be hopelessly divided. In the end, only Rhenius's death on 5 June 1838, made possible a reconciliation.[30] His son, Charles, was also to become a CMS missionary. Stephen Neill credits Pettit in his handling of the quarrel with 'great qualities of tact, modesty, and firmness': 'the twelve years of his residence at Palamcottah were a time of pacification, stabilization and progress'.[31] Pettit himself wondered if the seemingly gratuitous nature of the quarrel, for so it must have struck Indians, might not have impressed Hindus and hence have encouraged conversions.[32]

Tinevelly and Palamcottah sat alongside one another, separated by the river Tambraparni. If Tinevelly was the larger town, Palamcottah was the district's administrative headquarters. A recently settled area, and a scene of considerable poligar (a warrior chief) resistance, there had to be a garrison in Palamcottah. The CMS was itself based in Palamcottah, with one missionary in charge of the seminary, the other, and this was Pettit's initial assignment, looking after the Indian Christians in Palam-cottah, as well as proselytizing the villages round about. In the immediate vicinity the land, as a rice-growing area for most of the year, was 'a most beautiful green to the eye'.[33] These were villages of extraordinary antiq-uity. As one modern missionary puts it: 'here in these villages there is still a pattern of life not destroyed by the ferment of western civilization. One can say that these villages belong to pre-history rather than to history. Or perhaps one should say that they are just emerging into history.'[34]

Pettit was to be plunged from one quarrel into another. He was at the centre of the storm that flared up between Hindus and Christians in the 1840s. He rightly perceived that the explanation for Hindu protest lay in their alarm at the withdrawal of government support for temples and its devolving responsibility to Indian trustees. But mounting conversions had also bred the suspicion that the CMS missionaries 'were meditating some secret measures for the overthrow of Hinduism'.[35] If effective

Hindu resistance was limited to a twenty mile radius around the temple complex of Tiruchendur, here was a serious confrontation, initiated by an inter-caste alliance in 1841, and brought to a head under the leadership of a Nadar soothsayer in 1845. Pettit had the honesty to report that it was the irresponsible intervention of a Christian schoolmaster, taking on the self-appointed role of a panchayat committee, that had antagonized local Hindus. He confirmed that amongst the most hostile were lapsed Christians. Here was a concerted attempt to reassert the primacy of Siva, exploiting every possible manoeuvre, playing on the sympathies of a newly appointed collector, and trying to win over Europeans against the Christians on grounds of their being low caste. Pettit's account is an alarming revelation of just how unpopular Christians had become.

Here is another example of missionary as proto-anthropologist. Pettit provides a very lucid account of popular Hinduism at the village level. For him, this was mere devil-worship. It was an expression of religion wholly separate from Brahminical Hinduism. Whereas the Brahmins worshipped the gods as good, here the demons were worshipped as evil: Brahmins did not offer blood sacrifice, the devil-worshippers offered animals and, though not in Tinivelly, human sacrifice. Pettit interpreted demons as the personification of diseases; he speculated on a comparison with 'the old mischievous and even malignant fairies of Europe'. There was no special priesthood: anyone, male or female, could be a devil-dancer. Maybe there was real possession.

But such an attempt at description gave way to mere condemnation. Here was a system which not only debased its practitoners to the same 'wild and cruel' level as the demons, but actually worked to their harm, for they ignored available medicines and those ordinary measures of hygiene which dealt with cholera and small-pox. Today, anthropologists would point to a greater overlapping of such folk culture and sanskritic Hinduism, but this may have been a consequence of cultural changes over time, and Pettit could have been closer to the truth in emphasizing its discrete character in the 1840s.[36]

There was a pleasing open-mindedness to Pettit. Once he encountered a Brahmin, rolling himself along the ground, three to four miles a day, from Benares to Cape Cormorin and back, a stout man, of some forty years of age, and none the worse for his activity. Pettit took the trouble to discover that this was a self-imposed penance, in thanks to the gods for the birth of a son: 'it is impossible not to admire the constancy of purpose this exhibited; though when all the motives of it are weighed, it is not more extraordinary, and not a whit more religious, than that which thousands manifest in the common concerns of life.'[37]

He died in January 1873.

Tinevelly: John Pickford, CMS

After his arrival in India in December 1853, Pickford was posted to the Mission station at Pannaivelei, to the south-east of Tinevelly. Here he stayed till February 1858. It was a time of unease. Christian communities fell in and out of Hinduism. There was to be a major conflagration in 1858. Here was a missionary who began to see in caste the greatest obstacle to Mission. He spent more time with his Christian community and it is a sign of the greater maturity of Mission that more time was devoted to the needs of Indian Christians than to the quest for more converts.

Even so, itinerating was his passion. When required to transfer to the theological department of the Training Institute at Palamcottah, he begged that this should be given priority: 'there is no department of the work in which I find more enjoyment and so persuaded am I that so long as God is pleased to give me strength to labour this is my post, that no consideration with which I am at present acquainted would tempt me to give it up.'[38]

There was but a fragile frontier between being a low caste Hindu and a convert Christian. If economic factors go far to explain this transitoriness, more intriguing was the way villagers juxtaposed these competing loyalties. For Pickford the acid test was whether the converts rubbed on the sacred ash: 'I feel an increasing unwillingness to expel from the congregation unless ashes (the devil's own mark) have been rubbed on the forehead.'[39] He could even make fun of this. Confronted by a group of villagers, 'all marked very ostentatiously with ashes', and who validated their power by referring to the story of a dog, lying on a fire but disturbed by another dog, and who had then left his mark on a sick man, who had promptly recovered, he riposted: 'if such properties were contained in ashes we never ought to see a sick person in India.'[40]

In Pickford's journal we can find useful evidence of how deeply entangled Indian Christians were in the economic life of the village. One Hindu complained to Pickford at the way four Christians were trying to deprive him of his share in a palmyra tree, indicative to Pickford not only of extreme poverty—and in fact seventeen had shares in the tree—but also throwing 'a little light upon the source of the innumerable disputes which are perpetually agitating the Tamil mind'.[41]

There were to be endless land disputes. Despite his attempts to concentrate on matters of Mission, Pickford was invariably manoueuvred into dealing with these. If a court case went against them, this, Pickford dryly observed, would sort out the true believers, the chaff from the wheat. He had to do battle on their behalf with the naik or village headman. One had starved some forty-seven Christians into apostasy by denying them all employment.[42] On one occasion, he bearded the headman in his own home, 'an ample homestead', with 'a large colony of children belonging to different branches of the family', reminding Pickford 'of the patriarchal age'. If he had come on a visit for the sake of Mission, he still took time to remind the naik 'that it was the privilege of the powerful to assist the weak—and so our Christians depended very much upon him for employment, I hoped he would not act unjustly towards them'. And clearly his intervention worked. Not only did the headman give him a large supply of milk, but Pickford was later able to report: 'the Christians are very happy and thankful now that the Lord has turned the heart of the principal family towards them.'[43] Sorting out such grievances over property was clearly the primary role of a missionary.

Nevertheless, the missionary task of evangelism went on. Once, to get through to some local potters, Pickford drew on memories from home. Whereas there, to get a hearing from the weavers, he had had to pitch his voice against the noise of their shuttles, here it was simply a matter of presenting his case. One tack was flattery: 'my friend, I could not if you were to give me a hundred rupees make a pot as nicely as you.' The response was to offer him a lesson in pottery. Pickford rose to this challenge: 'I did not come for this purpose but if you have no objection you shall teach me what you can and I shall teach you what I can and I will begin.'[44] But in another village, the potters, informed of God's coming, 'only laughed and said it did not concern them'.[45]

At another village, shepherds offered, were he to pay them five rupees each, to think about Christianity. On the face of the shepherd, Pickford saw 'the conflict going on in his mind between the Hindu politeness and Hindu hatred of the gospel'.[46] However, exchanges could be friendly. In another village, when shepherds denied any recollection of his telling them of the good shepherd, he reminded them that he had been 'almost knocked down by a buffalo . . . they laughed and said they remembered that very well'.[47] Interestingly, some villagers were anxious to have their children vaccinated by a government vaccinator.[48]

But often the response was hostile. One mirasadar (a coparcenary landholder) 'thought it was a pity we should come so far especially to the Tamil people who possessed all the knowledge they required'.[49] Brahmins were perfectly happy to discuss innocuous subjects as the weather, even politics, but the moment he got onto serious things, such as man's fallen condition, 'they always decline to make any reply and go away as quickly as possible'.[50] Pickford delighted in the iconoclasm of converting a temple into a church, but when villages relapsed and there was a role reversal, 'a deep feeling of hatred stirred up against the gospel' would be left behind.[51] And when Pickford rashly took the faith to the centre of resistance at Tirenchedur, there was outright retaliation: 'as I was returning shreds of torn tracts together with dust were showered about me on every side.' The sanyasins were 'exceedingly violent . . . each shouting at the top of his voice.' Just a few had listened.[52] This was close to the events of 1857.

Post-1857, Pickford was to write to friends: 'God has been pleased to cast my lot in a province where order had been maintained—we have only been permitted to hear the fierce rumbling of the storm but how near we have been brought to murder and rapine is only known to him who can alone control the unruly wills of sinful men.'[53] And given the violence later on in 1858, Pickford was perceptive in his voicing such uncertainty.

In Pickford's writings we begin to see that increasing missionary claim that the explanation for their failure lay in caste. Indians believed that the British were just as caste conscious. One tahsildar drew attention to the differentiation between European and East Indian and claimed that punishment was devised to fit social rank. This led Pickford to ruminate that quite probably Brahmins and some Vellalas did see caste as a religious distinction, but that Nadars drew a distinction between the religious and the social.[54] But Vellala insistence on caste superiority was 'irritating': 'there is something particularly offensive to an Englishman's feelings in the ignorant pretensions of the Vellalas to superiority on account of their caste.'[55] He was uncomfortably aware of the extent to which caste sentiments still lingered among converts and recognized that were Christianity to take root, 'caste feelings, the grand barrier to the extension of the visible church as well as the great impediment to the growth of individual personal piety, must be thoroughly abandoned'. And when this occurs, 'they speak, act and think like free men'.[56] He was to end his mission to Panneivellei on a sour note, seeing caste as rampant and corruption widespread.

The role of women, for Pickford, was critical. Not that education was necessarily the way forward: 'those who have been educated even in our boarding schools go with the stream of custom after marriage.'[57] But were the wives of Indian priests and catechists to be 'God-fearing, educated and energetic women it would be a greater furtherance to our work than the introduction of a whole band of catechists'.[58]

There was a rare encounter with Islam. Pickford met an educated young man from Madras, on a visit to a village 'to cause a revival': many Muslims, through lack of a teacher for years, 'had forgotten the doctrines of the prophet'. They exchanged views on the means of salvation. The young Muslim put his faith in the four duties of prayer, alms, fasting and pilgrimage. But what, Pickford wanted to know, was 'acceptable prayer', and branded his reply of the five daily prayers as 'complacent': 'I gave as far as I was able the scriptural view of acceptable prayer, dwelling upon the broken heart and the suppliant eye of faith which looks only to the blood of Christ and not to alms or fasts or pilgrimage for acceptance.' Clearly an exchange between the evangelical, with an emphasis on inner spirituality, and one who placed more weight on outward observance, was never likely to come to any agreement: 'it is not necessary', ended Pickford, 'to give his reply.'[59] He left India in January 1868 and he died on 30 March 1882.

Masulipatam: Henry Watson Fox, CMS

In early 1842 missionary interest in south India in the new Telugu Mission was 'greater than in any other',[60] but the choice of Masulipatam (fish-town) or Bander (the port), as it was more popularly known, was somewhat strange. Once the virtual capital of Andhradesa—the French had occupied it from 1750 to 1759—and a major conduit of trade, its European garrison had been withdrawn in 1834, its Indian was to follow in 1864, and Cocanada (Kakinada) and Vizagapatam (Vishakapatnam) were to replace it as commercial entrepots. The CMS were not the first in the field. The LMS had been at Vizagapatam since 1805. In August 1836, inspired by Anthony Groves, Plymouth Brethren, George Beer and William Bowden, had come to Masulipatam, but were to move up the coast to Narasapur.[61] This narrowed the choice for the CMS. However, this was a landscape peculiarly sacred for the Hindus. Wherever rivers join the sea the land is especially sacred, and Masulipatam lay between the deltas of the rivers Kistna and Godavari. In Masulipatam alone there were twenty temples. On the river banks were the sites of many festivals. Here was an old story of Mission symbiotically attracted to the leading centres of Indian religions. The city was almost annihilated by a tidal wave in 1864.

Henry Fox, born near Durham on 1 October 1817, was along with Robert Noble, was to be one of the most highly regarded of the mid-nineteenth-century missionaries[62]. He well exemplified the new style, public school, Oxbridge recruit to Mission. Arnold's Rugby had left a deep impression: 'Rugby is my polar star, and I think of it daily.'[63] At Rugby he had already felt the call through reading Henry Martyn's memoir, though China beckoned rather than India. He had also met Charles Simeon at Cambridge. Later, Arnold was to try and persuade him that the needs of the church at home were greater than those of Mission abroad. He went up to Wadham as an exhibitioner in October 1836. At the time the university was torn apart by the Tractarian dispute. At Oxford his vocation took clearer shape: 'there is an overwhelming call, he wrote, for missionaries to the heathen, and we, the Church of England, have been bringing down punishments on our heads, by our neglect in not heeding the call; that thus some one *must* go, he who hears the call (peculiarly adapted for the service or no) must go; I hear the call, for indeed God has brought it before me on every side and go I must.'[64] In January 1840 he was told of Tucker's plans for a Telugu Mission: 'everything is ready', wrote Fox, 'except the missionary.'[65] Why, he queried, had England been granted its trade and empire if not to evangelize? He arrived in Madras on 8 July 1841.

His was to be a troubled mission with personal tragedy and serious ill-health. His wife, Elizabeth James, whom he had married on 30 December 1839, died on board ship on 6 November 1845 en route home. His son, Mark, died on the same journey. 'You know what it is to be lonely', he mourned, 'but you do'nt know what loneliness is after five years of such close and affectionate intercourse as I had with my dear wife. It is a terrible gap; nothing as yet fills it.'[66] Later, he wrote to his parents: 'at times I feel downcast by my loneliness and at such times it is an inexpressible relief to look across the water and feel your affectionate sympathy.'[67] But on the Mission trail this despondency was to vanish: 'to my astonishment (and it was all *His* doing) my loneliness, for I scarcely spoke a word of English all the while or saw a white face, was so far from being a burden, that I actually enjoyed it.'[68]

But Mission could induce depression. 'Sometimes', he confessed, 'the temptation assaults me on the way of utter distaste and disinclination to my work . . . I go as one *driven* there by conscience instead of being driven by love.'[69] He doubted his capacity. To himself he ruminated: 'I had more freedom of tongue than usual, but I long for that freedom and full command of the language to enable me to enlarge on the *fulness* of Christ . . . I fear that my method of conveying the gospel message is a very dry one.'[70] To Ragland, doyen of CMS evangelists in Tinevelly, he admitted: 'my trial and difficulty is not that of fear or danger, as St Paul's was, but first of sluggishness in going to work, and the inability, dullness and a tied tongue when in my work.'[71]

Intriguingly, it was his milleniarianism which kept him going. Until Mission spread the world over there could be no second coming: 'he who wishes to have a peculiar part assigned to him in hastening the return of his Lord, let him pray to be made a missionary'[72]; 'for myself it is a subject of frequent joy that with all my imperfections and inability I am yet an instrument in hastening the great day.'[73]

Yet he came to love India. First impressions were unfavourable. 'Everything here is', he reported, 'novel to us but not much different from what we had been led to expect.' He was particularly shocked by the plight of women: 'they seem mere miserable drudges.'[74] This was to be a constant theme in his writings. In his letters home, though, he always insisted that he lived comfortably in India, and that life on tour was particularly invigorating. On leave from 1845 to 1846, to recover his health, he wrote to Noble: 'my thoughts are continually returning to Bunder, full of happy memories and painful recollections.'[75] There is an astonishingly vivid description of a walk he took above his bungalow at Bezwada: 'here there burst on my sight a view as beautiful as it was unexpected . . . as I looked westward, lay the great river Kistna, a couple of miles in width, and studded with small islands. I had not seen so fair a scene since I left the Neilghery hills . . . I think I know none more beautiful.'[76]

Fox may have laid claim to good health, but here he did not know himself. By late 1847, he was desperately ill with dysentery. A period at sea did not help matters. According to medical opinion, 'his constitution is altogether unsuited for the tropical climate'.[77] There was no alternative but to return to England. By April he was back in Durham. Although he delighted in the English spring, 'not for one moment can these enjoyments compete with thoughts and regrets of India'.[78] He was appointed assistant-secretary to the CMS. He died on 11 October 1848.

If Fox and Noble were sent to Masulipatam both to evangelize and teach, here again itinerating took precedence. 'Our dear brother Mr Noble', he wrote to his brother, George, 'is tied up with the management of the English school . . . it is a most interesting and important sphere, to which if he did not give his time it would be my part to give mine.' But he went on: 'and this because no one will come out from England to take his work off our hands.'[79] Clearly teaching was but second best. Later the school was held responsible for controversial conversions (to be discussed below) and Fox reported how the citizens of the town viewed the school 'as thoroughly opposed to their religion'.[80]

Initially, Fox kept to the villages and, at best, to the outskirts of the town. This was in part through lack of confidence in his Telugu and in part out of fear for the Brahmins. Masulipatam was evidently a difficult city to get to know: 'I am trying to get acquainted with my diocese but ten years wo'nt suffice me for my purpose, for the blind alleys are the rule and streets the exception, and people are suspicious and do'nt like to see a European wandering in and out about the privacy of their narrow lanes.'[81] He rather dreaded the prospect of encounters with 'glibly speaking, noisy, unbelieving scoffing fellows . . . I assure you I am often afraid of a noisy Brahmin'.[82] Meetings in private homes were preferable: here, 'instead of wrangling about negative truths as I have often to do in the villages and streets when showing up idolatry', he could enjoy 'invaluable opportunities of delivering positive truth'. Admittedly, even so, partly through his faulty grasp of language, partly what one would 'naturally expect when with idolatrous minds they begin first to grasp divine truths', there were misunderstandings, e.g. one Hindu interpreted the admonition to join God's family as advice to become a sanyasin (surely a not unreasonable response).[83] Half his time was spent in the town, half 'in my snug tent. . . . very joyful'[84] on tour.

One major challenge was the festivals. There was the great three day festival, Siva-Ratri or Siva night, at Callapilly. Just a few people would visit his tent, though he was glad not to have to distribute too many tracts, for he doubted that they would be read: 'it is a serious reflection that I am here alone in the middle of Satan's kingdom . . . here he is rampant and triumphant; not a soul out of the thousands here but is a sworn servant of his.'[85] At one point, some Brahmins told him to get out of the way as 'the god was coming'; even the spearmen of the zamindars 'began to press up against me', and he deemed it wise to take evasive action: 'I was more astonished than annoyed at this rudeness which is so unusual towards Europeans.'[86] If he was to enjoy more success at the annual festival at Manghalagherry, this, he realized, he owed to a pro-missionary collector, 'but it was a subject of great rejoicing that I have been permitted to preach Christ to such great numbers, who have never heard of him before, without obstruction or opposition'.[87] Visits to Bezwada, a leading Brahmin centre on the Kistna, became a peculiar challenge: 'wherever any pickings or stealings are to be found, either from festivals or from visitors to sacred spots, there are abundance of lazy, vicious Brahmins to be found.'[88]

Inevitably, Fox came to doubt the efficacy of this itinerating strategy. What could one hope to communicate in ten minutes or so on the hoof? 'My hope', he recorded, 'is that by going frequently at short intervals to the same spots and speaking to the same people I may convey from time to time a new idea, so that at last they may get drummed into their ears and understanding some slight knowledge of the way of salvation.'[89] There were just too few missionaries: 'I daily feel my insufficiency here, single-handed among so many thousands.'[90] 'I rode 250 miles in a straight line, through a populous country, passing through villages every three or four miles, and seeing many others in all directions . . . but in all that district there was not a single Christian missionary.'[91] Besides, there were so many varied tasks: 'who is sufficient to unite in his own person these multifarious duties—preacher, teacher, superintendent of schools, translator, not for hundreds but for tens and hundreds of thousands.'[92] He had to live with the knowledge, conveyed by one of Noble's students, that 'the people crowd around you, not because they care to hear what you have to say, but they think you are mad, so they come for mere curiosity's sake'.[93] Alternatively, they were seen as but emissaries of the Company.

Increasingly, indeed, Fox blamed the Company for his lack of success: 'how great is the blood-guiltiness on the head of the East India Company, for not having sent missionaries and established Christian Bible schools.' But he also faulted the Church and the universities for not sending out more missionaries.[94]

However cussidly, Fox did make an attempt of sorts to grapple with Hinduism, in all its expressions. He had this to say on his servants, both Hindu and Muslim, and their faith: 'I do not think they have any system of belief to be overcome but will be willing to believe what "Master" tells them is true . . . However, the belief would go but a very little way; for the obstacles of disbelief, caste, etc, are but mere trifles compared with the opposition of the natural heart which is to be found in every land.' But could one get through when 'lightness of mind, half-belief, want of seriousness are the almost universal characteristics of the people regarding the idols?'[95] There was no naivety here about any easy conversion and exasperation began to surface. He came to the conclusion that Hindus exhibited a greater faith the less the proof and the more impossible the belief: 'the utter ignorance not only of history but of the very existence of such a thing as *history* prevents a Hindu from at all appreciating the value of external evidence.'[96] He held the Puranas in particular scorn: 'a set of books holding very much the position of the semi-fabulous monkish tales and lives of the saints.'[97] In the end, his judgement was bleak: 'with the people, high and low, Brahmins and Pariahs, their only ideas are of the world, low, material, grovelling, fleshly, or else bare, cold, intellectual, fruitless abstraction of the mind.'[98] Here mere prejudice prevailed.

One opportunity for theological debate came with his munshis. These he was to change quite frequently. There was a Vaishnavite, a Nyogi Brahmin, with his one yellow and two white perpendicular streaks, and with a dread of pollution. They discussed salvation. The munshi failed to see how one man could take on the punishment of another: this would not be permitted in a court of law. Fox resorted to the metaphor of paying off someone else's debt.[99] Time and again Fox ran up against a Vedantist rejection of the Christian concept of sin: 'he stated a vile doctrine of Man's irresponsibility by stating that we are not free-will agents, that we have no power to do good or evil , that all our power is from God and so that God is the cause of all our sin.' On another tack, the munshi viewed sin as a transgression of custom: 'just because infanticide and adultery among the Todars and the Nielgherries or robbery among the maravers of Tinevelly were customary, they were not sinful: the shastras sanctioned such a view of custom.'[100] One munshi admitted that idols were but means to focus the thoughts of the 'poor and unlearned'.

Fox determined to have Vedantism out with one of his munshis who professed 'to be learned in this most empty of all vain philosophies'. If the soul dictates to the body, and here he was trying to get inside the mind of Vedantism, the body includes not just the flesh, 'but in addition to the senses, the mind, intelligence, feelings, passions, wisdom, energy and indeed every piece and part of man who we Europeans suppose to form the man'. The individual does not sin and is incapable of sinning: 'the soul neither feels joy nor sorrow, desire or aversion, in as much as he partakes of the general character of the eternal being who is without attributes, and of whom nothing can be predicted but existence.' Man has no responsibility. And as the soul is to be one day reunited with God, 'the body, viz that composite body of intelligence, mind, feelings and physical frame, all utterly perish at death. Hence the doctrine comes to deny what we mean by immortality of the soul, for what they call a soul is a phantom over and above what we understand by the term'. Here, indeed, was a total failure of understanding. 'I could not find much to say against so monstrous a system', Fox acknowledged, 'which starts on such totally various principles from ours.' Hardly surprisingly, when Fox begged the munshi 'to give me proof of its truths', he, in his turn, quickly abandoned the attempt.[101] There were to be many like unproductive encounters with Brahmins on his tours, especially in Bezwada.

Fox likewise tried to come to terms with popular Hinduism. He was to meet with less resistance. When he took up polytheism with some villagers, 'they had no objection to make and were not offended at what I said, so we parted good friends'.[102] Villagers might take evasive action: 'one very common state of mind seems to be to neglect your questions of fact and to wander into those of "how", "wherefore", and "whence".'[103] When weavers described the lingams tied around their necks, encased in a silver box, not as a piece of stone but as god, Fox rather surprised himself by thinking of 'the parallel case of substantiation'.[104] When warned that they would go to hell should they not pray, one fisherman replied: 'I have got no sense, this will do for people of understanding, what can I do about it.'[105]

Most promising was his contact with the outcastes. On one occasion, in conversation with pariah women, one explained that they could not visit temples. Instead, they worshipped a stone, Marilamma. Yes, they were, they admitted, sinful not to worship god. But how to get rid of sin? 'These people struck me very much as being of a different race from the upper castes; the women had all the vulgarity but at the same time the open familiarity of any fishwives in England.'[106] He discovered that the chuklus, the shoe-makers of Masulipatam, worshipped not a stone but a crude carving of the village goddess, Ammevaru, together with the carving of her husband.[107] But missionary work among the outcastes was so entirely different 'as to remind one much of missionary labours in lands where caste, civilization and a system of heathenism are all unknown'.[108] Fox was in no doubt of their abject poverty. He anticipated that they were the best prospect for Mission: 'a very poor, oppressed people, yet seem not to have that superstition or those religious lies and priestcraft to restrain them from a profession of the gospel, which the upper classes have.'[109]

Fox came somewhat closer than most missionaries to reading Hindu popular culture. His was a confused response to a wedding. The actions and dress of the dancing girl 'were not indecent, for she was much more clothed than the women usually are, but her appearance was bold and forward and the whole effect was most unpleasant'. He could discern no 'discoverable tune' in the music.[110] He witnessed a funeral. The brother of the deceased was pushing skull and ashes into the flame: 'he did this with the composure of a furious labourer stirring up a pile of burning weeds.' One family were 'talking and chattering as if it was an ordinary business and when we went to speak to them showed no sort of grief or concern'. When Fox took up the theme of judgement, they 'showed that they were in no wise impressed with seriousness or a sense of solemnity of the meaning of death'.[111]

On the occasion of Dussehra, all sought the blessing of the tools of their trade and Fox could not forgive the collector for allowing the paper-work in the cutcherry likewise to be blessed. On the final day, he had expected 'some little display of pomp and tinsel finery': instead, the crowds gathered as 'one might see a crowd collecting for a horse race or prize fight'. His is a clear account of the procession of the gods: 'Lakshmi the heroine was seated or rather lifted above a great white horse, beneath which crouched a figure of one of the asuras (devils). Another was Narasimha, incarnation of Vishnoo, a man-lion mounted on an uncouth monster-lion.' Breaking the small branches of a pipal tree was 'in some way emblematical or commemorative of the final slaughter of the asuras'. 'All the while the images were on the ground there were a number of people standing about them without a shadow of reverence in their manner towards the gods.' He concluded: 'after witnessing the whole scene I thought what a farce it was to talk of the "religious feeling of the Hindoos", as old Indians at India House have been wont to do: we might as well talk of religious feeling of your attendants at Greenwich fair . . . It reminded one very much altogether, mutatis mutandi, of an English fair: there was a knot of gamblers, squatted on the ground instead of standing around a table, here an old woman with her heap of sweetmeats spread out on the ground instead of a stall . . . I believe the same debauchery attends both occasions.'[112]

There is the makings of the anthropologist's field report in his account of bathing festivals, but, once again, the evangelical intrudes. He visited the annual Sivaratri festival at Collapilly. When he enquired about 'the tawdry image either Vishnu or Siva', why did they provide 'mere toys for worship, instead of serving god, they made the common answer of patting their stomach to show that it was their livelihood.' 'Men and women were mingled together promiscuously. The booths reminded me much, as did much of the scene besides, of the outskirts of an English race-course.'[113] The Mangelagherry Krishna festival struck him likewise as an English fair, 'without its riot or drunkenness, but instead of that defiled with idolatry'. In reply to his question as to why some inflicted self-torture on themselves, 'I was assured it was not for religion or devotion but simply to collect a few pence from the bystanders'.[114]

On a visit to a temple to Durga at Bezwada, a young priest offered him an orange from the offerings to the goddess. This prompted Fox to write: 'truly there is no life in these people, no sense of anything greater than themselves, or any belief in anything more important than this life.'[115]

Somehow the penny refused to drop that Hinduism was in many ways a this-worldly faith, deeply woven into the every day, in many ways mundane, even a sport, an entertainment, a way of escape. All that self-regarding, intensely serious, priggish, evangelical outlook could not perceive how Hinduism was a way of life.

Masulipatam: John Edmund Sharkey, CMS

For someone Indian-born, Sharkey could not share Fox's allusiveness to England, though he was to display a very English puritanism, or rather, Victorian prudishness. A nude statue at a festival of Krishna, 'in full figure', with the gopis, prompted the response: 'it was a melancholy picture of the entire depravity of the human heart, a savage disruption of all moral order, a fearful outrage on decency, hateful to God and pernicious to man'. Clearly he was outraged that the young of both sexes should see such an 'obscene figure' paraded about the streets.[116] Erotic temple sculpture 'with all their agglomerations of vile representations embracing every conceivable form and act of uncleanness' elicited the same response.[117]

He joined the Masulipatam Mission in 1847. 'Old Fox', as he called him, was to be his mentor in itinerating. On rare occasions, Sharkey suggested that events were getting on top of him: 'to me it was a season of much trial as I felt that surrounded as I was by a large party of excited heathens and assailed by men who endeavoured to confound me by an infinite number of Sanskrit phrases and allusions, my entire dependence was on one above who alone can give the wisdom which no man can gainsay or resist.'[118] But Sharkey had on that occasion just endured a formal dispute with four Vaishnavites. He was, in fact, exceptionally robust, and to be quite unfazed by any encounter, with Hindus and Muslims alike. Evangelical protestantism had embarked on its mission confident it could storm the citadels of Indian religions. In Sharkey's writings we can trace yet another missionary who was to scapegoat caste for its failure to do so.

With good cause, Sharkey complained at the shortage of missionaries. There were but five attached to the Mission, and two were school teachers. The population of Masulipatam itself was 52,000. In a typical winter tour Sharkey would cover an area of some 4510 square miles, taking in around 1600 villages, with a population of some 5,00,000. This was his method. They would pitch their tent in one central village and would visit all villages within a two mile radius. They would then move on and repeat the process. This he seemingly undertook without Indian assistants, for strikingly absent from his accounts, as also in Fox's, is any reference to Indian catechists, or any commentary of a need for an Indian clergy. (But this may just be an oversight in their journals.) Clearly a follow-up visit was crucial: a Brahmin might well, in the meanwhile, have been sent to undo his damage. In one village, where on the first visit four families had shown an interest, he found on the second, two had moved into another village, one had been 'considerably intimidated', the fourth had lost interest. Sharkey did see that here was a need for a suitable full-time agent and the opening of a vernacular school.[119] Interestingly, the new irrigation canal system of the Godavari and the Kistna very considerably facilitated Mission: 'instead of long, rugged roads and impassable marshes, a missionary might now with a small boat and with comparatively little expense and still less labour visit and revisit many a village and town.'

But was Mission getting anywhere? 'The missionary', stated Sharkey, 'is trusted by all and with civility and even kindness. The prejudice of caste and the worship of idols are evidently on the wane. The influence of mercenary priests and the veneration of their sacred books are by no means as strong as they were.'[120] Yet the evidence of Sharkey's own journal shows this to be self-deception.

Hindus regarded missionaries with suspicion. They believed they were agents of the Company and found it hard to credit that it did not pay their salary. Sharkey, with 'feelings of shame and pain', had to deny that they were paid a certain fee per convert.[121] Did they not come, they feared, on some revenue matter? Of course, such association with the Sircar (Company) could work to missionary advantage: the very word 'has a peculiar spell about it, possessing the power of securing a certain amount of external homage which may yet exist with the greatest disaffection and bitterness of spirit'.[122] Quite possibly the hostility of Salai Street had spread to the Andhra villages: 'some of the Brahmins of the village had been to Madras . . . and had brought with them the strong feeling against Christianity which the heathen community there cherished . . . The village had received instructions from Madras cautioning the people against affording the Christian missionaries the remotest encouragement.'[123]

In fact, Indians took greater pleasure in maligning the Company's administration of justice and the debauched lives of Europeans and comparing the constitution of civil society in Europe and caste rather than mulling over matters missionary. One young man was keen to discuss the rumour that 'British rule was rapidly approaching its dissolution'.

Nevertheless, missionary visits were seen as highly threatening. Theirs was a polluting presence. In one village, panic set in that Sharkey 'would impregnate the wells of the village with a medical ingredient calculated to win over the villages to Christ'. It took time for the villagers to conclude that the padre was 'a quiet, kind and harmless man'.[124]

But why indeed had they come? Would the villagers have to wear European clothes? One of the more damaging charges was that once converted, the missionaries would forget them: 'that our professions of kindness were empty and that if we studied to be benevolent it was assumed to cover certain evil designs on them and that all our charity and interest in the welfare of the natives terminates with their conversion.' Afterwards, 'it costs no pangs or sorrow to see them as prey to the torments of a violated conscience and to the distress and misery arising from excommunication from caste.'[125] And neglect of these new Christian communities was, indeed, one of the failings of Mission.

Sharkey was himself an excellent example of ideology in action. He came with an agenda: 'it is my plan on all occasions to dwell much on the disparity of man, the nature of sin and its punishment, the moral responsibility of man and the infinite character of god's attribution, his justice in particular. I then dwell on Christ, his nature, atonement and willingness to receive and pardon the vilest of sinners.'[126] He made several confident summary assessments of the opposition. He tried to square a this-worldliness in Hinduism with its mysticism. Only those thoroughly demoralized by a life-time of dissipation, he argued, took to contemplation. Hinduism was highly flexible: 'I am aware that Hinduism, like Popery, is an ever fluctuating system, now rigid, now lax, now lost in accommodation, now concentrated in persecution—and it is this elastic peculiarity which has saved it from ruin and extinction.'

Clearly no one visit to a village would suffice: 'the hammer of God's word must strike again and again. Idolatry still allures. Ignorance still besots. Superstition still overawes. Priestcraft still prevails. Caste still domineers.' But Christianity was a new challenge: here was 'truth supported by evidence, too strong to be overcome by any fair process of reasoning and at the same time too plain not to strike the most superficial observer'.[127] At the outset of his career, Sharkey had expected to storm the citadel.

In one long statement, Sharkey portrayed the nature of Hindu worship in the mission. In Masulipatam there were the twenty-four temples (had they increased?) to Vishnu and Siva. In the surrounding villages, on a calculation of two temples per village, there were a further 3200 temples. Amongst phenomenon worshipped, he listed the sun, the moon, the stars (said to be souls of dead ancestors); animals, e.g. bulls, bats, cobras, monkeys; vegetables, e.g. the tulasi, gooseberry, fig. 'They believe in god, but a god unknown, they admit sin but know not its origin, understand not its depth, malignity.' The Brahmins themselves were sceptical, even atheistical, but this they kept hidden. They had indoctrinated the middle classes. They believed in god as a supreme essence, but saw him as 'a silent spectator of what occurs, and this inevitably undermined any real fear of God'. Far preferable to Sharkey, far more sincere, was the worship of the poor.[128]

Sharkey's journal is studded with incidental observations on the institutional life of Brahmins and Hindus. If he recognized that Indian temples were homes for the gods rather than places of worship, he could still argue of the sanctum sanctorum: 'surely this miserably narrow, dark and confined pagoda can convey but a wretchedly false and altogether, dishonourable view of god's omniscience.' And if he saw that Hindus had come to the temple to sell, to petition, to render thanks, he could not refrain from observing: 'not one professed to have come to have his sins pardoned and removed.'[129] When one priest offered him fruit from gifts to the temple, this he saw to be the devil's work, to get him 'to honour before a hundred watching eyes what he had just been condemning'.[130] And if he grasped the limited role of temple priests, he still put it in a derogatory way: 'presiding at certain ceremonies, repeating a number of prayers without the understanding, smatterings of Manu's laws and flourishing some popular saying or moral in Sanskrit verse.'[131] But there was nothing here on their being in attendance on the gods.

Brahmins reacted in varying ways. One, in an agraharam (Brahmin village), when challenged on reading a Sanskrit grammar rather than a work of religion, retorted: 'I am already a religious man. I have inherited my religion from my ancestors who have examined it for me. Besides, I am no sinner, to trouble myself as to the means of salvation. All my exertions will not procure for me more than I already have.'[132] Some would not be drawn into conversation: 'as they surveyed us from head to foot I asked them if they wished to speak to me. With much indifference and in an insulting contemptuous turn of the face, one of them replied in the negative.'[133] Others, if quiet and attentive, would not concede that idolatry was wrong or that the Puranas were suspect. Some took the offensive: 'Show us God. Is the soul distinct from God? What is Hell? Why is transmigration not true? and many such questions. After a long discussion in which one of them was very noisy they parted.'[134] Whereas Fox had found the Brahmins in one village 'listless', Sharkey was to be agreeably surprised: 'they listened with attention, they questioned and enquired and moreover manifested what they never before did, civility.'[135] But Brahmins believed they were winning the battle: missionaries could only convert pariahs and, besides, were just as mercenary as themselves.[136]

Behind these varied human reactions from the 'learned class' lay that characteristically intermittent theological exchange. Preponderance of the subject of sin suggests that Sharkey gave the lead, but Vedantism was also the issue. Rather delightfully, one sastri found the whole concept of redemption far too complicated: why couldn't god simply remove sin at a stroke? One sanyasin, who believed that renunciation and contemplation sufficed for salvation from sin, was not at all pleased to be told of the atonement. Were he to read the gospel, this would imply that all his activities, his penances, his learning and his pilgrimages, had been pointless. 'Besides, he had read enough already.'[137] Sharkey had the nerve to ask another sanyasin whether he thought he was on the right track: was 'he answering the design of his maker by shutting himself up in a closet and so wantonly and violently diverting and deadening the powers of body and mind from their legitimate exercise'. He replied, 'with a mixture of angry indifference and obscure expression', and 'with curses', 'that he believed nothing'.[138] An old and learned pandit discussed the atonement and redemption but 'of course thought the old wine as good if not better': abstraction and meditation would lead to Nirvana.

But Sharkey failed to see, and here he grappled with Vedantism, how if matter was at the root of all evil, as Hindus believed, endless reincarnations through matter could lead to purity; how, if there be a multiplicity of sins in the first incarnation, there could possibly be less in the second.[139] In another exchange, he asked how Sankara could exercise equal salvific powers as Christ when he had not died for mankind and had the blood of a thousand Buddhists on his hands: 'love was never characteristic of Sankara's doctrine.'[140] Sharkey would have no truck with any parallel between Christ and either Krishna or Ram. One Brahmin reflected on the fact that in Hinduism incarnations came to destroy the wicked rather than to save, and that even if their own crimes were as obnoxious as those they had come to punish, the end justified the means.[141] But was not the concept of resurrection, Sharkey speculated, a new one for the Hindus?

In one formal encounter, a Brahmin, who expressed respect for Christ, quizzed Sharkey as to why he slighted their incarnations, 'since you cannot but admit God is in them also, unless you deny his omnipresence'.[142] And that was the rub. In the concept of Nirvana, Vedantism and Pantheism had a perfectly coherent analogue with the Atonement. Sharkey did his best. On one occasion he raised the question: if we are all one with god, 'how is it that we are so ignorant of one another's hearts? Is God then ignorant of himself? How is it that our ideas of right and wrong vary so much and that there should be so much difference in our respective pursuits and pleasures? Is God then a Being of such conflicting attributes?'[143] But these were points of view which refused to lend themselves to constructive dialogue and, all too often, turned to abuse. What is one to make of a man who rudely interrupted a public reading of the Ramayana to question 'if that book contained any clearly defined way of salvation'.[144]

In the same way as Fox, Sharkey felt closer to the outcaste. Their being forced to live apart in malas or pariah villages, drew them all the more to the attention of the missionaries. Was this not, Sharkey pondered, an example of 'wise providence' 'overruling the odious distinction' for the good, for had the pariahs been intermixed with the sudras, 'it is very probable they would not have heard the gospel'.[145] But what were the outcastes to make of the missionaries? 'We endeavoured to tell them of Christ. They scarcely knew what we meant, so little removed in knowledge they appeared to be from the brute creation.' They were too late to change for the better, they claimed, 'so they must remain as they were without security and temporal comfort and without any notion whatever of future judgement, hell and misery'.[146]

But the pariahs had their own priests. And Sharkey had much to say on their deities. They had as many female deities as there were objects in nature, he observed. Outcastes lived in fear of evil spirits. These had to be propitiated with gifts of rice, meat and toddy. There was a goddess of cholera with an insatiable thirst for human blood. When cholera struck, a wooden idol was carved, blessed and taken to the edge of the village and 'cast out, as a sign that the plague has left the village'. Itinerant pariahs carried the goddess, Amaravelu, a female Vishnu or Siva, from village to village, the idol a thanksgiving for those who had escaped the disease.

But some pariahs were to become better disposed to these missionary visits. The weavers in one village 'look upon me as their friend and this is a great point gained when in every other village the missionary is associated with fears and bodings of the worst kind'.[147] Clearly, the outcastes were not such easy spoils for Mission, but here two rejected groups were in time to find one another.

In the process, Sharkey acquired a new awareness of caste. 'Caste', he argued, 'warped everything', 'cramped the mental faculties'. It 'was a sore hindrance to the progress of the useful arts'.[148] And, of course, there could be no greater clash of cultural values than that between caste and the Victorian cult of individualism, the ethic of Samuel Smiles and the self-made man. Sharkey had become keenly aware of the hold of caste in a long battle for the conversion of a Brahmin (discussed below). This led to a long statement on caste, worth quoting in full.

He wrote:

Caste is indeed an iron hand from Satan's forge. No immorality can break it, no natural tie is so powerful. It controls conscience, influences opinion, and gives birth to habits and manners abhorrent to humanity, subversion of all rules of decency and fatally opposed to the religion of love which we everywhere preach and teach. In a Christian church its existence is poison and pain to members, grief and pain to the pastor. In heathen assemblies the missionary soon discovers his chief barrier to be something else than religious prejudice and superstitious tendentiousness. It is not some favourite idol god, some long cherished worship, some name of reverence or some bond of natural affection—all these exert indeed their sway and kill their thousands, it is caste, caste, which slays its tens of thousands, is the missionary's great obstacle.[149]

This was the critical shift in missionary explanation for its failure to win over the high castes, to dwell on the social dimensions of Hinduism rather than its metaphysical and religious.

Sharkey had such few dealings with Muslims that he was asked if he 'was preaching to them also'. In his usual abrasive way, Sharkey soon contrived to upset them as well. 'The suffering of Christ was to them', he observed, 'a subject of ridicule.'[150] Sharkey ran up against the usual arguments on the corruption of texts. There was 'a long and apparently fruitless conversation' with Muslims in Gudur, though not before Sharkey had denied Mahommed his miraculous powers, and brazenly accused Islam of being 'ill adapted to the spiritual wants of mankind'.[151]

He met an Afghan faqir, who, in despair at finding salvation through Islam, had burnt all his Persian manuscripts.[152]

Sharkey died at sea on 26 May 1869, en route from Masulipatam to Madras for medical treatment.

Through the neglect of 'old' mission in Tanjore in this text, this is a lop-sided account of mission in the south. Under George Pope (SPG), there was to be a contentious, but ultimately abortive, attempt to rejuvenate the Indian Christian community along Tinevelly lines. However, I have described this story elsewhere and will not repeat myself.[153]

1857 AND MISSION

There was no rebellion in the south in 1857. Sharkey thankfully wrote: 'thro this year of terrible anarchy and outrage in so many parts of our empire, all our households thro this Presidency have been preserved to us in peace and the good word of the Lord has gone on unobstructed by the heathen.'[154] This project has only incidentally set out to be a contribution to the historiography of 1857. Yet the rebellion profoundly reflected on the missionary enterprise and forced an anguished reappraisal of policy.

Mission was determined to demonstrate that it was not to blame for the rebellion. Did not, so the argument went, the lack of rebellion in the more deeply evangelized rural Bengal and the south prove that the attempted spread of Christianity had not destabilized Empire? On the contrary, had it not helped to shore it up? And did not the comparative weakness of Islam in the south compared with its militancy in the north, the epicentre of the rebellion, substantiate the claim of Mission that Islam was the true protagonist? Today's explanation that the severity of the rebellion in the north west lay in a preemptive strike against a dreaded foreign intervention—this incorporated a loathing of Mission—was not an argument at the time. But it still leaves open the question as to whether Mission should be held responsible for such an anticipatory move.

On the other hand, if one concurs with the the interpretation of 1857 by nationalist minded Indian historians as essentially an expression of cultural nationalism rather than, for obvious reasons, political,[155] it seems impossible to reject missionary provocation, however limited its extent, as a contributory factor.

Post-1857, missionary organizations took the offensive, and sought to reverse the policy they saw as the cause of rebellion, the Company's policy of religious neutrality. Had the Company actively supported Mission, the rebellion would never have happened. They determined to interpret all official statements, above all Queen Victoria's proclamation, in this light. But the supportive views of Chief-Commissioner, Sir Herbert Edwardes, and the Lieutenant-Governor of the Punjab, Sir John Lawrence, were more than outweighed by those of Sir George Clark, Permanent Under-Secretary of State for India, Lord Ellenborough, Secretary of State for India, and his successor, Lord Stanley.[156] They drew the opposite lesson, that Indians had risen in defence of their faiths, and enjoined the new administration of the Raj to implement the strictest possible policy of non-intervention.

One is tempted to argue that missionary organizations were so mortified by this defeat that, the better to legitimize their own account of events, they doggedly persisted with a strategy of itinerating, long after it had been shown that it would not work. Paradoxically, in Sir Charles Wood's education policy of 1854, Mission had been offered a quite extraordinary potential new access of influence—grants-in-aid to missionary schools. Although the offer was in part taken up, Mission, perversely, was not at this stage to change its strategy and did not fully grasp this new opportunity until the 1880s. Here is striking proof of just how obstinate and persistent an ideology can be.

NOTES AND REFERENCES

1. For summary statements, see *The Church Missionary Atlas*, London: 1896 (eighth edn), pp. 137–51; Eugene Stock, *History of the Church Missionary Society*, vol. I, London: 1899; H. P. Thompson, *Into All Lands*, London: 1951; Stephen Neill, *A History of Christianity in India 1707–1858*, Cambridge: 1985, pp. 215–22. For a detailed and impartial account of Tamilnadu, see Hugald Grafe, *Tamilnadu in the Nineteenth and Twentieth Centuries: History of Christianity in India*, vol. II, part 2, Bangalore: 1990.

2. Grafe, p. 24.

3. Fred Clothey, On the Study of Religion in South India: An Assessment, in G. A. Oddie (ed.), *Recent Writings on the Social and Cultural Aspects of Modern South Indian History*, p. 327.

4. C. J. Fuller, *Servants of the Goddess: The Priests of a South Indian Temple*, Cambridge: 1984, p. 8.

5. Reginald Heber, *Narrative of a Journey*, vol. III, London: 1828, pp. 451–2.

6. Grafe, pp. 140–4.

7. Ibid., p. 146.
8. Grafe cites Caldwell's *Comparative Grammar of the Dravidian and South Indian Tamil Languages* (first published in 1856) and Pope's English translation of the *Tirrukkural* (first published in 1886). See Grafe, ch. VII.
9. Tucker to Venn, 22 February 1843, Correspondence of the Secretary of the Committee, CMS 12 F 20 (UTC: Bangalore).
10. Tucker, 13 January 1845, ibid.
11. 22 September 1841, CMS 5.
12. Tucker, 19 July 1843, CMS 12.
13. Tucker, 22 July 1845, ibid.
14. Tucker, 13 October 1846, ibid.
15. Eric Stokes, C. A. Bayly (ed.), *The Peasant Armed: The Indian Rebellion of 1857*, Oxford: 1986.
16. Tucker, 15 January 1846, ibid.
17. This whole episode now tends to feature in any account of proto-nationalist activity in Tamil Nadu. R. Suntharalingam got there first in his *Politics and Nationalist Awakening in South India 1852–1891*, Tucson: 1974.
18. He was to die quite literally from shame for some sexual misdemeanour with a sailor on the lower deck. See William Golding, *Rites of Passage*, London: 1980.
19. Revd James Joseph Haydn Louis, 9 March 1838, CI 2/091/1 (CMS: Birmingham).
20. Louis, Journal, 3 August 1838, CI 2/091/5.
21. Louis, Journal, 6 August 1838, ibid.
22. Louis, Journal, 29 July 1838, CI 2/091/15.
23. Louis, Journal, 7 October 1839 CI 2/091/8.
24. Louis, Journal, 2 November 1838, CI 2/091/7.
25. Louis, Journal, 7 October 1839, CI 2/091/8.
26. Louis, Journal, 30 December 1848, CI 2/091/14a, b.
27. Louis, Journal, 8 December 1839, CI 2/091/7.
28. George Pettit, 8 April 1834, CI 2/0 188/4 (CMS: Birmingham).
29. George Pettit, *The Tinevelly Mission of the CMS*, London: 1851. Grafe reads it as a work of 'a missionary of long standing and with a deep sense for the social and sociological dimensions of the impact of the Christian faith', Grafe, p. 6.
30. For one account, see M. E. Gibbs, 'Catechists in the Tinevelly Mission in the first half of the 19th century', *Bulletin of the Church Association of India*, no. 8, September 1965.
31. Neill, p. 221.
32. Pettit, *Tinevelly Mission*, pp. 134–5.
33. Ibid., p. 83.
34. J. E. Lesslie Newbiggin, *A South Indian Diary*, London: 1951, p. 44.
35. Pettit, p. 251.
36. Pettit, 482–95.
37. Ibid., p. 300.
38. Revd John Pickford to Revd Knight, 24 September 1858, CI 2/0 189/3 (CMS: Birmingham).
39. Pickford, Journal, 22 June 1856, CI 2/0 189/13.

40. Pickford, Journal, 4 July 1856, CI 2/0 189/14.
41. Pickford, Journal, 23 November 1856, CI 2/0 189/15.
42. Pickford, Journal, 24 October 1855, CI 2/0 189/12.
43. Pickford, Journal, 7 February 1856, CI 2/0 189/13.
44. Pickford, Journal, 15 February 1856, CI 2/0 189/10.
45. Pickford, Journal, 10 March 1856, ibid.
46. Pickford, Journal, 10 October 1855, CI 2/0 189/12.
47. Pickford, Journal, 26 October 1855, ibid.
48. Pickford, Journal, 19 January 1855, CI 2/0 189/13.
49. Pickford, Journal, 12 July 1855, CI 2/0 189/12.
50. Pickford, Journal, 12 April 1855, CI 2/0 189/11.
51. Pickford, Journal, 21 March 1855, CI 2/0 189/10.
52. Pickford, Journal, 5 March 1857, CI 2/0 189/16.
53. Pickford to London friends, 10 February 1858, CI 2/0 189/22.
54. Pickford, Journal, 23 July 1856, CI 2/0 189/14.
55. Pickford, Journal, 24 January, CI 2/0 189/16.
56. Pickford, Journal, 24 January 1857, CI 2/0 189/16.
57. Pickford, Journal, 17 July 1855, CI 2/0 189/12.
58. Pickford to Knight, 27 January 1860, CI 2/0 189/3.
59. Pickford, Journal, 17 August 1856, CI 2/0 189/14.
60. John Tucker, 21 October 1842, CMS 20 F20 (UTC: Bangalore).
61. For their story, see E. B. Bromley, *They were Men Sent from God,* Bangalore: 1937. Groves did not accompany them. He stayed behind in Madras to earn his keep as a dentist.
62. For biographical information, see his brother's account, Revd George Fox, *A Memoir of the Revd Henry Watson Fox,* London: 1850.
63. Fox's Journal, 20 October 1837. He kept a journal long before he was required to do so as a missionary, quoted ibid., p. 74.
64. Fox to John Emeris, 9 January 1840, quoted ibid., p. 82.
65. Ibid., pp. 88–9.
66. Fox to Noble, 6 November 1845, quoted ibid., p. 161.
67. Fox to his parents, 22 March 1847, quoted ibid., p. 240.
68. Fox to John Emeris, 27 March 1847, quoted ibid., p. 243.
69. Fox to his brother, George, 20 April 1847, quoted ibid., p. 245.
70. Fox, Journal, 8 September 1847, quoted ibid., p. 294.
71. Fox to Ragland, 7 September 1847, quoted ibid., p. 316.
72. Fox to Revd J. Y. Nicholson, 25 February 1857, quoted ibid., p. 232.
73. Fox to his brother, George, 9 July 1847, quoted ibid., p. 306.
74. Fox, Journal, 8 July 1841, C1 2/0 100/2 (CMS: Birmingham).
75. Fox to Noble, 17 July 1846, quoted George Fox, p. 179.
76. Fox, Journal, 28 August 1847, quoted ibid., pp. 285–6.
77. T. Ragland, 14 January 1848, CMS 13 (UTC: Bangalore).
78. Fox to Sharkey, 9 May 1848, quoted George Fox, p. 334.
79. Quoted ibid., p. 145.
80. Fox to his brother, George, 20 April 1847, quoted ibid., p. 248.
81. Fox to his brother, Robert, 9 July 1845, quoted ibid., p. 152.

82. Fox to his brother, George, 21 April 1845, quoted ibid., p. 150.
83. Fox, Journal, 25 March 1845, C1 2/0 100/6.
84. Fox to his brother, George, 17 February 1847, quoted George Fox, pp. 226–7.
85. Fox, Journal, 13 February 1847, quoted ibid., p. 199.
86. Ibid., pp. 201–2.
87. Fox, Journal, 3 March 1847, quoted ibid., p. 218.
88. Fox, Journal, 19 August 1847, quoted ibid., pp. 270–1.
89. Fox, Journal, 2 July 1845, C1 2/0 100/6.
90. Fox to his brother, George, 15 January 1845, quoted George Fox, p. 144.
91. Fox to Revd Nicholson, 25 February 1847, quoted ibid., pp. 229–30.
92. Fox to his brother, George, quoted ibid., p. 146.
93. Fox, Journal, 8 July 1847, quoted ibid., pp. 251–2.
94. Fox, Journal, 3 March 1847, quoted ibid., p. 218.
95. Fox, Journal, 13 June 1842, C1 2/0100/2.
96. Fox, Journal, 19 August 1847, quoted George Fox, p. 280.
97. Fox, Journal, 23 August 1847, ibid., p. 282–3.
98. Fox, Journal, 8 September 1847, quoted ibid., p. 295.
99. Fox, Journal, 13 June 1842, C1 2/0 100/2.
100. Fox, Journal, 28 October 1844, C1 2/0 100/5.
101. Fox, Journal, 11 June 1845, C1 2/0 100/6.
102. Fox, Journal, 15 October 1844, C1 2/0 100/5.
103. Fox, Journal, 23 November 1844, ibid.
104. Fox, Journal, 26 December 1846, C1 2/0 100/5.
105. Fox, Journal, 25 April 1845, C1 2/0 100/6.
106. Fox, Journal, 27 November 1844, C12/0 100/5.
107. Fox, Journal, 15 July 1847, quoted George Fox, p. 254.
108. Fox, Journal, 15 August 1847, quoted ibid., p. 266.
109. Fox to his brother, George, 9 July 1847, quoted ibid., p. 317.
110. Fox, Journal, 24 May 1842, C1 2/0 100/1.
111. Fox, Journal, 8 April 1845, C1 2/0 100/6.
112. Fox, Journal, 23 October 1844, C1 2/0 100/5.
113. Fox, Journal, 13 February 1847, quoted George Fox, pp. 194–205.
114. Fox, Journal, 3 March 1847, quoted ibid., pp. 215–17.
115. Fox Journal, 27 February 1847, quoted ibid., p. 212.
116. Revd John Edmund Sharkey, Journal, 10 May 1852, C1 2/0 222/13 (CMS: Birmingham).
117. Sharkey, Journal, Ellore, November 1852, C1 2/0 222/15.
118. Ibid.
119. Sharkey, Journal, 23 March 1851, C1 2/0 222/12.
120. Sharkey, Journal, 2 January 1855, C1 2/0 222/19.
121. Sharkey, Journal, 29 August 1848, C1 2/0 222/4.
122. Sharkey, Journal, 13 July 1849, C1 2/0 222/16.
123. Sharkey, Journal, 13 January 1848, C1 2/0 222/3.
124. Sharkey, Journal, 14 February 1853, C1 2/0 222/15.
125. Sharkey, Journal, 31 August 1848, C1 2/0 222/4.
126. Sharkey, Journal, 18 October 1847, C1 2/0 222/2.

127. Sharkey, Journal, 9 December 1850, C1 2/0 222/8.
128. Sharkey, Journal, C1 2/0 222/18.
129. Sharkey, Journal, 19 February, C1 2/0 222/3.
130. Sharkey, Journal, 11 December 1851, C1 2/0 222/11.
131. Sharkey, Journal, 11 December 1850, C1 2/0 222/8.
132. Sharkey, Journal, 20 November 1847, C1 2/0 222/2.
133. Sharkey, Journal, 30 March 1851, C1 2/0 222/9.
134. Sharkey, Journal, 4 February 1852, C1 2/0 222/12.
135. Sharkey, Journal, 9 February 1852, ibid.
136. Sharkey, Journal, 30 September 1852, C1 2/0 222/14.
137. Sharkey, Journal, 11 January 1848, C1 2/0 222/3.
138. Sharkey, Journal, 28 August 1848, C1 2/0 222/4.
139. Sharkey, Journal, 31 July 1849, C1 2/0 222/5.
140. Sharkey, Journal, 2 August 1849, ibid.
141. Sharkey, Journal, 4 July 1850, C1 2/0 222/8.
142. Sharkey, Journal, November 1852, C1 2/0 222/15. This was in his formal encounter with the Vaishnavites at Ellore.
143. Sharkey, Journal, 2 August 1849, C1 2/0 222/5.
144. Sharkey, Journal, 17 December 1851, C1 2/0 222/9.
145. Sharkey, Journal, 1850, C1 2/0 222/6.
146. Sharkey, Journal, 23 March 1851, C1 2/0 222/9.
147. Sharkey, Journal, 14 February 1853, C1 2/0 222/15.
148. Sharkey, Journal, 23 February 1850, C1 2/0 222/6.
149. Sharkey, Journal, 11 December 1850, C1 2/0 222/8.
150. Sharkey, Journal, 28 August 1849, C1 2/0 222/5.
151. Sharkey, Journal, 23 December 1847, C1 2/0 222/2.
152. Sharkey, Journal, 26 December 1850, C1 2/0 222/8.
153. See my essay on George Uglow Pope versus Vederanayagam Sastri: A Case-Study in the Clash of New and Old Mission in Geoffrey Oddie (ed.), *Religious Conversion Movements in South Asia: Continuities and Change 1800–1900*, to be published by Curzon press.
154. Sharkey, Journal, C1 2/0 222/22.
155. See the essays by Talmiz Khaldun and P. C. Joshi in the collection of essays, *Rebellion 1857: A Symposium*, New Delhi: 1957.
156. For a clear, if biased, pro-missionary account of the debate, see Eugene Stock, vol. II, ch. XLVI.

PART III
Indian Christians and Conversion

CHAPTER 7

Conversion: Case-Studies from the South

The story of Indian Christian converts is more significant than their numbers imply. In an earlier chapter, one paradigm of the conversion process, a push-pull model, has been explored, transposing a model conventionally used for migration from a poorer to a wealthier country to cultural migration, a journey from one faith to another. In the nineteenth century, missionaries began by concentrating their attentions on the high castes, for here were the exponents of the rival faith, and only by bending their knees could they demonstrate the superiority of Christianity. Here was yet another example of that British belief in downward filtration, that the conversion of the high castes would have a knock-on effect throughout the caste hierarchical system. In fact, when conversion did occur on any scale, missionaries were taken by surprise, for it came from below. If initially excited by this hint of fulfilment of their millenarian dreams, they became suspicious, doubting that the low castes did indeed seek spiritual enlightenment, and suspecting a merely material motive. And the minority aspect of conversion will be the more exaggerated in this account, for greater attention is given to the study of high caste converts, even more numerically insignificant. However, theirs is a story which demonstrates well the intriguing complexities of cultural migration.

Although this Indian Christian elite was but one small sector of India's elite in a far more widespread Indian cultural encounter with the West, theirs was in many ways the most substantial initial compromise with European values. In their subsequent troubled endeavour to fashion a more comfortable balance between their own traditions and the claims of an exclusivist Christianity, they were amongst the earliest to fall victim to that cultural crisis that was to beset so many of India's westernizing elite. But, more significantly, they were also in the vanguard of its resolution.

If I begin in the south, I do so on the grounds that Christianity here has a longer history than in Bengal and the north, and was, over time, to attract a much larger Christian community.

THE HISTORIOGRAPHICAL CONTEXT

Discovering appropriate paradigms for the story of conversion itself is easier than characterizing the historical circumstances in which it occurred. Burton Stein and David Washbrook berate recent attempts to do so. Looking in particular at the history of Vijayanagar, Stein laments the lack of any genuine historiography of south India. He is particularly fierce on 'Indologism', a species of Indian nationalism, the subject of much recent scholarship, and not even Nilakant Sastri quite escapes his critique. David Washbrook is even more condemnatory. He both dismisses 'modernization' as a paradigm and faults so-called 'ethno-historians' for their failure to carry through their attribution of an indigenous vitality into the history of the colonial state. If we are to understand the cultural dynamics of the nineteenth century, we have to, he asserts, recognize that communities constantly renew themselves, and that creative individuals can at any stage make a critical contribution. And if the nationalist historiography might seem quite obviously to be making that concession, this he also criticizes, for its over-simplification, its failure to recognize how multi-layered Indian culture is, and its oversight of conflict within Indian society.[1]

Yet historians of religion in south India display a more confident historiography. Out of recent writings on religion in south India, Fred Clothey believes that one could make the claim that 'the history of religions' is coming of age.[2] The history of religion is seen as a particularly indicative means of assessing change, be it 'heterogenetic', as a response to outside influence, or 'ontogenetic', from within. Clearly Clothey is addressing Mission history and, in a very direct way, the story of conversion, when he puts the question: 'what happens to a people's religion when one group of people are in contact with another or enter into a period of social and political change?'[3] There is syncretism. There is intratraditional confrontation. Clothey's peculiarly suggestive paradigm is that of liminality, 'the experience of transition'. He likewise is unhappy at the simplistic contrast between tradition and modernity: 'in any case', he asserts, 'modernity is scarcely the opposite of tradition. Religion proves to be neither dead nor dying in the contemporary era.'[4]

One way in which a historiography specific to conversion has come about has been through the application of the insights of an Africanist, Robert Horton, to the Indian situation. In his scenario, the 'outside' world religions of Islam and Christianity are often but catalysts of cosmological beliefs within African belief systems. Just because African religions already held a belief in a High God, these outside world religions could obtain a hold. The application of Horton's model to South Asia seems to work best for tribal religions. Oddie and Schreider have argued for its wider application, but concede that there is always an element of mystery about conversion, that it is 'deeply problematic', and that any account of conversion from Hinduism has to recognize 'the nature of pre-Christian cosmology and on the way in which the ideas such as those in Hinduism acted as a constraint, a linkage, an inducement or facilitating factor in the individual's turning to Christianity—the way in which a convert understood and contributed to development in the Christian faith'.[5] In an interesting attempt to formulate a taxonomy of conversion, Robert Frykenberg expressed his doubts about the application of Horton's model to Hinduism: there was, for a start, the awkward fact of the role of those powerful, intermediary gods or spirits.[6] Oddie has remained faithful to the Horton paradigm,[7] but it seems better adapted to shed light on so called 'mass' conversion movements from among the lower castes or outcastes than that of an individual from the higher castes.[8]

There is no intention here to minimize the significance of so called 'mass' conversion movements. Admittedly, there has been considerable scepticism expressed about motives. Kooiman, for example, has suggested that fear of cholera was as likely to be the reason for conversion as for apostasy.[9] There is a considerable body of evidence that low caste peasants turned Christian the better to draw missionaries as their apologists into land disputes with local zamindars.[10] But the charge of 'rice Christians' is open to abuse and Duncan Forrester, for one, has argued passionately that low caste, and especially untouchable, conversion was out of a genuine search for spiritual improvement.[11] Recent research on the history of Dalits (the new word for untouchables) suggests that untouchables had their own distinctive literature and theology and that it would be possible also to talk of both a cultural and a social dimension to the migration story of their conversion.[12] So it is partly on grounds of a more accessible documentation that this study focuses on high caste conversion.

THE RELIGIOUS AND CULTURAL CONTEXT

Why should an Indian convert? It took enormous courage. Due to the inextricable link between society and religion in Indian life, to reject one's religion was to reject one's society, and hence to inflict on oneself that most punitive of sanctions, ostracism. Most bitter was the divide from one's own family. On sons fell all kinds of customary obligations to the family, especially in shradda or funeral rites, and hence their conversions were particularly dreaded and resented. We can only circle around all the predisposing factors for conversion. If we accept the push-pull model, we have to ask both negative questions, such as, why did converts reject their own religion and culture (though, as will become clear, one did not necessarily entail the other), and positive ones such as, why were they attracted to Christianity? Society and religion were not, of course, so closely entwined in British or European culture (or was the Victorian era exceptional?) so it was possible to separate an attraction for Christianity from an attraction to western culture. It was possible to be 'westernized' but not to convert. However, by mid-century, it would have been difficult for a convert, particularly for someone educated in an English-medium school, to have kept them apart. But if conversion was often in consequence to be both to Christianity and to western culture, this inevitably set up conflicting loyalties, not only in matters of faith, but also to social values or mores.

Why should a convert in the south have turned against his own religion and/or culture (for this discussion of the south, although there were to be converts from Islam, it will solely concern converts from Hinduism). What kind of a religious tradition and practising faith would the convert have formerly experienced and can we find here the explanation for conversion?

Hinduism came later to the south and here the syncretism with an indigenous or Dravidian culture was even more complex than in the north. Conventional wisdom has dwelt on tension between a high or Sanskritic culture and a folk or popular culture but, as already mentioned, a revisionist view now stresses their interaction and entanglement. At both the village level and in the great temple cities of south India, Dravidian and Aryan cults syncretized. Nilakanta Sastri put it wittily: 'a Pariah body with a Brahmin head is an apt description of the cults of Siva, while a Pariah head with a Brahmin body might well describe some of the cults of the ancient Dravidian deities, modified by Brahmin ideas and influence.'[13] The mid-nineteenth-century missionaries were probably wrong to see the worship of grama devatas as mere devil worship. Sakti, or the worship of the female, reflected in part the pre-dominant role of women in agriculture.

Bhakti, or devotionalism, was another fundamental contribution of Dravidian culture to Hinduism. From the late fifth century onwards, it made a major contribution to Hindu revivalism through Saivite saints, the Nayanars, and through Vaishnavite saints, the Alvars. The climax were the Bhagavata Puranas of the tenth century. Admittedly here, to quote Sastri, was 'a bhakti very different from the calm, dignified devotion of the bhagavatas of the early centuries before and after Christ in Northern India'.[14] And a better application of the Horton model to south India might well lie in the redeployment of his argument about a high god to the contents of bhakti, for bhakti comes close to many assumptions of Christianity. It also seeks a personal relationship between the worshipper and a personal god, though one in which both retain a separate identity (contrast the pursuit of moksha, or fusion, at the heart of Vedantism).

But from the south also, of course, came the inspiration for Vedantism in its three major forms, the core belief structure of modern Hinduism. Maybe for a Hindu experiencing religious doubts in the nineteenth century, this intellectual achievement would have seemed as distant a legacy as thirteenth-century Thomism to a nineteenth-century Catholic, but then this was a religious tradition which had not been waylaid by a Renaissance or Reformation, and it must have seemed an awesome tradition to reject.

The question has then to be posed, but one which is very awkward to answer: had this great tradition so deteriorated by the nineteenth century that it had become no more than metaphysical nit-picking? Was the nineteenth-century convert rejecting a very arid version of a great original? If missionary accounts suggest that such a deterioration may have occurred, we are still left with the paradox that learned Hindus were to prove more than a match for these new opponents.

In the south, more than in the north, Hinduism was dominated by its great temples. Interestingly, even the temples had Dravidian, pre-Aryan, origins. Presler has calculated that in Tamil Nadu alone there were some 52,000 temples.[15] What kind of worship was practised in these temples and have we here an explanation for conversion?

It is a question that raises one controversial aspect of Hinduism, that of idolatry, as well as the role and status of priests. Temples were at the heart of a great political row between evangelicals and the Company, and there can be no doubt that missionaries, with a declared policy of 'withdrawal', did everything possible to denigrate the temples. Probably more than any other factor, missionary propaganda explains a convert's alienation from the life of the temple.

Protestant missionaries projected onto the Hindu concepts of idol, temple and priesthood, their own versions of idol, church and clergy, and, in terms of their ability to read Hinduism, went seriously wrong. No aspect of missionary ideology was so highly charged as their anathema for idolatry. Yet, in actuality, Hindus do not worship the idol as such, but the power of the gods that lie in the images: 'temple ritual', to quote Chris Fuller, 'is incomprehensible if it is thought that the images themselves are objects of worship.'[16] Admittedly, in so multifarious a faith, there are bound to be exceptions, and it is not surprising to find that in at least one branch of Vaishnavism the idol is seen to be a real form of Vishnu.[17] Ram Mohun Roy, in his response to the missionary charge of idolatry, had to concede that for the uneducated, the worship of idols was a useful means of aiding concentration.[18] But this was not an idolatrous faith. Missionaries wrongly branded it as such, and indeed, this was the mainspring in their denunciation of Hinduism.

Temples were, quite simply, abodes for the gods. At a certain stage, the Aryan rituals for sacrifice had been transformed into the temple rituals of worship, enshrined in the sacred texts of the Agamas. These were Siva's own directions for temple worship. At the heart of the temple was a dark cell, the sanctum sanctorum, where the gods resided and slept. There followed the complicated daily ritual of their lives. Each temple had its annual car festival. Ritual broke down the barriers between men and the gods. Not that the gods needed such service, for they were self-sufficient, but it was a way men could please the gods. Without bhakti, or genuine devotionalism, however, ritual would be inefficacious. The gods dispensed grace in exchange for man's devotion: 'the entire religious atmosphere of the temples is dominated by positive devotion rather than negative fear.'[19] Why did this form of worship so often prove antipathetic to converts? How far did this derive from missionary contempt for the temple priests?

Missionaries in the nineteenth century consistently misunderstood the role of temple priests. They drew false comparisons with themselves. In fact, priests were essentially the servants of the gods. Rarely were they educated. Not all temple priests were Brahmins, but when they were, they were the most despised of the Brahmin sub-castes. Missionaries saw the priests as venal and rapacious, but not one perceived that this receipt of gifts was in itself polluting, that it was, indeed, a form of self-sacrifice, for, in so doing, priests took on the sins of the donors. In the south though, in contrast to the north, priests did not have to accept gifts associated with death, and hence peculiarly inauspicious and unclean.

Temples had become integral to society and polity, the temple itself was a microcosm of the city, kingdom and universe. But with the destruction, by and large, of Hindu kingship, both temples and priests incurred a loss of status. By the time the missionaries arrived, there was a real sense in which their role had been depreciated in the eyes of their own communities. Maybe the converts developed a keen sense that here was a class whose status was indeed inferior to that of the Protestant clergy.

Just how far had standards of venality and literacy declined amongst the priests by the early nineteenth century? Fuller concedes that there was little evidence of the impact of any reformist movement before the 1890s.

But there is a further qualification. The priests of temples should be differentiated from the swamis or monks of the mutts or monasteries. Invariably they were much more educated, were held in high esteem socially, and took on the role of a guru or spiritual adviser. Did the missionary or convert appreciate this distinction? One can, of course, ask the same question: had their standards of venality and literacy seriously declined by the nineteenth century?

The story was further complicated through temples becoming a political battleground. The Company policy of neutrality did not imply neglect of temples. On the contrary, the new colonial administration saw itself as taking over the traditional kingly role of the preserver of dharma. This involved the maintenance of temples, though it was not, of course, coincidental, that it also brought in a considerable share of the not inconsiderable temple wealth. Through inam gifts or tax-free endowments, temples had acquired some of the best agricultural land. Evangelicals in the nineteenth century were horrified by the way Company officials both helped to run the administration of temple estates and, worst of all, assist their religious life, most conspicuously by organizing the recruitment of labour for the car festivals. Under Regulation VII of an Act of 1817, officials became the supervisors of temple trustees.

In part, missionaries were simply repelled by the very character of temple life: 'noisy, chaotic, full of extraneous activity which distracted quiet worship.' This was of a piece with missionary failure to accept a different way of life. Would missionaries have felt any different had temples resembled their more sombre protestant churches? But, as Presler has phrased it, a bitter conflict ensued between the missionary, with 'their ideology of withdrawal, and the Company, with its "concept of protection for south Indian traditions".[20] Ostensibly in 1841 the Company gave way, when powers were handed back to the Indian trustees, but historians differ on the scale of disengagement, e.g. some would argue that they never lost control of the estates. But might not this political bickering have led converts to look on the life of temples with contempt?

This squabble broadened out into a larger conflict, on the threshold of cultural nationalism, and one which placed converts in the wholly invidious context of competing loyalties. It rumbled on throughout the nineteenth century. It drew together rural and urban protest. We have already seen how provocative missionary activity in Tinevelly had brought together Hindu organizations in Tiruchendur and Madras. This led to overt political protest, and we should separate the protest of the Salur Veda organization of Salai Street from the one organized in October 1836 by the merchant, Lakshmanarasu Chetty. Here was protest by a merchant élite, active patrons of temples, genuinely angry at the government's reneging on neutrality. The Tweedale administration had given every cause for such concern, both through its support for a more Christian education in both state and missionary schools, and its paving the way for Christian converts to inherit property through the lex loci draft act of January 1845. (This did not become law until April 1850.)

In February 1852, a Madras branch of the British Indian Association, set up in Calcutta in October 1841, known as the Madras Native Association, was established. Its brief was not just religious; it criticized the Company's judicial and administrative systems. It also attacked the Company's grants-in-aid to missionary schools. Clearly, these were grievances of the same merchant élite. Possibly its most dramatic intervention came over the Tinevelly riots of 1858—Hindus had taken to the streets because of permission given by a magistrate for a Christian burial party to transit a street occupied by high caste Hindus—when it organized, in January 1859, a protest rally in Madras. The new governor, Charles Trevelyan, normally an outspoken advocate of the missionary cause, saw fit to judge that missionaries had unwarrantedly created widespread fear among south Indians. In fact, the MNA was on the wane and became defunct in July 1862. Maybe, as Suntharalingam suggests, anti-missionary zeal was itself on the wane. A more limited social reform movement, inspired by a small westernized elite in the Presidency capital, took its place.[21] Mid-century converts could not have ignored such proto-nationalist protest and it must have induced some unease at any uncritical regard for foreign rule.

A more noisy resistance flared up again in the 1880s. The arrival of

Madame Blavatsky and Colonel Olcott, leaders of the Theosophical movement, with their praise for Indian religions and ridicule of Christian Mission, did much to galvanize Hindu resistance. With marvellous irony, the first branch of the Theosophical Society in south India was set up in Tinevelly and Olcott gave a lecture in the inner precincts of its Saivite temple. Various other organizations took up the Hindu cause, the non-brahmin Hindu Preaching Association, and the Brahmin Hindu Tract Society. In 1886, some 64 Protestant priests were let loose on the streets of Madras, in a concerted effort to meet this challenge, preaching morning and evening, some six hours a day. The Hindu Tract Society in particular took up this challenge and by a curious symbiosis in reverse, sent its agents to all the main centres of protestantism. The outcome was that the Protestant Mission effectively contained this Hindu resistance and it was to fizzle out in the 1890s. Oddie sees it as 'the last great confrontation of its kind in the history of Hindu-Christian relations in South India'.[22]

And so converts found themselves throughout the nineteenth century in a context in which politicized Hindu revivalism could but deepen a sense of guilt at the betrayal of their own culture. Some Indians who embarked on a process of westernization did so without apparently looking back, but for many, caught up in this emergent cultural nationalism, it could but intensify a growing crisis of cultural identity. Clearly, in their response to their own religion and culture, converts were exposed to forces that could well alienate them, though this would have owed much to missionary propaganda, but were equally exposed to ideas which must have contributed to a sense of unease.

To what extent was conversion a positive attraction to Christian and western values? Was it more a case of pull than push? One key theatre for acculturation was education, and here I can draw on an Eriksonian pathography to explore the cultural dynamics of conversion. Education became a highly contentious aspect of Company policy. Might education be the means for fashioning a loyal and incorruptible administrative elite? Missionaries had already pointed the way. Charles Rhenius had in particular encouraged the spread of schools. By 1858, Mission had some 500 schools in south India, with an enrolment of 38,607 students. Governor Munro had envisioned a national structure for education, driven by an 'upward percolation' from village notables. Advocate-General Norton, who took over the cause from Munro on his death in 1827, favoured, instead, a 'downward filtration' from an urban elite. The setting up of the Madras University in 1839 and the founding of its High School represented a start in the fulfilment of these aspirations. But private education was always to be the more active contributor, be it Hindu schools financed by the Pachaiyappa Trust, or missionary schools, John Anderson's Scottish Free School, set up in 1837, being the most prominent. During Tweedale's governorship from 1841–46, this threatened to deteriorate into a rancorous dispute between missionary and government schools, though Frykenberg claims it never quite became a battle of 'Hindu' or 'Christian', 'Native' or 'European'. The outcome was an educational system for the making of an elite, though one based on merit. It was in this English-medium educational system that the real battle for acculturation took place.

This was always to be a painful process and it is hard to see how converts could come at all easily to Christianity and western values. If we adopt the Eriksonian paradigm,[23] here were young men caught up in an identity crisis, having to internalize negative, British stereotypes of Indians, and embarking on a process in which they could never wholly succeed: 'acculturation never made one a sahib as the British were.'[24] Many students flirted, Judith Walsh suspects, with Christianity 'as much from loneliness . . . as from conviction'.[25] Yet the objective of the English-medium school was the transmission of 'an entire cultural gestalt'.[26] Here was to be the locale for a quite extraordinary ideological endeavour.

Missionaries in the south differed about how far they should Europeanize their converts. Some recognized the danger of alienation from their own culture. 'Let us give him', one wrote, 'all that is really worth having from our western civilization, all the refinements which Christian modesty and taste bring with them, all that will really and truly elevate him in the social scale. But why do him the grievous injury of making him ashamed of his own nation or his own mother tongue? Why rob him of his national costume or innocent usages, when there are subjects of so far deeper and more permanent interest before him?'[27] Others were far less hesitant. The kudumi or tuft of hair, should be cut off. Should they not try to 'explode' all those Indian habits, as they saw them, of 'fostering bugs, of blowing the nose with the fingers, and wiping them on their clothes, of squatting most indecently around the town, of going half-naked . . .; those of eating not with the fingers but with a spoon and fork, of cleanliness in the person in the house, are to be encouraged.' But where did one draw the line? : 'the habit of wearing earrings and nose-rings and bangles on the wrist, the ankles and the toes—are they to be discountenanced?' 'Pride and idleness and want of business habits', this cultural imperialist let on, 'I greatly fear.' There should be a change in diet. Diet and the wearing of some items of clothing explain an Indian proneness to skin complaints. Converts should also enjoy more privacy in the home. 'I would suggest', he added for good measure, 'for respectable young men good clean clothes, a clean house, books, and where the means admitted it, a watch, with a few additional household utensils.'

But the editor felt this was going too far. Such advice could only have come from someone with little experience in the training of converts. It was, in fact, very difficult to effect such changes in mores. Besides, this smacked of cossetting. Not only would it alienate converts from their own communities, it would rob them of self-reliance; 'if native youth, by being too tenderly fostered, grow over delicate, they will be poorly prepared for rough conflict with the natives, even in missionary labours, and especially for any exertion for their own support, which a change of circumstances may render necessary.'[28]

This was a debate which exposed the intolerable predicament of converts: on the one hand, cut off from their own society, on the other, never wholly accepted into the European. They had entered a social and cultural no-man's land.

How could converts recover a sense of wholeness? If they had been attracted to Protestant Christianity in the nineteenth century for its offer of a personal relationship with Christ and for its humanitarianism, why should these necessarily be seen as European? Was not Christianity itself an Asian religion? The way out of brokenness lay in both an Indianization of the nascent churches and an indigenization of the faith. The paternalism of Mission had to be shaken off. And quite quickly, moves were made to set up a 'national' church.[29] In time, of course, both an exclusivist as well as its successor, an inclusivist theology, were challenged in the name of both an Indian Christianity and pluralism. 'In no other country', writes one pluralist, 'does the claim for "the uniqueness" of one particular religious tradition seem to be so rude and out of place, and the assertion of the "normativeness" of one particular faith over the other sound so theologically arrogant, as in India.' 'Exclusivism put fences around the Mystery.' 'Inclusiveness while being seemingly generous, actually co-opts other faiths without their leave.'[30] 'Indian Christianity', so this argument goes, 'had to be grounded in Indian culture: religious life is deeply grounded in cultural life and is in diverse ways shaped by our own cultural structuring of life.'[31] Behind these expressions of twentieth-century pluralism lay an earlier struggle by the nineteenth-century converts to find some way back from a European missionary exclusivist Christianity to a link with their own culture and faiths.

Lives of converts became experiments in liminality, in living through transition. Hugald Grafe tellingly encapsulates this conflict at the individual level:

The Hindu concept of dharma, the family duty that can be neglected at the risk of one's salvation, clashed with the Christian insistence on fulfilling the commandments of the one true God. But more was at stake: there was also a head on collision between the Hindu dharma, to be fulfilled by the whole family for the sake of their collective salvation, with the Christian concept of the sole determinative decisiveness of an individual conscience for his or her individual salvation.[32]

In the eyes of the Hindu community, conversion was a living death. The convert was cut off from his family and socially ostracized, maybe formally outcasted. And such was the nature of Christian exclusivism in an age of Empire that Mission sought to drive converts as far as possible from their former social and religious loyalties.

For converts peculiarly sensitive to the claims of caste, preserving caste practices became one way of maintaining some loyalty to their own culture. We shall see how this worked in the case of the Vellalas.

The best documented accounts of conversion are those of Hindu boys in English-medium schools. They came under exceptional cultural pressure and it was very hard for them not to go all the way and become thoroughly anglicized and alienated from their own society and culture. Here we have stories of converts in the English-medium school under the blind Cruickshanks at Tinevelly, from the Scottish Mission School under John Anderson in Madras, and from the CMS school under Robert Noble in Masulipatam. These mid-century conversions in south India seem to have been more thoroughgoing than their counterparts in Bengal.

As these were all conversions that derived from the missionary strategy of education, to restore the balance towards the alternative strategy of itinerating, I will end with examples of conversion by this method, certainly examples less well documented, and for the high castes, maybe for obvious social reasons—they would be less likely to expose themselves to missionary propaganda in the bazaar—to be comparatively rare.

The Vellalas

A particular cluster of Vellala converts has been very thoroughly investigated and it is not intended here to repeat their story at any length.[33] These were the conversions of the Pillai brothers, poet Krishna Pillai, and his younger brother, the future businessman, Muthiah. Muthiah converted in 1857, Krishna a year later. Together with Muthiah had converted another Vellala and one who claimed Kshatriya status, and Grafe has identified such conversions as one specific form of sisher (disciple) conversion. The point to be made here is that this was a peer group conversion, theirs was a decisive interaction with one another, and one would be wrong to attribute the conversion directly to missionary intervention. There were, however, elements of a more paradigmatic sisher conversion through the influence of the saintliness and instruction of Cruickshanks on Muthiah.

Another factor, and not uncommon amongst élite converts, was the early loss of their father. Krishna was but sixteen at the time, Muthiah, nine. Both, in consequence, came under greater pressure as sons to fulfil customary family ritual. But it also left them more susceptible to, and more in need of, surrogate father figures.

With the failure of missionaries to convert Brahmins in any large number in Tamil Nadu, their next most targeted group, with their Vedic learning, were the Vellalas. Given their distinctive social and religious status as Hindus, pull factors towards their own culture continued to operate long after conversion. Hudson has shown how the peculiar caste status of the Vaishnava Vellalas—the Brahmins looked on them as but clean sudra castes, but they laid claim to Vaisha or twice-born status and looked down on the majority of non-Brahmin castes as unclean—both led to an exaggerated respect for ceremonies, indicative of their claim to . higher caste status, and also to feelings of social alienation. This was a vital factor in the social dynamics of their conversion. Their belonging to a Vaishnavite minority in a Vellala Saivite majority compounded their sense of social alienation.

Throughout the nineteenth century a fierce debate raged amongst missionaries as to whether caste was intrinsic to Hinduism and would have to be abandoned by the convert, or was but a social phenomenon and could thus be retained. If, over time, some missionaries were to relent on their insistence that converts should surrender caste, Vellalas had, in the meanwhile, come under intense pressure to toe the line.

Converts themselves learnt to draw a line between what they saw as acceptable demands of the Christian marga or way of life, and the merely personal foibles of the missionaries. Muthiah, for example, refused to cut off his kudumi. As late as in the 1890s, he was still defending such traditional mores. Socio-economic forces unleashed by Company rule had posed awkward choices for the family: Krishna, for example, manager of the family estate on his father's death, had to face mounting low caste, Nadar protest at Vellala and Maravar control. In this multi-layered conflict situation, certain insights paved the way for conversion, some negative, for e.g. the limitations of the Puranas, and some positive, for e.g. the concepts of atonement and grace. This led, in both cases, to a personal encounter with Christ.

Muthiah found it impossible to maintain a double life, both fulfilling the demands of family ceremonials, and expressing his new but still inward leanings towards Christianity. His break was never complete. Hudson concludes:

As a Hindu Muthiah Pillai had been part of the Bhakti tradition of Sri Vaishnavism where the stress on faithfulness to Vishnu as the 'Protector of the Soul' modified, but did not abrogate, the dharmic observance of purity and pollution in caste relations among Sri Vaisnavas.

And here was an example of continuity between two faiths, for, as a convert, Muthiah:

seems to have brought with him a secularized version of his formerly Hindu point of view: the Christian Marga teaches faithfulness to Jesus Christ as 'Protector of the Soul', which faithfulness eliminates the notion of purity and pollution, but does not necessarily abrogate the observance of caste distinction among Christians.[34]

Continuities in Hindu spirituality can also be found in Krishna's Christian poetry. Fascinatingly, Hudson points to the influence of the Ramayana in his Tamil version of the Pilgrim's Progress. Hudson concludes: 'in the end Krishna Pilai remained a true Bhakti of the Tamil tradition, although a Christian.'[35]

Rajahgopaul

Rajahgopaul converted together with a Brahmin, A. Venkataramiah, and fellow Mudaliar, S. Ethirajaloo (though he was less closely linked) and hence this conversion, together with the conversion of a group of friends, bears some similarities to that of the Pillais. But in his case, the role of a European missionary, his teacher and Scottish missionary, John Anderson, was paramount. His was a far more extreme rejection of Hinduism and a far more thoroughgoing embrace of Christianity, and this was testimony to the extraordinary influence teachers from this Mission had over their pupils. Anderson himself felt that these three converts, with their subsequent successful careers as ordained priests and missionaries, validated his missionary career in India. But theirs had been a heavy responsibility, for they had borne the burden of those exceptional hopes for education in the Madras Presidency.

The Mudaliars were a Chingleput branch of the Vellalas. Rajahgopaul was born in the village of Poonamalee, some thirteen miles to the west of Madras. In translation his name means 'royal shepherd', one of the titles of Krishna. His father, a munsiff or village headman, a kind of petty magistrate, had died when he was young.[36] Caste does not seem to have posed the same problem of conflicting loyalties for Rajahgopaul as it had for the Pillais. He had no trouble dining with Anderson, a mleccha, after his conversion. But he had been brought up in a very orthodox household. 'His people', we learn, 'were idol worshippers and caste ruled their relations with their fellow men.' 'The home atmosphere was one densely superstitious in which floated continually such frightful notions as the evil eye, lucky and unlucky days, the occurrences of unfavourable omens.' He had been exposed to pantheism, 'that scepticism which underlies every Hindu creed'. Strong emotional bonds tied him to his parents: 'a mother's influence was the strongest fetter which bound him, a Hindu, to idolatry.' In the opinion of a contemporary foreign missionary, all this led to 'an exaggerated respect for the opinion of society . . . in place of the individual conscience'.[37] Certainly his family had no fear of his becoming a convert when they entered their son in Anderson's school as a pupil in 1839. There were so few warning precedents, anyway. Ambition led them to do so, for an English education was seen to be the passport to administrative employment.

Rajahgopaul would have needed a very strong personality to resist John Anderson.[38] Here is a frightening example of the suzerainty European missionaries could exercise over their converts. Born on 22 May 1805, Anderson was the eldest son of a blind father. He was educated at Edinburgh University. He had been won over to the missionary cause by Alexander Duff's famous address to the General Assembly in May 1835. Ordained on 13 July 1836, after a visit to Duff's school in Calcutta en route, he had arrived in Madras on 22 February 1837. His was a strongly emotional personality. His biographer wrote of his 'high, though not particularly logical order of intellect, a flowing style of conversation proceeding from an overflowing heart'.[39] Bishop Caldwell, a close friend, observed: 'one of his chief characteristics was his almost womanly tenderness and affection towards his students which were one of the things that conduced to the great number of conversions of educated young men with which his work was marked.'[40] And an Indian susceptibility to kindness from Europeans was indeed to be a common strand in conversion stories. Anderson did not marry till 1847 and his wife, a Miss Margaret Locker, daughter of a Swiss pastor—it was noted that 'she had only eight days alone with John Anderson during their married life'[41]—was equally close to Rajahgopaul. They indeed became his surrogate parents. She played an important role in encouraging female education and inspired Rajahgopaul in the same direction.

Initially Anderson was cautious at the prospect of conversion: 'it is not a conversion or two, but in the imbuing of their minds thoroughly with God's word that the main strength of the undertaking appeared to me at the present to lie.'[42] By 17 January 1840, however, he wrote: 'conversion is our aim and the scope of our daily prayers and should this be wrought, wrought by truth and the power of Christ's Spirit, then we may count on enmity and a terrible storm of opposition.'[43] Meanwhile the young Rajahgopaul came under more intimate guidance through Anderson's Sunday classes, a select group of some thirty students: 'this work with my little flock by myself is the most refreshing of any. Some of them are beginning to show affection to me.'[44] Anderson's Socratic teaching method, of questions and answers, induced a response from students. He also put them to work through the monitorial system. Students were to acquire the 'throughly Andersonian flavour of their writing and speech'. Possibly Rajahgopaul proved to be the most malleable of his students: 'young Rajahgopaul was a nature', we learn, 'that lent itself readily to his master's influence. Throughout his life he was remarkable for his strongly affectionate nature and John Anderson was just the man to win and keep his love. Respect for his teacher's character and affection for his person were important factors in bringing about the change that gradually took place.'[45] Both the Andersons encouraged social intimacy and Anderson comes across as an egalitarian—'his Hindu sons in the gospel were not members of a lower race to be treated with lofty condescension but real blood relatives of the soul'[46]—and this was an important factor in shaping Anderson's and Rajahgopaul's excellent future working relationship. The same could not be said of Alexander Duff and Lal Behari Day.

But the impress of Anderson's personality was clearly too strong: 'in many ways the relationship between these two seemed almost too ideally perfect, but may be questioned whether enough scope was left the young men for the development of their own personality. Anderson's was a strong and masterful character which bent or broke all those who came under its influence.' But this commentator saw some countervailing element: 'however, Rajahgopaul had a strongly marked individuality of his own which was powerfully swayed through the affections but not obliterated.[47]

The conversion was accompanied by characteristic family and legal rows. Hindu parents must have looked on such conversions much as parents do today when their children are taken over by cults such as scientology. Rajahgopaul was grateful that his mother, to whom he was very close, had not come in person to plead with him to change his mind: she begged him, at the least, to put off his conversion until her death and then he could fulfil his obligatory rites at her funeral. 'The one point on which we were weak', he admitted, 'was our fond attachment to our mothers.'[48] He was baptised on 20 June 1841. He was to betray no ambivalence at this change in cultural loyalties. Anderson had seemingly pulled him too entirely across the gulf.

A quite extraordinary training was to follow, 'amazing in its depth and diversity'.[49] One is struck by the precocious character of his Christian faith. There was an extraordinary authority displayed at those open public examinations at the school. In an answer to fellow convert, Venkataramiah—the monitorial system was in use—he stated: 'the more we look into ourselves with a clear eye, the eye of revelation, we see nothing but darkness and emptiness, the more we look to ourselves and our own works, the more our wretchedness increases, but the more we look into Christ and trust in Him, it brings us nearer and nearer to God in a way we cannot fully understand.'[50] He had mastered well the evangelical doctrine of salvation by faith alone. On 25 March 1846, he became a licenced preacher of the Free Church Presbytery of Madras. Following a visit with Anderson to Scotland in 1848–49 (Mrs Anderson stayed behind), he was ordained.

How does one assess the respective elements of a push-factor from his own religion and culture and a pull from Christianity and the West in his conversion? Political factors have also to be taken into account. Rajahgopaul's perception of idolatry in Hinduism does much to explain his sense of alienation. Frequent visits to Conjeevaram (Kanchipuram), one of India's most sacred cities—a subsidiary school had been opened there in 1840—did much to instill this attitude. Writing to 'the Christian ladies of Scotland who have taken an interest in the Hindus, especially in the condition of Hindu females', he fulminated: 'idolatry arises like smoke from the inlaid and long deposited masses of corruption in the human heart.' 'Vishnu, Siva, Durga and other popular gods and goddesses', he railed on, 'are visible personifications of the hidden man, viz. impurity, licentiousness, theft, lying, these are the gods that crowd the country.' A missionary triumphalism followed one such invective: 'the religion of the Vedas with its cold deism and elementary worship is no more a system. It has fallen a long time, dead and powerless by the rising of a new power.'[51] It is difficult to know whether this is Anderson speaking through Rajahgopaul or the authentic voice of the new convert. But clearly a sense of sin at his perceived former practice of idolatry had been a dynamic in his conversion.

Rajahgopaul was soon to share in the missionary sense of a failed endeavour. Conjeevaram, where there had still been no converts by 1852, was a particular cause for despondency. He confessed: 'the question occurs to my mind again and again, what is the result of our teaching and preaching?'[52] But he persisted with his critique of idolatry. To an audience at Chingleput, for example, attended by some two hundred Brahmins, he attacked the worship of Krishna in favour of the true saviour, Christ: 'when we are guilty of adultery we sin against our fellow man; when we are guilty of theft by depriving our neighbours of his goods, we sin against him; when we lie and deceive, we sin against our friends and against one another, but this sin, this sin of idolatry is directed against God, against his glory, against his spirituality, against the purity of his nature.'[53]

By comparison, caste hardly featured in his diatribes, though one of his grounds for championing British rule was its inroads into 'the monstrous system of caste'.

He was a thorough convert to British rule: 'we cannot read the history of British India, her small beginnings, her steady growth and her ultimate sovereignty throughout the length and breadth of the country without seeing the finger of God in it . . . I rejoice that we are under the banner of the British government because it is Christian.'[54] One can but speculate on the respective weight in pull factors of an evangelical Christianity and the fact of Empire.

But he was to lose that millenarian belief that Hinduism was on the brink of collapse. Indeed, he was to blame a second generation of missionaries in the 1850s for holding such views: 'because visible success does not seem to come up to the romantic expectations they formed at home', he chided, 'they are ready to conclude that everything is wrong, that Missions are a failure in India.'[55] He recognized that conversion would be a slow process: 'no, the training and formation of the Christian character is the plodding work of years.'[56]

This suggests that he drew closer to the realities of his own society. If he valued Christianity for its social compassion, and this he had been unable to find in Hinduism, in later life he applied it to his own people. He adopted such causes as female education and education for the poor.

He opened a school for Chetti girls in Madras and the Rajahgopaul Poor School in its slums. He became more sensitive to the intellectual needs of a younger generation, confused by the new ideas of western education, and started the Indian Christian Literary Society.

After a second visit to Scotland, he died on 9 June 1887.

Telugu Converts: Manchala Venkataraman

On 21 November 1843 Robert Noble opened an English school in Masulipatam. Duff's Institute in Calcutta was its inspiration, but its enrolment was confined to students from the 'upper classes', which meant from just Brahmins and some sat (clean) Sudra castes. In the autumn of 1846, David, a sudra, was his first convert, though he almost lost him. Friends had forcibly abducted him from the school compound, and Noble had had to give chase. The accompanying scandal had halved the school numbers, though these were quick to recover. The school fulfilled too great a local need for the élite. But the conversion of a Brahmin, Manchala Venkataraman, together with a Velama, Nagabushanam, in the autumn of 1852, caused greater scandal.

Venkataraman's parents were well-off Nyogi Brahmins.[57] His father had been in government service. His mother had died in his infancy and his father had become an invalid and was bed-ridden. In 1847, at the age of fourteen, he entered Noble's school as a day-boy, staying with his uncle, Manchala Adinarayana, a clerk in the Sessions court. His was a child marriage with one Narasamma. She did not join him till 1852. Through his influence, she was also converted. If Venkataramam and Nagabushanam were close friends, and in this sense, their conversion has some similarity with those of Rajahgopaul and his friends, they kept their intentions from one another, and when Nagabushanam did eventually broach the subject, Venkataraman chose to play the devil's advocate. Eventually, however, he came clean on his own faith, and together they informed Noble of their wish to be baptised. Rather cunningly, Noble, irked by the boasting of some students that for all his preaching not one student had converted, assembled the whole school and declared that there were now two ready to do so. This forced Venkataraman and Nagabushanam to come forward and make a public declaration. In July, both sought refuge in Noble's house, always an open house for converts. Near the time of baptism there were angry attempts to seize the young men from Noble's house, and he decided to anticipate a court meeting which had been fixed for 1 August 1852 to challenge their would-be conversion.

He baptised them the previous evening. Hindu aspects of their names, offensive to Christian sensibilities, were excised: Venkataraman lost Venkat, meaning Vishnu, Nagabushanam, Naga, a Hindu serpent god, and they became Ratnam and Bushanam.[58] The next day, Noble accompanied them to the court. The judge allowed them to return to his house. A few days later, however, when yet another Brahmin sought baptism, there was such a furious attack on Noble's house that the would-be convert lost his nerve. There was some cloak-and-dagger stuff before Narasamma was able to join her husband. At one stage she declared herself widowed though, rather oddly, it was the family priest who advised her to go to her husband.

These were conversions that overwhelmingly sprang from the extraordinary spell which Noble cast over the young. He was born on 9 March 1809; his father was at the time a vicar in the Cumberland parish of Frisby. His mother was the greater influence, 'all quickness, energy and versatility', 'always urging her children forward in the race of honour'. She taught him 'the habit of precision and attention to the minutest details of duty', 'his neatness in dress, his strict attention to diet, his punctuality and regularity in his engagements, and his inflexible determination not to be diverted from an object he desired to obtain.'[59]

As with so many Victorians, sisters were another important influence. His eldest sister, Letitia, gave him the grounding of his education; his youngest sister, Anne, encouraged him in his career as a missionary.

Symptomatic of a driven nature was his break-down at Cambridge; he was never to take his degree. He also chose not to marry. Later, en route to India, he wrote to his mother: 'I rejoice daily I am a single man.'[60]

Noble's was a life wholly dedicated to education. He never took home leave, never left his school until his death in 1865. Not that he fell in love with India. En route to Masulipatam in November 1842, for example, he found the temples 'dirty, shabby, uninteresting', and the presence of devadasis disgusting.[61] Only slowly did he master Telugu. Early on he regretted that it was only through an interpreter that he could silence a Brahmin: 'I feel myself most at a loss in refuting their doctrine of metempsychosis.'[62] It was the school that claimed his loyalty.

Noble was that rare CMS missionary, permitted, and seemingly without pressing urgency, to concentrate on teaching at the expense of itinerating. Beyond some misguided theory of 'downward filtration', it is not clear why he insisted on favouring a Brahmin enrolment. Not that he was opposed to the education of lower castes in some other, more vocational, institutions. But two students joined the school on the day of its opening on 21 November 1843.

In an obvious sense, European teachers usurped the Hindu role of guru in the lives of their pupils. But Noble was clearly possessed of an exemplary spirituality. He was a man of quite exceptional self-discipline. For eight hours a day, a habit unbroken for twenty-two years, he was to attend the school. To quote fellow missionary, Mr Darling: 'the natives regarded him with great respect and esteem; they looked on him as a holy man.' His brother wrote of his relationship with his pupils: 'yes, he loved them with a parent's love and to live and die in striving to do them service was the one great object of his life.'[63] 'Patient and gentle as a nurse cherishing her children and so affectionately desirous of their true happiness and Christian enlightenment, that he was willing not only to impart the Gospel of Christ to them, but even his life also, because they were dear unto him.'[64]

Others fell under his influence. In 1855, there were two more Brahmins, S. Mulaya and G. Kristaya, and a Muslim, Jahni Ali. Noble was well aware of the pain such conversions caused their families: 'nothing but a deep sense of man's perishing state while alienated from God, of the awful realities of eternity, and the infinitely superior claims to obedience which God has over parents . . . can fortify one to go through such painful scenes.'[65]

But it led to a delightful household for Noble, surrounded by his converts. They participated in every social activity in the house. Here was a quite exceptional sociability between European and Indian.

Ratnam probably never broke free from Noble's influence. He turned down a promising career in local administration as a tahsildar, a local revenue collector. Instead, he became an assistant master in the school, going on to the CMS's Anglo-Vernacular College at Ellore. Both he and Bushanan then trained for the priesthood. Noble taught them Greek and Revd Sharp, Theology. Ratnam became a competent preacher in English. In February 1864, they were ordained deacon, and in March 1866, priest.

Maybe Ratnam found a way back into his own culture through his work on a revised version of the Telugu book of Common Prayer. But he never quite got back on normal terms with his family. When he went on a visit, he was required to eat apart, as if he were an outcaste which, of course, he was. Tall and handsome, Rajaiah Paul saw him as 'the very beau-ideal of a high-caste native gentlemen'.[66] Increasingly, he took on senior church responsibilities in Masulipatam. This may have accelerated an early death at fifty-three on 10 November 1886.

Telugu Converts: Venkata Ananta Padmanabha Rao (Anantam)

A psychologically more revealing account of Noble's relationship with his converts is contained in the story of Anantam's conversion. Noble died before the conversion, but it was he who inspired it and he who shaped Anantam's life.

Anantam was by birth a Madhva Brahmin, a small but self assertive community. In the words of his biographer:[67] 'there was an air of self-complacency about them, born of the conviction that they are the top-dogs amongst the Brahmins. They are more inclined to command than to persuade.' His grandfather had fought and lost against the British, had ever afterwards sulked and kept out of the way in a remote village, near Nellore, 'so isolated that he could hardly meet the hated whiteman'.[68] His father had been in government service. He had died of an abscess when Anantam was but seven, though not before he had arranged his son's upanayana, the sacred thread ceremony, and just in time for him to light his father's funeral pyre; in his own words, 'to go through all the painful ceremonial'. Anantam had then to witness the enforced widowhood of his mother, youngest of a family of five brothers and three sisters: 'I cried bitterly when I saw my mother's beautiful long hair being removed and her head shaved by the barber's razor.'[69] She was pious and devout and he had to bear the burden of her expectations that he would become 'an ideal Brahmana gentleman'. Although his father had been careless with money, the family was landed and well-connected, and the mother and son were taken in by her brother, Janikiramanna, another Company employee. It was his transfer that brought the young Anantam to Masulipatam.

Seemingly he was surrounded by religious role models. Apart from his mother and his equally devout uncle, there was a cousin on his mother's side, Manuri Venkata Krishnamma, 'intensely religious, up-right and pure in his private life'. Never would he travel without his own household goods, avoided the train 'for fear of contamination' and went long distances on foot. 'He was known to practice great self-control as a husband.'[70] But he was the one to keep in touch with Anantam despite his conversion. Another was a Vaisha, Addepalli Sastrulu: 'he was great at reading and expounding the puranas and he purposely remained a bachelor to be able to live on his small income derived from lands and serve others.'[71] Anantam saw him as a closet Christian.

Such were the numerous Hindu pressures exerted on both Anantam and his cousin, Seenayya, who was to share his conversion. None proved comparable to those of Noble and his school.

A village pial, and he its first student, had been Anantam's first school: 'within a year I was taught all that the teacher knew and he averred that he could teach me nothing more.' In Masulipatam he was to go back and forth between the Hindu High School and Noble's school. The appointment of a catholic priest, the Revd Father O'Brien, as its English teacher, subsequently its headmaster, had revitalized the former. O'Brien had taken a shine to both Anantam and Seenayya and 'soon discovered our leanings towards Christianity'. 'Once or twice he threatened to inform our uncle of our religious views but never did.' His preference would have been their becoming Catholic and he had 'proposed to take us to Calcutta and educate us there'. But he saw that they belonged to Noble.[72] And whichever school they were at, his was always to be the more formative influence.

Anantam first met Noble in 1863. His 'first impression was one of awe and reverence. He was almost always dressed in satin-coloured silk and thus in my mind seemed that he was always surrounded by a halo of peculiar sanctity'. Noble had an extraordinary way with boys. 'Both cousin Seenayya and I soon took to him and he encouraged us to visit him at home.' Boys would visit Noble at noon between lessons: 'he would take several boys with him in his spacious bullock coach to school in the afternoon and I had the proud privilege of a ride frequently on his knee.' Once, when his hands and thigh were covered with itch, Noble 'took me into his bathroom and washed the sores with warm water and soap; then softly applied with his own fingers sulphur ointment gently as a mother would. This endeared him to me all the more'. Noble 'made the serious and thinking boys feel that there was something in him that was lacking in their own homes and lives'. Anantam came to recognize that Noble, the bachelor, had taken the school as his wife and the converts were his children.

Noble had pointed the way to Christ. On one of his visits to Noble from the Hindu school, sitting him beside him on the couch and 'stroking my back affectionately', he had remarked: 'I wonder my boy Anantam, if I would live to see you as a child of God serving him?' 'These words were lodged in my heart and they were fulfilled in my later life.' Admiration for Noble was to become admiration for Christ.[73]

By the 1860s Noble was already prematurely old. The dreadful cyclone that struck Masulipatam on 1 November 1864 finished him. Four days later, on a visit, Anantam found Noble still scraping mud from his books: 'he came out with tears of joy trickling down his sunken cheeks and asked each one of us if we and our people were all well and how we escaped.'[74] The great tidal wave had killed some 35,000 to 40,000 as it struck the coast and a further 15,000 in the town itself. Noble was never to recover from this disaster and died on 17 October 1865.

The dynamics of Anantam's and Seenayya's conversion had all the usual features, an alienation from the performance of Hindu ritual, a belief in Christ. Another schoolmaster at Noble's school, Mason, a former Company soldier, completed Noble's work: 'his simple and self-denying life and his love to us assured us that his interest in our spiritual well-being was sincere', and 'eventually this led to our baptism.' This Sharkey was to do on 28 May. Seenayya was just short of eighteen, but Anantam not yet sixteen, and this led to a severe grilling by the collector in his office. Anantam's replies in Telugu were greeted 'by a tremendous outbreak of hisses of disapprobation and anger from the crowd'. But Anantam prevailed, and was given the choice of staying with his uncle or going to stay with Sharkey. His conversion proved the destruction of his mother's hopes: 'in one of her paroxysms of grief she violently knocked her face against the wall where she was sitting.' She was never to reconcile herself to his conversion right till her death on 17 November 1879. Sharkey comes across as less abrasive in this context, for he sought to comfort her. Anantam's own Madhva Brahmin community did not formerly go through a performance of the ghata sradha ceremony, a funeral ceremony for those who abandon the Hindu faith, to ostracize him. But 'God alone knew what inward struggle took place', Anantam subsequently admitted, 'and I felt more than once I would break down.'[75]

There was a dreadful moment on first living with the Sharkeys in Noble's school. An untouchable served him at table: 'a cold shiver crept down his spine. For a moment his spirit swayed between earth and heaven.' But a still, small voice told him, god is no respector of persons, and his caste prejudice gave way. His Hindu wife would not join him and lived on as a widow. He was to marry Minnie, the Sharkeys adopted daughter, a Vaishnava Brahmin. She died on 15 December 1882. In January 1884, he married, for the third time, the daughter of a Tamil Vellala convert who had worked for Ragland in Tinevelly. Such was the restricted world of the converts.

Noble's influence remained paramount. Anantam also turned down a career in local administration. The Revd Sharp had wanted him to take up medicine (a profession, in fact, to be pursued by his son). He chose, instead, to become a schoolmaster in Noble's school. A reading of Henry Martyn's memoirs had encouraged him to become a missionary. Not till January 1881 did he take his BA degree. He was ordained and later became the headmaster of the CMS school at Bezwada. On tour, together with some other Brahmin converts, he had taken to playing Indian musical instruments to accompany the singing of Christian songs. These did not seek, he would insist, to denounce caste and Hindu social institutions, but to bring god to the Hindus: 'my knowledge of the Hindu system deepened and my sympathy with my people increased.' One of his fellow Brahmin converts 'could keep his rustic audience spell-bound for hours narrating puranic stories and comparing and contrasting them with Christ's life, death and resurrection.'[76] But they exercised little influence over the higher castes. As a headmaster, he was to imitate Noble and play the role of guru. He worked on a Telugu translation of the Bible. Here was another convert seeking a way back into his own culture. He lived till 1949.

There is, of course, a suggestion of a sublimated pedophilia in Noble's relationship with his pupils. Any celibate teacher, as the Catholic church has learnt to its cost, is open to such suspicion. The English may always have looked on Empire as an escape from intolerable sexual constraints at home, and pedophilia was not unknown among the civilians.[77] Mission could not hope to escape such aspersion. There had been a serious case at the SPG Sawyerpuram seminary in 1852, when the principal, Mr Ross, had been obliged to flee the country to escape arrest. All the boys had been sent home, and Caldwell, invariably called on to sort out such troubling occasions, had been dispatched, to talk to the boys and to find out how far the problem had spread. The local secretary, Symonds, wrote home: 'though some grounds of dissatisfaction was apprehended nothing serious was suspected and no one dreamt of so enormous an evil as that discovered.' But he then went on to make a surprising admission: 'We have had in this affair to go through a calamity that almost every educational establishment in India at one time or another has been afflicted with.'[78] It makes the innocence of Anantam's account, which one has no cause to doubt, just a little surprising.

Sharkey's Brahmin

Conversion stories such as these occur far less frequently in the journals of the itinerators. There was always less likelihood of a high caste conversion by an itinerator than by the schoolmaster. Élite families, though they had learnt of the risks involved, valued an English education so highly for their sons that they persisted in sending them to missionary schools. They persuaded themselves that they would recognize the danger signals and withdraw their children in good time. However, itinerating missionaries might find Brahmins amongst their enquirers, and one such Sharkey was to convert.

The first reference to him was on 12 July 1849. 'I have no desire to judge his motives' Sharkey reported, 'nor would it be right to do so. I have, however, reason to hope well of him.' 'He feels it very difficult to understand the scriptures aright. His old motives and associations, his erroneous views and prejudices, are all painfully in his way, and seriously oppose his viewing with meekness and simplicity the engrafted word.' For a while there were almost daily reports of their conversations. On 31 July, 'he looked dull and vague. He interrupted me and said he could not follow me. "We had better pray, Sir", he continued enquiringly . . . The poor distressed man kneeling by me repeated each petition after me and with so devout an air and earnest a manner that it filled me with comfort and strengthened me greatly.' On 1 August, 'he was much struck with Judaic treachery and covetousness and our blessed Lord's patience under all his trials and sufferings'. By 3 August Sharkey reported that the Brahmin 'is now almost a Christian. God grant that he may not stop here'; on 9 August, 'the Brahmin was quite struck with the account of the resurrection.' But there was not to be steady progress. On 20 August: 'a long and trying conversation with the Brahmin. I was somewhat surprised to find him still unsettled and even ignorant in regard to some of the simplest truths . . . He receives nothing with sluggish credulity or complementary flattery. This is a good sign.' Then there was a recovery. On 17 September: 'it is really very edifying to observe the process of grace in the man.'[79]

But all was, in fact, proceeding slowly. By 31 July 1850: 'the Brahmin is still halting between two opinions. He is retrograding and there does not appear to be in him that effort and desire to acquire Christian truths in which he once delighted.' He failed to keep his promise to convert once his wife had given birth: 'the Lord keep him from deceiving himself on us.[80]

We next hear of him on 11 December 1850: 'I had a companion in the Brahmin who now for two years and more had been wishing to learn and put on Christ. He accompanied me of his own accord. I do not think his purpose to embrace Christianity has suffered any change, nor has anything occurred to lead me to suspect his sincerity. But his knowledge and sense of sin appear defective. A sort of distant discipleship is evidently what he has been calculating upon. To give up caste, mother, sister and son, and follow Christ is still a dear sacrifice to him.[81]

But he must have converted, for Sharkey was to report in November 1852 a visit to his father: 'so anxious was he to hear of his son and the great spiritual change wrought on him that his visit was of some hours' duration. His regret which he repeatedly expressed and expressed with many a deep sigh was not that his only son had embraced Christianity but that he had broken caste.' He had not dared to visit his son in Masulipatam.[82]

A Brahmin convert was a great prize, and hence the time Sharkey gave to him, and the fullness of his reports home. An impressionable Brahmin schoolboy was one thing, an adult Brahmin another, and one can see from the protracted nature of this conversion how uphill a struggle it had been. It was, of course, from this experience that Sharkey drew the conclusion that caste was the real barrier to conversion.

A Christian Dacoit

Even more encouraging evidence that itinerating was not just scattering seed on barren ground was the conversion of one Pagola Venkayya, a former dacoit of the mala caste. At the age of forty-seven, he had become disgusted with his dacoity and settled down in the village of Raghavapuram, some thirty miles from Bezwada. Attending the Sivaratri festival on the Kistna river, which, as we have seen, the CMS missionaries used to frequent, a Hindu priest had asked him if he was a Christian. 'I am not a Christian', he had replied, 'but desire to be so.' No longer did he believe that bathing in the river would cleanse his sins. Later, weavers from his village, who had witnessed a Christian burial in a nearby village, brought back news of Christian belief in an after-life. When Darling visited his village three days later, on 9 March 1859, Venkayya, together with his wife and five children, requested baptism. As a former dacoit and a convert, he became something of a celebrity.[83]

NOTES AND REFERENCES

1. See the essay by Burton Stein, Reapproaching Vijayanagar, and by David Washbrook, Modern South Indian Political History, in Robert E. Frykenberg and Pauline Kolanda (eds), *An Anthology of Recent Research and Scholarship*, Madras: 1985.
2. See Fred Clothey, 'On the Assessment of Religion in South India', ibid.
3. Ibid., p. 327.

4. See his introduction in Fred W. Clothey (ed.), *Images of Man: Religion and Historical process in South Asia*, Madras: 1982.

5. See Deryck Schreider and Geoffrey Oddie, 'What is Conversion? History, Christianity and Religious Change in Colonial Africa and South Asia', *The Journal of Religious History*, vol. 15, no. 4, December 1989.

6. R. Frykenberg, 'On the Study of Conversion Movements: A Review Article and a Theoretical Note', *The Indian Economic and Social History Review*, vol. XVII, no. 1.

7. See his paper, 'Old Wine in New Bottles?': Kartabhaja (Vaishnava) Converts to Evangelical Christianity in Bengal 1835–45, given to the 13th European Conference of Modern South Asian Studies, Toulouse, August 1994.

8. Or so I argued in my article, 'The Conversion Experience of India's Christian Elite in the mid-19th century', *The Journal of Religious History*, vol. 18, no. 1, June 1994.

9. D. Kooiman, *Conversion and Social Equality in India: The London Missionary Society in South Travancore in the 19th Century*, New Delhi.

10. Certainly this was a major element in the Retti conversions in the Sawyerpuram Mission of the 1840s. I discuss this in my piece on G. U. Pope in the forthcoming collection of essays on conversion edited by G. A. Oddie.

11. Duncan Forrester, 'The Depressed Classes in Conversion to Christianity', G. A. Oddie (ed.), *Religion in South Asia: Religious and Conversion Movements in South Asia in Medieval and Modern Times*, London: 1973.

12. I base this comment on some very interesting conversations I enjoyed in October 1991 with members of CISRS (The Christian Institute for the Study of Religion and Society). Dr Abrahama Ayzookuzhiel is compiling a collection of Dalit writings.

13. K. A. Nilakanta Sastri, *Development of Religion in South India*, Orient Longman: 1963, pp. 25–6. I have largely followed his account of religion in the south.

14. Ibid., p. 40.

15. Franklin A. Presler, *Religion under Bureaucracy: Policy and Administration for Hindu Temples in South India*, Cambridge: 1987, p. 2.

16. C. J. Fuller, *Servants of the Goddess: The Priests of a South Indian Temple*, Cambridge: 1984, p. 10.

17. Sastri, p. 67.

18. Dermot Killingley has argued this point.

19. Fuller, p. 17.

20. Presler, p. 16.

21. I have relied here on R. Suntharalingam, 'The Madras Native Association: A Study of an Early Indian Political Organization', *Indian Economic and Social History Review*, IV, 3, 1967. For an excellent contextualization of this conflict in terms of educational policy, see Robert Eric Frykenberg, 'Modern Education in South India 1784–1854: Its Roots and Its Role as a Vehicle of Integration and Company Raj', *The American Historical Review*, vol. 91, no. 1, February 1986.

22. Geoff Oddie, 'Anti-Missionary Feeling in Hindu Revivalism in Madras: The Hindu Preaching and Tract Societies c. 1886–1891', Fred W. Clothey (ed.), *Images of Man*, p. 233.

23. Judith Walsh does so in her *Growing Up in British India: Indian Autobiographies on Childhood and Education under the Raj*, New York, London: 1983.

24. Ibid., p. 68.

25. Ibid., p. 58.

26. Ibid., p. 37.

27. Anon, 'Family Names among the Natives of India', *The Madras Church Missionary Record*, vol. XXII, no. 9, September 1855, p. 252.

28. Anon, 'Treatment of Native Converts', *The Madras Church Missionary Record*, vol. XXII, no. 20, October 1855.

29. For one general account of this theme, looking back to the earliest struggle of the Thomas Christians, see A. M. Mundadan, *Indian Christians Search for Identity and Struggle for Autonomy*, Bangalore: 1984.

30. See Stanley J. Samantha, 'The Cross and the Rainbow: Christ in a Multi-religious Culture', Somen Das (ed.), *Christian Faith and Multiform Culture in India*, Bangalore: 1987, pp. 29, 34, 36.

31. Eric J. Lott, 'Religious Faith and the Diversity of Cultural Life in India', ibid., p. 50.

32. Hugald Grafe, op. cit., p. 155.

33. The following literature can be consulted: Denis Hudson, *The Life and Times of H. A. Krishna Pillai 1827–1900*, Claremont: 1970 (unpublished Ph.D.); John V. Sundaram, *A Study of the Protestant Christian Impact on the Vellalas of the Tinevelli Area in the Eighteenth and Nineteenth Century*, MA Theology, UTC, Bangalore: 1980; Dennis Hudson, 'Christians and the Question of Caste: The Vellala Protestants of Palaiyankottai', Fred W. Clothey (ed.), *Images of Man: Religion and Historical Process in South Asia*, Madras: 1982; Dennis Hudson, 'The Conversion Account of H. A. Krishna Pillai', *India Church History Review*, vol. II, June 1968.

34. Clothey, p. 254.

35. Hudson, Life and Times, p. 490.

36. For biographical sketches of Rajahgopaul, see Rajaiah D. Paul, *Chosen Vessels: Lives of Ten Indian Christian Pastors of the Eighteenth and Nineteenth Centuries*, Madras: 1961; Revd A. Alexander, *Rajagopaul. A Memorial Sketch*, Paisley: 1888, Church of Scotland Publications, F 136B (UTC: Bangalore).

37. Alexander, pp. 4–5.

38. The standard biographical source for John Anderson is Revd John Braidwood, *The Yoke Fellows in the Mission Field: The Life and Labours of the Rev John Anderson and the Rev Robert Johnson*, London: 1862.

39. Ibid., p. 10.

40. Quoted in *Stories of Our Madras Mission*, Edinburgh, n.d. (early 1900s), p. 46.

41. Quoted in Sketch of Miss Margaret Locker Church of Scotland, Madras Mission, F 12 a 109 (UTC: Bangalore).

42. Braidwood, p. 59.

43. Ibid., p. 112.

44. Ibid., p. 72.

45. Alexander, pp. 8–9.

46. Ibid., p. 12.

47. Ibid., p. 13.
48. Ibid., p. 10.
49. Paul, p. 97.
50. *The Native Herald*, vol. II, no. 2, June 1843, p. 11.
51. Rajahgopaul's career can be followed in the columns of *The Native Herald*, copies of which, possibly uniquely extant, can be found in the Archives of Madras Christian College. I have been tempted to quote more extensively here, but in the end, it would merely make the same points. For this letter, see vol. III, no. 3, 3 February 1844, pp. 60–8.
52. *The Native Herald*, vol. XI, no. 3, January 1852, p. 20.
53. *The Native Herald*, vol. XI, no. 3, January 1852, p. 21.
54. *The Native Herald*, vol. XII, no. 6, August 1853, p. 126.
55. *The Native Herald*, vol. XVIII, no. 2, February 1859, p. 35.
56. *The Native Herald*, vol. XVIII, no. 2, February 1859, p. 35.
57. There is no substantial biography of Venkataraman. I have relied on a brief mention of him in S. Sathianadhan, *Sketches of Indian Christians*, London, Madras: 1896; a longer account in Rajaiah Paul. There are observations also in Revd John Noble, *op. cit., A Memoir of the Rev Robert Turlington Noble*, London: 1867.
58. Finding suitable names for Christian converts from Hinduism was always a bit of a problem. It was all part of the debate as to how far you should try to Europeanize. One proposal was to pick names from Milner's Church History, though the same person opined: 'we are not indeed prepared to advise the convert's keeping his birthname after baptism, when the name is the title of some vile and filthy object of idolatry; but why might it not otherwise be retained and transmitted from father to son?' and Noble seems to have acted in this spirit. See 'Family Names among the Natives of India', *Madras Church Missionary Record*, vol. XXII, September 1855, no. 9.
59. John Noble, pp. 5–6.
60. In a letter, 7 April 1841, quoted ibid., p. 119.
61. In a letter to a friend, 20 November 1842, quoted ibid., p. 133.
62. In a letter, 20 November 1843, quoted ibid., p. 156.
63. Ibid., p. 164.
64. Ibid., p. 230.
65. In a report to the CMS Committee, March 1855, quoted ibid., p. 252.
66. Paul, p. 136.
67. I consulted a manuscript copy of D. S. Ram Rao's biography of Venkata Ananta Padmanabha Rao (Anantam) in the archives of the UTC, Bangalore. This incorporated Anantam's own memoirs.
68. Ibid., p. 1.
69. Ibid., p. 19.
70. Ibid., pp. 25–6.
71. Ibid., p. 26.
72. Ibid., pp. 46–7.
73. Ibid., pp. 38–44.
74. Ibid., p. 44.

75. Ibid., pp. 48–53.
76. Ibid., pp. 173–7.
77. A theme explored by Ronald Hyams in *Empire and Sexuality: The British Experience*, Manchester: 1900. I have already referred to such assertions about the Punjab civilians in the 1840s and 1850s.
78. Symonds to Hawkins, 14 August 1852, The Madras Diocesan Committee Correspondence 1832–1917, 1 12 A 12 (UTC: Bangalore).
79. John Edmund Sharkey, Journal, C12/0 222/4 (CMS: Birmingham).
80. Sharkey, Journal, C12/0 222/17.
81. Ibid.
82. Sharkey, Journal, C12/0 225/15.
83. This story is described in both Sathianadhan and Paul.

CHAPTER 8

Conversion: Case-Studies from Bengal and the North

No city felt the pull of the west so strongly as did Calcutta and in this great, if desperate, Dickensian capital of British India there was to occur in the nineteenth century a quite extraordinary intellectual ferment, approached elsewhere, in a Bombay or a Madras, but here of a richness and complexity that continues to fascinate. Indian Christians were caught up in this maelstrom. Those questions of identity that haunted the new intelligentsia were equally theirs. Here we will study Baptist converts, and two outstanding Indian Christians, Krishna Mohan Banerjea and Lal Behari Day. If the north cannot lay claim to a movement of such intellectual vitality as the Bengal Renaissance, there was to be a distinctive encounter between Indian Islam and Christianity. This, however, has been fully investigated,[1] and if for reasons of symmetry it has to be discussed here, it will be but briefly. The focus will once again be on the élite, though neither region lacked mass conversion movements.

QUESTIONS HISTORIOGRAPHICAL

A variety of interpretations of the Bengali intelligentsia more than matches the complexity of the intellectual history itself.[2] Two themes dominate: how the intelligentsia related to their own traditional culture; how they responded to a western culture transmuted through an ever more oppressive colonialism. This led, on the one hand, to a variety of religious reform movements, and on the other, to emergent nationalism. Previously, the former were seen as preceding the latter. Increasingly, they are seen as overlapping and convergent.[3] It is none too difficult to see how a push-pull model might work for the Indian intelligentsia as a whole. Here was one beginning for Indian nationalism. It was peculiarly acute in Bengal. And in Bengal, even more so than in the south, Indian

Christians were in the vanguard. As much in their predicament as in their answers, they can be seen as proto-nationalists.

One obvious problematic about all these approaches in the risk that the intelligentsia becomes too abstracted from the context of social change, and, indeed, such abstraction was, in many ways, the very Achilles heel of this elite. Bardwell Smith tried to get round this flaw when he suggested that intellectuals cannot escape a group identity, and this, he saw, as inevitably entailing some engagement with a traditional religious culture: 'the problem at its deepest is inescapably religious, for the identity is corporate as well as individual in nature. And if so, the dignity of no one is finally enhanced except by working for the dignity of all.'[4] Panikkar's is the most polemical critique of this limitation. We have become too obsessed, he argues, with the origins of ideas, too mesmerized by the syndrome of impact and response, and too insufficiently critical of the failure of the intelligentsia to reach out to matters social and political, and indeed, to emerge earlier on as nationalists. However, he is also concerned to show that the mid-nineteenth century Bengali intellectual had a greater awareness of the destructive consequences of colonial rule than has been recognized.

THE RELIGIOUS CONTEXT IN BENGAL

One initial stratagem for drawing converts into this debate is to ask whether Christianity anyway had any inner connection with indigenous religion in Bengal. If, in the south, it was of such long standing that Christianity could almost claim to be an indigenous faith, this was true neither of Bengal nor the north.

Hinduism in Bengal was profoundly influenced by a regional version of Vaishnavism.[5] Its inspiration came from Caitanya (18 February 1486–29, July 1533), a Brahmin pandit from Nadia (Nawadwip). On his return from a visit to Brindavan he had a vision of Krishna and this was to inspire an extraordinary bhaktic cult of Krishna, one whose worship transcended caste and sect, and was to leave a lasting impression on Bengal. Here was the origin of the vairagi or celibate, Vaishnavite devotees of Krishna. Vaishnavism itself in Bengal was of an even greater antiquity, dating from as early as the eighty century AD, providing an answer both to the challenge of Buddhism, and in the twelfth century, to that of Islam and the crumbling of a more orthodox Hinduism. Caitanya's Vaishnavism was an attempt to steer this movement away from Tantrism and, indeed, in a more orthodox direction.

During his time, Nadia became one of the great intellectual centres of Bengal. Learning, though, was less important than devotion, and this explains its populism: 'slowly but surely', states Chakraborty, 'Vaishnavism became an essential element of the Bengali way of life.'[6] It spread out to both the middle and low castes, and beyond: Chakraborty writes of 'those nameless Vaishnavas who converted, the untouchable, the prostitutes, the pariahs and the neglected pariahs'.[7] It is a language which has clear overtones of a similar appeal of Christianity to the outsider and the oppressed.

One example of this proto-Christian content to Bengali Vaishnavism was its sectarian off-shoot, the Kharta bhoja (worshippers of the lord) movement. Whereas most mass conversion movements in Bengal have an economic explanation, a response, very often, to famine, there was a strong, predisposing religious explanation for the Kharta bhoja conversions of the 1830s. Converts saw in Christ an echo of their own belief in incarnation, in the karta or guru, the prime mover. Their first leader, Ram Saram Pal (he died *c.* 1783) was seen as a reincarnation of Caitanya and hence, by extension, of Krishna himself. Oddie has listed a number of other factors which drew the sect towards Christianity, their openness to further truth, their worship of the one god, their rejection of idol worship and of Brahmins, their millenarianism. Here was a sect attractive to all castes and to both Hindus and Muslims. Its followers, however, were outwardly conformist and only expressed their beliefs in secret worship. But the CMS missionaries were to touch a chord and from 1838 onwards, substantial numbers were to come forward, and by October 1839 some 4000 had become enquirers or been baptised.[8]

Have we a clue in this continuing hold of Vaishnavism in Bengali society as to why some members of the intelligentsia were so sympathetic to Christianity and even became converts? It did not work in the case of Ram Mohun Roy. He faulted Vaishnavism for its bhaktism and its indifference to jnana or knowledge. But the conservative Hindu spokesmen, Radhakanta Deb, was to promote Vaishnavite festivals in Calcutta, though he, of course, was a champion of orthodoxy and displayed no Christian leanings. Keshub Chunder Sen was to be drawn deeply to the 'god-maddened Caitanya', and this could well be the explanation for his positive response to Christ. His bhakti ecstasy was to divide him from Debendranath Tagore and cause the first of the splits in the Brahmo Samaj. But Bankim Chandra Chatterjee turned Vaishnavism away from Christianity and into a proto-nationalist movement. Krishna became a warrior-figure; 'the symbol of the cosmic struggle against the forces of disorder and tyranny.'[9] But there is positive evidence of the links between Vaishnavism and Christianity in the conversion of Lal Behari Day, who felt a warm affection for rural Vaishnavism.

Vaishnavism competed with both Shaktism, the cult of Durga or Kali, and with Tantrism. And if the new élites of the late eighteenth and early nineteenth centuries took to Vaishnavism, this was in part to distance themselves from the old zamindari elite, with their Shaktism, and the better to identify themselves as a new comprador elite. In the long run though, this reflected a process of upward mobility, of sanskritization, which took them in a more conservative, Brahminical direction.

In many ways, Vaishnavism, which had always bordered on the heterodox, was on the wane in nineteenth-century Bengal. If religious orthodoxy itself came under threat from more secular attitudes, Chakraborty can still conclude:

But English education and western concepts could not weaken Hinduism in Bengal. There is no evidence of languor, neglect or depression at any time during the nineteenth century. The impressive durability of Hinduism as a way of life remained unquestionable. Krsna, Siva, Durga, Kali, and many other lesser gods were very popular. The priests enjoyed great authority in the towns and villages. The middle class Hindus in the urban areas observed all sorts of sacraments and rituals.[10]

Just how vulnerable, anyway, was Bengal to evangelical Mission? Many Europeans in the eighteenth century saw a degenerate society, one worn down by continuing warfare and famine. Indians might well agree, but they would see the cause as that appalling period of Company rapine in the 1760s and 1770s. Was it the case that popular Hinduism had never been so violent and cruel? Revisionist historians argue that eighteenth-century decline has been much exaggerated, that here was a society still with a strong intellectual tradition, especially at Nadia, and that this was a society not in decline but in flux.[11]

Ye the nineteenth-century Bengali intelligentsia felt peculiarly threatened by critique from the west and recognized a paramount need for social and religious reform. Brahmoism was in mid-century the most significant voice for reform and in Brahmoism Christian Mission found its greatest rival for the mind of Calcutta's bhadralok élite. Given the anxiety about the condition of society and religion, the more likely response was to become a Brahmo rather than a Christian.

BRAHMOISM

Brahmoism was a multifarious movement. In one direction it leaned heavily towards rationalism, and turned towards secularism. In another, it became metaphysical, even mystical, and reactivated the Hindu faith. Did it provide sufficient grounds for staying within Hinduism and turning aside from Christianity?[12] Whereas European missionaries had hopes that both Ram Mohun Roy and Keshub Chunder Sen would convert, it seems for more obviously the case that they effectively vaccinated Hinduism against Christianity. This was only just in time, for in the 1830s, above all through Alexander Duff, it was to come under exceptional assault.

There was a running battle between Brahmoism and Mission. Ram Mohun Roy himself, founder of the Brahmo Samaj in 1830, rejected all expressions of dogma. He would have no truck with either the divinity of Christ or the Vedantic concept of maya. His was an eighteenth-century deist approach, a rationalist approach to religion. Out of anger at the abusive language of the missionaries, he, however, defended popular Hinduism, especially the worship of images. He also tackled social issues, in particular, the condition of women. Through Roy's apologetics, Hinduism acquired a rationalism and a humanism, those very qualities which attracted the intelligentsia to Christianity in the 1830s.

Under the leadership of Debendranath Tagore the Brahmo Samaj sensed the imperative need to resist Mission and so adopted an alternative theist line. In the Dharma Grantha of 1850, Debendranath drew up a new statement of Hindu faith. Even so, Brahmoism remained poised between rationalist and metaphysical alternatives: Akshay Kumar Datta, for example, pushed it in a more rationalist direction. To quote Sisir Kumar: 'this strong sense of reason made the Brahmo Samaj a possible alternative to popular Hinduism as well as Christianity.'[13] Keshub Chunder Sen took Brahmoism farthest in a Christian direction. Not that he was ever to recognize any unique claims for Christ. But this was still too much for Debendranath and the movement split in 1866 into the Adi Brahmo Samaj and Sen's New Dispensation. Sen's was a theological inclusivism, but with a twist: no faith has all the answers, one fulfilled the other. Given Sen's high regard for an Oriental Christ, an inner and invisible but universal Christ that prevailed over the merely external western version, could not anyone with Christian proclivities accommodate these within Brahmoism? He incorporated Christian practices of congregational prayer. Sen got curiously close to a Christian concept of sin, so much so that Sisir Kumar sees here a Christianized Hinduism, one that 'dammed the waves of Christianity and also prepared the ground for a more militant religious thought'.[14]

The movement divided yet again in 1878, with the setting up of the Sadharan Samaj. This had a far more committed programme of social reform. It had broken away in protest at Sen's seeming betrayal of his reformist views on marriage. Only in the 1880s, Sisir Kumar claims, was there a new political element added to this theological debate: 'no one before Vivekananda made patriotism a living element of religion.'[15]

So here in Calcutta was a confused intelligentsia, torn between the more secular culture of the West and their own traditions. Often cut off from the countryside, they underestimated the resilience of popular Hinduism. They projected onto society their own internal fears.

PROTO-NATIONALISM

Nationalism was the ultimate defence against the West. It was, of course, a turning of one of Europe's more dubious offspring against itself. Given Calcutta's longer and more ferocious exposure to western values, if more in the shape of Bengali patriotism than an all-India variety, its intelligentsia were to be the first to adopt this ideology. In the south converts had also faced an accusation of betrayal of their culture, but nowhere near so fiercely as in Calcutta. Bengali Christian converts on this score could but experience a strong sense of unease.

Quite deliberately the Bengali intelligentsia took a stand against Mission. Maybe Mission itself drew up the battle lines. Mohar Ali points out that between 1833 and 1857 30 out of 171 Mission stations were based in Calcutta.[16] Admittedly, the response of the Bengali intelligentsia was ambivalent: the decades from 1830 to 1870 were probably those in which they were most well disposed towards the West. Had not the British rescued them from Muslim tyranny and was there not the hand of province in their introducing a more liberal regime into India? It was only by the 1870s, claims Tapan Raychaudhuri, that 'the Bengali intelligentsia had developed an extreme sensitiveness in matters affecting their relationship with the English'.[17] Only then did they grasp how denationalizing western education had been.

But one could predate this perception. Christian missionaries became a target. With his invidious tract, *India and Indian Missions*, published in 1839, Alexander Duff was seen as a special threat.

One organization that set out to defend a reformed Hinduism against the missionaries was the Tattvabodhini Sabha, set up in 1838. Through its merger in 1842 with the Brahmo Samaj, it became a quite powerful counterweight. Its most famous tract was *Vaidantic Doctrines Vindicated,* published in 1845. In time, though, the rationalist mind of Akshay Kumar Datta was to dissuade Debendranath from such claims to the infallibility of the Vedas.[18] The vernacular press turned increasingly anti-Christian: to quote from the *Calcutta Review:* 'all these publications have a decided anti-Christian tone and must produce a considerable sapping effect upon the minds of their 20,000 readers who show the value they attach to them by paying for them.' There was a very considerable, if unsuccessful, agitation in Calcutta against the Lex Loci Act of 1850. (Oddly, the leaders of the Tattvobodhini Sabha did not sign the petition.) Even so, Mohar Ali has argued that the missionaries were pushed into a defensive position. Clearly the converts were caught in the crossfire. Was there a way out for them from this charge of denationalization?

Beyond the chronology of this project, and so too late in time to be included as a case-study, yet too important to be overlooked, is the extraordinary story of Brahmabandhab Upadhyay (1861–1907).[19] On 10 September 1907, he was arrested on a charge of sedition. In fact, he was to die a free man. Prior to his coming to trial, he died from tetanus, following an operation for a hernia. Here was both a Christian and a nationalist. 'We have said over and over again that we are not Swadeshi only so far as salt and sugar are concerned', he wrote. 'Our aspirations are higher than the Himalayas. Our pain is as intense as if we had a volcano in us. What we want is the emancipation of India.'[20] Yet if he belonged to the extremist wing of Congress, he never belonged to any terrorist group and did not advocate violence.

Bhavani Charan Banerjee, the youngest of three sons of a policeman, Debicharan, was born in 1861 in the village of Khanyam, some thirty-five miles north of Calcutta. Grandmother Chanramoni, fiercely proud of her Brahmin caste, exercised a strong influence. Kali was the family tutelary deity, though a circumambient Vaishnavism did something to soften her presence. He studied at Bhatpara, a nearby famous tol. One dominant influence on the young Banerjee was Keshub Chunder Sen and he became a Brahmo in 1887. Sen inspired in him a deep reverence for Christ. Another influence was that of his uncle, Kali Charan Banerjee, who had joined the INC in 1885 and in 1887 set up the non-denominational Protestant organization, the Christo Samaj. Banerjee went on to teach in the Free Church Institution of the Scottish Mission in Calcutta and various CMS institutions in Sind. He was to be present at his father's death in 1891 in nearby Multan. There he came across Joseph Faa Di Bruno's Manual on Catholic belief. On his conversion, he took the name Upadhyaya Brihmabandu, to become Brahmabhandhab, a Hindu version of Theophilus or friend of Brahma.

He should be seen as one inspirer of an Indian Christianity. He refused to denationalize. He wore the clothes of a sanyasin, a conscious harking back to Robert de Nobili and his policy of inculturation. But he fell out with the papal delegate, Mgr Zaleski, over his plans to set up a monastery on the banks of the Narmada. His was a wish to behave as Hindu but to believe as a Catholic, to separate Hindu culture from Hindu religion.

He became an exponent of a natural theology. Whereas Protestantism saw man as fallen, Catholicism has a belief in man's powers of reason, and this was his starting point. 'To destroy the religion of nature and reason', he wrote, 'you destroy the supernatural religion of Christ.'[21] He wanted as well to draw out the natural theology in Hinduism and to purify it. Vendantism could play just the same role in shaping an Indian Christianity as Greek philosophy had in shaping Thomism. It led him to tolerate many aspects of Hinduism, caste, the worship of idols, the avatar status of Krishna, the social and psychological, if not theological, value of festivals, all condemned by missionaries and Indian Christians. This was all a part of his insistence that conversion must not denationalize. He was raising fundamental questions about the relationship between Indian culture and Christianity. Are not other religions, he asked, to be seen as sources of salvation in their own right?[22]

When Upadhyaya, on his return from a year long stay in England in 1903, went through a ceremony of ritual atonement for crossing the dark waters, the prayascitta, he had seemingly abandoned Christianity for Hinduism. He did not see it this way. 'He felt that culturally he was a Hindu whilst being at heart a Christian.'[23] Did the mid-nineteenth-century converts in any way anticipate this attempt at a new synthesis, this kind of Indian Christian nationalism?

Given the extent to which members of the Bengali intelligentsia themselves fell under the spell of the West from the 1820s onwards, converts had cause to wonder why their acceptance of one aspect of the West should have put them so peculiarly beyond the pale. Was there no way back from what Duncan Forrester has perceived as their 'ideological marginality'.[24]

Estranged from their own community by its social ostracism and only partially accepted by the European, theirs was an especially painful position. There were very strong pressures to discover a new Indian Christian identity. Was it any help that missionaries believed their own ideology would revitalize Indian society rather than Ram Mohun Roy's 'milk and water' compromise with Hinduism or Derozian scepticism? They looked to the converts to be the 'Pauls, the Luthers, the Knoxes of their native land', pioneers of both an Indian Renaissance and a Reformation. But how could converts find a way back into their own traditions through an evangelical exclusivism which rejected both India's social structures and its religions? Paradoxically, it was just the imperial and racial arrogance of European missionaries which proved to be the catalyst. We will have to see how such outstanding Indian Christians as Krishna Mohan Banerjea and Lal Behari Day did arrive at some new creative synthesis between Christianity and Hinduism. Banerjea indeed was to claim, 'we are better patriots than the Brahmos'.[25]

BAPTIST CONVERTS IN BENGAL

By January 1854 there some 1200 converts in the Baptist Mission in Bengal and north India. Together with their dependents, this constituted a community of some four to five thousand. Half came from agricultural families though with some fishermen from areas south of Calcutta, Jessore and Barisal, and half from the towns, from a more disparate social background. Rural converts found it easier to carry on with their old activities and proved the more self-sufficient; the urban had often to begin again. But here was a dispersed community and, in George Pearce's view, one very dependent on European missionaries and quite unable to support their own priests.[26]

Given Pearce's prominent role in conversion stories, through his connection with the school at Entally, it is appropriate to begin with his reflections on the problematic of conversion and its aftermath.[27] So great was the material gulf between European missionaries and Indians, exacerbated by language, that missionaries were 'exceedingly liable to mistake'. Pearce saw idolatry as a greater barrier than caste. He had a low opinion of the energy and drive of converts: 'a deficiency of emotion, a distrust of themselves with regard to enterprise, a shrinking at difficulties, little or no ambition to imitate foreign customs, and perhaps little expectations of any immediate or considerable enlargement of their numbers.' This was of a piece with a general disparagement by Europeans of the Bengali character. But whatever their caste, converts betrayed no sense of regret or degradation at their conversion: 'on the contrary, a strong conviction of superiority to the heathen is universally apparent.' Unlike Muslims, once they had converted, Christians no longer attended local Hindu festivals. But Baptists did not expect converts wholly to escape their backgrounds: 'can it create surprise if there should cling to the new disciples some rags and remnants of the old clothing?'[28] But they did not apostasize.

Some Baptist Muslim Converts

Given that east Bengal was a Muslim majority area Muslims featured less than might have been expected among converts. A model convert was Sujatali, from the ashraf elite—his father was the physician to the prime minister of Awadh. He was baptised in the Ganges on 8 May 1824. Most Baptist conversions came through the Bible. A crucial intermediary for Sujatali's encounter with the New Testament was Bagchi, a converted Brahmin. Despite his mother threatening suicide, he persevered. Following conversion, one irate Muslim collared him: 'it is as well for you that you are in a country under the government of Christians; I would', he threatened, snapping his finger and thumb together, 'have cut you bit by bit, in this manner.' Sujatali went on to be a missionary preacher in both Hindustani and Bengali, a deacon under W. H. Pearce in a native church, and, if unable to speak English, a distributor of tracts to European soldiers and sailors.

Another Muslim convert came from a merchant background. His father had traded with Réunion. He also was a well educated, Bible convert. 'Having been well acquainted with the Koran and the tradition among Mohammedans', George Pearce reported, 'he is able to compare the two systems and has evidently done so carefully and by the blessing of God with good effect.' He was baptised in September 1847.[29]

There was a Delhi-born Muslim, Unwar Ali. When Pearce showed reluctance to let him marry a Christian convert, he took himself off in umbrage to Murshidabad, there to marry a Muslim girl. But he drifted back and refusal to rise to abuse from his wife finally convinced Pearce of his sincerity; 'there is nothing so difficult for a native to bear as abuse', yet he did not beat her. He also came from an educated ashraf background. He went on to be a munshi and a corrector of proof. Baptist converts quite often made a living in the Mission's press.[30]

Baptist Hindu Converts

The Chitpur Native school, later moved on health grounds to Entally, was often the context for Hindu conversions. Many had come from

Pearce's Mission at Luckyantipur. It provided a course of liberal education in Bengali and English.[31] Students could stay for a four year course in Theology. One Chitpur convert was Gunga Narayan Sil. Three years of education at the school had convinced him of the 'emptiness' of Hinduism, and a reading of Sale's translation of the Koran had done the same for Islam. He read the Bible and 'became, if not altogether, at least an almost Christian'. He wished to help his fellow Bengalis: 'I thought that a man would be truly charged with cruelty in a country ravaged by a dreadful disease who possessed a remedy that would cure but kept the same by himself, and refused to give it to his dying fellow-creatures.' Hence his publishing a newspaper article, favourably comparing Christianity with Hinduism. This led to public opprobrium, to his own loss of faith and to his atheism. But the evidences for Christianity told against him, and he reverted. Interestingly, a decisive factor had been his realizing that Bacon, Newton and other scientists 'had not thought Christianity beneath their attention', and Voltaire, Paine and other 'infidels' had undergone death-bed conversions. He went on to become a distinguished Bengali preacher, but died young, in 1843.[32]

Hurry Hurr Sandal: A Baptist Convert Turned Anglican

Another Hindu convert was a Kulin Brahmin, Hurry Hurr Sandal, born in 1820, from Jessore. Following on English-medium education, it was a lecture by Baptist missionary, Revd J. Penny, comparing Kali and Milton's Moloch, that alerted him to idolatry. Some writings by Ram Mohun Roy accelerated the conversion process. He now read a Bengali translation of the New Testament. Ganga Narayan Sil, already a convert, was the confidante of these doubts. Sandal accompanied him on his missionary visit to Luckyantipur. It was the threat by an anxious family to dispatch him to Benares that hastened his conversion. He went to live with Sujatali.

There then followed one of those cloak and dagger stories to achieve a reconciliation with his wife, Rammoni. At first she rejected him. After three months, however, her feelings altered, and it was in the aftermath of a Durga festival, 'when most of the people were weary with their orgies, and were fast locked in sleep',[33] and after bribing the servants, that she made her escape. Hers was a far more exceptional conversion story than her husband's. At this stage she was illiterate—it was taboo for women from wealthy backgrounds to be educated—but quickly she learnt to read. She was the first of her kind from a Bengal landed background to be converted.

In 1843, Sandal turned Anglican. He taught under K. M. Banerjea in Christ Church school. In 1856 he was ordained a deacon, and in 1857 a priest. Bishop Wilson appointed him as his first Cathedral missionary.

Intriguingly, in his Mission Journals,[34] we can see the way he fended questions from his erstwhile co-religionists. Questions ranged across all aspects, from idolatry to caste. They were particularly angry at this apostasy by a Brahmin. There were questions related to Hindu worship and Hindu values. Clearly Sandal felt personal distaste for the Durga festival and this prompted his own attack on idolatry, based, he claimed, on the shastras. One Brahmin response was to argue that one had first to learn the alphabet before one could read. Sandal endorsed European missionary abuse of the gods. Why worship the inferior, he challenged? Was not Rama a mere king and warrior? Incarnation in Hinduism was often only for carnal satisfaction. On another tack, how could you prove, he queried, the doctrine of karma?: 'the tenet is quite contrary to reason and the laws of nature.' And should one not at least know for what sins you now suffered?

Caste was another area of debate. How, one Hindu wanted to know, could a low caste illiterate convert understand religion? Sandal replied that 'almost all Hindu saints were born by Brahmin fathers and Shudra mothers.' Even the Bhagavad Gita affirmed that caste had nothing to do with the worship of God. 'In my worship', he asserted, 'the distinction of sex, caste, name, profession, avails nothing, but faith is all prevalent.' Despite his ability to draw on Hindu texts, Sandal was every bit the evangelical exclusivist: 'as Hinduism, Mohammedanism and Christianity are quite opposite to each another, how can all be true? Did you at any time hear of a governor who enacted different laws for each of the divisions of Calcutta and all of them diametrically opposed to each other?' Sandal had learnt his lessons well.

Inevitably Sandal incurred personal abuse. Just to look on him, one Brahmin stated, was 'to incur the displeasure of the gods'. Those who renounced the sacred thread had no right, his opponents asserted, to quote the shastras. 'My apostasy', Sandal saw, 'is so great and heinous that it is sin to see and talk with me.' But there were exceptions, and members of all classes permitted him access to their homes: 'most of them confess at least in words that the Christian shastras are better than the Hindu are.'

But he was bound to want to undo some of this alienation. One can see the slow working out of a Bengali, even an Indian patriotism. He later endorsed Banerjea's opposition to Henry Maine's 1866 Remarriage of Native Convert's Act, distressed at the way this would enforce widowhood on the Hindu wife and alienate the Hindu community. He sought to put the Native Church on its own two feet, initiating an endowment fund for the congregation to pay for its own pastor, and trying to raise enough money to build its own independent church. He died on 4 September 1887.[35]

Many factors could be the catalyst for conversion. For one Kayasth convert it was distaste for the churruck or hook swinging festival: 'these atrocities could form no part of true religion.'[36] One young man, on the road from the age of fourteen to twenty, from one sacred Hindu site to another, finally rebelled at 'the wretched conduct' of a priest at Benares,[37] another did so on discovering in a Baptist tract that Krishna could lie.[38]

But no action of the Baptists was to match the fury that Alexander Duff and his conversions were to arouse in Calcutta.

Krishna Mohan Banerjea

All the cross currents of ideas in Calcutta came together in the life of K. M. Banerjea, intellectually the most distinguished convert of his generation.[39] All of Young Bengal's almost visceral loathing for Hinduism and Hindu society was there, but in his case, it was followed by both a profoundly Christian phase and a later quest, through an Indian anticipation of an inclusivist theology, to rediscover something of his Indian identity. His often uneasy relationship with European Mission does something to explain these deep intellectual disturbances.

He was born on 24 May 1813, in the village of Nevagram, four miles south of Barvipur, 24 Parganas. His father, originally dependent on the rental income of his father-in-law, when this was withdrawn had to make his way as an assistant abkari superintendent. His mother, Sri Srimati, was a lady of punctilious piety. For example, she refused to eat any cooked food on pilgrimage to Puri, for fear it should be defiled by the gaze of anyone from the lower castes. She and her father, Ramjay Vidyabushan, a Sanskritist of some local standing, tugged the young Banerjea back towards his own traditions. Here was the source of his love of Sanskrit and his interest in the Hindu classics.

But he was a Kulin Brahmin by caste and this in time bred real distress at the plight of women in Hindu society. The Kulin privilege of practising polygamy had considerably swollen the number of widows: to maintain caste, Kulin families, with so few suitable husbands available, were forced to marry off their daughters to elderly Kulins, often soon to die and leave their wives child widows. Krishna was shocked on his own marriage in 1828 to discover the penances his widowed mother-in-law had to undergo.

If humanitarian concern for women was one key dynamic leading him in another intellectual direction, his education accelerated the process. He was a scholarship boy, educated from the age of six to eleven at Hare School, and from eleven onwards, financed by the Calcutta School Society, at Hindu College. Both schools had a strongly secular flavour. But he also attended classes in Sanskrit College (the two schools shared the same building). On leaving Hindu College in 1829, he returned as a teacher to Hare's Potuldanga or Central Vernacular College.

Through this education he encountered the two most formative influences in his early life, the great philanthropist and atheist, David Hare,[40] and the mercurial, half-Portuguese, Derozio, appointed in March 1827 to teach history and literature at Hindu College. Scepticism rather than atheism, itself a long term constituent of Hinduism, proved to be for Young Bengal the true corrosive of Hindu belief—or so Amales Tripathi suggested to me in a conversation—and Banerjea acquired this cast of mind from Derozio. A questioning, at times iconoclastic, rationalism underlay the revolt of Young Bengal.

The notorious incident of throwing cooked beef into the quarters of a neighbouring Brahmin household took place in Banerjea's Calcutta home, though he was absent at the time. By 1831, through his editorship of *The Enquirer*, one of the many radical journals of the day, Banerjea had become a leading spokesman of Young Bengal. Subsequent persecution forced him to leave home. One can see that social alienation, which led to bitter attacks on the Brahmin priesthood and caste, together with social persecution, would have been enough to explain his rejection of Hinduism. But should we agree with Dr Abhijit Datta that Derozian writings were 'as much responsible for the reception of Krishna Mohan and Mohesh Ghosh as were the spirited endeavours of Reverend Duff on the score'?[41]

At the outset of his career in India, Duff was at his most formidable, and it was at this point that he and KMB met.[42] One biographer believes his finest hour was at the age of twenty-four, in 1830, when he drew up his educational project for India: 'the rest of his life was spent in working out the full implications of this first momentous choice . . . He is a young man's hero.'[43] In many ways Duff was driven by a quite terrifyingly simple idea: Mission had to destroy Hinduism and the only means was through the agency of an indigenous, anglicized, Indian elite.[44] Duff did not reject out of hand the alternative strategy of itinerating and vernacularism—indeed, his own strategy depended on the anglicized elite turning vernacularism to the cause of Christianity—but, at this stage, his was the shuddering alternative of an English-medium higher education. Everything hinged on the conversion of the likes of Banerjea. For a young man already in the grip, in Kopf's account, of an Eriksonian identity crisis, had Banerjea any hope of resistance?

Born on 25 April 1806 in Moulin, Perthshire, Duff was brought up under the influence of strongly Calvinist parents, together with that of the local presbyter, Dr Stewart, a Charles Simeon man. This was to be an all-enveloping evangelical upbringing. Following his early education at Perth Grammar School, in November 1821, at the tender age of fifteen—and this early exposure to college explains Duff's later-readiness to exploit the precocity of the youth of Calcutta—he joined St Andrews University. Until the appointment in 1823 of Thomas Chalmers to the Chair of Moral Philosophy, the University, for Duff, was something of an intellectual backwater. His was to be the inspiration for Duff's sense of an undivided philosophical, scientific and revealed truth. Together with his younger friend, Urquart—and it was his premature death in 1828 that triggered Duff's decision to become a missionary—he took to teaching in Sabbath schools for the poor, his 'first experience of missionary work',[45] and displayed an active interest in foreign Mission. They started the St Andrews University Missionary Society.

The idea of a Scottish Mission to India had come from a Moderate in the General Assembly, John Inglis, and his appeal for a volunteer had reached Duff's ears by the winter of 1827–28. But Chalmers had already been won over—Dr Marshman had visited him at St Andrews. The pressure was on Duff to come forward. On 9 July 1829 he married, on 12 August he was ordained, and on 9 September he set sail.

It was a journey memorable for two ship-wrecks. The first was on Daffen Island off Good Hope, when Duff lost his entire library but his Bible and prayerbook, all highly symbolic for a man so emotionally charged. The second was on Saugor Island, at mouth of the Ganges. By the time he arrived in Calcutta on 27 May 1830, he might well be excused for supposing that he was a man of destiny. In Duff there was a man of a 'certain massive Puritanism', driven by a 'Carlylean duty', humourless, and to be for 'hundreds of Bengalis the embodiment of intellectual fearlessness and faith.'[46]

Events happened in rapid succession. Baptist Carey gave his blessing to Duff's vision of a Christian higher education. The Home Mission had foreseen a school in the mofussil. Duff opted for Calcutta. Ram Mohun Roy, quick to sense the driven nature of Duff, found him a site in the premises of the Brahmo Samaj he was just quitting, and on 13 July 1830, on Chitpur Road, the Assembly Institute, generally called Duff's Institute, opened.

He became notorious through his offering, in August 1830, a series of lectures for the students of Hindu College. These were to take place in his own house in College Square. After a rather innocuous opening lecture by James Hill, on the moral qualifications necessary for investigating truth, the College banned the attendance of their students.

Duff was quick to spot the potentiality for conversion among the disturbed and rebellious students of Hindu College. He invited Banerjea to visit him at his home. He had heard Hill's lecture. But it was Duff's reproving him for his 'serious neglect' of Christianity and his 'not inquiring into its evidences and doctrine' that had moved him. 'This word "inquiring" ', he recorded, 'was so uttered as to produce an impression upon me which I cannot sufficiently well describe.'[47] He attended Duff's second, unaborted series of lectures. On 28 August 1832 *The Enquirer* reported the conversion of Mohesh Chunder Ghose. Banerjea's followed on 17 October 1832, but only after a long mental battle with the concepts of the atonement and the trinity which he could not square with reason. 'What brought Krishna Mohan to the point of final decision', accepts Rajaiah Paul, 'we do not know.'[48]

Can we read into his own conversion his account of that of his friend, Mohesh Ghose?[49] At the Hindu College, 'his understanding', Banerjea preached, 'became too enlightened to submit to the monstrous dogmas of Brahmanism'. 'From worshipping many gods he ran to the opposite error of worshipping no god—and thus he shook off the trammels of superstition and idolatry merely to put on the still more galling chains of infidelity and atheism.' Then, 'prompted by a natural disposition to metaphysical speculation and partly impelled by the evidently rational calls of several friends, he undertook to enquire into the evidences of Christianity'. He discovered that 'the evidence of Natural and Revealed religion were too overwhelming not to produce some impressions upon his mind.' But was he sincere Mohesh still asked? 'His conscience convicted him. He found that there had been no sincere enquiry on his part; he became humbled at the idea—and he prayed for divine forgiveness and direction.' Then came conversion: 'A flood of light rushed into my mind.'

Even so, for Banerjea, there had to be a necessary leap of faith. Here Duff's overwhelming presence was surely the determining factor. Paul continues: 'one can well imagine those eight weeks of preparation for baptism— the daily meeting between Krishna Mohun Banerjea and the

Scottish missionary, the intimate soul-searching conversations between the two, the praying together, the gradual conviction in the young Hindu's mind, culminating in the absolute and final surrender of body, mind and soul to the keeping of the newly found saviour.'[50] Banerjea chose to be baptised in Duff's lecture room in his house.

But Banerjea soon put some distance between himself and Duff. He was not to take over his personality to the same extent as Anderson had that of Rajahgopaul. Preferring Episcopalianism to Presbyterianism, he turned Anglican. Mohesh had already betrayed Duff through his baptism in Calcutta Old Church. Duff had to swallow his pride. He looked on the conversion of Banerjea, together with those of three other boys from Hindu College, as the legitimizing of his life's work. On his return to India in 1841, he greeted Banerjea's ordination with these words: 'what is wanted to inspire under God the rapid and extensive spiritual regeneration of India is not an exotic artificially sustained life, but an indigenous, self-sustaining self-propagating life.' With Banerjea's priesthood, 'the process of indigenous self-propagation may be said to have begun'.[51]

Banerjea's career in the Church of England was invariably fractious. Foreign missionaries and churchmen did not always share that high sense of his own worth. From his becoming superintendent of the CMS school in Amherst Street (Mirzapur) and Bishop Wilson's admitting him as a candidate for Holy Orders in 1833 until his ordination in 1839 and his becoming the priest of Christ Church, in Cornwallis Square on 27 September 1839, a church specially built for him, Banerjea quite frequently ran up against the authorities.

Clearly he resented the time he had to spend at the expense of his preparing for ordination as a catechist. This all blew up in 1837.[52] In a letter of 16 January he refused to go and work as a catechist either under Weitbrecht at Burdwan or Deer at Nadia. The secretary of the CMS Corresponding Committee, Henry Chapman, reported that Banerjea 'adhered strenuously to his determination to obey the instructions of the Committee as his temporal patrons only so far as he may consider them consistent with due subordination to his Ecclesiastical superiors.' The Committee stood by its conviction that 'no native candidate for Ordination' should be presented 'who have not purchased to themselves "a good and great boldness in the faith which is Christ Jesus" by preparatory labour as catechist'. Dealtry had already in a letter of 1 February conveyed Bishop Wilson's insistence of at least a three month stint as a catechist, all the more needful in Banerjea's case 'as he has the advantage of no regular system of education, either collegiate or otherwise'. (Clearly, Hindu College did not count.) Banerjea's supervisor at Mirzapur school, Revd Sandys, came to his defence, but it was quite apparent that he had not taken on the duties of a catechist. The Committee were offended by his attitude: 'great allowance should be made for his situation and for the habits of respectful deference to the Archdeacon (Dealtry) and though his letters are certainly not such as might have been addressed by a young candidate for ordination to a body of gentlemen, his elders and temporal superiors, and the representatives of the Society who have long supported him, I should be very willing to consign them to oblivion, on his expressing his regret for having written them.' How could they give their consent to ordination 'to a young man whom we do not consider qualified in his present frame of mind for the humble, laborious, and self-denying duties of a missionary'. 'He had much to learn—much to unlearn before he would be qualified to do service and credit to the cause.' One can see how utterly galling to an ambitious and gifted Indian missionary paternalism would have been.

And the real fears of the local committee were precisely about status:

It would tend to encourage all sorts of extravagant expectations among young Christian converts or orphans, it would lay the first stones towards the establishment of a Native ministry very nearly as expensive as a European one and therefore utterly inadequate for the wants of this land, and worse even than these it would demonstrate to the hundreds of educated and Hindooized young men in Calcutta that as Christian missionaries were far better paid than Brahmin priests the profession of the faith of the Gospel would be better paid than Brahmin priests.

Even Charles Trevelyan, so keen to advance the missionary cause, signed this statement. Could they have been genuinely alarmed at the prospect of so many false vocations?

Banerjea's career could have been held up, not only to save money at a time of cutting costs, but to set a precedent against converting on merely material grounds. Banerjea saw it as a racial snub, a way of preventing Indians from acquiring the same status as Europeans. If Bishop Wilson was to rescue Banerjea's cause, clearly this had always been more than a mere boundary dispute between a missionary organization and the ecclesiastical establishment. This was a quarrel between the colonizer and the colonized. In fact, Banerjea had some cause to be grateful to the local committee for insisting that he spend time as a catechist. He went to Burdwan, some seventy-two miles north west of Calcutta. Weitbrecht, a Basle missionary, a good friend of Leupolt, and a not unsympathetic man, had, together with the active support of the late and present raja of Burdwan, taken over an ambitious scheme for local education. Burdwan is one of the most beautiful parts of Bengal and Banerjea should have enjoyed his time there.

But an even more absorbing experience lay ahead, for in 1838, just to the north, in Krishnagar, the kharta bhoja conversions began. Banerjea was there at the start. As an insider, he was likely to have a greater insight than the European missionaries into the true dynamics of such a movement. He subsequently wrote to Weitbrecht: 'I cannot help regretting that such glowing accounts were sent to England and must regard this as premature . . . We had no time for full enquiries when we were at Krishnagar and the little enquiry we made brought to light much that was painful to us, as well as much that was cheering.[53] He was beginning to shape up as quite a good missionary!

If the Anglican establishment, in the form of Bishop Wilson and Bishop's College, was to claim Banerjea as one of its own, and clearly Banerjea was a respected pastor of Christ Church, his relationship with both bishop and college was to be uneasy. In the early 1840s, he took on the running of Seal's College: it would seem he was more sensitive to the claims of caste of its students than the Jesuits had been.[54] In August 1847 he turned down Wilson's invitation to be a native missionary of the new St Paul's Cathedral. Banerjea had insisted on the same salary as the European missionaries. Wilson was outraged: 'he has been poisoning all the minds of the native students with the same spirit of conceit and unthankfulness.'[55] This still rankled three years later. Reporting the appointment of one Revd C. Davies, Wilson added: 'I only delay the filling up of the foundation for a native missionary because I have not yet found one suitable individual amongst our converts. The only one whom I had long intended to nominate refused the offer on the most miserable plea of not having the same advantages and allowances as the English clergymen.'[56]

But clearly the issue of quality of pay was more pervasive. It was a question which beset Bishop's College. Professor Street deplored the former agreement to give equal salaries to all those educated in the college. For Street it was obvious that the material needs of Indians were less than those of Europeans: 'though they have chairs and tables they will sit in the native fashion, though they own knife and fork and spoon they will prefer their fingers; though they have boots and pantaloons to appear abroad in, they will sit in dhooti and shudder when quite at home.' One explanation was pressure from those of a mixed race, acutely sensitive to any snub. But he also put it down to 'the infidel democratic spirit spread abroad by the non-religious educational schemes and institutions rife in India'.

And then he picked on Banerjea. The rot set in through 'the ill-judged manner which the conversion of Revd K. M. Banerjea (to whom and justly they have all looked as their leader and pattern) was hailed by the Europeans of Calcutta. He and his wife were and have continued to be involved in everything that is European, a course for which moreover he and his comrades were prepared by their previous training in the Hindoo College'. But Street recognized that Banerjea's stand on the St Paul's post had been an isolated one; he had not made equalization of salary a condition for accepting the ministry.

Street was not in the least impressed by the candidates Banerjea was putting forward for the college from schools in his care. The Revd Long, to prove himself one of the more radical CMS missionaries, worried that, should Indian Christians ape the mores of Europeans, it would merely strengthen the prejudice that 'Christianity is an English religion connected with their Saxon race as Hinduism is associated with India'.[57] Banerjea, for his part, was simply looking for employment for Indian Christians. He had hoped that, through the renewal of the Company's Charter in 1853, chaplaincies would no longer be filled through patronage, but, failing this, might not Indian Christians at least be appointed to sub-assistant chaplaincies, if at a lower salary?[58]

Bishop Wilson had to eat his words when Banerjea was appointed to a professorship at Bishop's College. He was too much the high churchman for Wilson, but, he conceded: 'I have no kind of prejudice against him. He is cold but sound in faith and of very fair abilities and requirements.[59] Ironically, he had been appointed on 31 May 1851 as Street's successor. He reminded the college that prior to his appointment as deacon in 1837 he had been a student there. Nothing in his opening speech could give the authorities any cause for alarm. He would 'fight the Lord's battle in this land of idolatry and pantheism, of superstitious credulity on the one hand and of philosophical scepticism on the other'; he would fight 'the elemental polytheism of the Vedas, the pantheism of the Vedanta, the infidelity and sophistry of the Sankhya, the idolatry and hero-worship of the Puranas and the Tantras, and all the moral, social and spiritual evils which have accumulated in the country by the prevalence of those monstrous errors and ungodly practices for many centuries.'[60] Here was an insider who could tackle head-on all those 'errors' which an exclusivist foreign missionary could only dimly grasp.

The new principal, Professor Kay, approved the appointment. The question of pay came up, with Banerjea giving it a twist by wondering if Europeans might not live on less. Should he go on running Christ Church? The recent conversion of Gyanandra Tagore encouraged him to do so, and this was, in fact, to be the case.[61] Not until 19 March 1852 was his appointment as third professor to be confirmed. By February 1853 he had been promoted to second. Other honours followed. In March 1853 he was appointed examiner in Sanskrit at Fort William College, the first Indian to hold the post. Grudgingly, the Bishop conceded this to be an honour for the college. Banerjea remained at the college until his retirement on 20 December 1867.

There was something almost Pauline about the way Banerjea attacked Hinduism at this stage. He reported a number of polemical encounters.[62] Some Vaishnavites paid a friendly visit to the college. He was not convinced of their liberalism on caste or Brahminical ritual and ridiculed their wish 'to see the Lord face to face'. He queried the theism of Nyoga philosophy with a visiting Brahmin; were not the aphorisms of its founders 'mutually contradictory' and were there not 'sentences which are seemingly opposed to theism of any kind?' He spurned claims in the local press for the compatibility of the Vedanta with human reason. It was 'in some important points essentially opposed to known and ascertained truth'. But his position was to change.

Here is not the space to do justice to the way Banerjea in time sought some realignment with Hindu culture. The clue lay in the manner of his critique of social practice. The plight of women, for example, should not be blamed on the Puranas but on custom.[63] The traditional Vedic texts did not sanction caste or idolatry. In his post 1865 writings there was an anticipation of fulfilment theology. To quote T. V. Philip: 'it was no longer Christianity and Hinduism contrasted, but Christianity as fulfilment of Hinduism. For him, no one could be a true Hindu without being a true Christian.'[64] For someone who had been one of the most scholarly critics of Hindu thought, and whatever the limitations of fulfilment theology, this was a major shift.

And this took on a political complexion. He played a major role in setting up in 1868 the Bengal Christian Association. In 1875 he was the president of the India Association. If not quite a damascene conversion in reverse, Banerjea's neophyte zeal had given way to a much more tolerant attitude towards his own culture: 'to him was mainly due the reincorporation of Christian converts into the national fold. Indeed, the progress of assimilation developed itself to such lengths that in every movement of national importance his services and even his leadership came to be regarded as a necessity.'[65] He died on 11 May 1885.

Lal Behari Day

Next to Banerjea, Day was the most highly regarded of the Bengali Christian converts. His life was also to be entangled with Duff's, less in terms of conversion and more in terms of the recovery of his Bengali identity.[66]

He was born in 1824 in the village of Talpar, some sixty to seventy miles north of Calcutta, in Burdwan, a part of Bengal he never ceased to love. His mother, but sixteen at the time, does not seem to have exercised a great influence, though Day was to record her distress at his leaving at the age of nine for Calcutta: 'that night she had not a wink of sleep, she tossed from one side of her bed to the other, and every now and then hugged me to her bosom as I was sleeping in the same bed as her.'[67] His father, from Dacca, over forty at the time of his birth, was the dominant parent: 'as I was the son of his old age he loved me excessively, though he was too wise to spoil me with fond affection. As I was not fond of play I was always beside my father, excepting when I was at school, and both morning and evening I had the inestimable privilege of listening to his advice in all matters relating to the conduct of life.'[68] His father was an orthodox Vaishnavite, 'diligent in all the practice of his religious duties.'[69] In keeping with his Suvarna-Vaik or banker's caste, he made a living in Calcutta as a bill and stockbroker. Day's biographer, Macpherson, states: 'he was not a man endowed with great strength of will or force of character in any form, but he possessed distinct individualism and many of the incidents of his life engraved themselves on his son's memory.'[70] The son was to experience great guilt at being asleep when his father died in 1837. One can but speculate on the role Scottish missionaries were to play as surrogate father figures.

Day never ceased to feel the loss of this family background. On returning as a missionary to his village in 1849 he wrote in his journal: 'it would be impossible for Europeans to form an adequate idea of the sacrifices which a respectable native makes when embracing the Christian religion. We speak not of pecuniary sacrifice but we speak of the rending of the social, paternal, filial and fraternal ties which is the immediate effect of the conversion of a Hindu youth.' It was to spare his extended family the pain he knew his conversion would bring that he continued to profess Hinduism 'long after he had ceased to believe in it as a religion.'[71] Even before conversion he was winning prizes at school on such themes as 'The Conversion of St Paul', viewed as an argument for the truth of the Gospel (1841), and 'The falsity of the Hindu Religion' (1842). Day's conversion was marked by profound continuities, both social and cultural, with his background.

There are curious analogies between the Vellalas and Day over the role of caste in the dynamics of their conversion. Day's was a caste which aspired to higher Vaisha status, denied that they were of Sudra or mixed (varna-sankara) caste, saw themselves as superior to Kayasths and Vaidyas, and only recognized Brahmins and Kshatriyas as their superior. If one of the richest castes in Bengal they were 'looked upon as amongst the most degraded': 'indeed it is properly said that if a Brahmin were accidentally to put his foot on the shadow cast by the body of a Suvarna-Vaik, the Brahmin must expiate the vile pollution by ablution in the holy river Ganges.' All this went back to Bellal Sen and his reprisal against the caste for their refusal to attend a banquet he had given and their ridiculing his liaison with a basket-weaver; in retaliation, he had accused them of killing a cow and purchasing stolen gold. It was Sen who had introduced Kulinism into Bengal in the thirteenth century.[72] Such a caste background could well have engendered a sense of social alienation. But Day wrote the story of his caste not through any lapse in his Christian rejection of caste but as an antiquarian.

Day's was a comparable education to Rajahgopaul's. It began in the local village school or pathshala, the admission preceded by a solemn religious ceremony in honour of Saraswati, the goddess of wisdom: no man could, his father believed, acquire knowledge without her blessing.[73] 'We met', Day related, 'under the open sky on a spot of ground in front of the temple of Siva.' His teacher, 'an arithmetician of the first force', though a Brahmin and a pedagogue . . . was ignorant of Sanskrit.'[74] Determined that he should not suffer the same handicap as himself, his father desired that he should study in an English-medium school. David Hare would not let him into his school on the grounds that he was already 'half-Christian', and would 'spoil my boys'.[75] In consequence, Day lost the opportunity of following Banerjea's example, with a scholarship to go to Hindu College. This left the General Assembly's Institution. But his father was only anxious that he master English, a strictly utilitarian education; 'real knowledge was not to be found within the range of English literature, it being confined to the Sanskrit which was the language of the gods.'[76] Nor was he afraid of conversion, intending to withdraw his son 'long before I was able to understand lectures on Christian religion'.[77]

Duff was to have three spells in Calcutta, from 1830–34, 1840–49 and 1856–63, and Day was to encounter him in all three. Though a force for conversion in stages one and two, his was not the decisive influence. Prior to his departure in 1834, Duff had little contact with the young Day, though clearly he had left an indelible impression: 'I cannot say he walked into the class-room—he *rushed* into it, his movements in those days being exceedingly rapid . . . He scarcely stood still for a single second, but kept his feet and his hands moving incessantly, like a horse of high mettle . . . He had his white pocket handkerchief in his hand, which he was every now and then tying round his arm and twisting it into a thousand shapes. He was later to drop the habit of constantly shrugging his shoulders.[78]

On his return—and for Day this was a moment of excitement: 'we all turned out of our classes to catch a glimpse of the prince of educators and of missionaries'[79]—he took up where he had left off, lecturing, both in the school and at home, on chemistry, psychology, ethics, the theology of revelation. This was a time of great upheaval. After the split in the General Assembly in 1843, the school had to abandon its existing precincts and move to Neemtollah Street. There it reopened on 4 March 1844, as the Institute of the Free Church of Scotland. Two months after the split, on 23 July 1843, Day had converted, and may be the final decision was out of loyalty to Duff: 'my path of duty was plain—namely to stick to those who had shown me the way of salvation, and who were then my spiritual fathers.'[80]

Day went to live with the Duffs. He recalled the atmosphere of their home in almost bizarre terms: 'I at the time as a young convert experienced sensations which it is almost impossible to describe. I felt as I had never before felt. I seemed to breathe the atmosphere of heaven.'[81] In time, he moved to a special home for converts in Calcutta's Grub Street, Bartala Street. As a teacher, a friend, and above all, a surrogate father, Duff had seemingly played a major role in his conversion.

But the nature of his education and the role of other teachers should be given precedence. Day had come under the full weight of an extraordinarily personalized form of education—Duff was a great believer in the Socratic method—whose unashamed intent was to convert. If one bears in mind current interpretations of the anglicist inspired secular education, that the study of English literature was to be the inspiration for a new secular ideology of Empire, one can see that the young Day was caught in a double bind.[82] One can but wonder at the resistance of his fellow students, given that so few were to convert.

Day acknowledged his debt to other teachers. First there was Ewart: 'he was a tall young man, about six foot high, well built, stalwart, bolt upright; though his complexion was fair, his cheeks were ruddy; on the whole he appeared to be a man exceedingly lovable and I felt I could, without the slightest hesitation, open up to him and talk to him—a thing which at that age I could hardly think of doing to any European.'[83] Later he was to reflect on 'the perfect equanimity of his temper, his freedom from all prejudice, the philosophical coolness of his judgement, the rigid uprightness, gentleness, which more resembled that of a woman than of a stalwart man upwards of six feet high'.[84] Converts were curiously susceptible to the female in their teachers. There was Thomas Smith, who taught him in the junior classes, and whose return from South Africa Day was to await—he had gone there for his health—so that he could bapitise him. In Smith's response to Day one can hear echoes of Arnoldian values of education; 'my personal attention soon fell on him as out of sight the best scholar in the class, and still more as exhibiting a manliness of character and fearless truthfulness which was unhappily rare . . . Boyishness. A proper boy, with his recklessness and affectionateness, is to me and I suppose to most others the model of humanity at its best and I never found among Bengalis those qualities so happily blended as they were in him.'[85] There was also John Macdonald, his instructor in the Bible and theology: 'no minister of the Gospel in Calcutta, of whatever denomination, exercised so much spiritual influence as John Macdonald of the Free Church Mission.'[86] Duff clearly has to take his place alongside other teachers.

Oddly, for a man so keen on autobiography, Day left no account of his conversion. 'His mental struggle at the time', explains his biographer, 'was not a side of his experience he cared to dwell upon.'[87] Was it the case that for Day 'the author of the universe was almost from the first rather Christian than Hindu',[88] as his biographer supposed?

In fact, Day was strongly drawn to Brahmoism. 'I myself was once', he admitted, 'a Brahmo, though not in name yet in reality. I conscientiously believed in those Brahmoistic doctrines.' But Brahmoism could not answer his acute sense of sin. Its concept of the atonement was no match for the Christian. 'Brahmoism represents God', he observed, 'as being incapable of being displeased with a sinner. Let him violate all his commandments. This is the dogma of Brahmos and it is the cornerstone of the edifice of the Brahmo atonement'. 'I began to to feel that I was a great sinner, a vile transgressor of God's law. My good works, such as they were, seemed as like filthy rags. Formerly I comforted myself with the thought that I was better than many of my neighbours and this laid flattering unction to my soul. But now I appeared before myself in all my naked deformity.'

Here we have all the hallmarks of a self-punitive evangelical conscience at work, and it may be one he simply owed to his Scottish teachers. He provided some of the explanation, but may have chosen not to tell all of the truth.

In 1837, following his father's death, he went through a bad patch. He had joined a gang at school: 'they wanted me to go along with them to perdition, they smoked hemp, they visited houses of ill-fame.'[89] But significantly closer to the time of his conversion, there was a great moral scandal in the school. The brightest and oldest of the converts, Dwarkanath Basu, who had been sent to London to study medicine, was caught in an adulterous relationship with the wife of a CMS catechist. His allowance was forfeited and he was suspended. It had led to a truly Victorian outbreak of moral panic in the Mission: 'under a deep sense of the afflicting dispensation which had befallen the Mission, the (Missionary) Council (see below) resolved to hold a special meeting for prayer and humiliation before God in reference to this mournful affair.'[94] Duff's personal sexual puritanism was depressingly strong.[91]

Only two other converts were now left, Jagadishwar Bhattacharya and Prasanna Kumar Chatterjee. Day was close to them. Was it anxiety over sexuality that drove his sense of sin, rather than, as seemed to be the case with Rajahgopaul, idolatry, and that here we have the true catalyst for his conversion? Day merely observed: 'but they soon found a new companion, for I felt it my duty publicly to profess my faith in Christ in whom I had believed for some time past.'[92]

In contrast to Rajahgopaul's harmonious career in the Scottish Mission, Day's was one of conflict. A confrontation with Duff came during his final spell in India. He had left in 1849, and returned to Calcutta in February 1856. If never a racist, during the troubles ahead, Duff revealed himself at his imperialist worst. Day was to experience himself as a colonial subject.

In the meanwhile, Day had, in 1846, been appointed a catechist and had turned missionary in his own home region of Burdwan. The Scottish Mission had in 1841 taken over a CMS station at Kulna (a part of Duff's drive to evangelize rural Bengal). In 1848 he had been attached to the

Bengal Native Church in Calcutta, and whilst there had been licenced to preach in November 1851, and in September 1855, had been ordained. Had the iron entered his soul when Duff refused his request in 1849 to take him to Scotland?

Day crossed swords with the Mission in 1852 over rates of pay. He was a joint signatory to a letter, undated, but first discussed in the Missionary Council on 5 February,[93] protesting that rates of pay were fifty years out of date. Even Duff had recommended higher rates of pay in December 1840. 'By this statement we do not mean to insinuate', asserted the converts, 'that a young Bengali magistrate should be the model of a native missionary. But neither can we admit what has been asserted that an old pandit of simple habits should constitute the pattern of an educated preacher. It is surely possible to stake out a just milieu between these extremes.' Those of 'a cultured intellect and liberal education' necessarily had more expensive needs. All they desired was 'a position in society which avoids contempt and commands respect and ensures usefulness' and this the recommended salary would not provide. 'The scantiness of our salaries often involves us in pecuniary difficulties which materially destroy the tranquility of our minds and interferes with our devotion to the social cause in which we have embarked.' Whether Day was the ringleader, or indeed what decisions were taken on pay, the records do not divulge. Disputes over remuneration was a prelude to a far more serious dispute over status.

Following ordination on 25 July 1855, the Missionary Council authorized Day's release from teaching at the Institute to take up a missionary post at Chinsura. Day proceeded on a winter tour of Burdwan and Hooghly. Duff returned just in time to face a request from Day and two other recently ordained converts to join the Missionary Council. It should be explained that this was the crucial policy making body, set up in 1841, in which all European missionaries sat as of right. Here was an issue about which Day felt passionately and despite a highly manipulative attempt by Duff to get him to change his mind, he stood firm, and in the long run, it was probably the grounds for his leaving the Mission.

Duff chose to see this as a challenge to his authority. He turned the request down on the rather dubious grounds that the Missionary Council was an offshoot of the Home Foreign Mission Committee and 'so in my proper view of the case no ordained missionary from here is ipso facto and of right a member of the Council'. An analogy could be drawn between the home government and the Company.

Day fought a clever battle, turning all the moral claims of the Scottish

Mission against itself. Given that its primary object was the training of an Indian ministry, he asked, in his letter of 24 May, should not the convert presbyters enjoy the same rights and privileges as European missionaries? Did they not possess a coordinate authority? 'In other words should the native missionaries become members of the Missionary Council or should they not? Not to recognize presbyter parity would be repugnant to the constitution of our church.' With lethal shrewdness, Day played on some of Duff's deepest convictions: to assign an inferior status 'virtually creates two classes—I had almost said two castes'. 'Even the British India government, confessedly one of the most slow-going machines in the world, repudiates all distinctions of country, colour and race, the Bengal civilians (and there will soon be such a class) enjoying the same rights and privileges *in every respect* with their brethren of the far west.' (Day's was a highly optimistic interpretation of the open competition on offer in the renewed Charter Act of 1853). Had not equal status been granted in Madras? He had then to get round Duff's point about the Home Committee. 'The argument that the Home Committee would be ignorant of the minds and abilities of Indian priests would not hold water for they had been under their constant scrutiny for years and were far better known than their European recruits.'

He then addressed matters of status:

The ill-consequence of subordination were all too foreseeable. When we consider the corrupt nature of fallen humanity and remember that in his best state is but vanity, it is not too much to say that under the above supposition the European missionary would be apt to look down upon the Native missionary and the Native missionary to regard their European coadjutors with jealousy. Stress, bickerings, dissatisfaction and hostile feelings would be produced and the cause of Christ would suffer . . . There would be a deterioration of the native agency, for an inferior position is apt whatever people may say to cramp the powers and dwarf the capacities of those who hold it.

Few clearer cases could be made against colonialism.

The quarrel threatened to pull the Mission apart. Were this demand to be rejected, the converts planned to rally round the newly ordained presbyters and break away from the Council. Interrogated by Duff as to whether as not he knew of these plans, Day admitted that he had been approached and 'had thanked his native brethren for their sympathy, whist at the same time warned them against any imprudent conduct in the matter'. At a crisis meeting in the Institute on 5 May, some converts stuck by their resolve, while others opted to hold another meeting the following day. At this meeting they surrendered and, in a cringing submission, admitted one by one: 'I feel therefore that I have sinned against God and you (Duff) in not having set my face against the conspiracy from the very beginning.' This Day could not stomach and it led to a highly charged, personal encounter with Duff.

In a letter of 17 May, Day made a submission of sorts to the Council. His request was 'right and proper in itself', but he had set about in a way 'precipitate and impolitic': 'he sincerely repented of his connection with the movement which unknown to other missionaries had been for some time in progress among the converts.' He was now willing to go on with his work 'without taking any further step in the matter'. But he was not ready to commit himself to any long-term future relationship with the Mission. In a letter to Duff, he begged him not to challenge his views on the composition of the Missionary Council. 'Recant them I will not for they are my honest convictions.' 'I allow I may be mistaken', he conceded. 'I have good reason to suspect the soundness of my conclusions when I see a great and good man like yourself and your excellent colleagues all differ from me. I am persuaded you would be the last person in the world to ask me to recant. I withdraw my letter to the Missionary Council.' He could hardly have gone further without loss of all personal integrity. He still craved Duff's approval. 'If you ever thought I was actuated by ambition or love of power in the matter before us', he deferred, 'you did me an injustice . . . Pile as much work on me as you will; the more work the better. I am in the prime of manhood. I am blessed with health and strength and with the blessing of the Lord a long prospect of humble usefulness lies before me.' Could all this be undone? 'Look upon me and trust me as your son: let Mr Ewart kindly do the same . . . I have no feeling against you. Believe me, look upon yourself and Mr Ewart as my fathers. I owe you a great deal under God. I owe you all!'

But Day had seriously underestimated Duff's unyielding if highly emotional wilfulness. He was a prima donna and brooked no opposition. Day had to endure just that personal show-down he had tried so hard to avoid. Duff found his account of his future plan of action 'rather vague and unsatisfying'. There followed an appalling meeting. Duff begged him to stay for at least a year. He offered Culna 'unfettered, unhampered, free'. He had, Day recalled, 'burst into tears . . . I agreed.' They knelt down and prayed. Duff gave him a hearty shake of the hand and went away. 'I shall never forget that scene in my room in the converts home. How he trembled in every limb of his body. How his eyes reddened. How he sobbed.' Though this was emotional blackmail of the worst kind, Day could still admit: 'I felt for him greater reverence and love than ever.'[94]

But Day did not recant. In a second letter, dated 24 May, he stated: 'ever since Monday evening I have been laboriously thinking on the subject which you brought before me . . . I see little reason for changing my opinions'. Given the failure of the Mission to grant his right to membership, he retained the right to leave the Mission, 'providing he feels that his missionary usefulness will be compromised and his situation will be rendered insupportable and provided that he has honestly no intention of either leaving the Church or ceasing to be a Missionary.' Might, in fact, the object of Mission be better fulfilled were he to break away and preach the gospel on his own? But he stepped back from the brink: 'I do not wish to pledge myself to any particular course.' He would not give 'a certain pledge, yet there is room I think for harmonious co-operation'. Everything was contingent: 'You may look on me if you please as an invalid missionary—invalid not as far as the quantity of the work to be imposed is concerned but invalid so far as the continuance of that work is concerned.' On grounds of ill-health, he asked to be sent to Kulna.

At best, this was a pyrrhic victory for Duff. Whilst he clutched his musket in defence of his property in Cornwallis Square during the days of 1857, Day worked as a missionary in Kulna, even agreeing to edit the journal *Arunady* there rather than in Calcutta. Duff left India for the last time on grounds of ill-health in July 1863. In Edinburgh, he took on the convenorship of the Foreign Mission Committee and inspired a Mission to the Gonds and Santals—proof that Duff was never narrowly concerned with just the education of the elite. He died on 12 February 1878.

Day returned to Calcutta in 1860 and took over the Native Presbyterian Free Church in Cornwallis Square and stayed there until 1867. But his friendship with Duff faded. In 1860 he married and the financial pressure of bringing up a family on a Mission salary—three of his children died—was the given reason for leaving the Mission and becoming, at double the salary, headmaster of Berhampore College.

But the process of Day recovering his Bengali identity, never wholly lost, was driven by the events of 1856. His was not so radical an assertion of patriotism as Upadhyaya's, but here was further proof of the strength of continuities in the lives of Bengali converts. He was to work for a new Bengal Christian Church: 'Native Christianity', he argued, 'is stretched on the procrustean bed of European forms of church polity: no wonder, therefore, it does not grow.'[95] If he also shared the delusion that Hinduism was on the verge of collapse, Christianity, he believed, could not hope to advance unless it was indigenized.

Not that Day ever lost a sense of loyalty to Empire. 'Bengal above all', he averred, 'had cause to be loyal. It would in our opinion be an act of blackest ingratitude if Bengalis showed any disaffection to that very government to whose beneficence they owe their present advance over the rest of India . . . Physically the weakest in all India without exaggeration and the least warlike they would be an easy prey to any adventurer that chose to lord it over them.' But if he thought Dadabhai Naoroji absurdly naive in supposing that Empire was not about self-interest, he still criticized the government for over-taxation, for the wasteful expenditure of the Public Works department—'it can at any time be done by private companies at half the price'—and for failing to relieve the peasantry of their financial burdens and develop mass primary educating.[96] On this evidence, Day might best be seen as a laissez-faire Victorian, rather than as a supporter of the moderates in the Congress, let alone the extremists.

But it was his empathy for the Bengali peasantry in his later writings that defines him as a Bengali patriot. This was most famously so in his *Govinda Samanta* (*Life of the Bengal Peasant*), published in 1871. This was also a humane plea to address the plight of the Hindu widow. Not that this was an exposure of Hinduism: 'it was first and foremost a plain tale of peasant life and sincere Christian that he was, he had too tolerant a catholic mind not to recognize that the Hindu religion in some instances at least, had a humanizing effect and helped to sweeten existence.'[97] He died on 5 November 1894.

CASE-STUDIES FROM THE NORTH

Nilkanta (Nehemiah) Goreh

In Goreh's conversion we probably come closest to discerning the problematic of Hindu conversion in the mid-century.[98] A Chitpavin Brahmin, born in the village of Kashipura in the Deccan on 8 February 1825, he had become a pandit. In various capacities his family had served Indian princes; his uncle, for example, had been an adviser to the nawab of Banda. His father had retired to Benares to look after a charitable trust for pilgrims. His uncle became head of the family. Rather than expose young Nilakantra to the anti-Hindu education of Benares Sanskrit College, he had been privately educated.

Evangelicals would wish to attribute his conversion to bazaar preaching, but this would be disingenous. On the contrary, it was out of a genuine sense of anger at such intrusion that Nilikantra sought out

William Smith in April 1844, not as an enquirer, but to defend his own faith. Far from being converted, he went away to write a major work of Hindu apologetics, *Sastra Tattvavinirvaya* (*A Verdict on the Truth of the Shastras*).

Almost for the first time we encounter here a Hindu-Christian herme-neutics, and if this is putting it too strongly, then, at the least, to quote Fox Young, 'a conflict between religious persons of particular persua-sions'.[99] Nilikantra's was to be one of several responses to John Muir's polemical work *Mataprakisha* (*An Examination of Religion*), published in 1839. At the time of this crucial juncture in Nilikantra's career, Muir, an Orientalist, a company official and a member of the Thomasonian circle, if not quite of their evangelical persuasion, was principal of the Sanskrit College. However 'acerbic', to quote Fox Young, this was a work of 'dispassionate rationality', dependent on William Paley's evidential approach, a theology of conciliation.[100] It was written in Sanskrit. How else, Muir wondered, could you expect the pandits to respond? Nilikantra did so, and his readiness at least to defend Hinduism against Christianity was a crucial breakthrough into a Hindu perception of religious plurality. Nilikantra had already made one religious shift, from Saivism to Vaishnavism. Would this prove to be a predisposing factor for another? If by way of a 'resistant Hinduism', responding to Muir's rational exposi-tion proved far more suggestive than listening to Smith's Calvinist apologetics.

Fox Young doubts that Goreh ever became a convinced Christian. He never ceased to be plagued by doubts: 'he would settle for nothing less than full certitude, rationally based assurances upon religious truth.'[101] He came back to Smith in April 1845. He still saw many contradictions. How could you square a Christian view of the after-life with a Hindu belief in transmigration? How was god's love compatible with eternal damnation? Regrettably, Smith was to win him over to a Victorian con-cept of hell and Goreh was not to subscribe to Frederick Maurice's broad church view that those who did not believe in Christianity might still be saved. Was the crucial catalyst a sense of sin, sexual guilt at taking at nineteen a second wife, aged but seven? (such child marriages would be consummated at the onset of puberty.)

One disincentive was his father's amused scepticism at his interest in Christianity. But once he had attended a service in CMS church on 5 September 1847, a serious family row broke out. His uncle beat him. Together with a friend, Balkrishnapant Thatta, another enquirer, he went off to Jaunpur. A false rumour that they had dined with a CMS missionary was to blight his friend's life, never to become a Christian, but still to be outcasted by his community until death. Doubts remained. Should he try endless repetition of the gayatra? He followed Smith on leave to Calcutta but still hung back. He was not baptised till 14 March 1848.

Had a suspension of his reason or, as the evangelical would put it, a suspension of disbelief, alone permitted conversion? Monier Williams recorded: 'he does not attribute his own conversion to any human instrumentality, although there was a certain Mr Smith at Benares with whom he was in the habit of arguing. He traces his conversion entirely to his own reading on the grace of God.'[102] In a conversation with Goreh on 6 June 1846, Smith admitted: 'I fear I have been reasoning the matter too much with him.'[103] At the very end, in 1888, however, Goreh refuted any such suspension, and in so doing admitted the continuing ambiguity of his Christian faith: 'however I have begun to think that it is not by going through a regular process of reason that man renounces one religion and embraces another, though that was certainly the case with me, and that is the very reason why my faith in Christianity is so poor.'[104] He died on 29 October 1895.

Muslim Converts in the North: Abd-al Masih, Imad-ud-in

Mission looked on Islam as more recalcitrant than Hinduism. Yet Muslim converts were disproportionate to their share of population in the Gangetic core region.[105] Conversion tended to be more final, with less inclination to seek out roots with the past. By mid-century, members of the ashraf elite, increasingly threatened both politically and culturally by the Company, saw India less as dar-al-Islam and more as dar-al-harb. No longer confident of their cultural moorings, a few were bound to experience religious doubt. Is there a case for arguing that converts from one exclusivist faith will more probably be totally reconciled to the claims of yet another? 'Most of their writing', it has been observed, 'took the form of either apology for the Christian faith or the refutation of the claims of other faiths.' No hybridism here. Theirs was a greater ascetic puritanism and a greater insistence on personal salvation. On the other hand, they were to acculturate less.[106] Here I will explore but two conversions, one of which demonstrates how prolonged and anguished a cultural migration from Islam to Christianity could be.

Abd-al Masih was the protestant Mission's first prestigious Muslim convert. Born Sheikh Salih, *c.* 1769, in Delhi, to a family of middling ashraf status, his family moved to Lucknow, and by the 1790s, Salih himself, clearly down on his luck, had to earn his living as a paint manufacturer. Was revulsion at the violence he had witnessed whilst on military service on behalf of Ibrahim ali Khan—there was the murder of the Mahratta, Rao Sevak Singh—the trigger for religious doubt?

His story links with those of Henry Martyn and Daniel Corrie. Sheikh's father was tutoring a neighbour of Martyn's in Kanpur. Sheikh, taking an interest in his preaching, sought employment in Martyn's household as a copier of Persian manuscripts. On binding Martyn's Urdu translation of the New Testament, he found himself drawn to the Sermon on the Mount. If Martyn was reluctant to baptise him, David Brown did so in Calcutta on Whit Sunday in 1811. He took the name Abd-al Masih, servant of Christ. Corrie chose him as his scripture reader and superintendent of schools when opening his mission in Agra in 1813. He would happily have remained a catechist, but he took Lutheran orders in 1820 and was ordained by Bishop Heber on 30 November 1825.

None of this seems to have prompted the usual violent wrench from the family. He took over the congregation at Kuttra, near Agra. He was not to Europeanize. When charged with becoming a 'feringhee' he replied: 'I was born a Hindoostani: my colour is black, my dress different from that of the Sahibs, and I have a beard like yourselves: how then can you call me a feringhee? If you call me a Christian you will call me right.'[107] He died on 4 March 1827.

Imad-ud-in's conversion was a more troubled affair.[108] Born in *c.* 1830, in Panipat, some fifty-three miles north of Delhi, he was the youngest of four sons in a family of good ashraf standing. They were sunni and sufi, with a tradition of learning and piety, who traced their descent from the saint, Qutub Jamal. By the 1840s, they were running into economic difficulties. At the age of fifteen, he had gone to the Government College, Agra, where his brother, Karim-ud-in, was a lecturer in Urdu. Conversations with Christians had raised some doubts, but when he aired these with fellow pupil, Safdar Ali, he was strongly reprimanded. Later, however, it was Safdar Ali's conversion which triggered his own.

He was drawn into the munazara, the theological dispute between Muslim theologians and CMS missionaries in Agra. For ten years he read on his own, in the meanwhile teaching at the mosque in Agra. Strangely, it was Wazir Khan, one of the key disputants in the munazara, who pointed him in another direction, suggesting that behind all the outward observance and self-discipline lay another awareness, the 'secret science' of mysticism. 'As soon as I was entangled in this subtle science I began to practice speaking little, eating little, living apart from men, afflicting my body and keeping awake at night . . . I constantly sat on the graves of holy men in the hope that by contemplation, I might receive some revelation from the tombs.' For the time being, with the outwitting of Pfander, Christianity was buried, and his religious quest took an extreme direction.

Haunted by the verse from the Koran, 'every mortal necessarily must go once to hell; it is obligatory on God to send all men once to hell; and afterwards He may pardon whom he will', he turned faqir, and was to spend ten years of his life travelling in the jungles and plains of northern India. His books on mysticism became more highly valued than the Koran and he himself was worshipped as a saint.

But none of this was leading anywhere and he came to look on all religions as 'but vain foibles'. In the 1860s he was employed by the Normal School at Lahore; his elder brother was the city's deputy inspector of schools. Hearing of Safdar Ali's conversion at the hands of Goreh, to reconvert his friend, he set about reading Christian texts, but this proved to be the beginning of his own conversion. Robert Clark baptised him on 29 April 1866, in Amritsar. In the second version of his autobiography, emphasis is laid on the interventionist role of Christians, especially Mr Mackintosh, headmaster of the Normal School, but the real origin is surely in his long personal quest.

But once converted, he had no doubts and sought no hybridism with Islam. He turned down the offer of a post as extra-assistant commissioner. He was ordained deacon on 3 December 1868, and priest on 15 December 1872. He never left Amritsar, and died on 18 August 1900 in the same room in which Clark had baptised him. Bishop French of Lahore became a close friend. Once they shared a police bungalow for a week while evangelizing together along the river Beas. He wrote some thirty books, the best known being his Urdu translation of the Koran. In 1884 the Archbishop of Canterbury conferred on him the title of Doctor of Divinity. He addressed the anti-Christian ideas of Sayyed Ahmed Khan.

The Punjab was the first province to have its own indigenous Church Council and Imad-ud-in gave its inaugural sermon on Easter day, 1877. At the Allahabad Missionary Conference in 1873, he spoke of the need for true friendship between the European missionaries and the Muslims: 'this yearning after this is better than bazaar preaching.' 'It is necessary to show them', he added, 'that the Christian religion does not interfere with the customs of the country and of olden times—it has only to do with the heart.' He himself was not to acculturate.

Sikh Converts

Over time the Sikhs have been divided between seeing themselves as but a reformed sect of Hinduism and as a distinct faith. Revivalist Hinduism, through viewing Sikhism as a corrupt faith—by rejecting caste they had become polluted—induced the Sikh community towards the latter view, and does much to explain the communal divide of the twentieth century.[109] But this was only on the periphery of the community in the mid-nineteenth century, one seriously demoralized by military defeat and by the absorption of the Sikh state by the Company, and one threatened by an aggressive Christianity.

Mission, wrongly, foresaw the large-scale conversion of Sikhs, initially to either Islam or Hinduism, and in the longer term, to Christianity. The CMS missionary, Fitzpatrick, saw two approaches towards the Sikhs: on the one hand, a cautious one—'it would be more advisable to avoid for a while collision with the Priests and leaders of the religious systems of this country and rather to seek converts from the less prejudiced and the more simple'; and a confrontational one—'the Sikh religion is a system fast decaying' and to ascribe a strength to Sikhism it does not possess, merely 'serves to impede rather than to advance the end in view'.[110] Both he and the Revd Keene, deemed an expert on Sikhism, clearly belonged to the second camp.

One convert was David Singh, the first Sikh to be ordained. Born to a local zamindar family, with lands between Lahore and Amritsar—his uncle owned some twenty villages—he had started out in life as a soldier. He was severely wounded in the Sutlej campaign. Subsequently, he enrolled in the Company army and it was whilst he was posted in Kanpur that he began to take an interest in Christianity. He stumbled on a tract in Punjabi, became an enquirer, and begged his CO to let him 'go to Benares and learn the way of salvation'. Under William Smith, he was led to baptism on 29 September 1850.

Fitzpatrick read his character 'as clear and unequivocal; naturally bold and fearless, of extraordinary energy, independent and high-spirited; he is yet tender and simple and possesses a good deal of Christian humility'. In the streets of Benares, however, as a catechist, his naturally confrontational style upset the Muslims: 'we have therefore forbidden him to speak in this way or enter into any controversy.'[111] Was his ordination 29 October 1854 in Allahabad premature? 'He knows no English, little history and less geography—he is surprised by some in other places even in his knowledge of the Bible and by many in his acquaintance with Mahomedan controversy.' 'He is not quite the man for European society but well qualified to take a high place amongst Natives.'[112] But quite soon Fitzpatrick reported that 'David has exceeded my highest expectations as a native pastor'.[113]

First conversions, with David acting as the intermediary, bred the usual excitement. On a visit to villages only two to four miles from Amritsar, a local granth reader came to hear them preach. The village at the time was very worked up at the prospect of a visit from the deputy commissioner. They entered into a conversation, and as he was literate, gave him two books in gurumukhi—'From Pentecost to Exodus', and the 'Pilgrim's Progress'. Despite their warning him of the social risks he ran, he came to stay with David to learn more. But he had to wean himself off opium and this he did too fast, suffering 'bodily trial', and was tempted to return to the village: 'he was excited against David, the chief instrument of his conversion, and reproached him as the cause of his mis-deeds'.[114] But he persevered and was baptised, though 'he is now somewhat depressed in spirit. Satan is not leaving him untried. We do not however doubt his real conversion'.[115]

The conversion of Kharak Singh gives a greater sense of the spiritual journey a Sikh had to undertake. His father was the lambardar or headman of the village of Uddoke, near Batala. He had served in both the Sikh and Company armies. At the age of eleven, he had fallen under the influence of a Hindu faqir and had taken the Hindu name, Narain Das. There followed another of those extraordinary religious quests, which took him to Jammu, Rishikesh, Benares, Kashmir and the Kangra hills. To escape sin and sorrow for all time he learnt to control his breath for up to twenty minutes: but 'I found no nearness to God and no comfort in my soul'. In Benares he read the sacred Hindu texts and became a Vedantist. He was an anti-Christian and saw the missionaries in the streets of Benares as 'leading the people astray. I despised them altogether, for they knew only the Gospel and I knew all the Shastras'. In the Kangra hills, he encountered John Lawrence, then Commissioner of Jullundur, who appointed him his teacher of Sanskrit. In 1857, he turned soldier again: 'I met with many Europeans but not one of them ever spoke to me of my soul or of Christ, and I never saw them go to church.' Post-rebellion, he returned to his village and, on his father's death, succeeded him as headman.

His very pugnacity was to engender doubts. He had met a Revd

Nathaniel in Indore: 'I went solely to oppose him and to stop his mouth, and all that he said made no impression on me.' There was a Hindu in the village who quoted the Bible's findings on the age of the world. He wrote a tract to prove him wrong: 'in this way I stopped his mouth, or thought I did, but still I began to think.' Should he be maligning a book which he had not read? He acquired a Hindi Bible from Amritsar: 'I became a Christian through reading the Bible.' At the age of 52 on 1 March 1874, Robert Clark baptised him.

But he was to recant. Baptism had failed to rid him of his sins. He then encountered Dayanand Saraswati. It was a case of going back go the shastras and adopting, once again, Hindu practices, such as the recitation of *om* 50,000 times a day. But reading a passage from the fifty-first psalm—'believe in Him whom I have sent'—led to the Pauline moment. Disillusionment with Dayanand, however, was probably the decisive factor. Even Dayanand had admitted that he gave a false reading of the shastras: 'he had tried to make the Vedas say what was not in them.' 'He said that we must not expose the weaknesses of Hinduism or else it would fall, if it became generally known what it really was.' Kharak lost his faith in Hinduism. Dayanand, he believed, 'to be a hypocrite. He knew he was preaching deceit and fraud. When I discovered this I was utterly discouraged and sorrowful and all hope left me'. His younger brother replaced him as lambardar and he went on to study at the Lahore Divinity School. He wrote tracts against the Arya Samaj. Ordained deacon on 21 December 1887, he was never to become a priest. Marriage to a much younger girl brought his private life into disrepute. He died on 5 February 1900.

It was more than a little strange that a falling out with the founder of the Arya Samaj, a movement which more than any other was to bring about a Hindu revival, should have led to a conversion.[116]

There were, of course, to be lapsed converts. Fitzpatrick recorded two, one but a few weeks after baptism, and the other after 'walking with us for fifteen months' and 'for the most part disorderly'. 'Both are now miserable. They would come back to us without true repentance if we were inclined to receive them—but we prefer to wait and see.'[117]

NOTES AND REFERENCES

1. By Avril Powell. See her paper, 'Processes of Conversion in Nineteenth-Century North India', given to the 13th European Conference of Modern South Asian Studies, Toulouse, August 1994, to be published in a collection of essays, edited by Oddie.

2. For these, consult David Kopf, *British Orientalism and the Bengali Renaissance 1773–1835*, Berkeley: 1969. Amales Tripathi, *Vidyasagar: The Traditional Moderniser*, New Delhi: 1974; Gerald James Larson, 'Modernisation and Religious Legitimation in India 1835–1885', Bardwell Smith (ed.), *Religion and Legitimation of Power in South Asia*, Leiden: 1978, pp. 33–9; Bhikhu Parekh, *Colonialism, Tradition, and Reform: An Analysis of Gandhi's Political Discourse*, New Delhi: 1989 (in particular, ch. 2); Kenneth Jones, *Socio-Religious Reform Movements in British India (The New Cambridge History of India III.1)*, Cambridge: 1989.

3. K. N. Panikkar makes a persuasive case for convergence. See his chapter, 'The Intellectual History of Colonial India: Some Historiographical and Conceptual Questions', Romila Thapar (ed.), *Situating Indian History*, New Delhi: 1986. Also his article, 'Culture and Ideology: Contradictions and Intellectual Transformation of Colonial Society in India', *Economic and Political Weekly*, 5 December 1987.

4. Bardwell Smith, *Religion and Social Conflict in South Asia*, Leiden: 1976, p. 12.

5. For information on Vaishnavism in Bengal, see Durgadas Majumdar, *Nadia: West Bengal District Gazetteer*, Calcutta: 1978, and Ramakanta Chakraborty, *Vaishnavism in Bengal 1486–1900*, Calcutta: 1985.

6. Chakraborty, p. 303.

7. Ibid., p. 340.

8. See Geoffrey Oddie, 'Old Wine in New Bottles? Kartabhaja (Vaishnava) Converts to Evangelical Christianity in Bengal 1835–1845'. 13th European Conference of Modern South Asian Studies.

9. Chakraborty, p. 427.

10. Ibid., p. 402.

11. For example, see Peter Marshall, *Bengal: The British Bridgehead. Eastern India 1740–1828*, Cambridge: 1981, pp. 25–34.

12. One very perceptive analysis of the interaction between the Bengal reform movement and Christianity is Sisir Kumar's *The Shadow of the Cross*, New Delhi: 1978.

13. Ibid., p. 77.

14. Ibid., p. 100.

15. Ibid., p. 132.

16. Mohammed Mohar Ali, *The Bengali Reaction to Christian Missionary Activities 1833–1857*, Chittagong: 1965, p. 10.

17. Tapan Raychaudhuri, 'Bengali Perceptions of the Raj in the 19th Century', *Itinerario 1*, 1989, p. 92.

18. See Arundhati Mukhopadhyaya, 'Attitudes Towards, Religion and Culture in Nineteenth-Century Bengal: Tattvobhini Sabha, 1839–59', *Studies in History*, vol. III, no. 1, January–June 1987 (in particular pp. 24–7).

19. There is a substantial literature on Upadhyay. I have consulted R. H. S. Boyd, *Indian Christian Theology*, Madras: 1969; Julius Lipner, 'A Modern Indian Christian Response', H. G. Coward (ed.), *Modern Indian Responses to Religious Pluralism*, New York: 1987, ch. 13; Julius Lipner, 'A Case-Study in Hindu

Catholicism: Brahmabdhanab Upadhyay (1861–1907)', *Zeitschrift fur Missionwissenschaft und Religionwissenschaft*, January 1988; Julius Lipner and George Gaspert-Sauch (eds), *The Writings of Brahmabandhab Upadhyay*, Bangalore: 1991.

20. Quoted Boyd, p. 269.
21. From his journal, Sophia, January 1895, quoted J. Lipner, *A Modern Indian Response*, p. 308.
22. Julius Lipner explores this theme in his essay, 'Facets of the Relationship between the Gospel and Culture', *International Review of Mission*, April 1985.
23. Boyd, p. 66.
24. Duncan B. Forrester, 'Christianity in Early Indian Nationalism', 6th European Conference on Modern South Asian Studies, Leiden, July 1978.
25. Quoted, ibid., p. 5.
26. George Pearce, 'The Social Conditions of Native Converts in India', *The Missionary Herald*, vol. CLXXVI, January 1854.
27. I tracked down Pearce's *On the Extent and Character of the Conversion to Christianity among the Natives in the Presidency of Bengal, 18 November 1846*, in the library at Serampore College (BR 3 33). It is quoted extensively in an article, 'Character of Native Converts in Bengal' in M.H., vol. CLXXII, September 1853.
28. See W. H. Pearce, Brief Account of Sujatali, M.H., no. 11, July 1839.
29. George Pearce, 6 September 1847, M.H., vol. CIII, December 1847.
30. George Pearce, 31 May 1850, M.H., vol. CXXXVI, September 1850.
31. Pearce's account, M.H., no. III, August 1839, p. 52.
32. For information on Gunga Narayan Pal, see M.H., vol. CCXL, December 1838, vol. LX, December 1843, vol. LVII, February 1844.
33. M.H., vol. CCXLIII, March 1839, p. 17.
34. See H. H. Sandal to Dr Kay, 15 January, 30, July 1857, 19 April 1858, C Ind 1(14), Calcutta (SPG: Rhodes House).
35. See an obituary, *The Indian Churchman*, 17 September 1887.
36. M.H., vol. CXXVII, December 1849.
37. M.H., vol. CXXXVI, September 1850.
38. M.H., vol. XCV, April 1847.
39. For the life and thought of Krishna Mohan Banerjea, I have consulted S. Satthianadhan, *Sketches of Indian Christians*; Rajaiah Paul, *Chosen Vessels*; Ramchandra Ghosha, *A Biographical Sketch of the Rev K. M. Banerjea*, Calcutta: 1892 (rpt. edn, 1981); T. V. Philip, *Krishna Mohan Banerjea. Christian Apologist*, Bangalore: 1982.
40. In his *A Discourse on the Hare Anniversary*, June 1849, given at Hindu College, Banerjea stated: 'at the age of six I became his boy, an honour which I continued to enjoy as long as any other friend now present in the hall.'
41. This is the theme of a series of articles by Dr Abhijit Datta, 'Nineteenth Century Urban Elitist Reaction to Christian Missionary Enterprise in Bengal', *The Quarterly Review of Historical Studies*, vol. XXVII, 1987, no. 2. vol. XXVIII, nos 1 and 2.

42. There is a classic Victorian biography, George Smith, *Life of Alexander Duff,* vols I–II, Edinburgh: 1879. There is a more recent one: William Paton, *Alexander Duff: Pioneer Missionary,* London: 1923.
43. Paton, p. 234.
44. This was the thrust of his major Indian statement, *India and Indian Missions,* Edinburgh: 1840.
45. Paton, p. 38.
46. Ibid., p. 227.
47. Widely quoted, but see Paul, p. 148.
48. Ibid., p. 150.
49. K. M. Banerjea, 'A Funeral Sermon Preached at the Old Church, Calcutta, 12 October 1837, on the decease of Baboo Mohesh Chunder Ghose. Calcutta (Bishop's College Press): 1837.
50. Ibid., p. 150.
51. Quoted George Smith, vol. I, p. 446.
52. I was lucky to come across the material for this incident in the Proceedings of the Corresponding Committee of the CMS, vol. VII, 1836–40, pp. 48–132 (St Paul's College: Calcutta).
53. Quoted in Mrs Mary Weitbrecht (ed.), *Memoirs of the Rev John James Weitbrecht,* London: 1854, pp. 203–4.
54. Kenneth Ballhatchet, 'Missionaries, Empire and Society: The Jesuit Mission in Calcutta 1834–1846', paper to the 6th European Conference of Modern South Asian Studies, July 1978, p. 7.
55. Bishop of Calcutta, 13 August 1847, CLR 13 (SPG: Rhodes House).
56. Bishop of Calcutta, 1 November 1850, ibid.
57. Revd J. Long, 2 May 1850, ibid.
58. Banerjea, 16 July 1853, ibid.
59. Bishop of Calcutta, 3 September 1851, ibid.
60. Banerjea, 31 May 1851, ibid.
61. Kay to Hawkins, 19 September 1851, ibid.
62. K. M. Banerjea, Calcutta, 18 November 1854, C Ind (14) (SPG: Rhodes House).
63. K. M. Banerjea, *Native Female Education,* Calcutta: 1841.
64. T. V. Philip, p. 113. His is an able summary of these late writings.
65. Ramchandra Ghosha, p. 53.
66. There is a rich biographical and autobiographical literature for Day (De), see G. Macpherson, *Life of Lal Behari Day: Convert, Pastor, Professor and Author,* Edinburgh: 1900; Lal Behari De, *Recollections of Alexander Duff,* London: 1897; Lal Behari De, 'Recollections of My Schooldays', *The Bengal Magazine,* vol. I, August 1872–July 1873, vol. II, August 1873–July 1874, vol. IV, August 1875–July 1876.
67. Day, *Recollections,* p. 42.
68. Quoted Macpherson, p. 18.
69. De, *Recollections,* p. 39.
70. Macpherson, p. 3.
71. Quoted ibid., pp. 52–3.

72. Lal Behari De, 'The Banker Caste of Bengal', *The Bengal Magazine*, vol. I, pp. 281–91, 324–39.
73. Macpherson, p. 16.
74. De, 'Recollections of My Schooldays', *The Bengal Magazine*, vol. II, pp. 324–39.
75. Macpherson, p. 16.
76. De, 'Recollections of My Schooldays', p. 332.
77. Macpherson, p. 12.
78. De, *Recollections*, p. 50.
79. Ibid., p. 111.
80. Ibid., p. 162.
81. Ibid., p. 164.
82. The controversial interpretation of Gauri Viswanathan, *Masks of Conquest: Literary Study and British Rule in India*, London: 1989.
83. De, *Recollections*, p. 66.
84. Ibid., p. 222.
85. See Thomas Smith's *Introduction to Macpherson*, p. xiv. For an insight into education in England at the time, see David Newsome, *Godliness and Good Learning*, London: 1961. Duff shared many of Arnold's ideas on education.
86. Day, *Recollections*, op. cit., p. 46.
87. Macpherson, op. cit., p. 43.
88. Ibid., p. 46.
89. De, *Recollections*, p. 79.
90. See Missionary Council Minutes, 14 June, 25 June 1841 (Bishop's College: Calcutta).
91. He was clearly genuinely horrified at the prospect of viewing a performance by the devadasi on a visit to the Srirangam temple in Trichnoploy in 1849. See George Smith, vol. II, pp. 148–9.
92. Day, *Recollections*, p. 160.
93. I have compiled this account from the Missionary Council Minutes, 1840–57, Calcutta Diocese, no. 1, box 12 (Bishop's College: Calcutta), supplemented by Day's own account in *Recollections*.
94. See Day, *Recollections*, pp. 214–16.
95. Revd Lal Behari Day, *The Desirableness and Practicality of Organizing a National Church in Bengal*, Calcutta: 1870. This was a speech delivered to the Bengal Christian Association, 13 December 1869.
96. Lal Behari De, 'The State of the Empire', *The Bengal Magazine*, vol. I, pp. 1–9, Dr Dadabhai Naoroji on the Condition of Empire, *The Bengal Magazine*, vol. X, pp. 171–80.
97. Macpherson, p. 122.
98. I have balanced the evangelical account of the biography by C. E. Gardner, *Life of Father Goreh*, London: 1890 with R. Fox Young's brilliant, scholarly study, *Resistant Hinduism: Sanskrit Sources on Anti-Christian Apologetics in Early 19th Century India*, Vienna: 1981.
99. Fox Young, p. 49.
100. Ibid., p. 169.

101. Smith's Journal, quoted Gardner, p. 45.
102. Quoted Gardner, p. 43.
103. Smith's Journal, quoted Gardner, p. 45.
104. Quoted Fox Young, p. 172.
105. A third of the converts, though only 10 per cent of the population. See Avril Powell.
106. John, W. Sadiq, 'Muslim Converts in the Indian Church', *Indian Church History Review*, vol. x, no. 1, June 1976, p. 76.
107. Quoted Avril Powell, op. cit.
108. Apart from Avril Powell's account, I have followed those of S. Satthianadhan and Rajaiah Paul. Both quote extensively from A. Muhammedan, *Brought to Christ, Being the Autobiography of a Native Clergyman in India.*
109. For an interesting discussion of this theme, see Cynthia Keppley Mahmood, 'Sikh Rebellion and the Hindu Concept of Order', *Asian Survey*, vol. xxiv, no. 3, March 1989.
110. Revd Fitzpatrick, Journal, 21 June–9 July 1852, CI/0 106/26 (CMS: Birmingham).
111. Fitzpatrick, Journal, 21 June–9 July 1852, CI 1/0 106/26.
112. Fitzpatrick to Venn, 8 June 1854, CI 1/0 106/11, 12.
113. Fitzpatrick to Venn, 14 June 1855, CI 1/0 106/13.
114. Clark to Fitzpatrick, n.d. CI 1/0 106/9.
115. Fitzpatrick to Venn, 6 July, CI 1/0 106/8a.
116. The account of Kharak Singh's conversion was recorded on 21 December 1887. See ch. ix of R. Clark, *The Mission of the CMS and the CEZMS in the Punjab and Sindh*, London: 1905.
117. Fitzpatrick, Annual Letter, 19 June 1855, CI 1/0 166/30.

Epilogue

There was a shift in missionary strategy in the 1880s. Maybe the experience of a counter-confrontationalism from a strident, neo-orthodox and more highly organized Hindu opposition led missionaries to have second thoughts about the pleasantness of evangelism, as well as demonstrating just how urgent it was to address this new intelligentsia. This text began with an attempt to relate the mid-nineteenth-century missionaries to an earlier generation of Europeans in India, both lay and missionary; it should end with a similar endeavour for their successors, though only the missionaries will be covered. An exclusivist theology gave way to an inclusivist theology. Connected with this was an effort to bring Mission into line with the moderate position in Congress. Interestingly, William Miller, educationist par excellence, would not go along with this political tactic, fearing that nationalism would ultimately destroy Mission. At the Edinburgh World Mission Conference of 1910, if its blessing was given to inclusivism, there was to be a further hiatus in strategy. Despair at the revivalist character of the extremist wing of Congress led Mission to turn from the elite to the poor and to take up so-called 'mass' or, as Sundaraj Manickam has suggested more appropriately, 'group' conversion movements:[1] evangelism was back in fashion.

A close reading of J. N. Farquhar's *The Crown of Hinduism*,[2] the Bible of inclusivist or fulfilment theology, does not suggest that it lives up to its name. Even if a more liberal theology has to be welcomed, not only were there worrying continuities with exclusivism, at its heart was hiatus rather than 'fulfilment' between Hinduism and Christianity. There was the same charge of Hinduism in decline, though blame fell on the scepticism of an Indian westernizing intelligentsia rather than Mission: 'Hinduism is being disintegrated. This is the great fact which has to be recognized.' Christianity, indeed, would have to stay on 'to sow the seeds of spiritual religion and healthy moral life.'[3] 'Hinduism must die in order to live. It must die into Christianity.'[4] In the same way as Ram Mohun Roy, Farquhar looked back to an earlier Vedic age as a means of faulting the present, though with the missionary twist that it stood 'much nearer to Christianity than it does to Hinduism'.[5] If, in that sense, Christianity could be seen as the crown of Hinduism, it legitimized an attack on contemporary Hindu practice every bit as hostile as that of the mid-nineteenth-century missionaries. Here was a critique of Hindu social mores, the plight of women, of caste, Kathleen Mayoesque in tone. Just as ferocious was the portrait of alleged idolatry, 'one of the chief hindrances to the progress of India',[6] a denial of any divinity to Ram or Krishna—'all Indian stories of incarnation are baseless'[7]—together with scorn for the ascetics and their monastic life. Hinduism was branded 'the dark apocalypse'. There was a gap rather than a bridging between the faiths, for only Christ could save. His conclusion that 'the missionary who fails to acknowledge the presence of these right ideas amidst all the vice, cruelty and superstition does not deserve to get the ear of the educated classes' feels flat and unconvincing.[8]

But inclusivism had some interesting off-shoots. It inspired the SPG missionary, Father Jack Winslow, to take an Anglican model of missionary brotherhood one stage further and initiate the Christian ashram movement. Here was an adaptation of bhakti to an Anglo-Catholic tradition. But the Christo Seva Sangh, which had its origin at Ahmednagar in 1922 only to move near Poona in 1928, was to divide into those wishing to go over to Franciscan monasticism and those loyal to Winslow's more this-worldly approach. But not even Winslow was ready to follow Verrier Elwin in his radical identification with Gandhi and Indian nationalism, one that led him in 1934 to break away from the Anglican establishment.[9] Anglo-Catholicism could take quite different routes to the Evangelical.

Not that inclusivism always prevailed. At the Tambaran Conference of 1938, through the influence of a Dutch missionary from Indonesia, Hendrick Kraemer, a Christ-centred exclusivism was reasserted in its place. Christianity was not deemed the same as other religions.

Describing the careers of two twentieth-century missionaries is one way of assessing their nineteenth-century predecessors. For the young Lesslie Newbiggin, Winslow's Poona ashram was 'first to awaken' his interest in India. He came out to India in 1936 as a Scottish missionary. Almost immediately, he was plunged back into the world of the mid-nineteenth century: entering his bungalow at Chingleput was to step 'out of the life of the twentieth-century student into that of an eighteenth-country gentleman'.[10] He discovered the same old rancorous divisions between European missionaries and their Indian colleagues. In October 1938 he came to Kanchipuram. Anderson's school, set up a hundred years earlier, was still the only attempt to establish a Christian presence in this holy city of the Hindus. Newbiggin's predecessor, Maclean, had dome something to put the school on the map. He was to follow his example of street preaching, especially during the great May festival. When appointed Bishop of Madura in 1947, he stumbled on old missionary rivalries: 'the depth of the chasm which separated the SPG from the CMS.'[11] Here was a missionary in an ancient mould; 'our fundamental task, from which nothing ought to deflect us, was the preaching of the Gospel.'[12]

But Newbiggin saw that his real mission was to the village and to the poor, above all to the adi-dravida, to help fashion a new self-reliant village Christianity; a commitment to Church rather than to Mission. Nevertheless, his was a classic Christ-centred missionary approach: 'I still see the cross of Jesus as the one place in all the history of human culture where there is a final dealing with the ultimate mysteries of sin and forgiveness, of conflict and peace, of death and life.'[13]

In the writings of Roger Hooker an entirely new voice is heard, a missionary who went to India, not to convert, but to listen and learn. Ordained in 1960, in 1965 he went as a CMS missionary to India, first to Bareilly and then to Varanasi. Quickly he concluded that though the Christian faith had made an impact on north India over the last 150 years, 'we have not yet touched the heart of traditional Hinduism. The real Mission has hardly begun.'[14] If through both being minority faiths, Islam and Christianity should be more accessible to one another, this should be through prayer and not the nineteenth-century munazara: 'the normal results of these was that each side convinced themselves, but that neither convinced the other.'[15]

Looking back to the mid-nineteenth century, he recognized how little Hindus had ever listened to Christian Mission. The principal of the Sanskrit College in Varanasi, Ballantyne, had been exceptional in his readiness to work with 'my friends the pandits'. Christians had come, Hindus believed, but to debunk, and 'at some point the Christian ministry to the educated of the city petered out'.[16] There had to be a radically different approach: 'is it too much to claim that for too long Christianity has tried to make itself impregnable and that it now has to learn to be vulnerable?'[17] All the misconceptions of the nineteenth century had to be unravelled: 'we have often seemed to Hindus—and others—to be cerebral, sterile, dogmatic and intolerant.'[18] His was an extremely subtle exploration of how Mission had failed to understand Hinduism. 'The trouble with Exclusivism', he writes, 'is that it too easily became hardened into a harsh negative judgement on all that lies outside the boundaries of Christian belief and belonging.'[19] He is a little kinder to Inclusivism: 'which is the more insulting to Hindus, to tell them that they are benighted heathen, destined to everlasting perdition unless they become Christians, or to tell them that they are really Christians without knowing it?'[20] Hindus had been alienated by the hard-edged in Christianity: 'In Vedantin eyes, the Christian insistence on particularity, on dogmatic statement, on personality in God and in humanity, merely affords proof that we are still on an inferior and lower plain of reality.'[21] (Wilhelm Halbermas has, of course, questioned if Hinduism is itself a faith which tolerates others.) Hooker did not go all the way with pluralism, though this is the direction of his approach.[22] He still saw a need to respect one's own cultural upbringing. One should not lose one's own identity by 'going native in another tradition'.[23] But a missionary should only come to learn from Indians: 'I am not in the business of trying to manipulate them, still less of trying to convert. I honour them too much for that.' He also remained loyal to the person of Christ, but 'even that final claim must be made in vulnerability and openness'.[24]

Meanwhile, Indian Christians persisted in their quest to free themselves from the constraints of Mission's paternalism and to found their own independent church. On the one hand, they opened themselves to a more inclusivist, even pluralist, acceptance of their own culture, and on the other, they sought a closer kinship with Indian nationalism.[25] One way through to a greater sense of nationality was to try to break down denominational boundaries. But how could they both identify with the poor and outcaste and yet get back in touch with the Hindu intelligentsia? One Christian expressed this dilemma in an interesting way: 'a great many of our missionaries and Christian workers are total strangers to the ideology of the country. This is because they have come to view their work as connected with the masses, almost to the exclusion of the "intellectuals". The "intellectuals" are becoming one of the outcastes of India so far as the missionary is concerned'.[26] In many ways, Indian Christianity chose to go along the Dalit path, though in terms of social uplift rather than conversion.

Can we come to any conclusions on the mid-century missionaries? In a recent study, Jacob Dharmaraj has sought to deliver a body blow to their reputation.[27] A 'colonial epistemology' and a 'racist hermeneutic' have obscured, he argues, a true understanding of the history of Christian Mission in India. It has been 'culturally conditioned', 'politically one-sided', 'missiologically limited'. Only a 'dehegemonized history' will let the 'mute inarticulate' discourse of the colonized be heard. Even William Carey does not escape his net. Had he not for five years managed an indigo plantation and received a monthly salary of a thousand rupees (a monthly wage for a fully employed Indian worker was four) from that agency of the Company, Fort William College?'; 'the Serampore Mission was carried out with colonial monetrism and with the help of the colonial government.'[28] Far more fairly, Alexander Duff comes in for an equal drubbing: 'to negate culture is to deny power and a legitimate identity to people.'[29] Presumably, he sees the missionary presence as lethal for he refers by 1857 to 'a nearly doomed Indian religious culture'.[30]

This has been the story of an encounter, bitter and invariably one of mutual incomprehension, between a largely evangelical, Protestant Mission (at this stage the Anglo-Catholic voice was very understated) and Indian religions. It confirms Raghavan Iyer's metaphor of looking through a glass darkly. Yet there was that curious symbiosis between Christianity and Indian religions. Mission seemed, like moths to the flame, drawn to the centres of Indian faiths. Was there in fact any shift in ideology, and growth in cultural understanding?

To be a missionary was often a lonely and depressing activity. It needed considerable self-deception to keep going against the odds. Many missionaries preferred to plough their own furrow, to be 'loners', to follow that romantic model conjured up by Edward Irving and Anthony Groves.[31] Individual missionaries came to recognize the absurdity of the itinerating strategy and to see a more promising alternative in education. However, Mission, as a whole, doggedly pursued the evangelical trail long after its vanity had been exposed. This is a good example of the stubborn persistence of an ideology in action. But, in the process, Mission stumbled on its best long-term prospect. Having set its heart on the conversion of Brahmins, it found, instead, that its future lay in the conversion of the outcastes and the tribals, exiled communities as they themselves were, fellow outsiders in India's society.

Some missionaries did attempt to compensate for their initial ignorance of Indian faiths. At the very least, and this is surprising for a people so notorious for their reluctance to learn languages, they made an exceptional effort at mastering the Indian vernaculars. Admittedly, with a strategy of mass propaganda, they had no alternative. Some learnt, or saw the need to learn, Sanskrit. Just how negative did their attitude to Indian society and culture remain? Did they approximate in any way to the curiosity of the Orientalist (in the best sense) or the more 'romantic' response of a Heber? Did they show themselves to be proto-anthropologists?

Many were to discover a genuine attachment to India. They identified with the region in which their Mission station was based. In a sense, given the long missionary tours and their length of service, theirs, at the time, was the greatest commitment of any European to India. They did reach out, however confrontationally, for a greater knowledge of Indian culture. Yet it is difficult to see, as the missionary found out more about the Hindu, Islamic and Sikh way of life, an exclusivist theology giving way to an inclusivist. Not that inclusivism had so much to recommend it.

But in the 1880s there seems to have been a genuine shift in attitude. Maybe this emerged from missionaries more committed to an educationalist approach, though there are plenty of examples of educational missionaries, better informed, maybe, about Indian religions, but still with absolutely closed minds. Alexander Duff was one such.

On the whole, a reading of the cultural contact between Mission and India's culture is a gloomy one. Whether a case has been made that Mission, rather than admit that its millenarian belief in the superiority of Christianity over India's religions was ill-founded, scapegoated caste for its failure, the reader will have to judge.

This has also been the story of a minority, of a Christian élite, converts from the high castes. Not that conversions from the low castes have been overlooked, but they have not been brought into such sharp focus. Mission always claimed that there was a much greater number of sympathizers among India's élites, closet Christians, who, for fear of social ostracism, were reluctant to come out. Mission began to wonder if there was not some temperamental gulf between the European Christians and the Indians: 'is there something inherent in the prevailing Indian temperament that will be likely to produce striking differences between his religious experience and that of the average Western Christian?'[32] Maybe the evangelical appeal to the conscience, to the inner man, was always less likely to exert an appeal than a Catholic sacramental approach. This had been recognized by Anglo-Catholic missionaries working in centres of 'old' Mission.

Yet, as we have seen, the young did prove susceptible, may be as much to the man as to the doctrine, to the kindliness and the feminine in the European missionary. If one has to be wary of applying Freudian insights to the Indian extended family, there is a case, following Erikson, of seeing the young in the grip of an identity crisis and in search of alternative father figures. They also responded to a rationalism and a humanitarianism in European Christianity as they saw it. They were critical modernizers rather than mere modernizers, to use Parekh's terminology. Theirs was often an intolerable position, caught, as they were, between two cultures, or, as Gramsci and Edward Said have put it, subject to 'a mutual siege'. Did they go on to fashion a new 'hybridism', a new synthesis between Indian culture and the West?

Their response varied. Whereas some almost entirely assimilated, others sought a way back into their own culture. One could risk the generalization that the degree of assimilation was always greater in the south, where Christianity had put down deeper roots and larger Christian communities offered a closer sense of belonging, than in Bengal, where Bengali Christians were more exposed to the force of an emergent cultural nationalism. One very important expression of this was the quest for a more independent church. But this was not exclusive to Bengal.

One paradigm for their story has been a push-pull model. But as the story has developed, an alternative, of continuity and discontinuity, becomes more revealing. Indian Christians began to back away from the cultural demands of European Mission. One can only speculate how different this story would be if the case-studies had been chosen more from those who lived their lives outside Mission and in the secular world.

Indian religions weathered attack and desertions. Again, only the reader can judge if a case has been made for the critical role played in this survival by traditional institutions and their personnel. I come back to Swami Ranganathananda's insight that Hinduism is always strong, just stronger at certain times. At a deeper level, this had been a clash between an individualist and a communitarian ethic and the latter had prevailed. Even so, Hinduism could never be the same. Once the Bible and the Church became open to all, no longer could the Brahmins claim exclusive access to the sacred texts and the temple entry movement was bound to follow.

The history of Mission is a window on the religious pluralism of India. Through the story of the missionaries we can see both the rich variety of faith within Hinduism itself and the vitality of other faiths. Sadly, nineteenth-century Mission addressed this pluralism in a spirit of confrontationalism. This is a story which has revealed the toughness and resilience of the traditional institutions and their adherents. More than the religious reform movements, they took the brunt of the missionary assault. The future of India's unique form of secularism lies in the continuing vitality of its religious pluralism.

NOTES AND REFERENCES

1. Sundaraj Manickam, *The Social Setting of Christian Conversion in South India*, Wiesbaden: 1977. (See, in particular, ch. III, The Trichinopoly Mass Movement from 1913 onwards.)
2. J. N. Farquhar, *The Crown of Hinduism*, London, etc.: 1913.
3. Ibid., pp. 42–3.
4. Ibid., p. 51.

5. Ibid., p. 75.
6. Ibid., p. 342.
7. Ibid., p. 423.
8. Ibid., p. 451.
9. See A. Webb, 'The Christo Seva Sangh Ashram 1922–1934', *South Asia Research*, no. 1, May 1981, pp. 37–50.
10. Lesslie Newbiggin, *Unfinished Agenda*, London, Michigan: 1985, p. 40.
11. Ibid., p. 103.
12. Ibid., p. 144.
13. Ibid., p. 254.
14. Roger Hooker, *Uncharted Journey*, London: 1973, p. 18.
15. Ibid., pp. 23–4.
16. Roger Hooker, *Journey into Varanasi*, Rushden: 1978, p. 35.
17. Roger Hooker, *Themes in Hinduism and Christianity: A Comparative Study*, Frankfurt am Main: 1989, p. 181. Another example of a more enlightened approach to Hinduism is Klaus Klostermeier's *Hindu and Christian in Vrindaban*, London: 1969.
18. Hooker, 'Themes in Hinduism', op. cit.
19. Ibid., p. 347.
20. Ibid., p. 351.
21. Ibid., p. 357.
22. Its most authoritative statement is by John Hicks, *An Interpretation of Religion*, London: 1989. Hick's claim that 'the real in itself' transcends the differences in faiths is, at an ideal level, wholly acceptable, but it does underestimate the passionate attachment of faiths to their prophets, avatars, gurus, and claims to a unique incarnation.
23. Hooker, p. 366.
24. Ibid., p. 367–8.
25. There is a useful collection of essays along these lines edited by G. V. Job *et al.*, *Rethinking Christianity in India*, Madras: 1938.
26. Ibid., p. 237.
27. Jacob S. Dharmaraj, *Colonialism and Christian Mission: Postcolonial Reflections*, Delhi: 1993.
28. Ibid., p. 56.
29. Iid., p. 72.
30. Ibid., p. 84.
31. Not that this was just a European preference. Arulappen, a palla converted by Rhenius, inspired by Anthony Groves, was to break away and, unattached to any Mission society, evangelize on his own. See G. H. Lang, *The History and Diaries of an Indian Christian*, Lowestoft: 1939.
32. E. A. Annett, *Conversion in India: A Study in Religious Psychology*, Madras, etc.: 1920, p. vi.

A Select Bibliography

MANUSCRIPTS

The Church Missionary Society (CMS) Archive, the Heslop Room, the Library, the University of Birmingham:

Journals, Letters, etc.

Revd William Bowley	CI 1/0 133
Revd Thomas Fitzpatrick	CI 1/0 106
Revd Henry Watson Fox	CI 2/0 100
Revd Samuel Hassell	CI 1/0 133
Revd James Joseph Haydn Louis	CI 2/0 091
Revd James Leighton	CI 1/0 176
Revd Charles Leupolt	CI 1/0 77
Revd John Pickford	CI 2/0 189
Revd John Edmund Sharkey	CI 2/0 222
Revd William Smith	CI 1/0 265

The United Society for the Propagation of the Gospel (SPG) Archive, Rhodes House Library, Oxford.

Correspondence Local Received (CLR), Calcutta, vols 12–14.
Correspondence Local Received, Madras, vols 46–8.
Letters, etc., C Ind (1) 1–63.
K. M. Banerjea, C. E. Driberg, H. H. Sandal, Samuel Slater, W. O. Brien Smith.

The Baptist Missionary Society Archive, the Angus Library, Regent's Park College, Oxford:

Letters, etc.
George Pearce	IN/29
Richard Williams	IN/11

The Mission Archive, the Library, the United Theological College (UTC), Bangalore:

Correspondence of the Secretary of the (CMS) Committee, 1818–1928.

The Madras Diocesan Committee Correspondence (SPG), 1832–1917:
D. S. Rama Rao, Biography of Venkata Ananta Padmanabha Rao (Anantam), 1850–1949. In manuscript.

The Archive, Bishop's College, Calcutta:

Missionary Council Minutes, 1840–57, Calcutta Diocese (Scottish Mission).

The Archive, St Paul's College, Calcutta:

Proceedings of the Corresponding Committee of the CMS, vol. VII, 1836–40.

PRINTED MANUSCRIPTS

Journals

The Missionary Herald, 1830–58 (BMS Archive).
The Native Herald, 1840–58 (Archive, Madras Christian College).

Pamphlets, etc.

Revd A. Alexander, *Rajahgopaul: A Memorial Sketch.*
Paisley: 1888 (Church of Scotland Publications, UTC).
Anon Sketch of Miss Margaret Locker (Church of Scotland, Madras Mission, UTC).
K. M. Banerjea, *A Discourse on the Hare Anniversary,* January 1849.
———, *A Funeral Sermon Preached at the Old Church, Calcutta, 12 October 1837, on the Decease of Baboo Mohesh Chunder Ghose.*
Lal Behari De (Day), *The Desirableness and Practicality of Organizing a National Church in Bengal,* Calcutta: 1870.
George Pearce, *On the Extent and Character of the Conversion to Christianity among the Natives in the Presidency of Bengal,* 18 November 1849 (Carey Library, Serampore).

Articles

Anon, 'Family Names among the Natives of India', *Madras Church Missionary Record,* vol. XXII, no. 9, September 1855 (UTC).
Anon, 'Treatment of Native Converts', *Madras Church Missionary Record,* vol. XXII, no. 20, October 1855.
Lal Behari De (Day), 'Recollections of My Schooldays', *The Bengal Magazine,* vol. I, August 1872–July 1873; vol. II, August 1873–July 1874; vol. IV, August 1875–July 1876.
———, 'The Banker Caste of Bengal', *The Bengal Magazine,* vol. I.
———, 'The State of the Empire', vol. I, Dr Dadabhai Naoroji on the Condition of Empire, *The Bengal Magazine,* vol. X.

Missionary Conference Reports, etc.

Proceedings of the General Conference of the Bengal Protestant Missionaries, Calcutta: 1855.

Proceedings of the South Indian Missionary Conference, Ootacamund, 19 April–15 May, Madras: 1858.

Report of the Punjab Missionary Conference, December 1862–January 1863, Lodiana: 1863.

Report of the General Mission Conference, Allahabad, 1872–73, London: 1873.

The Missionary Conference, South India and Ceylon, Bangalore, 1879, London: 1880.

Report of the Second Decennial Missionary Conference held at Calcutta, 1882–1883, Calcutta: 1883.

Baptist Periodical Accounts, 9, London: 1839 (BMS Archive).

Baptist Handbook, 1886.

Indian Missionary Manual, 1864.

Reprint Editions

The Imperial Gazetteer of India. vols I–XXV (first edn, Oxford, 1908), New Delhi, 1974.

Reginald Heber, *Narrative of a Journey through the Upper Provinces of India*, vols I–III (first edn, London: 1827), New Delhi: 1985.

Unpublished Theses

Bennett, Clinton, *19th Century Christian Views of Islam: Evidenced by Six British Approaches*, Ph.D. thesis, University of Brimingham (Selly Oak Library).

Hudson, Denis, *The Life and Times of H. A. Krishna Pillai 1827–1900.* Ph.D. thesis, Claremont: 1970 (UTC: Bangalore).

Sundaram, J. V., *A Study of the Protestant Christian Impact on the Vellalas of the Tinevelli Area in the Eighteenth and Nineteenth Centuries*, MA, Theology, UTC: Bangalore, 1980.

Interviews

Dr Abraham Ayzookuzhiel, CSIRS, Bangalore, 7 November 1991.

Father Augustine, Dharmaran College, Bangalore, October 1991.

Professor Chakraborty, Rabindra Bharati University, Calcutta, 5 December 1991.

Binoy Chowdury, Calcutta, 29 December 1991.

Father Ephraim David, Bangalore, 28 October 1991.

Professor Barun De, Calcutta, 5 December 1991.

Professor Fred Downes, Bangalore, 7 October 1991.

Dayanand Francis, General Secretary of the Christian Literature Society, Madras, 21 November 1991.

Swami Lokeswarananda, the Abbot, The Ramakrishna Mission Institute of Culture, Calcutta, December 1991.

Professor Mahmood, Presidency College, Calcutta, 23 December 1991.

Dr Nizami, Director of the Centre for Islamic Studies, Oxford, 5 September 1991.

Professor Peter, St Joseph's College, Bangalore, 7 November 1991.

Professor Ramaswamy, Presidency College, Madras, 22 November 1991.

Swami Ranganathananda, Abbot, the Ramakrishna Math, Hyderabad, 27 November 1991.

Professor David Scott, Bangalore, 22 October 1991.

Professor Sirajuddin Syed, editor of *Islamic Culture,* Hyderabad, 28 November 1991.

Father Sundaram, Loyola College, Madras, 20 November 1991.

Amales Tripathi, Calcutta, 24 December 1991.

SECONDARY SOURCES

Ali, Mohammed Mohar, *The Bengali Reaction to Christian Missionary Activities 1833–1857,* Chittagong: 1965.

Andrews, Charles, *North India,* Oxford: 1908.

Annett, E. A., *Conversion in India: A Study in Religious Psychology,* Madras, etc.: 1920.

Appasamy, A. J., *Christianity as Bhakti Marga: A Study of the Johannine Doctrine of Love,* Madras: 1930.

Laird, M. A., *Missionaries and Education in Bengal 1793–1837,* Oxford: 1972.

Baird, Robert (ed.), *Religions in Modern India,* New Delhi: 1981.

Bayly, C. A., *Indian Society and the Making of the British Empire,* Cambridge: 1988.

Bayly, Susan, *Saints, Goddesses and Kings: Muslims and Christians in South Indian Society 1700–1900,* Cambridge: 1989.

Bebbington, D. W., *Evangelicalism in Modern Britain: A History from the 1780s to the 1980s,* London: 1989.

Bhattacharyya, Haridas (ed.), *The Cultural Heritage of India,* vol. IV; *The Religions,* Calcutta: 1956.

Birks, Herbert, *Life of T. Valpy French,* vol. I–II, London: 1895.

Boyd, R. H. S., *Indian Christian Theology,* Madras: 1969.

Bose, P. N., *Hindu Civilisation and British Rule,* vols I–III, Calcutta: 1894.

Braidwood, Revd John, *The Yoke Fellows in the Mission Field: The Life and Labours of the Rev John Anderson and the Rev Robert Johnson*, London: 1862.

Breckenridge, A. Carol and Van der Veer, Peter (eds), *Orientalism and the Post-Colonial Predicament*, Philadelphia: 1993.

Bromley, E. B., *They were Men sent from God*, Bangalore: 1937.

Cannon, Garland, *The Life and Mind of Oriental Jones: Sir William Jones, the Father of Modern Linguistics*, Cambridge: 1990.

Cassels, Nancy, *Religion and Pilgrim Tax under Company Rule*, Riverdale: 1988.

Chakraborty, Ramakanta, *Vaishnavism in Bengal 1486–1900*, Calcutta: 1985.

Chopra, P. N. (ed.), *Religions and Communities*, New Delhi: 1989.

Clark, Henry M., *Robert Clark of the Punjab: Pioneer and Missionary Statesman*, London: 1907.

Clark, Robert, *The Mission of the CMS and the CEZMS in the Punjab and Sindh*, London: 1885.

Clothey, W. Fred, *Images of Man: Religion and Historical Process in South Asia*, Madras: 1982.

Corrie, Henry *et al.*, *Memoirs of the Right Revd Daniel Corrie, compiled by his brothers*, London: 1847.

Coward, H. G. (ed.), *Modern Indian Responses to Religious Pluralism*, New York: 1987.

Cragg, Kenneth, *The Call of the Minaret*, New York: 1956.

Daniells, Norman, *Islam, Europe and Empire*, Edinburgh: 1966.

Das, Somen (ed.), *Christian Faith and Multiform Culture in India*, Bangalore: 1987.

De (Day), Lal Behari, *Recollections of Alexander Duff*, London: 1879.

Dharmaraj, S. Jacob, *Colonialism and Christian Mission: Postcolonial Reflections*, Delhi: 1993.

Drew, John, *India and the Romantic Imagination*, Delhi, etc.: 1987.

Dubois, Abbè and Beauchamp, *Hindu Manners, Customs and Ceremonies*, third edn, Oxford: 1924.

Duff, Alexander, *India and Indian Missions*, Edinburgh: 1840.

Dyson, K. K., *A Various Universe: A Study of the Journals and Memoirs of British Men and Women in the Indian Subcontinent 1765–1856*, Delhi, etc.: 1978.

Embree, Ainslee, *Charles Grant on British Rule in India*, London: 1962.

———, *Imagining India: Essays on Indian History*, Oxford: 1989.

Endo, Shusaku, *Deep River*, London: 1994.

Erikson, Eric, *Identity: Youth and Crisis*, London: 1968.

Farquhar, G. N., *The Crown of Hinduism*, London, etc.: 1913.

Forrester, D. B., *Caste and Christianity: Attitudes and Policies on Caste of Anglo-Saxon Protestant Missions in India*, London: 1980.

Fox, Revd George, *A Memoir of the Revd Henry Watson Fox*, London: 1850.

Frykenberg, Robert and Kolanda, Pauline (eds), *South Indian Studies: An Anthology of Recent Research and Scholarship*, Madras: 1985.

Fuller, C. J., *Servants of the Goddess: The Priests of a South Indian Temple*, Cambridge: 1984.

Gardner, C. E., *Life of Father Goreh*, London: 1890.

Ghosha, Ramchandra, *A Biographical Sketch of Rev K. M. Banerjea*, Calcutta: 1892 (rpt. edn, 1981).

Golding, William, *Rites of Passage*, London, 1980.

Grafe, Hugald, *Tamilnadu in the Nineteenth and Twentieth Centuries: History of Christianity in India*, vol. II, part 2, Bangalore: 1990.

Grewal, J. S., *The Sikhs of the Punjab*, Cambridge: 1990.

Halbfass, Wilhelm, *India and Europe: An Essay in Understanding*, New York: 1988.

Hicks, John, *An Interpretation of Religion*, London: 1989.

Hooker, Roger, *Uncharted Journey*, London: 1973.

————, *Journey into Varanasi*, Rushden: 1978.

————, *Themes in Hinduism and Christianity: A Comparative Study*, Frankfurtam-Main: 1989.

Hughes, Derrick, *Bishop Sahib: A Life of Reginald Heber*, Worthing: 1986.

————, *The Mutiny Chaplains*, Salisbury: 1991.

Hutchins, Francis, *The Illusion of Permanence: British Imperialism in India*, Princeton: 1967.

Hyam, Ronald, *Empire and Sexuality: The British Experience*, Manchester: 1990.

Job, G. V. *et al.* (eds), *Rethinking Christianity in India*, Madras: 1938.

Jones, Kenneth, *Socio-Religious Reform Movements in British India*, Cambridge: 1989.

Kakar, Sudhir, *The Inner World: A Psycho-analytic Study of Childhood and Society in India*, Delhi, etc.: 1983.

Kejariwal, O. P., *The Asiatic Society of Bengal and the Discovery of India's Past 1784–1838*, Delhi, etc.: 1988.

Kennedy, James, *Life and Work in Benares and Kumaon 1839–1877*, London: 1884.

Khaldun, Talmiz and Joshi, P. C. (eds), *Rebellion 1857: A Symposium*, New Delhi: 1957.

Klostermaier, Klaus, *Hindu and Christian in Vrindaban*, London: 1969.

Kooiman, D. *Conversion and Social Equality in India: The London Missionary Society in South Travancore in the 19th century*, New Delhi: 1989.

Kopf, David, *British Orientalism and the Bengal Renaissance: The Dynamics of Indian Modernisation 1770–1835*, Calcutta: 1969.

————, *The Brahmo Samaj and the Shaping of the Modern Indian Mind*, Princeton: 1979.

Kunte, K. M., *The Vicissitudes of Aryan Civilisation in India*, Bombay: 1880.

Lang, G. H., *The History and Diary of an Indian Christian*, Lowestoft: 1939.

Laird, M. A., *Bishop Heber in Northern India: Selections from Heber's Journal*, Cambridge: 1972.

Laue, Theodore von, *The World Revolution of Westernisation: The Twentieth Century in Global Perspective*, Oxford, New York: 1987.

Lefever, Henry, *The Vedic Idea of Sin*, Travancore: 1935.

Leupolt, Revd C. B., *Further Recollections of an Indian Missionary*, London: 1884.

Lewis, Norman, *The Missionaries*, London: 1988.

Lipner, Julius and Gaspert-Sauch, George (eds), *The Writings of Brahmabandhab Upadhyay*, Bangalore: 1991.

Lott, Eric, *Vedantic Approaches to God*, London: 1980.

Mcleod, W. H., *The Evolution of the Sikh Community*, Oxford: 1972.

Macpherson, G., *Life of Lal Behari Day: Convert, Pastor, Professor and Author*, Edinburgh: 1900.

Majeed, Javed, *Ungoverned Imaginings: James Mill's the History of British India and Orientalism*, Oxford: 1992.

Mallett, Chibli and Connors, Jane (eds), *Islamic Family Law*, London: 1990.

Manickam, Sundaraj, *The Social Setting of Christian Conversion in South India*, Wiesbaden: 1977.

Marshall, Peter, *Bengal: The British Bridgehead. Eastern India 1740–1828*, Cambridge: 1981.

Mathew, A., *Christian Mission Education and Nationalism: From Dominance to Compromise 1870–1930*, Delhi: 1988.

Moor, Edward, *The Hindu Pantheon*, London: 1810.

Nazir-Ali, Michael, *From Everywhere to Everywhere: A World View of Christian Witness*, London: 1991.

Neill, Stephen, *Bhakti: Hindu and Christian*, Madras: 1974.

————, *A History of Christianity in India*, vol. I: *The Beginnings to 1707*, Cambridge: 1984; vol. II: *A History of Christianity in India: 1707–1858*, Cambridge: 1985.

Newbiggin, Lesslie J. E., *A South Indian Diary*, London: 1951.

————, *Unfinished Agenda*, London, Michigan: 1985.

Newby, Eric, *Slowly Down the Ganges*, London: 1966.

Newsome, David, *Godliness and Good Learning*, London: 1961.

Noble, Revd John, *A Memoir of the Rev Robert Turlington Noble*, London: 1867.

Oddie, Geoffrey (ed.), *Religion in South Asia: Religions and Conversion Movements in South Asia in Medieval and Modern Times*, London: 1973.
————, *Hindu and Christian in South East India*, London: 1991.
Panikkar, K. M., *Asia and Western Dominance*, London: 1953.
Parekh, Bhikhu, *Colonialism, Tradition, and Reform: An Analysis of Gandhi's Political Discourse*, New Delhi: 1989.
Paton, William, *Alexander Duff: Pioneer Missionary*, London: 1923.
Paul, Rajaiah, *Chosen Vessels: Lives of Ten Indian Christian Pastors of the Eighteenth and Nineteenth Centuries*, Madras: 1961.
————, *Triumph of His Grace*, Madras: 1967.
Pemble, John, *The Mediterranean Passion: Victorians and Edwardians in the South*, Oxford: 1987.
Pettit, George, *The Tinevelly Mission of the CMS*, London: 1851.
Pfander, C. G., *The Mirzanu'l Haqq: Balance of Truth. Thoroughly Revised and Enlarged by W. St Clair Tisdall*, London: 1910.
Philip, T. V., *Krishna Mohan Banerjea: Christian Apologist*, Bangalore: 1982.
Piggin, S., *Making Evangelical Missionaries 1789–1858*, Sutton Courtenay: 1984.
Potts, E. Daniel, *British Baptist Missionaries in India 1793–1837*, Cambridge: 1967.
Powell, Avril, *Muslims and Missionaries in Pre-Mutiny India*, London: 1993.
Presler, A. Franklin, *Religion and Bureaucracy: Policy and Administration for Hindu Temples in South India*, Cambridge: 1987.
Radakrishnan, Sarvepalli and Moore, Charles (eds), *A Sourcebook in Indian Philosophy*, Princeton: 1957.
Raychaudhuri, Tapan, *Europe Reconsidered: Perceptions of the West in Nineteenth Century Bengal*, Delhi, etc.: 1988.
Robb, Peter (ed.), *Dalit Movements and the Meanings of Labour*, Delhi: 1993.
Robinson, Vaughan, *Transients, Settlers and Refugees: Asians in Britain*, Oxford: 1986.
Rocher, Ludo, *The Puranas*, Wiesbaden: 1986.
Rowell, Geoffrey, *Hell and the Victorians*, Oxford: 1974.
Said, Edward, *Orientalism*, London: 1978.
————, *Culture and Imperialism*, London: 1995.
Sargent, Revd John, *A Memoir of the Rev Henry Martyn*, London: 1831.
Sastri, K. A. Nilikantra, *Development of Religion in South India*, New Delhi: 1963.
Sathianadhan, S., *Sketches of Indian Christians*, London, Madras: 1896.
Schimmel, Anne-Marie, *Islam and the Indian Subcontinent*, Leiden, Koln: 1980.
————, *Mystical Dimensions of Islam*, Chapel Hill: 1975.
Scott, C. David (ed.), *Keshub Chunder Sen*, Madras: 1979.

Sharpe, J. Eric, *Faith Meets Faith: Some Christian Attitudes to Hinduism in the 19th and 20th Centuries*, London: 1977.

Sinha, Pradip, *Nineteenth Century Bengal: Aspects of Social History*, Calcutta: 1965.

Sinha, N. K. (ed.), *The History of Bengal 1757–1905*, Calcutta: 1967.

Smith, Bardwell, *Religion and Social Conflict in South Asia*, Leiden: 1976.

——, *Religion and Legitimation of Power in South Asia*, Leiden: 1976.

Smith, Donald Eugene, *India as a Secular State*, Princeton: 1963.

Smith, George, *Life of Alexander Duff*, vols I-II, Edinburgh: 1879.

——, *The Conversion of India*, London: 1893.

Spear, Percival, *India, Pakistan and the West*, Oxford: 1958.

Stanley, Brian, *The History of the Baptist Missionary Society 1792–1992*, Edinburgh: 1992.

Stock, Eugene, *History of the Church Missionary Society: Its Environment, its Men and its Work*, vols I-III, London: 1899.

Stokes, Eric (ed.), Bayly, C. A., *The Peasant Armed: The Indian Rebellion of 1857*, Oxford: 1986.

Suntharalingam, R., *Politics and Nationalist Awakening in South India 1852–1891*, Tucson: 1974.

Thapar, Romila (ed.), *Situating Indian History*, New Delhi: 1986.

Thompson, F. M. L., *The Rise of the Respectable Society*, London: 1988.

Thompson, H. P., *Into all Lands: The History of the Society for the Propagation of the Gospel in Foreign Parts 1701–1950*, London: 1951.

Tripathi, Amales, *Vidyasagar: The Traditional Moderniser*, New Delhi: 1974.

Viswanathan, Gauri, *Masks of Conquest: Literary Study and British Rule in India*, London: 1989.

Walsh, Judith, *Growing Up in British India: Indian Autobiographies on Childhood and Education under the Raj*, New York, London: 1983.

Watson, James (ed.), *Between Two Cultures: Migrants and Minorities in Britain*, Oxford: 1977.

Weitbrecht, Mrs Mary, *Memoir of Rev John James Weitbrecht*, London: 1854.

Wilson, H. H., *Religious Sects of the Hindus*, Varanasi, Delhi: 1972 (rpt. edn).

Young, R. Fox, *Resistant Hinduism: Sanskrit Sources on Anti-Christian Apologetics in Early 19th Century India*, Vienna: 1981.

CONFERENCE PAPERS

Ballhatchet, Kenneth, 'Missionaries, Empire and Society: The Jesuit Mission in Calcutta 1834–46', *6th European Conference of Modern South Asian Studies*, Leiden: July 1978.

Forrester, Duncan R., 'Christianity in Early Indian Nationalism', *6th European Conference.*

Oddie, G. A., 'Old Wine in New Bottles? Kartabhaja (Vaishnava) Converts to Evangelical Christianity in Bengal 1835–1845', *13th European Conference of Modern South Asian Studies,* Toulouse: August 1994.

Powell, Avril, 'Processes of Conversion in Nineteenth-Century North India', *13th European Conference.*

ARTICLES

Bayly, C. A., British Orientalism and the Indian 'Rational Tradition' *c.* 1770–1820, *South Asia Research,* vol. 14, no. 1, Spring 1994.

Carson, Penny, 'An Imperial Dilemma: The Propagation of Christianity in Early Colonial India', *The Journal of Imperial and Commonwealth History,* vol. 8, no. 2, May 1990.

Copley, Antony, Hinduism Revisited, *Religion,* vol. 11, January 1981.

————, 'Projection, Displacement and Distortion in 19th Century Moral Imperialism: A Reexamination of Charles Grant and James Mill', *The Calcutta Historical Journal,* vol. VII, no. 2, January–June 1983.

————, 'Indian Secularism Reconsidered: From Gandhi to Ayodhya', *Contemporary South Asia,* vol. 2, no. 1, 1993.

————, The Conversion Experience of India's Christian Elite in the mid-nineteenth century, *The Journal of Religious History,* vol. 18, no. 1, June 1994.

————, 'In Quest of Indian Religions: A Journey to India 1991', *Indo-British Review,* vol. XX, no. 1.

Datta, Dr Abhajit, 'Nineteenth-Century Urban Elitist Reaction to Christian Missionary Enterprise in Bengal', *The Quarterly Review of Historical Studies,* vol. XXVII, 1987, no. 2, vol. XXVIII, nos 1 and 2, Frykenberg, Robert Eric, 'On the Study of Conversion Movements: A Review Article and a Theoretical Note', *The Indian Economic and Social History Review,* vol. XVII, no. 1.

————, 'Modern Education in South India 1784–1854: Its Roots and Its Role as a Vehicle of Integration under Company Raj', *The American Historical Review,* vol. 91, no. 1, February 1986.

Gibbs, M. E. Catechists in the Tinevelly Mission in the First Half of the Nineteenth Century, *Bulletin of the Church Association of India,* no. 8, September 1865.

Daniel Corrie, *Indian Church History Review,* vol. IV, no. 1, June 1970.

Hatcher, Brian, 'Eternal Punishment and Christian Missions: The Response of the Church Missionary Society to Broad Church Theology', *Anglican Theological Review,* vol. LXII, no. 1, Winter 1990.

Hudson, Denis, 'The Conversion Account of H. A. Krishna Pillai', *Indian Church History Review,* vol. II, June 1968.

Lipner, Julius, 'Facets of the Relationship between the Gospel and Culture', *International Review of Mission*, April 1985.

———, A Case-Study in 'Hindu Catholicism': Brahmabandhab Upadhyay (1861–1907), *Zeitschrift für Missionwissenschaft und Religionwissenschaft*, January 1988.

Mahmood, Cynthia Keppley, 'Sikh Rebellion and the Hindu Concept of Order', *Asian Survey*, vol. xxiv, no. 3, March 1989.

Mukhopadhyaya, Arundhati, 'Attitudes towards Religion and Culture in Nineteenth-Century Bengal: Tattvobhini Sabha, 1839–1859', *Studies in History*, vol. iii, no. 1, January–June 1987.

Oddie, G. A., 'India and Missionary Motives c. 1850–1900', *Journal of Ecclesiastical History*, vol. xxv, no. 1, January 1974.

Panikkar, K. N., 'Culture and Ideology: Contradictions and Intellectual Transformation of Colonial Society in India', *Economic and Political Weekly*, 5 December 1987.

Sadiq, W. John, 'Muslim Converts in the Indian Church', *Indian Church History Review*, vol. x, no. 1, June 1976.

Schreider, Deryck and Oddie, Geoffrey, 'What is Conversion? History, Christianity and Religious Change in South Asia', *The Journal of Religious History*, vol. 15, no. 4, December 1989.

Suntharalingam, R., 'The Madras Native Association: A Study of an Early Indian Political Organization', *Indian Economic and Social History Review*, iv, 3, 1967.

Raychaudhuri, Tapan, 'Bengali Perceptions of the Raj in the Nineteenth Century', *Itinerario*, 1, 1989.

Webb, Andrew, 'The Christo Seva Sangh Ashram 1922–1933', *South Asia Research*, no. 1, May 1981.

INAUGURAL LECTURE

Andrew Porter, Religion and Empire: British Expansion in the Long Nineteenth Century, 1740–1914, 20 November 1991, King's College, London.

Index